The LIGHTED ROAD

KENNETH N. PRICE

Published in Australia by Sid Harta Books & Print Pty Ltd,
ABN: 34632585293
23 Stirling Crescent, Glen Waverley, Victoria 3150 Australia
Telephone: +61 3 9560 9920
E-mail: author@sidharta.com.au

First published in Australia 2025
This edition published 2025
Copyright © Kenneth N Price 2025
Cover design, typesetting: WorkingType (www.workingtype.com.au)

The right of Kenneth N Price to be identified as the
Author of the Work has been asserted in accordance with the
Copyright, Designs and Patents Act 1988.

All rights reserved. No part of this publication may be reproduced, stored in a retrieval system, or transmitted, in any form or by any means without the prior written permission of the publisher, nor be otherwise circulated in any form of binding or cover other than that in which it is published and without a similar condition being imposed on the subsequent purchaser.

Kenneth N Price
The Lighted Road
ISBN: 978-1-7643861-7-3 (pbk)
978-1-7645125-3-4(ebook)

About the Author

Kenneth Price is a retired Vietnam veteran. When he was seventeen, he enlisted into the Australian Army and was trained as a medic. He was sent to Vietnam in 1968 and worked in a field ambulance and field hospital.

His grandfather served in the 9th Battalion in France from 1916 to 1918, and his father served in the Australian Army during WWII. Kenneth's uncle also served as a bomber pilot in WWII and was shot down and killed in 1944.

After returning from Vietnam, Kenneth married and went to university where he graduated with Distinction in an Arts Degree, majoring in History and Literature. He also has a Bachelor of Education and a Masters (with Distinction) in Australian Political History.

Kenneth spent fourteen years teaching History and English at Brisbane Grammar School and eight years as a lecturer in English in Singapore, where he helped his students obtain their O and A levels from Cambridge University.

Writing has always been his passion, and following retirement, he was inspired to research his family's military history. This led to writing his first book, *Broken Lives*, which covers some of the exploits of his grandfather's 9th Battalion.

Kenneth has six children and eleven grandchildren. He is currently married to his second wife and lives in Hervey Bay, Queensland.

The photograph on the cover of this book is of a lighted road which evokes a sense of longing, mystery, imagination and nostalgia. It is a metaphor for life's journey through life. The light dispenses with darkness revealing the profound mysteries of life while leading us in the right direction towards truth. We bask in the majesty and beauty of truth, yet, at the same time, fear its frightful reality. The lighted road demands of us the exercising of patience, courage and sharp vision. It draws us towards a higher purpose or profound understanding of life leading us towards personal growth and transformation.

You, too, with the still soul,
have your mission, for beneath the
dashing, noisy waves must ever
run the silent waters that give the tide
its course.

Max Ehrmann,
You with the Still Soul

This book is dedicated to
my grandchildren and their generation.

Content

Preface		1
Prelude		14
Chapter 1:	The Nature of Truth	40
Chapter 2:	The Three Levels of Truth	52
Chapter 3:	A Disciplined Mind, Controlled Emotions, and Acknowledged Empathy	114
Chapter 4:	Physical Fitness and Healthy Eating Habits	132
Chapter 5:	Personal Hygiene	155
Chapter 6:	Financial Security	159
Chapter 7:	Love, Marriage, and Family	217
Chapter 8:	New World Issues	253
To Summarise		530
Chapter 9:	Conclusion	539

Preface

I wrote this book for the youth of Australia, but it has application for people of all ages. I also realise that some of the material in it needs judgements regarding age applicability. Such decisions should be made by parents. The ideas revealed here have relevance for the wider community, because I have tried to capture a picture of what I believe were the most valuable elements of the society I inhabited, and the current changes being wrought upon Australia's society. Am I suggesting that my generation had things right while generations that followed have them wrong? No. Not at all, but I hope those who inherit Australia will be curious about what went before and look for ideas that they find valuable enough to hold on to. Remember the old adage –

> *Don't throw out the baby with the bathwater.*
> (German Proverb)

Every generation shapes the future in terms of its own image but change for change's sake has led to much suffering in the past, which I hope can be challenged by the ideas expressed in this book. Remember, every generation makes mistakes, and my generation made their share of mistakes too. In short, this book should be seen as a start to your lifelong journey of discovering truth. As such, it offers a broad consideration of the merits of some of life's values; it is not a deep dive into any one particular aspect of religion, philosophy, science etc. However, if you take the time to examine the trends and ideas pursued by my generation and yours, I'm sure you will find some gems worth preserving, and some issues worth pursuing in greater depth. Discovering the truth illuminated by the lighted road does not let others define truth for you. Rather it helps you to discover it for yourself.

Much of what is recorded here is disappearing and a new world is emerging that is very different from the one I grew up in. I hope my world will not be erased completely by this new world, which seems dedicated to a different path. I grew up believing in individual sovereignty (designed to measure the will of the people), liberty (especially the right to free choice, free speech, and the ownership of private property), equal opportunity (with empathy for those unable to compete), and limited government intervention in the lives of individuals. Let me quote Peter Costello (Australian Treasurer, 1996-2007) –

> *Big government will lead to smaller citizens;*
> *responsible citizens might lead to smaller government.*
> *Responsible citizens can turn the tide.*
> (ARC Conference, *The Credit Card No One Sees: Give young people a DEBT FREE start*, 2025)

Many of these ideas are under challenge today, and I believe your generation's hold on them is becoming tenuous. For example, whereas my generation prioritised liberty above all other values, your generation has been educated to give top spot to sustainability and government interference *in your best interest*. This has allowed your leaders to substitute new values over your liberty in the name of a greener future and equity over equality.

Much of your education has been directed towards replacing the individual with identity politics which replaces individual liberty with group conformity; equal opportunity with equity; and small government with big government. If you find these changes beneficial you would probably be reluctant to question their validity but please keep an open mind towards those who find some of these changes distasteful, especially for the sake of your descendants. Remember things can change in the future if you find the courage to face your fears with truth, hope, and optimism.

First, do you believe that the world is counting down to a climate catastrophe? Despite what you may have read or been told, there is much contention over the issue of human activity on climate. Do your own research on this topic. Do you think those scientists who are sceptical about *catastrophic* climate change emergency should be given a fair hearing or dismissed as climate change deniers? If you think you should give them a fair hearing, find those scientists who are sceptics and read what they have to say in combination with those who promote it. You might like to consider the following scientists.

Professor Freeman Dyson (1923-2020), renowned theoretical physicist and mathematician who held the position as Professor of Physics at the Institute for Advanced Study in Princeton. He believed that climate change models are incapable of predicting future climate owing to the complexity of the climate system and the limitations of current models. He argues that *fudge factors* are fitted into existing data which may not represent future atmospheric chemistry. He also argues that some positive effects of increased carbon dioxide in the atmosphere, such as increased agricultural yield, are not given adequate consideration.

Professor Emeritus of Princeton University, William Happer (1939-) who believes we are in a carbon dioxide drought. That the atmosphere needs more carbon dioxide not less, for the good of our earth's flora, the basic food source for all fauna on earth and the generator of oxygen in the atmosphere. Current discoveries about *the greening of the earth* by NASA confirm his belief.

Professor Ian Plimer (1946-), Professor Emeritus at the University of Melbourne, an Australian geologist who believes that carbon dioxide can only have a minimal effect on climate change, that the huge changes to climate have been wrought upon the earth over eons of time by super powerful events like enormous volcanic activity or the tectonic shifts of our continents. His latest publication is a book titled *Climate Change; The Facts 2025*, published by the Institute of Public Affairs (IPA).

Dr Patrick Moore (1947-) a world-leading biologist who was a founding member of Greenpeace. He believes that an increase in carbon dioxide in the atmosphere will be beneficial for the Earth's flora and will not lead to catastrophic climate change which, in Moore's mind, is nothing more than a fake, invisible catastrophe and threat of doom. Much like the doomsday prophecies of the past.

Professor Bjorn Lomborg (1965-), author, political scientists, eminent environmentalist and Professor of Statistics at the Aarhus University in Denmark, who believes that climate change due to human activity is a reality but not a catastrophic emergency. He believes we have more time than 2050 to adjust and, therefore, wants environmentally destructive renewable energy sources replaced with the least environmentally destructive nuclear power sources.

David Wilson (1947-), civil engineer and author, who believes that climate change is a serious, urgent problem whose solution can be found in combining renewable energy with nuclear power. His latest book, *Wind + Sun + Nuclear* (2025), tackles Australia's complex energy problem with practical solutions.

Professor Mark Jacobson (1965-), Professor of Civil and Environmental Engineering at Stanford University, who believes that the world should rapidly move to 100% renewable energy by using wind, water, and solar power to solve a climate change emergency (*Scientific American*, 2009) (*The Guardian, No Miracles Needed*, 2023).

You don't have to agree with their arguments, but don't you think you should at least approach what they say with an open mind?

Consider this. While it is true that renewable energy is carbon dioxide free when creating energy, it does have its problems. Renewable energy releases high concentrates of carbon dioxide into the atmosphere during the transport (iron ore and coal to China and solar panels and wind generators back to Australia) and the manufacturing phase of solar panels and wind turbines. It also has high costs associated with installation and transmission. Also, who will be responsible for dismantling the wind turbines is unclear, but it will be expensive. For example, decommissioning a wind turbine after its useful life has expired costs of up to $600,000 AUD (annewebster.com.au, *Hidden wind turbine decommissioning costs a risk to farmers,* February 7, 2024). Since the sun does not always shine and the wind does not always blow, renewable energy needs baseload power during its downtime. Current technology (batteries and green hydrogen) associated with stored power is expensive and has not been developed to a level sufficient to supply power during the downtime of renewable energy. Hydro power, which is subject to extended periods of drought and has limited locations in Australia, is also expensive (ref. Snowy 2.0). Fossil fuels are the cheapest form of energy production but emit carbon dioxide. Nuclear power is initially expensive and takes a long time to become operational. However, nuclear power produces massive amounts of carbon-free energy. It makes the least environmental impact and is generally considered the most energy-dense source of electricity available.

Australia has had a nuclear generator in operation at Lucas Heights since 1958 with the opening of the High Flux Australian Reactor (HIFAR). It produces radioisotopes for nuclear medicine, irradiated silicon for the semiconductor industry, and neutrons for scientific research. In 1998, the Howard Government passed the National Radiation and Nuclear Safety Act which placed a moratorium on nuclear facilities being built in Australia (sbs.com.au, *What we know about Australia's only live nuclear reactor, 19 June 2024*).

Under the AUKUS trilateral security pack (15 September 2021), Australia has placed an order to purchase an initial three Virginia-class nuclear submarines starting in the early 2030's with an option to purchase up to two more additional Virginia-class submarines. In February 2025, Australia placed its first downpayment of US$500 million for the Virginia-class, nuclear-powered submarines. Australia also intends to build conventionally-armed, nuclear-powered SSN-AUKUS submarines based on a UK design. America, Britain, France, Russia, and China have nuclear-powered submarines. They also have conventional nuclear-powered electric generators for their power grid.

It is the reality of baseload power that makes renewable energy among the most expensive and unreliable forms of energy generation, as all countries using renewable energy, including Australia, have experienced. Renewable energy is also more sensitive to frequency fluctuations, making the grid more susceptible to instability and possible grid failure without a reliable baseload power input.

My generation, the baby boomer generation, completed an electrical generation grid based on coal-fired power stations and a transmission grid that connected Queensland, New South Wales (including the Australian Capital Territory), Victoria, Tasmania, and South Australia. It provided these States with cheap, reliable, 24/7 energy that powered our industry, kept our homes lighted, and made Australian industry competitive on the world markets. The adoption of a net zero policy of carbon emissions by 2050 and Australia's investment in 82% renewable energy in our electricity grid by 2030 now involves us in a trade-off. These are some of the costs involved. We are currently sacrificing our energy security, our industrial and manufacturing base, our food production, our landscapes (natural, farm, and grazing), our koala habitats, our seascapes (including our whale migration paths), the living standards of our poorest people, and the mental health (climate change anxiety) of our youth in the name of our net zero and renewable energy ambition.

Are you prepared to make these sacrifices in the name of Australia's net zero, renewable energy targets? Ask yourself, how can renewable energy be cheaper if it needs expensive subsidies and baseload power? And why are China and India building coal-fired power stations, if renewable energy is cheaper?

Do some research on the facts. Are you aware that our actions to reduce carbon dioxide in our atmosphere has not achieved the desired effect on earth's temperature despite the actions of some countries to arrest it? That's the problem, you see. Carbon dioxide reduction only affects some countries and not others, so the carbon dioxide content in the atmosphere is not being reduced at the desired rate. In fact it has continued to increase (jpl.nasa.gov, 2021).

As of 2025, Australia had 19 coal-fired power stations operational and the Australian Energy Market Operator (AEMO) expects all Australian coal-fired power stations to close by 2038 (climatecouncil.org.au). On the other hand, China had 1,161 coal-fired power stations and were building the equivalent of two coal-fired power plants per week, while India had approximately 285 coal-fired power plants and were building 2 new plants per month (ARC Conference, *Solar Panels Made in China with Coal*, 2025). America has 212 coal-fired power plants (Wikipedia.org). Australia does not even make it into the top 10 countries with coal-fired power plants.

Do you think that if Australia was to close its 19 coal-fired power stations, it would have any meaningful effect on the amount of carbon dioxide entering the earth's atmosphere each year or achieve anything significant in attacking climate change? So the truth is that whatever Australia does to reduce its carbon footprint, it will have little, if any, effect on the world's temperature if the rest of the world does not also reduce theirs. Remember, China, India, and the USA emit 60% of global emissions (AI Overview, 2025). Australia produces 1.3% of the global human activity carbon dioxide emissions. When asked in a Senate estimates committee hearing in 2017 about how much the global temperature would be reduced if 1.3% of carbon dioxide emissions was eliminated, Australia's Chief Scientist, Dr Finkel replied, 'virtually nothing'. Subsequently, Dr Finkel offered a clarification of what he had said (chiefscientist.gov.au, Dr Finkel, *Clarifying the Chief Scientists' position on reducing carbon emissions*, December 2018).

To those who would say that we need to set an example for the rest of the world to follow, it needs pointing out that America has just pulled out of the Paris Agreement on Climate Change and intends to reinvigorate its energy industry with fossil fuel production and consumption so it can compete on world markets. To meet net zero by 2050 Great Britain proposes to increase its nuclear generating capacity by 4 times owing to the unacceptable trade-offs related to renewable energy. Australia has no nuclear powered electric generators and has a moratorium on the construction or operation of them.

Do you think China, India or America, by far the largest emitters of carbon dioxide, care about what Australia does in relation to climate change? If the largest emitters of carbon dioxide do not care, how can we expect to make any meaningful change?

Then there are the prophets of climate change doom. Go back to Al Gore's *An Inconvenient Truth* (2006) and the forecasts that he predicted would materialise by the summer of 2014. Have the polar ice caps melted causing the oceans to rise approximately 20 feet, generating coastal flooding and 100 million refugees, or have polar bears become extinct? Europe and America have seen mass-immigration into their countries but this has been driven by economics not flooding. In truth, atolls in the Indian and Pacific Oceans have increased in size by 61.74 square kilometres (sciencedirect.com, 2025) and between 2000 and 2017, the polar bear population has risen by more than 30% to about 30,000 bears (ginarinehart.com.au, 2025). Observations on a small polar bear population of Canada (which were under threat from hunting) are not representative of all the Arctic.

What about Greta Thunberg? She stated that people are dying from global warming (COP24 United Nations Climate Change Summit, 2018). Worldwide, people have always died from health-related problems like malnutrition, malaria, diarrhoea, heat exhaustion, and cold exposure (especially the elderly). In 1770 life expectancy worldwide was around 30 years of age. Since the 1900s it has steadily risen to a life expectancy of around 80 years of age in 2023, except for Africa which is around 60 years of age (OurWorldinData.org/

life-expectancy). If life expectancy continues to rise, how is it that more people are dying from climate change? Natural disasters like floods, fires, droughts and earthquakes have always been a part of global existence. The question is: has there been an increase in global deaths owing to an increase of these disasters due to climate change? The number of deaths from natural disasters has actually declined in recent times. It was highest during the period from 1918-42 when at its peak it reached a height of over 3.5 million. In the period 1943-2024 the death toll from natural disasters reached a peak of 1 million in 1958. The last decade's death toll is among the lowest recorded during the period 1918-2024, despite an increase in world population (OurWorldinData.org/natural/disasters, 2024).

Professor Tim Flannery, Melbourne Sustainable Society Institute, The University of Melbourne is one of Australia's leading writers on climate change who stated,

Even the rain that falls in Australia will not fill our dams and river systems.

(Tim Flannery, ABC Landline, 11 Feb 2007.)

Since 2007, not only have our rivers and dams filled, but we have experienced several floods.

Scientists have been predicting the demise of The Great Barrier Reef (GBR) since the 1960s. First it was the crown-of-thorns starfish that was eating the coral, then the bleaching, then the agricultural run-off and now it's acid water and cyclone damage created from climate change. Agricultural run-off is something we can and are tackling; the rest are all natural. Cyclones have always caused damage to the GBR, but it always recovers. The reasons alarmists give for its demise have varied, but the fear remains the same. The truth is that —

> *Coral cover has increased in all three regions of the Great Barrier Reef and is at regional highs in two of the three regions.*
>
> (www.aims.gov.au, 2024)

The latest report on the GBR released by the Australian Institute of Marine Science (AIMS) indicates a sharp decline in coral cover following a mass bleaching event in 2024. However, this decline has pushed coral cover back to *near long-term average levels*. In short, there is still more coral on the GBR than the long-term average levels.

Does this suggest a natural cycle or a catastrophic change? Does this history of doom prediction suggest that science has been compromised by a political agenda when it comes to the GBR?

What about the frequency of tropical cyclones in Australia?

> *There has **not** been an overall increase in the number of tropical cyclones impacting Australia in recent years.*
>
> (AI Overview, 2025)

Believers in climate change emergency point out that the intensity of the cyclones have increased.

> *It is important to note that the impact of cyclones **may** be increasing.*
>
> (AI Overview, 2025)

So the intensity argument by climate alarmists is speculation not scientific fact.

We also have a development that the prophets of doom never predicted. What NASA calls *the greening of the earth* is a phenomenon clearly observed by satellite data from the NASA Earth Observatory. Apparently, this has been known since at least 2016, by scientists who used satellite data from 1982 to 2009 showing that 25-50% of the earth's land surface had become greener and that –

Factorial simulations with multiple global ecosystem models suggest that carbon dioxide fertilization effects explain 70% of the observed greening trend, followed by nitrogen deposition (9%), climate change (8%) and land cover change (LCC) (4%).
(Zaichun Zhu, Greening of the Earth and its drivers, Published Online, 2016)

In 2017 another team of scientists stated that –

Satellite data show unequivocally that the land surface has been greening for the past 30 years, and that leaf area index (LAI) has increased by 8% globally.
(Zhenzhong Zeng, et al, Climate mitigation from vegetation biophysical feedbacks during the past three decades, 2017)

What do we make of these conclusions? Could it be that warmer temperatures, increased rain, and increased carbon dioxide in the atmosphere is actually good for the planet and not harmful?

Climate change due to human activity may or may not be a real problem, but the evidence shows that present climate change policies are not reducing the emission of carbon dioxide into the earth's atmosphere, and that the predictions of those promoting catastrophic climate change emergency have not materialised.

Go back to the research you did on Professor Bjorn Lomborg who has lectured and debated on this topic extensively. Do you think Australia should pursue net zero through 82% renewable energy regardless of cost and trade-offs? Why do Australians continue to push for net zero by 2050, and why do some Australians continue to push for 82% renewable energy when they know the sacrifices it is inflicting on the Australian people?

Germany and Spain aim for over 80% renewable energy by 2030.

They have both run into the reality that, for them, there is no viable baseload power other than fossil fuels or nuclear power for their renewable energy projects and that renewable energy is so expensive that it is destroying the economy of their counties. Both Germany and Spain rely on gas for their baseload power. On 16 April 2025, Red Electrica stated that their renewable energy source had momentarily supplied 100% of Spain's electricity demands with renewable energy. On Monday, 28 April 2025, a major power blackout occurred across the Iberian Peninsula, creating a power outage for Spain and Portugal for about ten hours owing to a drop in generation from renewable energy which caused frequency to fall and triggered load shedding. A subsequent surge in voltage led to further generation disconnections in a chain reaction. How do we fix this? What do you suggest we do about climate change? What would your suggestions cost the Australian public?

Here are two topics you can debate with friends and family, or you might like to suggest them to your teacher so he/she can set them up as a class debate –

That catastrophic climate change emergency is overstated.

And

That 82% renewable energy by 2030 is ruining Australia's economy.

Please indulge me here. I find it sometimes helps stimulate our imagination and encourage independent thought if we consider alternative arguments outside established norms. I believe that today's generation call this *thinking outside the box* or *pushing the envelope*.

Second, reject the resurrection of racism in your society. Judge people by their character not the colour of their skin (Dr. Martin

Luther King Jr., *I Have a Dream Speech*, 1963). Know that you are a unique child of the universe. No one else is exactly like you, and as such, you have purpose and dignity as a human being. Find your place in this wonderous, congenial cosmos. We are all at one with nature, so be comfortable in your situation. Furthermore, believe in yourself and shape your own destiny devoid of group identity; this is the only way to fulfil your individual potential. Above all else, discard any temptation you may develop towards victimhood; it will replace the love and joy in your life with envy and hatred towards others. Accept that all human beings experience injustice, setbacks, physical pain, and emotional suffering in their lives, even those outside your group. It is a fact of our existence. The question is not how we avoid these negative elements in our lives, but rather how we deal with them. If you stand up, square your shoulders and look these negative elements in the eye while developing the courage to confront them, you will develop the necessary strength of character to deal with these things for yourself, fulfil your potential and find true joy and happiness from your newfound self-reliance. Be assured, the shadows of your ancestors, who bequeathed you one of the great nations on earth, are still visible. Don't despair, and above all else think for yourself while questioning everything, even your own motives.

Prelude

Before we start, I need to define some of the words I will use in our discussion throughout this book. Largely, because the modern usage of these words have corrupted their meaning.

Conservative

The term 'conservative' originates from the Latin word 'conservare' meaning 'to keep, preserve or guard'. Conservatism, as a political concept, is linked with Edmond Burke's (1729-1797) opposition to the French Revolution in the 18th century. A definition of a conservative is –

> *A person who is adverse to change and holds traditional values like free enterprise, private ownership, and socially or culturally conservative values.*
> (Oxford Languages Dictionary, 2025)

Conservatives are more centrist than extreme. They promote and preserve traditional institutions, customs, and values. Things like traditional marriage with traditional vows, limited government, law and order, peace through strength, fiscal responsibility, and market-driven capitalism are conservative values.

Reformist

The term 'reformist' is derived from the Latin word, 'reformare' meaning to form again, change, transform or alter. Reformism is defined as follows –

> *Reformism is the belief that all efforts should be directed at the bit that needs reforming (with the economic system, society, State or political party).*
>
> (libcom.org, 2025)

A reformist is someone who advocates for change designed to solve a specific problem. Reformists work within the system to improve it rather than overthrow it. In this way they hope to initiate change that improves society, politics, or the capitalist system. Like conservatives they are more centrist than extreme in their approach. They usually are more practically minded than radicals and more inclined to solve pressing issues rather than change the system itself. Reformists are likely to uphold the principles of liberty like freedom of speech, religious worship, and free choice.

Radical

The word 'radical' originates from the Latin word 'radix' meaning 'root'. The concept of 'radical' promotes the idea of going back to the fundamental basis or origin of something. Radicals distinguish themselves by

> *believing or expressing the belief that there should be great or extreme social, economic, or political change.*
>
> (Cambridge Dictionary)

Radicals, then, believe in changing the system because they see problems, either social, economic, or political as being structural rather than incidental. That is, problems that are built into the system itself and not problems of a unique nature that can be tackled individually.

Radicals can be found on the far left (totalitarianism) or far right (authoritarianism) of politics. Radicals are sometimes referred to as extremists and are prepared to use uncompromising methods to achieve their ends. Radicals are often found in religion and ideology. Radical Christians, for example, seek a society run by a religion under a United Order (group self-sufficiency, income equality and the elimination of poverty), Radical Muslims seek the establishment of a world Califate run by Islamic clerics, and Radical Ideologues seek the adoption of their ideology regardless of the human cost involved. Socialists and communists are radicals as are religious cults or ideologues, because they all seek the radical elimination of liberal democracy and the capitalist economic system.

Partisan

'Partisan' comes to us via 16th century France which uses the Latin word parte, which translated means 'part'. A partisan is defined as –

> *A person who takes the part of or strongly supports one side, party, or person; often specifically an unreasoning, emotional adherent.*
>
> (Collins Dictionary, 2025)

Partisans are fervent supporters of a specific objective. For example, they are strong advocates of a particular political party, social group, or ideological cause and often have a closed mind about alternative opinions which displays bias or prejudice in their attitude. Extreme cases of partisanship exhibit intolerance even to the extent of violent and/or unlawful behaviour for their cause. Some partisans can even refuse to accept the decision of an election conducted in a liberal democracy.

The next two terms are ones I will discuss in more detail in Chapter 7, New World Issues. For now, I will provide only a brief overview.

Socialism

The term 'socialism' originates from the French word 'socialisme', which emerged in the 19th century. A definition of socialism is –

> *Social and economic doctrine that calls for public rather than private ownership or control of property and natural resources.*
>
> (Britannica.com, 2025)

A *socialist*, then, is someone who believes in equity rather than equality of opportunity. Socialists want to radically change society through the legislative process and overthrow the existing liberal socio/political establishment through *evolution*.

Communism

The word 'communism' originates with the 19th century French word 'communisme'. A definition of communism is –

> *A theory or system of social organisation in which all property is owned by the community and each person contributes and receives according to their ability and needs.*
>
> (Oxford Languages Dictionary, 2025)

A *communist* is someone who wants to radically change the political establishment through *violent revolution*. Communists want to end liberal democracy, private property, capitalism etc. through a destructive process and rebuild civilisation into a new classless society.

I will avoid using the term *progressive* since it was a term in popular use in America in the early 20th century then fell out of use. It has seen a revival lately. However, I find it a confusing term because it has positive connotations and is used by socialists, communists, partisans, religious extremists, and radical ideologues, all of whom are very different in nature but see themselves as progressive rather than radical.

I will also avoid using the term *traditionalist* since it is a term used to describe the upholding of religious values (particularly traditionalist Catholic values) rather than a political movement resisting change.

Two other concepts worthy of consideration are equity and equal opportunity.

Equity

Equity is derived from the Latin root 'aequus' meaning 'even', 'fair' or 'equal'. As a political concept, then, it refers to fairness and justice. It seeks to put in place a political structure that equals out discrepances created from the unequal start that all citizens make in their society. The problem with equity is that it robs individuals of the equal treatment of their potential while creating discrimination for individual groups within their societies. This robs aspiring individual citizens of their aspiration and ambition.

Equal opportunity

Equal opportunity brings together two words into a compound noun. The word 'equal' originates from the Latin 'aequus' which has the same meaning found in the words listed above in the meaning for equity. The word 'opportunity' traces back to the Latin 'ob portum veniens' which refers to a favourable wind bringing ships into harbour.

> *Thus, the phrase 'equal opportunity' signifies a concept of everyone having the same chance or access to something, without discrimination.*
>
> (AI Overview, 2025)

Equal opportunity, then, seeks the same outcome as equity but prefers to achieve it through providing all citizens with equal opportunity for their aspiration and ambition. The problem with equal opportunity is that it makes no allowance for the individual citizen's unequal potential at birth. Societies that adopt equal opportunity as a political structure for their society usually recognise the unequal distribution of wealth that this system produces and adopt welfare programmes for the needy.

Equity aspires to create an equal society while equal opportunity seeks a society with more social mobility. Both of these aspirations are noble. However, both systems, to some extent, create feelings of unfairness or grievance in their outcomes.

In addition, the difference between logic, reason, wisdom, and common sense should be made apparent.

Logic

> (Logic is) *a formal scientific method of examining or thinking about ideas.*
>
> (Cambridge Dictionary, 2025)

The word 'logic' originates from the Greek word 'logos' which encompasses many differing concepts like reason, word, speech, account, argument and relation. The scientific methods of logic are deductive and inductive reasoning (more on this later). Logic is more related to objectivity separate from emotion.

Reason

Reason has a slightly different definition which involves justification and sometimes feelings. The word 'reason' derives from the Latin word 'ratio' meaning reckoning, calculation or explanation.

> (Verb) *If you reason that something is true, you decide that it is true after thinking carefully about all the facts.*

> (Noun) *If you say that you have reason to believe something or to have a particular emotion, you mean that you have evidence for your belief or there is a definite cause of your feelings.*
>
> (Collins Dictionary, 2025)

Wisdom

Wisdom is more related to experience and judgement. The word 'wisdom' derives from two Old English words 'wis' meaning wise and 'dom' meaning judgement or decision. A definition of wisdom is –

> *The quality of having experience, knowledge, and good judgement; the quality of being wise.*
> (Oxford Languages Dictionary, 2025)

Common Sense

Common sense is defined as –

> *Good sense and sound judgement in practical matters.*
> (Oxford Languages Dictionary, 2025)

The term 'common sense' is derived from the Latin 'sensus communis' meaning a shared sense or understanding. The use of common sense requires a basic level of practical knowledge and the exercising of sound judgement. Common sense allows individuals to understand and respond to everyday situations in a reasonable way.

Essentially then, *logic* involves formal, objective thinking, *reason* is more concerned about justification for thoughts and feelings, *wisdom* arises from experience and judgement, while *common sense* allows us to make practical decisions.

Furthermore, the difference between prudent, empathy, and compassion needs clarification.

Prudent

A definition of prudent is –

> *Acting with or showing care and thought for the future.*
> (Oxford Languages Dictionary, 2025)

The word 'prudent' originates from a combination of two Latin words 'pro' meaning before and 'videre' meaning 'to see'. So to be prudent one must be able to see ahead. A prudent person is careful, cautious, and sensible about providing for the future.

Empathy

> *Empathy is the ability to understand and share the feelings of another person.*
>
> (AI Overview, 2025)

The word 'empathy' originates with a combination of two Greek words, 'en' meaning 'in' and 'pathos' meaning 'feeling' or 'suffering'. So to be empathetic with someone is to be in sympathy or understanding about their suffering.

Compassion

> *Compassion, on the other hand, is a feeling of deep sympathy and concern for others, often accompanied by a desire to help alleviate their suffering.*
>
> (AI Overview, 2025)

The word 'compassion' originates from the Latin word, 'compati' meaning to suffer with. It is driven by a desire to share someone else's suffering and offer support or help. It is this desire to help that most distinguishes the compassionate from the empathetic. Compassion, when taken to extreme measures, becomes radical and brings about structural changes to a compassionate society that produce unexpected outcomes.

Can you see how a compassionate person may not be acting prudently? In what way? Explain your opinion with examples of compassionate but imprudent behaviour.

Moreover, many today take offence at what some people say. In any conversation it is possible for offence to be taken when none was intended, so the difference between *offence* and *vilification* should be noted.

Offence

The word 'offence' originates from the Latin word 'offendere' meaning 'to strike against'.

> (Offence is an) *annoyance or resentment brought about by a perceived insult or disregard for oneself.*
> (Oxford Languages Dictionary, 2025)

Sometimes offence may be taken when none was intended, as in the case when someone says, 'no offence intended'.

Vilification

The word 'vilification' originates from the Latin word 'vilificatio' meaning 'the act of making vile or worthless'.

> (Vilification is an) *abusively disparaging speech or writing.*
> (Oxford Languages Dictionary, 2025)

Vilification is especially egregious when it involves hatred or contempt that can lead to violence directed towards an individual or group.

Clearly, offence is something that we have no control over, since we cannot predict what reaction others will have to the things we say and write. Vilification, on the other hand, is something that someone does deliberately to insult and provoke someone else. Vilification may involve defamation.

For example, someone might say, 'generally speaking, Jews have a natural affinity for finance and commerce'. Some Jews might take offence at that because European Jews were criticised for practising usury during the Middle Ages while for Christians it was condemned by their Catholic leaders. For example, the Second Lateran Council in 1139 AD and Pope Benedict XIV's 1745 AD encyclical *Vix Pervenit*, which definitely condemn the practice. Over time the distinction between sinful usury and legitimate interest-taking in commerce became more acceptable. Today, governments use monetary tools, like the Reserve Bank's cash rate in Australia, to influence overall economic conditions, which then indirectly affect market-driven interest rates set by banks and lenders. Market competition, lender costs, and borrower risks also determine the actual interest rates of lending organisations. While some Jews may take offence at being accused of having a natural affinity for finance and commerce others might not. Some Jews might even take it as a compliment towards their accomplishment in this endeavour. What is important is the speaker's intention, which may or may not have been intended to cause offence.

On the other hand, when the Nazis likened Jews to vermin, or Islamists preach that Allah wants Muslims to kill Jews, they are clearly engaged in vilification, because their statements cannot be taken any other way. Today there is also a vilification of white people because some white people were once engaged in racially based slavery. Also, blue-eyed, blond people are sometimes vilified because the Nazis once believed them to be part of a 'master race'. The thing is that those who vilify others are guilty of not recognising that individuals have no control over their appearance or the circumstances of their birth. Merely being born a Jew or white or a blue-eyed blond does not make someone reprehensible. Only their actions do that, and those who vilify others because of the way they were born are themselves reprehensible.

Do you agree with my reasoning? Do you have a different opinion? Give evidence for your opinion.

Integrity

Finally, we come to integrity. Something we all should desire.

'Integrity' originates from the Latin word 'integer' meaning 'whole' or 'complete'. Integrity implies a state of being undivided, unbroken, and morally or ethically sound.

Those who maintain their integrity always do the right thing in a reliable way. They are admired for their wholeness of character. Just as an integer is a whole number with no fractions, so those with integrity maintain their moral or ethical position and do not waver when placed in a difficult position. To maintain their integrity they must be honest and refuse to change their firmly held moral or ethical values and principles.

I would encourage you to view *The Tall Men*, a 1955 American Western movie staring Clark Gable, Robert Ryan, and Jane Russell. Towards the end of the movie, Robert Ryan's character says of Clark Gable's character –

> *He is the only man I ever respected. He is the kind of man every boy wants to be when he grows up, and what every old man wishes he had been.*

Enjoy the movie. Although movies are a different art form from poetry, this movie achieves what the ancient Roman poet and critic, Horace famously said was the purpose of poetry. That it should 'instruct and delight'.

Do you think Clark Gable's character exhibits integrity? Why? Give a detailed explanation of your opinion by reference to specific scenes in the movie.

Now that we have defined some of the terms necessary for our discussion, let us begin.

The purpose of this book is to provide some ideas and values for those who read it. Hopefully, the youth of Australia will be inspired to question some of the principles shaping their new world and their parents and grandparents will not only reminisce nostalgically about their past but also inspire their descendants to question rather than accept what they are told. Conceivably, if they have not considered these things before, they may find them interesting and consider adding them to their daily life.

The approach I will use is the same one I adopted during my career as a teacher. Namely, the Socratic tradition, that is, through the delivery of ideas and the posing of questions and, in some cases, presenting some possible answers for your consideration, which may be accepted, questioned or rejected.

Of course, any informed decision needs to be based on a body of knowledge. The knowledge base I offer here should not be considered complete, or even the most appropriate. I offer it merely as a starting point, not an end, and the conclusions about the ideas and values I present should not be considered as rules or commandments. Rather, I offer them merely as items for consideration.

Let me state from the outset that what we share here I consider a beginning to what I hope will become a lifelong endeavour on your part as it has been for me. I can provide you with some ideas and values that, if you decide they have applicability to your life, will put you on a path towards maintaining your integrity, fulfilling your potential and achieving your desired goals in life. I do not intend, in any way, to try and force my opinions on you. Accordingly, I encourage you to question everything I present to you and create some ideas of your own.

Remember, no one can demand you adopt any idea or value. They only become a reality if you accept them for yourself. Hopefully, after you have given these ideas and thoughts considerable deliberation by the application of logic, reason, wisdom, common sense, prudence, and empathy, you will reach decisions of your own. In other words, you must believe in them, because you can see wisdom or benefit in them for yourself and those around you. As you go through life, you will discover that many people will come to you and want you to adopt an idea or a value because it benefits them if you do so. Regarding this situation, I would advise you to ask three simple questions –

How will this affect the person offering the new value or idea?

How will it affect me and others?

And what are the long-term consequences of adopting these ideas or values?

I hope you will ask these questions of all the ideas and values I present you with in this book.

Of course, there are times when we adopt new ideas or values because we believe they will lead to a more just or better organised society. Even here, however, we need to be prudent in our judgement about the true benefits, because often there is a *hidden agenda* that becomes apparent later. Hidden agendas are difficult to discern, because others do not want us to know what they are, and so they do not tell us what they truly want and even try to hide or disguise the truth from us. People like this are usually motivated by one of two things, however, *money* or *power*, and if we direct our attention towards these two things, the truth usually becomes apparent.

Let us consider money first –

For the love of money is the root of all kinds of evil. By craving it, some have wandered away from the faith and pierced themselves with many sorrows.

(1 Timothy 6:10)

This warning was first presented to us over 2,000 years ago, yet we must keep rediscovering it. Notice we are warned that *the love of money* is the problem, not *money* itself, which is nothing more than a convenient means of exchange. In answering the following questions please substitute 'truth' for 'faith' in the above quote.

Do you believe that the love of money could compromise or corrupt a person's commitment to truth? If you believe it could, in what ways could this happen? Do you believe that some individuals could hide their true motivation for some new idea or value if they believed they would gain some monetary reward from it? Explain your opinion with reference to examples of how money has or has not corrupted someone's commitment to truth. Would you say that those who do not allow themselves to be corrupted by money maintain their integrity? How so?

If you do believe this, there is one logical rule that you can adopt to discover these hidden agendas –

Follow the money.

This term came into popular use in the 1970s, although the idea had been in circulation long before that. What does it mean? You could start by asking, would this new idea or value create a new flow of money? If it would, who would be the ultimate beneficiaries of this new flow of money? Who would be the losers? Then, ask yourself, are the people advocating for this change being truthful or are they hiding the truth about their motivation?

Let us now consider the following proverb regarding power –

Power tends to corrupt, and absolute power corrupts absolutely. Great men are almost always bad men...
(This English proverb is attributed to Lord Acton (1834-1902), when writing a letter to an Anglican bishop in 1887.)

What this proverb highlights for us is the pervasive, corrupting influence of power. Remember, tyrants and dictators tell their followers that they only take the actions they do in the interests of their followers. Some will even claim that they do what they do out of love for their followers.

Do you believe this? Do you think most leaders use power to get what they want from their followers? If you do, can you think of some examples of this happening? How can we identify when leaders begin to unreasonably exercise power over us? Do you think that when leaders begin to exhibit tyrannical behaviour over their followers, they have lost touch with moral clarity (more on this later) and truth?

As well as hidden agendas, there is also the danger of *unintended consequences* emerging after a society has made changes to its values. From the 1960s on, divorce rates began to rise in Australia, so in 1975 the Family Court was introduced, to enable couples to divorce from one another without incurring expensive costs and the stigma of social shame. Prior to this a person seeking a divorce had to prove that their partner had broken the vows of their marriage. This usually meant that it had to be proven that one or other of the partners had been unfaithful. This meant hiring a private detective and proving infidelity in court, which was costly and required the revealing of embarrassing evidence. What the Family Court enabled was for couples in a marriage to show that their marriage had irretrievably broken down (parties to a marriage had lived separately for a period of 12 months) and the divorce was automatically granted. This is still the only legal requirement for divorce today.

This was compassionate reform that was intended to save divorced people from the cost and shame of divorce, and most Australians supported it. It did, however, produce unintended consequences. Currently, the average marriage in Australia lasts for just 12 years, and the negative effects on children affected by marriage break-up remains mostly unsolved. Juvenile violence, for example, is now on the rise and has reached a level that produces serious social problems.

> *The Journal of Research in Crime and Delinquency reports that the most reliable indicator of violent crime in a community is the proportion of fatherless families.*
> (R L Maginnis, *Single-Parent Families Cause Juvenile Crime*) (From *Juvenile Crime: Opposing Viewpoints* P62-66, 1997, A E Sadler, ed – see NCJ-167319), 1997)

This is a significant structural change in marriages and the behavioural pattern of teenagers from generations before the 1960s. Also, fewer young people today are marrying than in times past.

The marriage rate began to fall steadily from the 1970s until 2000. Then it stabilised for a decade before falling again.
(aifs.gov.au, 2022)

It appears that marriage no longer offers young people the rewards that it did for their ancestors. Today young women claim that marriage is complicit in their subjugation while young men claim that marriage is a bad deal for them because the legal system favours women. The unintended consequence of this development is that birth rates have fallen below replacement levels. The medium age for first-time marriages in Australia currently stands at 32.9 years for men and 31.2 years for women (abs.gov.au, 2024). This is much later than in the conservative 1950s when the median age for men was around 23 years and for women around 20 years (AI Overview, 2025). This seriously limits the most fertile years for a female to fall pregnant (late teens to early 30s) in today's Australia.

These are some examples of the unintended consequences that can occur from well-intentioned, compassionate reform to a society's values.

Today, conservatives look back to the 1950s and reminiscence about a time when families remained intact and only one income could sustain a family – when mental health, obesity, asthma, autism, diabetes, and juvenile crime were at an all-time low – and wonder if their society has been reformed or radicalised.

Do you think these changes are examples of reform or radicalisation? Are they good for you or society generally? Have these changes improved or radically changed our society? What role did the compassionate, as opposed to the prudent, society play in introducing these changes?

Am I suggesting a return to a culture controlled by expensive divorces and shame? Not necessarily. What I am suggesting, however, is that changes to a nation's culture, driven by compassion, often results in unintended consequences, which need addressing by those who encouraged the reform in the first place. What, then, can be done? Before we consider better education, the most often suggestion of problem solvers addressing social problems, we need to recognise that changes to education have seldom led to planned solutions and usually contribute to further problems. Poor classroom discipline, schoolground assault, online bullying, increasing teenage suicide, declining academic standards, an increase in teenage sexual activity with the accompanying consequences – like rises in STD's, teenage pregnancy, and abortion – are just some of the unintended consequences that have arisen in Australia's schools since the introduction of reformist changes to education intended to improve education and solve society's problems. Again, do you think education in Australia has been reformed or radicalised over the past 50 years?

Is it good enough for us to shrug our shoulders and declare that these changes are the cost we must pay to live in a more compassionate society? Can you suggest any ideas about how to address these problems that do not lead to further, undesirable, unintended consequences?

I know that the truth revealed from an examination of hidden agendas and unintended consequences can be difficult or even hard to accept, but should that be a sufficient reason to ignore these issues? I think not, if we desire to live in a society with integrity. Also, in your pursuit of truth I would encourage you not to become cynical about what you discover regarding human nature, and the irony, irrationality, and hypocrisy so prevalent in it.

Changes brought on by compassionate reforms are one thing, radical change is something else and generally meets with more resistance from the public at large. For this reason radicals adopt a *pattern of dishonesty* to disguise their hidden agenda. It begins with *obfuscation* (making what they say obscure or unclear). Then moves to being *disingenuous* (being slightly dishonest or insincere in what they say). If that fails they will *lie* to achieve their desired goal (telling an untruth in order to deceive).

Obfuscating is an irritating technique used by radicals, and politicians generally. When asked questions that reveal an underlying inconsistency, incorrect action, or fallacy in their argument, they obfuscate endlessly about a tangential issue, hoping the interviewer will forget the actual question asked. If the interviewer does not continue to probe for an answer to the original question, the radical's technique has been successful. If a politician does not want to answer a question he/she should state why and not try to obfuscate.

Beyond obfuscation is the disingenuous statement.

In August 2025, Chris Bowen, Australia's Minister for Climate Change and Energy, stated on his Facebook page –

> *Just recently, for example, renewables overtook coal as the largest source of electricity for India.*

Whereas –

> *Currently, over 70% of India's electricity needs are met by coal-fired power stations.*
> (AI Overview, August 2025)

What conclusion do you draw from this evidence? Is Chris Bowen not across the detail of his portfolio, awkward in his expression, or being disingenuous?

There are also a number of techniques that radicals have adopted to convince you that they are right without having to present a coherent argument of their own or disprove their opponent's argument. Many of these techniques have been adopted by radicals from Sophist philosophy which first arose in Ancient Greece. A *Sophist* is someone who follows a philosophy that believes in atheism, relativism and rhetoric. For Sophists, truth is whatever they can convince the majority it is, since, in their opinion, truth has no reality other than what is in the mind of the individual.

One of these radical techniques is the use of the *strawman fallacy*. This occurs when the radical avoids the argument being presented and refutes an argument different from the one actually being discussed. You can recognise this technique because the radical goes off on a tangent, making all sorts of tenuous connections to try and shift the argument away from its original intention.

A good example of the strawman fallacy was when Senator Jacinta Nampijinpa Price tried to introduce legislation into the Senate of the Australian Parliament to establish a forensic audit on the government expenditure on aboriginal programmes designed to 'close the gap' and a royal commission into domestic violence and child abuse in remote Aboriginal communities. Her proposal was argued against on the grounds that Senator Price was trying to politicise the plight of aboriginal people generally. The issues of wastage, fraud and abuse were not even mentioned by radicals opposing the legislation.

Do you see how the issue of politicalisation became the focus of the Senate's discussion rather than the issue of government spending and domestic violence in remote Aboriginal communities?

The difference between *cause and effect* is also related to this technique. Radicals will often address the effect of a problem to make it appear like they are addressing the problem, when in fact, all they are doing is avoiding its cause. For example, in 2025 teenage gangs in Melbourne carried out a machete attack on the streets of Melbourne. The Victorian State Government responded by immediately imposing a ban on the sale of machetes and displaying 'drop bins' for citizens to hand over their machetes. The government did this to make it appear like they were addressing the problem.

Were the machetes the cause of the problem or was it the belief in the minds of some teenagers that it was appropriate behaviour for them to roam the streets of Melbourne carrying machetes? Since this behaviour had not occurred before, what had changed in Melbourne society that would lead these teenagers to believe that this behaviour was appropriate? These questions address the underlying causes of the problem and not its effects.

Yet another of these techniques is *gaslighting*. This occurs when radicals attempt to sow doubt or confusion into their opponent's minds. They do this by distorting reality and forcing their opponents to question their own judgement, intuition and reality. Their gaslighting usually involves *emotional abuse* with little attempt to provide evidence, fact, data or logic, and if evidence is provided it is usually in the form of quotes taken out of context. This allows them to shout abuse at their opponents and accuse them of being a racist, sexist, homophobe, Islamophobic, bigot or Nazi, among other things. During the Voice referendum (2023), for example, those wanting more detailed information about the issue, or who questioned the wisdom of giving one group of Australians a political right that other Australians would be denied were accused of being immoral and racists.

Another good example of this gaslighting fallacy occurred recently in Australia when a rise in antisemitism occurred on the steps of Australia's iconic Sydney Opera House (crowds were shouting, 'where are the Jews' while Israeli flags were burnt). Chris Minns, Premier of New South Wales, claimed that the Sydney Opera House had been 'overrun with people spewing racial epithets and hatred' (en.wikipedia.org, October 2023). This was condemned by some Australian citizens. Their condemnation was countered with a radical reference to Islamophobia, which avoided debating the issue of rising antisemitism within Australian society by accusing those who were alarmed by this evidence as promoting Islamophobia. Suddenly, those alarmed by the evidence of Jew hatred on their streets were accused of hating Muslims.

Similarly, another example of gaslighting was in 2025 when a Chinese three warship flotilla held two live firing drills 300 nautical miles off Australia's coast in the Tasman Sea without giving appropriate notice of their action and endangering private passenger aircraft. In an interview on Sky News, Australian Senator Sarah Hanson-Young blamed Australia's relationship with President Donald Trump as the reason for the CCP's belligerent attitude. So, according to Senator Hanson-Young, Australia deserved the CCP's bullying tactics because of our relationship with America. Thus, making the action of the CCP justified. This is a clear example of gaslighting because, according to Senator Hanson-Young, the Australian Government's security arrangement is at fault not the hostile actions of the CCP (skynews.com.au, 2025).

Would you like to be called a racist, sexist, homophobe, bigot, Nazi, or accused of being hostile towards Islam or Muslims? If you were none of these things, would you consider that your opponents were gaslighting you?

If these techniques fail, radicals usually turn to a strategy called 'shoot the messenger', whereby the radical will blame or punish those who deliver bad news, even though they are not the source of the problem. This takes the form of *an ad hominem* attack (character assassination) through the use of gossip, inuendo or false accusation to avoid discussing the issue at hand. The aim here is to throw as much mud as possible at their opponent and repeat it so often that some of the mud unjustly sticks. Defamation laws were created to compensate those whose reputation is harmed by demonstrably false statements. However, the person who deliberately made the false statement must be proven to be at fault. Defamation laws can be diluted by claiming that certain individuals have a right to be believed without having to prove their statements. The 'me too' movement, for example, operates on the principle that all women must be believed in cases of rape (apparently, only men are capable of lying or bearing false witness), thereby allowing accusation to rob a man of his right to a fundamental legal principle – innocent until proven guilty.

Obviously, the suffering of a woman who is raped by a man is horrendous and something that our justice system should address, and suitable punishments administered, after a man is found guilty in a court of justice. It should not be determined by accusation or trial by media.

Then there is *cancel culture*, including deplatforming, doxing, or blacklisting which are used to supress free speech. Cancel culture is a term which came into use in the 21st century, that has a negative connotation –

> *Cancel Culture is a cultural phenomenon in which an individual thought to have acted or spoken in an unacceptable manner is ostracized, boycotted, shunned, fired or assaulted, often aided by social media.*
>
> (wikipedia.com, 2025)

As you can see, this cultural phenomenon is designed to shut down free speech by conflating violence with offensive language. The language of conservatives is often deemed to be 'offensive' while that of radicals is deemed 'appropriate'. This clearly shows an unwillingness to engage in free and open debate that would challenge the radical agenda's attack on liberty and free speech.

The concept behind free speech is that it should challenge established social norms and ideas which, by its very nature, will be offensive to some. Do you think some social groups in Australian society have 'privileged offence' over others? In other words, does their offence have special rights over others? Can you identify these groups? Do you detect a hidden agenda here?

More recently we have seen the emergence of *mis/disinformation* laws designed to introduce political and bureaucratic censorship on free speech. This legislation treats the Australian adult public like children, believing they are incapable of intelligent, discerning decision making. There is a big difference between protecting minors from harmful information and censoring the free speech of adult citizens living in a liberal democracy. Once again, the hidden agenda is to protect the radicals' goals which must not be questioned by free and open debate.

In 2024, the Australian Government called for written submissions regarding the mis/disinformation laws they proposed to introduce. I felt so strongly about this issue that I sent in the following response –

Communications Legislation Amendment (Combating Misinformation and Disinformation) Bill 2024
The voting public in Australia is composed of intelligent, discerning voters capable of making these decisions for themselves. They do not need politicians or bureaucrats censoring what they say or read. I refer you to J. S. Mill: *On Liberty*. May I suggest you all read his thesis before voting on this bill. This mis/disinformation Bill is an attempt to introduce political censorship on Australian citizens. It belongs on the agenda of a third world dictator not in the Parliament of a free speech liberal democracy. Frankly, I am disappointed this even made it onto the floor of our liberty inspired Parliament.
Kenneth N. Price

Do you consider the purpose of cancel culture or mis/disinformation laws to be an attempt to hide the truth? If you do, why do you think the radical, partisan sections of society would fear a challenge to their established narrative? Do you think they might fear the exposure of their hidden agenda?

I have also noticed three new developments that trouble me. Radicals are now engaging in *deceptive editing* of so-called documentaries to promote their agenda. A good example of this is found in the way that the ABC edited footage from an operation led by commando commander Heston Russell in Afghanistan in 2012. Russell was awarded more than $400,000 after he sued the ABC for defamation. The ABC claimed that the editing mistakes were accidental and not deliberate. Nevertheless, their documentary claimed that Heston Russell was a war criminal and their edited version of the video footage supported their claim that Heston Russell was capable of such an action while the unedited version did not.

The second development is *redefining terms* to alter the statistical evidence highlighting the prominence of problems. For example, redefining an individual terrorist attack as being an attack from a mentally deranged individual. Clearly, this would be designed to hide the frequency of terrorist attacks.

The third is providing dilution to rules governing planned projects. For example, the controversy over the clubbing to death of koalas to make way for a renewable energy project at the Clarke Creek Wind Farm was raised in 2023 by an ABC Report, *Why claims about euthanising koalas to make way for a Queensland wind farm are missing context, Nov 2023*. In the report, the ABC states –

> *…the site's developers must protect threatened animals such as birds, koalas, and greater gliders, and minimise or offset the destruction of habitats.*

Then came the dilution of this requirement –

> *Also included in the plan, which was drafted and approved before Squadron Energy acquired the farm in March 2022, are details of how euthanasia will be conducted in cases where injured animals are deemed to be 'unviable'.*
> *'Euthanasia will be conducted using blunt force trauma,'*
> *it states.*
> *'This is a hard, sharp blow to the base of the back of the skull with a blunt metal or heavy wooden bar.'*

The Clarke Creek Wind Farm occupies a project area of approximately 76,300 hectares along a 55km stretch of the Broadsound Range. How can a project of this size 'minimise or offset' the destruction of habitats? Do you think the dilution in the plan, which includes the euthanasia of 'injured animals', to develop this project could be exploited by Squadron Energy? If you do think that, in what way could it be exploited?

There are many other techniques that radicals use, but these are the most common. As you become aware of these deceptive tactics, you will identify many more for yourself. A study of logical fallacies will help you with this endeavour. You might like to start with reviewing this topic on YouTube, or reading *Thinking, Fast and Slow* by Daniel Kahneman, 2011.

Try not to let this get you down, especially when you discover how successful deceptive radicals are. It helps if you develop the healthy habit of laughing about it. Remember the kings of Europe kept and protected their court jesters, so they could be kept in touch with any inconsistencies or hypocrisy with their rule, while comedians today are always pointing out the absurdity of our actions and the duplicity of our leaders (that is, of course, if they have not been cancelled), so follow their example and find humour in what you discover and make a conscious effort not to become bitter and angry. When developing your sense of humour don't forget to learn how to laugh at yourself. We are all subject to human frailty and imperfection, and mistakes can happen, so learn to laugh at those mistakes you make in your life and do what you can to correct them. This will also help in not taking yourself too seriously, which can lead to actions which you might later regret. Dictators and tyrants, for example, do not have the capacity to laugh at themselves. Power unchecked by humour can be very destructive, as history has revealed.

As a final warning I advise you to question everything and make decisions for yourself. Don't let others make decisions for you. Take advice, yes, but decide for yourself. When you question everything, don't forget to question yourself, especially your own motivation. Ask these questions of yourself –

Why do I want this?

What am I trying to gain by adopting this?

How will this affect others?

What I have said here applies to all the ideas and values I present in this book, so I do not intend to repeat what I have said each time I offer a new idea or value.

I will also present you with further reading relevant to the ideas and values under consideration. I have found that one book leads to another, so I hope this will be the experience of those of you interested in pursuing the ideas you find interesting. Also, I will present unanswered questions for you to ponder or discuss with others. Ideally, parents and their children could come together and share their thoughts and evaluations. Don't forget, my intention is to introduce you to ideas and values that you may not have considered before. It is not to lecture you on your shortcomings or browbeat you into accepting what I offer.

Let me close this section by pointing out that each generation shapes their world in their own image. This was true for my generation as it will be for yours. Do you want your generation's image to be based on truth or radical, partisan ideology?

With this understanding, let us begin our journey of discovery along the lighted road and see if we can reach some mutual understanding about fulfilling your potential and achieving your goals in life.

Chapter 1:
The Nature of Truth

And ye shall know the truth, and the truth shall make you free.
(John 8:32, *King James Bible*)

It may seem a biased start at discovering truth by quoting from the *Bible*, but my intention here is to link truth with freedom. I am not expecting you to accept any religious belief. It is just that I believe freedom to be the greatest benefit that truth seekers acquire from their efforts, and since this is not an original idea of mine, I need to quote my source.

Let us pose for ourselves a question vital for our understanding of the reality of our existence –

What is truth?

A good beginning is to consider what the Sophists of the fifth and fourth centuries BC Greece taught their followers. Sophists believed only in the value of winning and succeeding. For them, rhetoric, argument and conviction were of paramount importance, especially when used for political success. Protagoras (490-420 BC), one of their original founders, believed that the human mind is incapable of conceiving universal truth. Therefore, truth should be seen as nothing more than whatever the general population can be persuaded to accept as true. In modern terms, Sophists believe that truth is *personal* not *universal* or *objective*.

Distinctions need to be shown here concerning *personal, universal* and *objective* truth.

Personal truth is an individual's understanding of reality,

> rooted in their unique experiences, values, memories, and emotions, which forms their deeply held beliefs about themselves and the world.
>
> (AI Overview, 2025)

> Universal truth suggests an absolute truth that is true for all people, at all times, and in all places, without exception.
>
> (AI Overview, 2025)

> Objective truth refers to facts or knowledge that exists independently of individual minds, perspectives, and biases. In science, objective truth means descriptions that are verifiable through the scientific method and are not influenced by the scientist's personal beliefs or cultural background.
>
> (AI Overview, 2025)

Returning to Protagoras, he believed that virtue can be taught and absorbed by cultural absorption (socially constructed) and not by recognising that virtue is a universal truth. For a Sophist, then, virtue is dependent primarily on one's perspective or social (cultural) background. Socrates (470 BC-399 BC), on the other hand, argues that virtue is arrived at not from instruction but from personal character, because parents often succeed or fail in transmitting virtue to their offspring. Socrates, then, sought to discover universal truths through the application of logic and reason. From the reasoning of Protagoras (relative truth) and Socrates (universal truth) we arrive at an understanding of the difference between *personal* and *universal* truth. However, truth for us today is shaped by our understanding of personal, objective, and universal truth.

Do you swear to tell the truth the whole truth
and nothing but the truth?
(Sworn Testimony, used in a court of law)

This is how a court of law attempts to arrive at truth. If you fail to uphold your sworn testimony by not telling the truth, you commit perjury and this places you in serious legal trouble. How would this play out in a court of law?

Consider this. Two people claim ownership of a sheep. The one holding the sheep claims it is his, while the other claims that the holder of the sheep stole it from him. How do you know who is telling the truth? What is the truth regarding the ownership of the sheep? It is not possible to determine this since both claim ownership. Let us assume that the one claiming it was stolen produces a witness who claims he saw the sheep being stolen. A Sophist would attack the credibility of the witness, claiming that he is conspiring with or favouring the one lacking possession of the sheep. You can see here the importance of rhetoric, argument, and persuasion. In modern terms, we refer to this practice as *sophistry*, something played out in our own courtrooms daily and sadly even in our politics and media. Often sophistry clouds our judgement, making it more difficult to arrive at truth, but it can also reveal hidden truth.

This brings to mind the wisdom of Solomon. Recall the story of the two women claiming motherhood of the same child. Solomon tells a guard to cut the child in half and give half to each person claiming motherhood. The woman who stops the dividing of the child is claimed by Solomon to be the mother, since the mother would want the child to live. This sounds reasonable and would no doubt be generally true, but what if the genuine mother's hatred of her opponent is such that she is willing to sacrifice her child to get revenge? Think here of a radical Islamist mother who encourages her child to become a suicide bomber. Alternatively, what if the false mother has a genuine love for the baby or is so repulsed by violence that she is willing to release her claim on the child to halt it? Perhaps these two positions are so unlikely that they do not qualify for genuine consideration. But are they *possible*? You see sophist persuasion at work here. Remember we are seeking truth, but to be objective must truth be apparent in all cases? Our court rooms overcome this obstacle by applying the standard 'beyond *reasonable* (not possible) doubt' to jury verdicts. Scientists also have a way of dealing with these extreme *exceptions* to truth. They say that there are always exceptions to the rule, but that these exceptions prove the rule.

I would like to point out that, in fact, there is universal truth in both these cases – the sheep's owner and the baby's mother do exist. It is just that our powers of observation and perception make it difficult, if not impossible, to discover. We can conclude that although truth may be complex or hidden it is not *malleable*, it is only our perception of it that is.

Do you agree with my observations and conclusions regarding truth so far? Do you have any observations of your own to discuss? Why not debate it with your family and friends, or suggest the following debating topic with your teacher for a class debate –

That truth is universal, not personal.

Because of the elusive nature of truth, scientists, lawyers etc. have moved away from trying to discover universal truth. Those who undertake the search for truth, therefore, speak of the three degrees of truth: the *possible*, the *probable* and the *certain*. Almost anything is possible, fewer things are probable and almost nothing is certain. The possible takes us into flights of fancy (thinking outside the box or pushing the envelope). The probable involves the application of logic and reason, and the weighing of facts, data, and evidence. The certain is most often found in faith or ideology, but some laws of predictability have been discovered in mathematics, physics, chemistry, economics, etc. through logical and reasonable observation. This reminds me of an amusing axiom –

> *Nothing is certain except death and taxes*
> (Benjamin Franklin, 1798)

Using sophistry, one could conclude that there is no universal truth or virtue, and therefore, no such thing as good and evil, right and wrong, or lies and deception, since truth and virtue are relative to the perspective of the holder of them. In short, there is only personal truth and personal virtue.

Can you see any danger in this belief? Consider the 'truth' and 'virtuous behaviour' as perceived by the general population in Hitler's Germany, Stalin's Russia, or Mao's China. What happened to the Jewish community living in Germany at this time? What happened to the kulaks of Russia, or the landlords and middle class during the Chinese communist revolution, or the intellectuals and party officials during China's cultural revolution? Can you see any parallels in the politics and culture of today's countries? Is there a race or group of people today that those using sophistry have singled out for derision, vilification, and hatred?

A lot is said these days about *personal truth* and *objective truth*, and it is presented to us as an either/or proposition. Let me say that whenever I am presented with an either/or argument alarm bells ring in my mind, because it is seldom the case that there are only two alternatives to any given situation. Usually, one can think of a third option or see the solution as a combination of the two given alternatives.

Before we continue this discussion, let me relate an interesting actual event in my life. At one time I happened to witness a disagreement over a solution to a problem my mother and father faced. This rarely occurred, because they were usually of one mind. They had both stated their positions and could not come to an agreement.

Chapter 1: The Nature of Truth

At one point in their discussion my mother realised that my father's solution was more logical than hers. I will never forget her reply –

Well, just because you are right doesn't mean that I am wrong.

Of course, mother was right. Maybe they were both right. Maybe mother's solution was more reasonable while father's was more logical. Alternatively, there could be a third solution that neither of them had yet discovered.

Do you think this is probable? Explain your decision by way of example.

Could it be that truth can be found at the personal, universal, and objective levels? Solely seeing truth on a personal level, however, is likely to lead to bigotry or prejudice, neither of which is desirable, nor is viewing truth as solely objective because it can lead to conclusions that are devoid of empathy. Universal truth introduces the concept of *beauty* and *goodness* being related to truth. Given this, should we start from the axiom that to know truth is to seek the inherent beauty or goodness of it?

However, what if an objective truth is confronting. Is it possible for truth to be ugly and evil? Should we make a value judgement here? Should we seek the beautiful and the good over the ugly and evil, or should we accept that both are possible when seeking truth? Here I have presented you with an either/or proposition. What is your response? Could it be that we must accept that objective truth can be both beautiful and good or ugly and evil, but that to arrive at universal truth we *should prefer* the beautiful and good over the ugly and evil? But doesn't this make our universal truth personal by being dependent on our perception of the beautiful and good?

Do you see our dilemma? We may discover an objective truth but by making it subject to our preference it is no longer objective but has become personal. Should we perhaps reach a final judgement by evaluating objective truth against our personal experience?

Nevertheless, in doing this we also must accept that personal experience is limited in arriving at universal or objective truth. Furthermore, we must also accept that personal experience alone is not the only valid way of arriving at *personal truth*. For example, we are all capable of reading about or witnessing the experience and thoughts of others and then testing their conclusions against our own personal experience to arrive at their essential goodness or evilness. Does this exercise in reading influence our own perception of what we experience?

Moreover, there are obvious logical dangers associated with relying too heavily on *personal truth*. Among others, there is the *non-sequitur* fallacy. That is, where a general conclusion does not logically follow from one experience. A good example of this is found in trying to find the cause of the plague which hit Europe in the 14th century. It wiped out approximately one-third of Europe's population. Doctors and scholars who tried to fathom the cause of the plague noticed that the rat population first died, then people started dying, so they concluded, from their personal experience, that the rats carried the plague and passed it on to people. However, closer study in later years discovered that the rats did indeed die from the plague virus, but they did not pass it on to people. Instead, it was the fleas that fed on the rats that infected the rats with the plague, and after the rats died the fleas became ferociously hungry and consequently migrated to people who passed the plague on to people. So it is infected fleas, not rats, that infect people with the plague. Despite this new discovery we still control the flea population by controlling the rat population because we do not have an effective way of controlling the flea population alone.

I will add here that some of those who followed religious doctrine during the plague believed that God was punishing them for their moral wrongdoing. Consequently, a group of superstitious fanatics called flagellants began the religious practice of public flagellation, believing that such a public display would offer restitution for their sins and save them from contracting the plague. This is an example of how mistaken personal truth, based on religious superstition, can become.

What is more, there is danger in drawing a generalisation from only one experience. After all, *one sparrow does not a summer make*, and personal truth only amounts to *anecdotal evidence*. A good place to start an inquiry, but not to end it. Therefore, we should never draw generalisations from the experience of any one individual. Personal truth also can be manipulated by individuals. They may or may not be misleading us, but their memory of any experience could be inaccurate or misinterpreted.

I am reminded of a joke I heard many years ago. The Board of Directors of a company was conducting interviews for the position of managing director which had recently become available. First, they interviewed the manager of their engineering division. At the end of the interview, they asked the engineer what 2+2 equalled.

Why 4, he replied, *it can only equal 4 and nothing else.*

Next, they interviewed the manager of their sales department. At the end of the interview, they asked the same question.

Given the need for cost variations and profit margins, I would say it equals 5, was the sales manager's reply.

Finally, they interviewed the manager of the accounting department. Again, at the end of the interview, they asked their chief accountant what 2+2 equals. The accountant smiled and replied,

What do you want it to represent?

What is interesting about this joke is that it tells us what truth can represent for different people. For people of maths or science truth operates within the bounds of logic and verifiable fact. To flexible people truth is subject to the variability of their needs. Finally, for people with an ideological bias, truth is subject to an array of endless creative possibilities. Let's hope those who give top priority to their own needs or their ideological bias have the wisdom to stay within their own fields of expertise and not try to dominate the opinions of others or lead us into ethical behaviour that will compromise our integrity.

What is it to know truth?

What is truth? Pontius Pilate mockingly asks of Jesus Christ, who claimed to be the bearer of truth. For Pilate, a powerful Roman Governor, truth is optional, and of no consequence, since he can define it in any way he wants. Such is the prerogative of the powerful, much like the relative concept of truth espoused by the Sophists of ancient Greece and Idealogues of today.

Let me say that my conclusions about the nature of truth, which follow, have been arrived at by combining *personal, universal, and objective truth*. I am of the opinion that logic leads us to what is objectively true, while reason helps balance it with our own personal truth, and universal truth is discovered through wisdom, common sense, prudence, and empathy. How can we make what we discover about truth be right for us without changing the actual truth we have discovered? By all means, we should analyse the evidence, facts and data to arrive at objective truth, then apply our memory and reflection to arrive at a well-supported and reasonable belief, and finally use our wisdom, common sense, prudence, and empathy to make a final judgement about co-opting truth into our daily life. In this way, all three elements of truth work in unionism to provide us with a holistic view of truth and not the triumph of any one over the others.

You might like to examine how these different aspects of truth play out by considering the following evidence. Some people prefer flesh that is infused with adrenalin, because it makes it tender and tasty, so they prepare their meat while the animal is still alive, thus allowing the adrenalin to infuse into the flesh. For example, they scale and gut their fish while still alive.

I remember once being invited by some American friends to a restaurant that they said served the best chilli crab in Singapore. The chilli crab was indeed delicious, the buttered chilli being spread liberally outside the crab's shell, thereby necessitating one to lick one's fingers while eating. Quite an experience. However, as an entrée I was encouraged to try the frogs legs, which I did. Later, when going to the lavatory, I passed by the kitchen. The door was open so I looked inside and saw the chef preparing the frogs legs. He took a frog from a bucket full of frogs and slowly cut off its hind legs while it was still alive, then threw it back into the same bucket where it squirmed around with the other frogs. I never ate frog legs in Singapore again.

I won't go into the other myriad ways that some people prepare their food so as to infuse it with adrenalin, because it is so disquieting. Nevertheless, we can conclude that infusing flesh with adrenalin does, indeed, make it tender and tasty. This is an objective truth, so it would be logical to conduct these practices when preparing food. This may be logical, but is it reasonable? Does it offend our sensibility, our intuition? So is this a truth that our reason tells us not to practise? Again, for me it is, but clearly for others it is not. For me it is unreasonable because it lacks empathy for the frogs, but for those with less or no empathy it is not. Well, you might rightly ask, which is it, right or wrong? Actually, for some countries it is illegal to prepare food in this way and for others it is not.

The issue of sensitivity brings our discussion into the area of what our personal truth decides is an appropriate level of compassion for us to hold. Sometimes our compassion leads us into unsound decisions. This occurs when our empathy transforms into compassion. The compassionate believe they are showing pity, understanding and sympathy for those who suffer, while those who point out the probable harmful consequences of their compassion are deemed as heartless and uncaring. In this way the compassionate believe that they occupy a position of superior morality or ethical behaviour over their opponents. This is sometimes used in a self-righteous or manipulative way to gain an advantage. Again, this is another sophist technique. When taken to extremes this can include spending money on social projects that a society simply cannot afford. When such spending takes a society into intergenerational debt its compassion has led it to conclude that it is right and proper to steal from its descendants or destroy its country's economy with uncontrolled spending. The 'compassionate' do this because their personal truth tells them that their compassion is boundless and therefore above criticisms of prudence.

Compassion can also lead a society into making decisions that enable some privileged minorities to live dependent lives, thereby robbing them of the opportunity to fulfil their potential. Such is the case with drug dependent citizens, for example, who are assisted by the compassionate society to maintain their dependence.

Do you accept that logic can lead us into unwise conclusions? Do you accept that compassion can do the same? Explain your position in clear terms.

This brings to mind an insightful movie, *A Few Good Men,* which is a courtroom drama where Tom Cruise's character, Daniel Kaffee, shouts at Jack Nicholson's character, Colonel Nathan R. Jessup, who is in the court dock. Kaffee shouts,

I want the truth!

Colonel Jessup replies with as much conviction,

You can't handle the truth!

On the other hand,

To know truth is to know things as they are.

Chapter 1: The Nature of Truth

(St. Thomas Aquinas, *The Aquinas Catechism*, XV(B), 1273)

St. Thomas suggests that truth is knowable and that it is knowable by studying its reality. This becomes the foundation of our understanding the world as it truly is rather than as one might be led to believe it is through sophistry, deception, and lies. This truth also enables us to make informed decisions based on accurate information and break free of the false narratives imposed on us by radical ideology or boundless compassion.

Also, by viewing ourselves truthfully we come to see ourselves as we truly are, enabling us to accept our character flaws, mistakes and weaknesses. Thus, allowing us to grow our authentic self and build our integrity. Truth enables us to break free from ignorance and deception and empowers us to make informed choices that unlock our potential. It broadens our understanding of the world, which helps us develop empathy for others and not be overly swayed by compassion. By realising the truth about reality and ourselves, we develop integrity and authenticity. In this way truth sets us free. We come to recognise that our feelings guide us to a perception that something is true, our senses making the necessary objective observations and our mind applying logic, reason, wisdom, common sense, empathy, and prudence to affirm it. Of course, scientists would argue that this is the approach that artists make. That is for artists, intuition (a message from their feelings) gives rise to a theme and from the theme a story or narrative. Scientists, on the other hand, would argue that they receive a thought (a message from the mind) which leads them to objective experiment, a hypothesis, and ultimately a thesis.

So this is what our understanding about the nature of truth entails, but are there different levels of truth?

Chapter 2:
The Three Levels of Truth

Lately, I watched several lectures by Jordan Peterson in his *Biblical Series* on YouTube where he reflected on the three different levels of truth. In his lecture he skirted over this statement, so I have picked up on it here and attempted to flesh out its meaning for myself as best as I can. I have now concluded that truth does indeed exist on three separate levels, and each level needs careful consideration which is unique to that specific level. The three levels of truth that Jordan Peterson led me to discovered are –

The Transcendental Level,
the Existential Level,
and *the Archetypal Level.*

To discover the truth existing at each of these levels we need to read and understand the works of *sages through the ages* (the collective wisdom of wise individuals throughout history), while applying our logic, reason, wisdom, common sense, prudence, and empathy to reach judgements regarding their application in our lives.

The Transcendental Level

This level is accessible to us through imagination and inspiration. It is most prominently relayed to us through the works of prophets and saints, philosophers, poets, dramatists, and novelists. There are also other inspirational and creative enterprises like opera, ballet, painting, sculpture, architecture etc. that I have not covered here since I am primarily interested in storytelling or the use of words to communicate meaning on this level of truth. Of the three levels this level emerges first historically, because it was used to make order out of the chaos of our existence. It tried to explain why certain things happened, both in the physical world and in the world of human relationships. It also carries us to a place beyond our earthly realm. It is articulated to us through *revelation, logic, reason,* and *creative inspiration*. Its truth is transcendental. That is, concepts beyond ordinary or common experience. It is often expressed in narrative form. Heroic narratives, for example, are vital to a culture because they foster a shared identity, transmit collective values, and provide historical and moral benchmarks for members of a group. Again, Jordon Peterson has done a lot of work on the importance of storytelling to our understanding of who we are, the world we live in, and our place in it.

The Prophets and Saints
Prophets use revelation which is contained in religious works that provide us with a moral code that helps us live our lives in happy and fulfilling ways. It is designed to minimise the pitfalls in life that can result in us experiencing great suffering and pain and leads us towards goodness. The chief religious work of Christians is *The Holy Bib*le, for the Jews it's *the Torah,* Muslims have *the Quran,* Hindus *the Verda,* Buddhists *the Tripitaka,* and Taoists the *Tao Te Ching* to name just a few of the more prominent holy texts. The moral codes expressed in these holy texts are the foundational stones of the various civilisations that they inspired. Without a moral code, civilisation is not possible, and if a civilisation loses its moral code of behaviour it will be destroyed. This has been the cycle of civilisations for thousands of years.

These moral codes include explaining how we are responsible for the evil that we find in the world and how to deal with it.

The ancient Greek myth of Pandora's Box, for example, explains the origin of evil and suffering in the world. It is a cautionary tale warning us against excessive curiosity and tampering with the unknown. When Pandora opens the box that Zeus gave her she releases all of the world's evils, including disease, war and death. Hope remains trapped inside the box and offers solace and reliance against these evils.

The story of Adam and Eve in the *Holy Bible* is another example which suggests that evil originated from humanity's choice of free will over divine will. This highlights a determination of humanity to follow its own path rather than to follow God's instruction, leading to humanity's knowledge of good and evil and their ability to participate in it. Following this Adam and Eve become shameful and try to hide the truth from God. The consequences of their action are hardship, toil, and mortality.

Hindus explain the existence of evil in one's life as a result of it rising naturally from one's actions, and a misunderstanding of one's true spiritual nature rather than a divine imposition. The illusory nature of materialism, for example, obscures our ultimate spiritual reality.

One of the ways Jesus helped his followers to discover truth was by using parables. Of the many parables Jesus used, one that impacted me most, is the parable of The Good Samaritan, related to us in Luke 10:29-37. In essence, the story tells us that a man travelling from Jerusalem to Jericho is set upon by a group of bandits, who strip him of everything he owns, including his clothes, and beat him mercilessly. He is left lying naked and helpless by the roadside. A Jewish priest and Levite pass by without helping the distressed man. However, a Samaritan stops and cares for him. This includes taking him to an inn where the Samaritan pays for new clothes, accommodation and care for him.

We are relieved to know that the distressed man was eventually helped by the Samaritan, because he was in genuine need of help through no fault of his own, but the story's moral goes deeper than that. It is necessary for us to know that, at the time Jesus told this parable, the Samaritans were the despised enemies of the Jews. Does this information change the way you now understand this parable?

Could it be that Jesus wants us to understand that goodness does not reside in our religion, national identity, or race, but rather in our deeds to our fellow human beings? Is it our empathy and benevolence (well-meaning, kindness) for others that is the source of our goodness?

Then, there are the different religious beliefs found in these texts which can inspire us. For example, the *Ten Commandments* contained in the *Torah*. The Muslim belief in the five pillars of faith, *Shahadah* (Faith), *Salah* (Prayer), *Sawm Ramadan* (Fasting), *Zakat* (Almsgiving) *and Hajj* (Pilgrimage), or *Karma* (Fate, Destiny), *Artha* (Wealth, Property), *Dharma* (Right way of living, Path to rightness) and *Moksha* (Freedom, Liberation) as practised by Hindus. The cycle of suffering and rebirth until one reaches *nirvana* (release from the cycle of rebirth) accepted by Buddhists. To conclude, the adherence to *the way* (Inaction, Simplicity, Living in harmony with nature) as practised by Taoists. Unfortunately, I do not have the space here to explore all these sacred beliefs, but if you are interested, you should explore and discover those religious beliefs you feel would be valuable for you. Remember, your exploration is to understand the moral teachings of different religions. It is not necessary to adopt any one as being the arbiter of absolute truth.

I do, however, want to explore one of my favourite myths taken from one of these texts. It is the one about a group of blind men who encounter an elephant for the first time in their lives. It was first recorded on the Indian subcontinent around 500 BC. However, it is believed to have existed long before this, so we are unable to attribute it to either Hindu or Buddhist origins. The parable has several variations but broadly goes like this –

A group of blind men inspect an elephant using nothing but their sense of touch to reach an understanding of what an elephant truly is. The first blind man touches the elephant's trunk and concludes that an elephant is like a thick snake. The second touches the elephant's ear and decides it seems like a fan. The third touches its leg and thinks it is like a tree trunk. The last two touch the elephant's side and tail and believe it seems like a wall and rope respectively. What follows is a violent argument between the blind men, each being convinced the elephant must be what they had experienced.

This myth can be said to highlight the limitations our sensory perception and reasoning encounter when trying to reach conclusions about something as mysterious and remote as truth, when nobody can see, or even visualise, the totality of the subject under scrutiny. A cogent reminder of our limited capacity for understanding truth when using our senses and personal experience, and a warning about becoming violent about things we have only a limited capacity to understand.

Given this, do you think we should cease trying to discover something as difficult and remote as truth? Alternatively, do you think we should continue this fascinating quest, but refrain from violence to settle our differences of opinion? There's that pesky little either/or proposition again.

Saint Augustine (354 AD-430 AD) of Hippo located in North Africa was a highly influential theologian and philosopher whose writings shaped Western Christianity. His autobiography titled *Confessions* (late 4th century AD) chronicles his intellectual journey from a lavish lifestyle and sinful youth to his eventual conversion to Christianity. His views on sin, grace, freedom and sexuality had a profound effect on Western culture and are at odds with today's humanist, liberal, and feminist viewpoints. Saint Augustine's views on sin, for example, centres around the doctrine of original sin, which maintains a belief that all humanity inherited a corrupted nature and guilt from Adam and Eve's disobedience. This inherent character flaw in all human beings leads to nescience (lacking knowledge, unawareness), chaotic desires, misguided wants, a proclivity for further sin, and physical death, making human beings incapable of achieving true freedom or righteousness without God's grace.

Augustine was canonised by Pope Boniface VIII in 1298 AD as a result of his veneration and popular acclaim. Saint Augustine is the patron saint of brewers, printers, and theologians. His patronage of brewers stems from his own conversion from a life of loose living, a story that inspires those struggling with vices.

Sir Thomas More (1478-1535 AD), now Saint Thomas the patron Saint of politicians and lawyers, following his canonisation by Pope Pius XI in 1935, wrote a philosophical fiction called *Utopia* (1516 AD) in which he describes a perfect and imaginary world. The word 'utopia' is derived from the Greek phrase *ou topos* meaning 'no place' which is what Saint Thomas intended to describe. Utopia is a concept we perceive through our inspirational and creative appreciation of transcendental truth. It is not something available in an imperfect world inhabited by imperfect human beings. Ever since, the word *utopia* has been used to describe an impractically idealistic concept or planned society.

Do you believe that some ideas are utopian? Give a detailed explanation for your belief. Are idealism and realism antithetical to each other or do they require a trade-off for citizens of a liberal democracy? Are human rights an ideal (utopian concept) for us to aim towards or should we consider them absolute? If we do consider human rights to be absolute, should we enforce them on other cultures through cultural imperialism? What might be some of the unintended consequences that might arise if we attempted to impose our concept of human rights on other cultures?

Saint Thomas was executed by King Henry VIII for treason when he refused to take the Oath of Supremacy, making Henry VIII the head of the Church of England. Saint Thomas was a staunch opponent of Protestantism and willing to die for the principle of papal infallibility and the Pope's spiritual supremacy over the Kings and Queens of Europe and England. Clearly, Saint Thomas was a man of integrity who believed that once Christendom fractured it would splinter into an ever-increasing number of factions until it ceased to unite but rather divided Christendom and, by extension, Western Civilisation itself. For example, Saint Thomas blamed the Peasants Revolt in Germany (1524) on Martin Luther, the founder of Protestant Lutheranism. Such division (created by the supremacy of a secular ruler over a spiritual leader), Saint Thomas believed, would ultimately lead to the downfall of not only Christendom but also Western Civilisation. Saint Thomas' sacrifice, therefore, can be seen as his attempt to prevent this from happening.

Erasmus (1466-1536), a Christian humanist of the Northern Renaissance and first editor of *The New Testament*, described Saint Thomas as *omnium horarum homo*, a Latin phrase that loosely translates into *A Man For All Seasons*. A famous title that stuck and was used as the title of a play and movie describing the story of Saint Thomas' life.

Was Saint Thomas right to believe in the danger that Protestantism posed for Christendom and Western Civilisation? Do you think Saint Thomas was right to sacrifice his life for a principle? Do you detect a connection here with Socrates' concept regarding the preservation of one's virtuous soul?

Saint Thomas' Protestant critics point to his abusive treatment of Protestant heretics as evidence of his unethical behaviour. While holding the office of Lord Chancellor, Sir Thomas More was required to at least appoint Protestant heretics to courts of law which included physical torture during the pre-trial discovery stage and burning at the stake for convicted heretics. Saint Thomas defended his involvement in the persecution of Protestant heretics in his *Apologia* (1533) as being necessary to uphold the Catholic faith and maintain social order.

Justice Michael Kirby, Australian High Court Judge (1996-2009) and President of the International Commission of Jurists (1995-98), has this to say about Sir Thomas' action –

> *Doubtless he saw himself, as many judges before and since have done, as a mere instrument of the legal power of the State.*
> (Justice Kirby, *Thomas More, Martin Luther and the Judiciary Today*, speech to Thomas More Society, 1997)

Do you think Sir Thomas More was unethical in his participation of Protestant persecution or do you believe his action was justified? Do you think that judges should see themselves as 'mere instruments of the legal power of the State'? Did Saint Thomas see himself as upholding the legal power of the State or the spiritual supremacy of the Catholic faith? What role should justice play in the judgements of judges? Would justice always be on the side of the State, or, for that matter, the Catholic faith?

Today, many accuse judges of becoming politicalised by engaging in judicial overreach and a two-tiered justice system. Some even make the claim that politicalised judges create a revolving door of justice (because they encourage recidivism) for those who are treated too leniently by our justice system. What is your opinion about this? Do you think this is an accurate observation on the part of those who are critical of some of the judgements of our judges? Should limits be placed on a judge's power to exercise *mitigating circumstances*? Mitigating circumstances are factors that can lessen the criminal charges or punishment of criminals owing to a reduction in their criminal culpability.

Some have suggested that if judges are unaccountable for their mitigating-based decisions, and are incapable of making responsible decisions, perhaps they should be stripped of this capability and have it passed on to a criminal's behaviour in prison. That is, that a judge must hand down the same punishment for the same crime committed by any juvenile or citizen and that a reduction in his/her sentence should only be granted on their proven behaviour whilst in prison. That is, if they show genuine remorse, good behaviour, or co-operation whilst incarcerated.

What is your opinion regarding mitigating circumstances and reductions in sentencing? Here is another debating topic for you –

That sentence reduction for criminals
should be handled by prisons not judges.
This opens another discussion. The flaws found in human nature.

The Philosophers

Philosophers use logic and reason which is contained in the great philosophical works of the Greeks and other civilisations.

Socrates never wrote anything down. It was Socrates' followers, Aristophanes (450 BC-388 BC), Xenophon (431 BC-354 BC), and in particular Plato (428-348 BC) who wrote down what they remembered from the discussions Socrates had with his followers at their symposium (a school Socrates had established in Athens). I am reminded of the notes I took at the lectures my professors gave and can't help but wonder what Socrates actually said. For Socrates, caring for our soul, the reasoning part of our being that lived on after death, was of paramount importance. This meant becoming virtuous in order to achieve happiness. That evil acts were committed out of ignorance and that committing an injustice is far worse than suffering an injustice, because of the effect it will have on your soul. Socrates' idea of the soul was established before Christianity.

Another philosophical principle I admire is the existence of perfection and universal truth as explained by Plato in *The Republic* (around 375 BC), his book on political philosophy. From Plato's writing we discover that he believed that we are all aware of the perfect forms of things, but that we can never achieve their perfection. A perfect chair, for example, would be in the mind of a carpenter who would set out to build a chair. The chair that the carpenter builds, however, will only be a representation of a perfect chair we all can imagine. This is known as Plato's *doctrine of the forms* which highlight his belief in the concepts of perfection and universal truth, and the importance of ideals for us to stive towards without ever achieving them. For example, try to understand the significance of escaping from Plato's darkened cave (one of Plato's metaphors for discovering truth found in Book VII of *The Republic*). You can discover for yourself where Plato thought these perfect forms resided, and why we can only visualise them. Have I whetted your appetite? I hope so.

I have personal experience of this. I once had two carpenters come to dinner with my family and me when I was working in Mount Isa. I asked them what the most important factor was for their trade. Their answer was instructive. Before we start, they both agreed, we must first visualise what it is we are trying to build. This is Socrates' perfect form that we all can visualise but never reproduce. From this pursuit of perfection, the modern world has produced the amazing technical and scientific achievements that we all enjoy today.

Plato's book: *The Last Days of Socrates* (written sometime between 399 and 387 BC), which covers the trial and condemnation of Socrates on charges of heresy and corrupting young minds, reveals the Socratic belief in being responsible for oneself, and why this is necessary for preserving the integrity of our soul. It is a small book but packed with so much.

Turning back to universal truth, Athens, where Socrates and Plato resided, was a maritime City State, so shipbuilding was a much-respected enterprise. Let us, therefore, consider the building of a ship. You can try to persuade people all you like (as Sophists would do) about the superiority of a ship you want them to build, but if the design does not follow the natural (and universal) laws of buoyancy and flotation it is doomed to failure (consider what happened to the *Mary Rose*). You can even extend this truth further by observing that ships have often been used as a metaphor for the state. That is, ignore the universal truths about mathematics, science, economics etc. and your ship of state will be put in danger. I guess reality has a way of catching up on those who would put rhetoric above fact and data analysis. One can choose to ignore reality but not the consequences of one's ignorance. Such is the proof of universal truth as discovered by our mathematicians, scientists etc.

Of course, ideal or abstract truth is somewhat harder to prove, because it contains moral and ethical judgements. However, can some moral and ethical truths be universal? Can some moral or ethical values be considered good and some bad? On what grounds do you claim this? If this is true, should we move towards the 'good' in our lifetime? Why?

Socrates also left us with the Socratic Tradition, where people of reasonable intelligence can arrive at universal truth by posing questions and arriving at a reasonable agreement about the answers. As you can see, I am currently using the Socratic Tradition in our pursuit of truth. I present you with information then pose questions for you to use your logic and reason to answer. Hopefully, you are also discussing these questions with others you trust, enjoying their company, and arriving at agreed reasonable answers.

Plato's *Republic* also contains his further ideas about political philosophy. It deals with justice and why it is in our best interest to be just. Plato also rejects democracy, believing it is dangerous for the soul owing to its excessive freedom. Instead, he is in favour of dividing society into three sections –

> the *Guardians* (rulers) those who keep order in society (the philosopher kings and queens based on hereditary and educated in philosophy),
>
> the *Auxiliaries* (aristocracy and warriors) those who are courageous and skilled in warfare and who are loyal in protecting their society,
>
> and the *Producers* (workers) who make the goods and provide the services for society.

The main criticism of Plato's republic is its over-dependence on logic and lack of empathy. Another criticism is articulated in the common phrase –

> *Who guards the guardians while the guardians guard us?*

Which is the function that democracy is expected to perform.

Do you detect a connection between Plato's *Republic* and the emergence of European monarchies, their aristocracy and armies, and their peasant farmers? What is commonly referred to as the Feudal System?

Aristotle (384 BC-322 BC) was a student of Plato and the teacher of Alexander the Great (356 BC-323 BC). However, he rejected the doctrine of the forms as articulated by his mentor Plato. Aristotle is considered the father of empirical science since he invented the field of formal logic and categorised the different scientific disciplines, particularly regarding nature and biology. He championed a belief in causality with his most famous saying –

We do not say we truly know a thing until we know its cause.
(Aristotle, *Physics* and *Metaphysics*,
4th century BC)

For Aristotle, to discover why things exist, the key question to ask is what causes them to exist? So in terms of ethics, he believed the goal of human life is *eudaimonia*, which, when translated, means happiness or flourishing. From his perspective, then, we should ask, what causes us to be happy, and to flourish? Then we would discover the source of our happiness and become happy and flourish.

Another of Aristotle's great contributions to our understanding of the virtuous life is his theory of *The Golden Mean*. In its most basic terms this theory promotes the idea that virtue lies in the middle rather than the extremes. This suggests a balanced, moderate approach to life, as opposed to one of radical extremism. You can think of this in terms of violence at one extreme and compassion at the other. The golden mean would exist when there is moderation between the violence and compassion in our lives.

Another concept of classical Greece addresses the question as to whether there is a mythical force in the universe that rights wrongs. Classical Greek mythology believed there is. Greek mythology tells us there is a Goddess called *Nemesis* who pays back hubris (excessive pride or arrogance). The Hindus and Buddhists believe in *Karma*, which insists that our fate in future existences is determined by our actions in this life. The New Testament of Christians tells us to limit our actions when dealing with others –

> *Do unto others as you would have them do unto you.*
> (*The New Testament,* Matthew 7:12, and Luke 6:31)

What these three sources are warning us to avoid is excess in our actions and thoughts which encourage us to brag about our achievements and become arrogant, self-righteous, and fall into evil practice. In short, they are reinforcing Aristotle's *Golden Mean*.

Do you think the Universe has a way of levelling justice on the unjust? Do you believe in the saying that

> *the truth will eventually be revealed.*

Does the revealing of truth bring justice to the untruthful? Argue your opinion from personal experience and objective analysis.

For me, the most important Greek and Latin philosophical sources are the Stoic philosophers who articulated our place in nature and the Four Virtues (*Courage, Moderation, Justice, and Wisdom*) that a virtuous person should pursue. The original Stoic philosopher was Zeno of Citium around 300 BC. Other great Stoic philosophers include Cicero (106-43 BC), Seneca (4-65 BC) and The Roman Emperor, Marcus Aurelius (121-180 AD).

Virtue, as explained by the Stoics, is a quality worthy of understanding and emulation. Let me explain one aspect of their principles regarding Courage. Stoics believe that we are all subjected to pain and suffering during our lifetimes. Physical pain and emotional suffering seem constants in our lives, and we are tempted to believe that our pain and suffering is unique to us. The Stoics, however, believe that it is a condition of our existence. That is, everyone experiences pain and suffering at different times in their lifetime. Since we are unable to avoid pain and suffering in our lives, they believe the only control we have over it is our response to it. We can either let it crush us, or we can accept it and use it as an opportunity to grow. Through acceptance and overcoming the pain and suffering in our lives we can become more courageous and better able to face the hardships that life will throw our way in the future.

So if we cultivate the *Four Virtues,* we will become virtuous, and our virtue will enable us to handle better the vagaries of life. Do you think this Stoic belief has value for you in your lifetime? How so?

Given these different perspectives on what constitutes good virtue, what have you discovered that might lead you to a more virtuous life? What is your evaluation of Socrates' belief in the paramount importance of our souls, a life after death and his insistence in one's personal responsibility even to the point of sacrificing one's own life? Does Plato's doctrine of the forms or Aristotle's belief in causality and the golden mean leave you confused or wiser? Are the Stoics' four virtues worthy of your consideration? Should we maintain the integrity of our soul whatever the cost? Should we seek universal truth through Plato's doctrine or Aristotle's causality or both? Would it be fulfilling to cultivate the four virtues of the Stoics? Maybe you might like a compromise between the four. What would that be? How do you define happiness? Do you believe that the primary goal of life is to achieve happiness and to flourish? Why? Can you see any problems arising for a society whose individuals all pursued their individual conception of happiness? Should we adopt a moderate approach to achieving happiness as opposed to an extreme, obsessive approach? Would it be best to achieve happiness through the pursuit of a virtuous life?

One of the East's better-known philosophical principles is the concept of respect for elders contained in the Confusion Order. Asian people refer to this as *filial piety,* a concept that was first presented to them by the great Chinese philosopher, Confucius (551–479 BC). Filial piety urges us to accept the wisdom of our elders and defer to their superior position. This concept of superior/inferior order in our relationships provides stability for our society and the ability to benefit from the wisdom of our elders. It is worth noting here that Confucius articulated his concept of filial piety during a period of political fragmentation, social upheaval, and constant warfare among various feudal states led by Chinese warlords. Filial piety, therefore, was Confucius' way of trying to offer a means to restore social order and harmony to the Chinese people.

Confucius also recognised that our elders may be wrong, or even worse, tyrannical or malevolent. So he put a caveat on filial piety. That is, people of inferior status are not required to submit to the superior status of their elders if the elders ask them to do anything that would violate their integrity. This is the Confucian principle of *remonstrance* which prevents filial piety from requiring unconditional obedience to the point of violating one's own integrity. Rather, a truly pious youth would actively work to make their elders more upright, rather than simply comply with wrongdoing. One important aspect of filial piety is that it does provide limits on the excesses of youthful exuberance and inexperience and highlights the importance of good manners and decency to a civilised society.

Should we accept the Confucian Order for our society? Would you want to see restrictions placed on this Order? Would your restrictions apply to adults only or would you include minors as well? Would restrictions on minors be different from those placed on adults? What are those restrictions and how do you propose to enforce them?

Creative Inspiration is revealed to us through the works of drama, poetry, and prose. Obviously, the great works of Dramatists; Metaphysical, Romantic and Modern poets; and Novelists spring to mind. Again, I have greatly limited my observations here for the sake of expediency.

The Dramatists
Sophocles (about 496-406 BC), a famous ancient Greek dramatist, wrote many great plays. Two of those plays were *Antigone* (441 BC) and *Oedipus Rex* (429 BC). The plot line, based on Greek mythology, is a fascinating tale. Antigone is the daughter of Oedipus (King of

Thebes) who unintentional kills his father and marries his mother. Antigone and her two brothers (Eteocles and Polynices) are the product of this incestuous union. When the truth is revealed to Oedipus, he goes insane, takes out his own eyes and exiles himself. Eteocles and Polynices fight for the kingdom of Thebes. Both are killed in the ensuing battle and Creon, Oedipus' brother-in-law (and uncle) becomes king. Creon decrees that Eteocles will have a proper burial while Polynices, a traitor, will have his body left for the dogs and vultures to devour. Antigone decides to give Polynices a proper burial and performs the proper burial rights over him. Creon is enraged that Antigone has defied him and orders Antigone executed by burying her alive in a cave. Later, Creon has a change of heart and orders Antigone released, only to discover that she has hanged herself.

This punishment that Antigone suffers needs explanation. The Greeks did not believe in capital punishment, so when a guilty person had committed a crime worthy of capital punishment (in Antigone's case the crime was treason) they were entombed in a cave with a piece of rope. This meant that the guilty would either die from suffocation (a natural process) or commit suicide by hanging themselves.

There are many themes and pieces of advice that Sophocles' plays divulge. First there is the importance of fate in our lives. Poor Oedipus, through no fault of his own, has fate conspire against him and has him unwittingly commit the immoral acts of patricide and incest. The human suffering he cannot endure after discovering the truth is something that evokes our pathos (pity, sadness), and we fear what fate might send our way. Next comes the decision Antigone makes. Does she follow Creon's law or uphold the law of the Gods on behalf of her brother? What do we make of Antigone's free choice regarding Creon's decree? Is she really defiant or merely a victim of the cruel and devastating events in her life? Then there is Creon's decree. Should Creon make an exception for Antigone, or follow the legal principle that 'no one is above the law', as an example of his commitment to justice? Would a wise ruler admit fault and change his decree? Is it dangerous for a ruler to change his mind? These questions play with our minds long after the plays have ended.

What role, if any, do you believe fate or destiny plays in your life? How does this affect your free will? Are our choices in life limited by the circumstances we find ourselves in? Are we capable of changing the circumstances in our life by our own courage and determination?

The great works of the inestimable dramatist William Shakespeare (1564–1616 AD), show us the tragedy found in our character flaws. The tragedy that Macbeth faces because of his ambition –

> *I have no spur to prick the sides of my intent, but only*
> *Vaulting ambition, which o'erleaps itself*
> *And falls on th' other.*
>
> (Act 1, Scene 7)

is a warning to us all to temper our ambition with prudence.

Do you think a person's ambition can lead someone into evil acts? What would be justice in such a circumstance? What becomes of Macbeth in Shakespeare's play?

What Romeo and Juliet suffer from their obsessive love –

> *Did my heart love till now? Forswear it, sight, for I ne'er saw*
> *true beauty till this night.*
>
> (Act I, Scene 5)

warns us all not to be infatuated by the superficial attraction of beauty rather than a deeper contemplation of love at first sight. What fate awaits Romeo and Juliet as a consequence of their obsession over each other?

What Hamlet suffers from his procrastination and indecision –

> *To be, or not to be, that is the question.*
>
> (Act 3, Scene 1)

forces us to reflect on these traits in our own characters. Some dangers that we may face if we procrastinate or are unable to make decisions are missed opportunities, diminished self-esteem, strained relationships, and difficulty with self-discipline. Can you find these dangers being played out in *Hamlet*?

Finally, what Othello endures because of his jealous nature –

> *O, beware, my lord, of jealousy!*
> *It is the green-eyed monster which doth mock*
> *The meat it feeds on.*
>
> (Act 3, Scene 3)

reaches out to touch us throughout the ages, making us all consider the danger of losing our reasoning ability to destructive jealousy.

What truth do you see in Shakespeare's warnings about the character flaws of human beings (i.e., ambition, obsessive love, procrastination, and jealousy)? Of course, Shakespeare offers us so much more than this. Through his plays, can we come to better understand our own nature and the society we inhabit? Explain in detail, referring to your own personal truth and understanding of universal truth.

Hedda Gabler (1891), by Henrik Ibsen (1828-1906), explores the complexities associated with borderline personality disorder and repressed passion. Hedda is an upper-class woman who is bored with her monotonous life, and conservative husband and restrictive society. She is a jealous, narcissistic and self-involved young woman who constantly tries to manipulate others for her own self-gratification. She feels trapped in an unfulfilling life and her disappointment with life leads her to commit suicide. Some see *Hedda Gabler* as a feminist play displaying sex-specific roles, which are apparent in this play. However, do you think such a narrow focus on Hedda's personality limits our appreciation of this play?

These lines, delivered by Hedda, point to her desire for liberation –

> *These impulses come over me all of a sudden,*
> *and I just can't resist them.*
>
> (Act 2)

> *Oh courage...oh yes! If only one had that...*
> *Then life might be liveable, in spite of everything.*
>
> (Act 2)

> *Everything I touch seems destined to turn*
> *into something mean and farcical.*
>
> (Act 4)

Do you think Hedda Gabler is a pioneer for feminism or is she simply a deeply flawed young woman with a borderline personality disorder? Do you think you would like Hedda as a friend, lover or wife? If so, why? If not, why not? Give a detailed response.

Tennessee Williams' (1911-1983) play, *A Streetcar Named Desire* (1947) explores mental instability, sex roles, and morality in post WWII American society. Both Blanche and her sister, Stella, are trapped in their dependence on men for self-fulfilment. Blanche has a history of sexual promiscuity

> *I was just looking for someone to rest my head on.*
>
> (Scene 9. Blanche to Mitch)

This line displays Blanche's desperate desire for male attention to fill the void left by her husband's death.

Stella, on the other hand, is drawn to Stanley's (her husband) animal sexuality –

> *I was sort of – thrilled by it.*

> (Scene 4. Stella to Blanche, following Stanley's violent outburst)

The play's climax leads to Blanche's rape at the hands of Stanley and Stella's decision to commit Blanche to a state-run mental institution, taking Blanche's accusation against her husband as evidence of Blanche's insanity. Whatever else we take from this play, its display of the desire and manipulation found in women's lives in a modern society is evident. This is a thoroughly modern play with a strong feminist proclivity.

Are Blanche and Stella victims of a male-dominated society or are they deliberately participating in a life suited to their personalities? Do they try and get out of society what they want or does society dictate what they can have? Are Blanche and Stella victims of societal fate or are they agents of their own desires and choices in life?

Death of a Salesman (1949) by Arthur Miller (1915-2005) is the story of Willy Loman, a travelling salesman whose endless travels leave him exhausted and dissatisfied with the reward he has earned for his hard work. His frustration leads him into serious depression and he begins to lose touch with the reality of his circumstances, his job, his family and his failure to realise the 'American Dream'. He feels he has failed everyone, including himself. In this way, Willy represents *the tragedy of the commons*. That is, for a few Americans to realise the American Dream, the many must have dreams that remain unfulfilled, like Willy's dream which ends in disappointment and tragedy.

Two memorable lines from Miller's play are delivered by Biff, Willy's son, who, heartbroken and angry, tries to explain that he cannot fit into Willy's expectations –

> *I realise what a ridiculous lie my whole life has been.*
>
> (Act 2)

> *Why am I trying to become what I don't want to be ... when all I want is out there, waiting for me the minute I say I know who I am.*
>
> (Act 2)

Despite his infidelity and failures as a husband and father, we sympathise with and pity Willy, because he clings to his illusions regardless of what damage reality does to his mind.

Do you think you should have a dream to guide your life? If you do, what should your dream be contingent on? When settling on your dream should you rely on realistic ambition or should you 'aim for the stars'? Do you see dangers for dreams based on material gratification? If you do, what are they? Give a detailed explanation in your answer.

The Poets

When considering our great poets, one must first mention the epic poet, Homer (8th century BC) and his two great works *The Iliad* (750 BC) and *The Odyssey* (720 BC). *The Iliad* covers the Trojan War while *The Odyssey* deals with Odysseus' return home from the Trojan War. These works highlight the character traits that good Greeks should emulate. Things like honouring the gods, loyalty to the king, love and fidelity towards family, defending one's country, glory in battle, courage in adversity, accepting your destiny and showing hospitality to any guest, even strangers, are just some of the character traits on display in these epic poems. Memorable lines from these poems are —

> *No man or woman born, coward or brave, can shun his destiny.*
>
> (*The Iliad*)

> *Be strong, saith my heart; I am a soldier.*
>
> (*The Odyssey*)

These lines highlight the courage needed to accept one's destiny (fate) and duty.

Achilles, the greatest of all warriors, tells us about the necessity of *esprit de corps* in battle –

> *Let no man forget how menacing we are, we are lions!*
> (*The Iliad*)

Or Hector's (the Trojan Prince) famous lines, that reveal the code needed to live an ethical life in Ancient Greece –

> *All my life I've lived by a code and the code is simple: honour the Gods, love your woman and defend your country. Troy is mother to us all. Fight for her.*
> (The Iliad)

The Greek concept of hospitality (xenia) is portrayed in these lines from *The Odyssey* –

> *We're at your knees*
> *In hopes of a warm welcome, even as a guest-gift,*
> *The sort that the hosts give strangers. That's the custom.*
> *Respect the Gods my friend...*

These lines underscore the expectation that hosts should offer food, shelter and protection for guests, and that guests should not abuse this generosity.

What is you evaluation of Homer's portrayal of good Greek character traits? How relevant do you think they are in today's modern world? What fate would await any civilisation that turned its back on these traits? Give a detailed explanation for your answer. What is your opinion about Greek hospitality? Would this be beneficial for any society that adopted such hospitality? Would it be potentially dangerous for the host?

Then, we move on to the father of metaphysical poetry John Donne

(1572-1631 AD). Here I am reminded of his poem, *Death Be Not Proud*. In this poem, Donne personifies death, and in the final line of the poem Donne declares,

> *Death thou shalt die.*

Of course, Donne was referring to the day of resurrection, but it can relate to anyone who believes in life after death as, for example, Socrates did.

At thirteen I experienced a near death experience when I was trapped underwater by a broken waterwheel while on a boy scout camp. Luckily for me, the quick thinking and strength of other scouts pulled me to the surface. Nevertheless, it was a terrifying experience for me, which made me confront the vulnerable and temporary state of my mortal existence. I well remember having the joy of life sapped out of me.

I had just graduated from primary school and was to enter high school the next year, so Dad took me to a menswear shop and bought me my first pair of shoes and long trousers. Despite the significance of this memorable event, I could not get excited. What is the point in getting excited about anything, I thought, if my life will come to an end sooner or later.

In my despair, I turned to those works of classical literature with scenes containing death in an attempt to gain some understanding of this most haunting reality of my life. My search took me to Charles Dickens' *Tale of Two Cities*, and the courageous, noble sacrifice of its protagonist Sydney Carton when he substitutes himself for Charles Darnay at the guillotine. Carton's self-sacrifice is motivated by his love for Darnay's wife, Lucie, and his desire to secure for her a better future. Such courage and nobility in the face of what I now feared helped bolster my own courage.

Then, I explored the plain English translations of Shakespeare's tragic plays mentioned above. However, it wasn't until I read the last line of Donne's poem that I could visualise the death of death, that foul grim reaper meeting his demise, that I drew comfort from the hopelessness of my mortal position.

Can you draw comfort from such an idea (the possibility of a life after death) when confronting the certainty of your own mortality? Do you find truth in such comfort? Remember that the concept of an afterlife exists throughout history and across all cultures. That is, that it is a timeless and universal truth.

Zoroastrianism, the first known religion, believes in a dualistic afterlife where the good are rewarded and the wicked punished. Theirs was also the first religion to believe in an eternal war between good and evil played out here on earth.

The Egyptians envisioned a *Field of Reeds* that only those whose heart, after being weighed by Ma'at (the goddess of truth and justice) in the Hall of Truth, was found to be lighter than a feather could enter. If the heart was heavier than a feather it was devoured by Ammit, a monster god, and the soul of the reprobate ceased to exist.

The *Elysian Fields* of the ancient Greeks and Romans was where the righteous and heroic went to live after death. Others became mere shades of their former self and entered *the underworld* after paying the ferryman and crossing the river Styx. The underworld was ruled over by the Greek god Hades or the Latin god Pluto.

Hinduism believes in reincarnation (samsara) where one's soul (atman) is reborn with the purpose of liberating itself (moksha) from samsara through good karma and spiritual growth. The circumstances of one's previous life determines the circumstances of their new life. This is why Hindus believe in a rigid class structure for their society. For Hindus, *the untouchables* deserve their position in society because of the bad karma from their previous life.

Buddhists, like Hindus, believe in reincarnation. However, Buddhists do not believe in a rigid caste system, like Hindus. Buddhists reject distinctions based on birth and emphasise spiritual enlightenment and wisdom. For a Buddhist, a person becomes a 'Braham' or 'outcast' through their actions and deeds, not their birth. Furthermore, Buddhists embrace the continuous life cycle of birth, death and reincarnation that is driven by one's karma and will continue until a state of enlightenment (nirvana) is achieved when one escapes the cycle of suffering, desires and attachments. To reach nirvana, therefore, Buddhists must divorce themselves from any desires or attachments they may have with this world which would bring them back to this world after death. In freeing themselves of any attachments and desires with this existence their freed spirits can achieve an exalted existence. This conviction modifies a belief in a fixed, eternal afterlife of punishment and reward. That is, Buddhists believe that we continue to suffer the punishment of existence until we reach nirvana.

The *Heaven* and *Hell* of Christians are the places where the righteous and faithful or the unrepentant sinners receive their reward or punishment. Righteous Christians will dwell with God (heaven) while the unrighteous will experience eternal separation from God (Hell). Catholics also believe in *purgatory* where the souls of sinners go to expiate their sins before going to heaven. *Judgement day* for Christians is when all people, both the living and the resurrected, will be judged by God regarding their beliefs and actions, leading them into salvation or damnation.

Muslims believe that after death their souls enter *Barzakh*, a place of waiting for *judgement day* when Allah will judge them. The righteous will go to *Jannah* which the Qur'an describes as *gardens of pleasure*. Non-Muslims and unworthy Muslims are sent to hell for eternal punishment.

Taoists believe that death is a natural part of life and after death their spirit (shijie) transitions to a different dimension rather than a judgement and afterlife of heaven or hell. For the Taoist, their shijie is a part of the larger cosmos where they return to the Tao, the source of all things.

All of these religions are convinced that there is such a thing as an afterlife. Where they differ is in how one gets there and what awaits them when they do. Do these explanations about an afterlife confirm the reality of its transcendental truth? What is your opinion about the existence of an afterlife? Do these different explanations about the existence of an afterlife remind you of the parable of the elephant? Can it be said that the elephant symbolises an afterlife while the different features of the elephant symbolise the means by which we gain access to it? Do those who do not believe in the concept of an afterlife limit their purpose and meaning to this earthly existence? Which means they may or may not believe in transcendental truth, since transcendental truth exists in the realm of the supernatural not natural laws. What might be some of the consequences for a society dominated by people who do not believe in an afterlife?

Another of Donne's poems is *For Whom the Bell Tolls* which reminds us that we are all a small part of humanity (a supernatural not a natural concept), so when one dies it is a loss for all of us. The last lines of this poem read –

> *Therefore, send not to know*
> *For whom the bell tolls.*
> *It tolls for thee.*

Do you find any truth in Donne's vision? Do you think we are all a part of humanity? Should we mourn the loss of all those who die, because with their death a part of us dies as well? Is Donne asking us to mourn those who pass away or bringing to our attention the fact that one day we will join them?

It would be remiss of me not to mention the great works of John Milton (1608-1674 AD) at this point, but to read his metaphysical poems with understanding requires an informed and judicious knowledge of *The Holy Bible* and *classical mythology* because of the allusions he makes to them. If you are interested, his two outstanding works are *Paradise Lost* and *Paradise Regained*. Be warned, however, that you will need to seek explanations for many of his allusions. This will require a scholarly yet most rewarding enterprise on your part.

Then, we have the works of two prodigious Romantic poets, Wordsworth (1770-1850 AD) and Keats (1795-1821 AD), who draw inspiration from nature and love and what it reveals about truth. When Keats proclaims,

> *Beauty is truth, truth beauty - that is all*
> *Ye know on earth, and all ye need to know*
> (*Ode on a Grecian Urn*, 1819)

he is clearly leading us to an ideal beyond the reach of human sensory perception. After all, beauty is an ideal concept against which the observations of our sensory perception would be seriously limited if not for art. So, for Keats, it is in the beauty of art that truth can be found. He also sees truth in the love we express for both nature and those we love. *Bright Star* (1838) has these lines –

> *Pillow'd upon my fair love's ripening breast*
> *To feel forever its soft fall and swell*
> *Awake forever in a sweet unrest*
> *Still, still to hear her tender-taken breath*
> *And so live ever – or else swoon to death.*

These lines disclose Keats' discovery of truth found in human love, in this case his love for 'Fanny' Brawne Lindon (1800-1865). Keats also has great affection for nature. Read *Ode to a Nightingale (1819)* and discover this famous line –

> *Already with thee! Tender is the night.*

F. Scott Fitzgerald took *Tender is the Night* for the title of his 1934 novel. This line suggests that the nightingale is leading Keats into a more tender place than the harsh light of day. This tender place can be seen as the transcendental level.

This line from Keats' poem *To Autumn* (1820) –

Season of mists and mellow fruitfulness

describes Keats vision of a paradise as realised on earth. It demonstrates how natural beauty affects our feelings and thoughts, leading us to transcendental truth.

Can you see beauty in art? Does the beauty in human love and nature affect your feelings and thoughts? Does this beauty lead you to transcendental truth? If this is so, you are beginning to understand the importance of beauty in our search for moral or ethical truth. Do we spend so much time in creating a living environment (building our dream home, designing its interior, and shaping our gardens) because we aspire towards an ideal, a transcendental truth, concerning a beautiful, heavenly sanctuary, a place where we can achieve peace and harmony in our lives?

Possibly, the most touching of all Wordsworth's poems is *She Dwelt among the Untrodden Ways*. Surely, these words touch the heart of everyone –

> *She lived unknown, and few could know*
> *When Lucy ceased to be*
> *But she is in her grave, and, oh,*
> *The difference to me.*

Such words capture the suffering felt by those of us who have lost a loved one. Often, the best thing we can do for someone close to us who has lost a loved one is just to be there for them. To listen without judgement or offering advice. This can lead us to yet another transcendental truth – empathy for others.

Can you find truth in Wordsworth's sensitive words? Can you feel his deep sorrow? If you can, you are being empathic towards

Wordsworth's feelings and beginning to understand the importance of empathy in our search for truth.

Do these words of Keats and Wordsworth lead you to a more refined understanding of life's truth? Explain your decision.

T.S. Eliot (1888-1965) was greatly influenced by the destruction and suffering inflicted on Western Civilisation in WWI, and even more disillusioned and disgusted by the reaction of people to it in the post-WWI era. His poem *Preludes* (1917), contains his most famous line –

the burnt-out ends of smoky days

which is a vivid image of the alienation and disaffection of urban life, lived without purpose or meaning. That is, without transcendental truth.

His other, more famous poem, *The Waste Land* (1922), portrays a world desiring salvation yet beset with material hedonism (relentless pursuit of material gratification), constant anxiety and pointless lust. This poem achieved great acclaim and established Eliot's international reputation. Here are some notable lines from *The Waste Land* –

I will show you fear in a handful of dust

What are the roots that clutch, what branches grow

Out of this stony rubbish.

My nerves are bad tonight. Yes, bad. Stay with me.

Do some research into this period of Western Civilisation to gain a greater understanding of Eliot's theme. Do you think his message has any relevance for you today? How so? Provide modern details of any similarities and differences between his period of history and yours.

William Butler Yeats (1865-1939) was haunted by the Spector of a pending doom for Christianity in the aftermath of WWI and the 1918-1919 flu epidemic terrorising the world at that time. His poem, *The Second Coming* (1919) illustrates the Apocalypse and the coming of the Anti-Christ. These lines describe the coming epoch of history as a gyre (a circular pattern) –

> *Turning and turning in the widening gyre*
> *The falcon cannot hear the falconer*
> *Things fall apart; the centre cannot hold...*

and his last lines describe the coming of the Anti-Christ –

> *And what rough beast, its hour come round at last*
> *Slouches towards Bethlehem to be born?*

Was Yeats right? Do things fall apart when the centre cannot hold? How so? Did Christianity suffer a decline in the 20th century? Do you see a relationship between the centre not holding and the demise of Christianity in the post-WWI era? Did a new epoch dominated by material and sexual hedonism coupled with the emergence of societal alienation (separation from) and the unrestrained exercising of power emerge? Would these developments be the hallmarks of an Anti-Christ epoch?

Dylan Thomas' (1914-53) main concern seems to be how sexuality and death link the different generations. *Death Shall Have No Dominion* (1933) alludes to St. Paul's epistle to the Romans (6:9) –

> *For we know that since Christ was raised from the dead, he cannot die again; death no longer has mastery over him.*

In *Death Shall Have No Dominion*, Thomas links humanity's triumph over death by its continuance despite the death of individuals. However, his imagery concerning death is graphic and disturbing –

> *Dead men naked they shall be one*
> *with the man in the wind and the west moon*
> *When their bones are picked clean and the clean bones gone*
> *...Thou lovers be lost love shall not*
> *And death shall have no dominion.*

Notice that for Dylan Thomas it is not the idea of an afterlife that conquerors death but a continuance of humanity after we die that does. This theme is also found in love, for it is love that endures after we die not that we go to an afterlife.

His concern regarding sexuality can be found in these lines from *Twenty-four Years* (1922) –

> *Dressed to die, the sensual strut begun*
> *with my red veins full of money...*
> *I advance as long as forever is.*

Also, it is found in, *Light Breaks Where no Sun Shines* (1934) –

> *A candle in the thighs*
> *Warms youth and seed and burns the seeds of age.*

Here Dylan Thomas again displays his belief in the importance of sexuality confronting death.

These images of death and sexuality contrast sharply with those of beauty proffered by the Metaphysics or the Romantics who search for peace and solace in old age as they await the inevitability of their pending death.

Do you think that this idea that humanity and sex conquer death, whereas individuals do not, is one that echoes Donne's idea of us all being a part of a greater humanity, or Keats' observation about love found in *Ode on a Grecian Urn*? Does Dylan's message match the existential approach of his generation while Donne's and Keats' match their contemplation of the transcendental.

Thomas' most famous lines appear in his poem, *Do Not Go Gentle Into That Good Night* (1951) which highlight his anxiety about death –

> *Do not go gentle into that good night*
> *Old age should burn and rave at close of day*
> *Rage, rage against the dying of the light.*

Do you find a hint of anxiety in Dylan Tomas' idea that we should rage against death until we die? Do you want to rage against death in your old age or accept your mortal fate with peace and solace?

Compare Dylan's message with that of Eliot and Yates. Despite Dylan's insistence on the triumph of the human spirit, do you think his 'sensual strut' and anxiety about death would accompany anyone who lived in Yeats' new epoch? Do you detect any link between Dylan's imagery and your own society?

Why not also include an influential modern poet, Robert Frost (1874-1963). He was President John F. Kennedy's favoured poet, who wrote *Dedication* (1961) in honour of JFK's Inauguration.

The Road Not Taken is a poem where Frost asks us to consider the importance of decisions we make in our lives which ultimately determine our destiny. In the poem, Frost comes to a fork in the road he is travelling along and has to decide which road he will take. One road is well worn and the other not so. Frost takes the road less travelled. What do you make of the final lines in his poem –

> *Two roads diverged in a woods, and I –*
> *I took the one less travelled by,*
> *and that has made all the difference.*

Speculate on what 'difference' the 'road less travelled by' might have made to Frost's life. Why do you think Frost describes this as **'all** the difference'?

Frost's poem, *Design* asks whether there is design in a small thing like the spinning of a spider's web. Interestingly, Frost chose to deliver this message through the use of a sonnet. Perhaps the most heavily designed and structured of all the poetic forms. The sonnet is a 14-line poem featuring iambic pentameter rhythm, an eight-lined quatrain and a six-lined sestet with a two-lined couplet that ends the sestet, and a ABAB CDCD EFEF GG rhyming scheme. The quatrain develops the sonnet's theme or argument while the couplet offers a summary or resolution. In *Design* there exists what artists call a marrying of form and content. That is, the structure of the poem matches the message intended to be delivered. The rhyming couplet at the end of Frost's poem ask a question –

> *But what design of darkness to appal?—*
> *If design govern in a thing so small.*

Do you see any connection between Frost's topic and his choice of poetic form? What is the connection between a spider's web and 'darkness to appal'. Can you detect a larger meaning to Frost's sonnet?

Finally, Max Ehrmann (1872-1945) became popular in the 1960s when people rediscovered his poem, *Desiderata* (1927). His poem offers us a way of achieving inner peace while living in an unfair world –

> *Go placidly amid the noise and haste, and*
> *remember what peace there may be in silence.*

Why not read the lines from Max Ehrmann's poem, *Desiderata,* found in his book, *the Desiderata of Happiness.*

When reading his poem, did you detect an 'inner peace' emerging within you? Consider the Ehrmann quote at the beginning of this book – what do you think Ehrmann means by a 'still soul'? Do you have a 'still soul'? If you do, what mission do you think Max Ehrmann is calling on you to undertake?

Do you detect a growing anxiety and despair between the older poems and some of the modern ones in this collection? The 20th century saw the rise of post-modernism in Western institutes of learning which later spread to the wider society. So plays like *Hedda Gabler, A Streetcar Named Desire,* and *Death of a Salesman,* along with poems like *Preludes, The Wasteland, The Second Coming, Death Shall Have No Dominion, Twenty-four Years,* and *Do Not Go Gentle Into That Good Night* became popular with the learned class because they reflected the loss of faith, anxiety and despair that people had developed towards Western Civilisation. Do you believe this feeling that citizens developed towards Western Civilisation could lead to radical movements? If you do, what do you think might be the destiny of this cultural shift?

The Novelists
As far as fiction is concerned, I'm sure we all have our own favourites. For me, some of my favourites are the works of Jane Austen (1775-1817 AD), Charles Dickens (1812-1870 AD), Charlotte Bronte (1816-1855 AD), Fyodor Dostoevsky (1821-1881 AD), Leo Tolstoy (1828-1910 AD), F. Scott-Fitzgerald (1896-1940 AD), Ernest Hemingway (1899-1961 AD), George Orwell (1903-50 AD), and Aleksandr Solzhenitsyn (1918-2008 AD).

Let us consider Jane Austen for a moment. Her most famous novel is *Pride and Prejudice* (1813) which is a satirical look at 18th and 19th century English society with its rigid social and sex roles, and the prejudice that people displayed at that time. It also warns us about the danger of first impressions. The most famous line in this book drips with sarcasm –

> *It is a truth universally acknowledged that a single man in possession of a good fortune must be in want of a wife.*

For this reason, the mothers in *Pride and Prejudice* compete with each other to make their daughters known to rich men and push their daughters into relationships focused on securing wealthy partners. One needs to understand, though, the precarious financial situation families faced at this time. The motivation for mothers, therefore, was based more on need than greed. Elizabeth and Darcy, the two leading characters in the novel, get off to a rocky start. Elizabeth believes Darcy is guided by little but his pride and his prejudice. She vows never to marry him. However, as their lives become intertwined she comes to realise she has misjudged him.

Feminists point to the sexual stereotyping and lack of opportunity for women in 19th century English society presented in *Pride and Prejudice*. This is clearly present. However, focusing on these issues detracts from the real message of Jane Austen's work and undervalues the worth of love, marriage and family to Jane's beliefs. For me, the more important message of this novel is the danger we all face if we project our own prejudice onto those we meet for the first time, as Jane plainly does with Darcy.

For Charles Dickens the ideas of injustice, crime and corruption, as it existed in the society of his time (19th century England), interested him. In *Bleak House*, for example, Dickens critiques the legal corruption found in the Court of Chancery which illustrates an irresponsible and self-serving legal system rather than one seeking justice for their clienteles. These faults in the English legal system is illustrated in the line –

> *The one great principle of the English law is,*
> *to make business for itself.*

Much of the empathy found in his novels arises from his observation about the plight of children. Some of the main deprivations that Dickens' child characters experience are poverty, neglect, and poor education. Through his portrayal, we come to empathise with the plight of children generally. A reading of Dickens' novel *Oliver Twist* (1838), in which Oliver endures a meagre ration of food, overcrowded living conditions, and harsh discipline, elicits our sympathy. This line –

Chapter 2: The Three Levels of Truth

> *Please, Sir, I want some more.*

highlights the hunger that these poor children in a 19th century English workhouse had to endure. It also shows Oliver's courage to stand up to the harsh reality of his circumstances.

Hard Times (1854), which demonstrates how children conform to a rigid educational system that prioritises the learning of facts over imagination and creative thinking, creates in us a desire to help children from unfortunate or even tragic backgrounds. This quote encapsulates the priority of this educational system –

> *Now, what I want is, Facts. Teach these boys and girls nothing but Facts. Facts alone are wanted in life. Plant nothing else, and root out everything else.*

Do you find truth in Dickens' portrayal of the corruption found in the legal profession or the plight of his child characters? If you do, does this inspire you to undertake some action to seek justice in the legal system or alleviate the suffering of children? What action would you like to undertake? What might be some of the consequences of your action? Do you think your action, if taken too far, might have some unintended consequences?

Charlotte Bronte's most famous book, *Jane Eyre* (1847), depicts an English society with a rigid social class and the power of religious thought over thoughts of personal fulfilment. This is at odds with Jane's aspiration as she seeks love and belonging not alienation. Throughout the novel, Jane feels undervalued and excluded because of her social standing (she is an orphan). These words, spoken by Jane, display her deep desire for recognition as a person with feelings,

> *Do you think, because I am poor, obscure, plain, and little, I am soulless and heartless? You are wrong!*

Jane Eyre is considered by feminists to be valuable to their movement because the story depicts sexual inequality, discrimination and a lack of opportunity for females in 19th century English society. Again, this is clearly present in this novel, but for me the greatest value of the book is that Jane maintains her integrity by remaining true to herself, despite the many difficulties her circumstances bring upon her. In the end, she shapes her own destiny and overcomes the challenges that life throws at her.

Fyodor Dostoevsky is best known for the complex and ambiguous characters he creates in his writing. His works focus on the emotional and intellectual consequences of evil, the necessity of freedom for human dignity but also the burden of suffering it creates, and his character's craving for something to believe in.

A famous Dostoevsky quote from *Crime and Punishment* (1866) is –

> *To go wrong in one's own way is better than*
> *to go right in someone else's.*

This line is spoken by Razumikhin to Raskolnikov's mother to reassure her about her son's action even though Razumikhin does not fully understand the gravity of the situation Raskolnikov is in. Nevertheless, this line tells us to think critically for ourselves and do not blindly accept what others tell us, even if we make the wrong decisions that bring with them serious consequences.

Another famous line is spoken by Father Zosima in *The Brothers Karamazov* (1880) to Fyodor Karamazov –

> *Above all, don't lie to yourself.*

This emphasises the importance of self-honesty over self-deception. If we lie to ourselves we will never be able to discern truth and thus fail to show dignity and respect towards ourselves and others.

Chapter 2: The Three Levels of Truth

Here's a task for you that reinforces Father Zosima's words – consider the lyrics of two Charley Pride (1934-2020) songs, *All I Have to Offer You (Is Me)* and *I'm Just Me*. They both speak of the importance of being authentic by accepting, and letting others know, who you are.

Or as Polonius, a character in Shakespeare's play, *Hamlet* (Act 1, scene 3), puts it when giving advice to his son, Laertes who is leaving his home in Denmark to study in Paris –

unto thine own self be true.

Do you think it is important for you to be authentic in your life or do you want to follow others who tell you what is best for you? Of course, there is no reason for both these options to be true for you. That is, what someone wiser than yourself advises you to become may be the very person you desire to become. Alternatively, you may accept some of a wise person's advice while rejecting other suggestions.

The main themes of Leo Tolstoy's great works centre on Russian society, war, love, and death. His most famous works are *War and Peace* (1867) and *Anna Karenina* (1878). After reading *War and Peace*, an epic, historical novel, we discover the society of Tsarist Russia in the 19th century, its family dynamics, its love and marriage relationships, and its attitude to wealth among other societal values. The novel chronicles the French invasion of Russia and its aftermath. A major theme of the novel shows us how fate and historical circumstance impact the lives of all strata of society and all individuals within it. Here is a quote that illustrates how power structures and social norms can perpetuate violence through unequal power dynamics –

All violence consists in some people forcing others, under threat of suffering or death, to do what they do not want to do.

On the other hand, Anna's life experience, in *Anna Karenina*, leads her into depression, as she struggles throughout to maintain her rationality. She abandons her social standing and family for passionate love and her personal insecurities drive her into jealousy and paranoia.

> *She hardly knew at times what it was she feared, and what she hoped for. Whether she feared or desired what had happened or what was going to happen and exactly what she longed for, she could not have said.*

This lack of clarity in Anna's thoughts reveal her profound confusion and emotional instability. For Anna, the social ostracisation she endures ushers her into isolation, despair, and ultimate tragedy. Towards the end of her life, Anna believes that everyone is deeply unhappy.

Do you think Anna is suffering from a Borderline Personality Disorder like Hedda Gabler?

Levin, the other protagonist in this novel, has a different experience. Although socially awkward, his interest in farming, agriculture, and rural life provide him with the serenity of a faith-driven life. Despite being born into the Russian aristocracy, the life he leads is far outside the social norms of its 19th century values, especially his respect for humanity and love of the natural experiences of life. His lack of self-centred superiority, so prevalent in the aristocracy of this time, makes of him the exception, not the rule. His life is Tolstoy's archetype (original example) for a better human existence.

We can conclude from our reading of these novels that Tolstoy believes human motives and the societies they inhabit are greatly impacted by fate and circumstance and are essentially irrational.

Do you ever find yourself struggling to keep your sanity when confronted with the irrationality of your lived experience? If you do, you can appreciate Tolstoy's message. However, I hope you will not let this truth lead you into despair but rather strengthen your courage to meet its challenge.

F. Scott Fitzgerald takes a different tack from his contemporaries when examining American society by showing us the futility of trying to achieve happiness through material gratification. His works are a criticism of the hedonistic materialism he observes around him. He is credited with creating the term 'Jazz Age' to describe the age in which he lived. There is some irony when contrasting this theme in his books with the actual life that he and his wife, Zelda, lived. Perhaps it was the chaotic, pleasure seeking, materialistic life he led with Zelda that inspired him with this vision.

Gatsby in Scott Fitzgerald's novel, *The Great Gatsby* (1925), tries to win back Daisy's lost affection for him with a display of wealth and opulent parties. How successful do you think this approach is? What sort of relationship do you think would develop between two people if one of them tried to impress the other with a display of wealth? One key moment occurs when Gatsby displays *a mountain of* (floral) *shirts* for Daisy to see. Her response is telling –

> *It makes me sad because I've never seen such,*
> *such beautiful shirts before.*

What is your evaluation of Daisy's character? Many see her as a rich, spoilt brat, who believes she is entitled to everything she has and unappreciative of what others do for her. Is she a shallow woman with an immoral nature? How do we react to those who have allowed themselves to become corrupted through material gratification?

Hemingway is famous for creating a new style of writing. He believed that to have a reader develop an emotional response from his writing, he needed to describe an incident with dispassion and objectivity, then have the reader's empathy arise naturally. This spawned a new rule for writing – *show don't tell* – and led to authors reducing their writing to vivid descriptions. In today's terms this is known as the reductionist's view of writing, summed up in the concise phrase,

> *less is more.*

Also, Hemingway has his characters seek to find sufficient courage to face the hardships that life throws their way. Here Hemingway returns to the message of the Stoics mentioned before. A reading of *The Sun Also Rises* (1926) and *A Farewell to Arms* (1929) reveals his protagonists' struggle to achieve this courageous approach to life.

At the end of *The Sun Also Rises,* Jake says to Brett,

Isn't it pretty to think so.

This highlights their struggle to find the necessary courage to accept a lack of fulfilment in their lives.

These lines from *A farewell to Arms* reinforce the necessity of courage to face life's challenges –

The world breaks everyone and afterwards many are strong at the broken places. But those who will not break it kills. It kills the very good and the very gentle and the very brave impartially.

Have you ever found yourself struggling to acquire enough courage to face the challenges and hardships in your life? Do you have friends who struggle with this? What can you do for your friends to help them find their courage? When faced with this problem yourself, do you think you should seek help from your family and friends?

George Orwell (1903-50) wrote two popular and influential books, *Animal Farm* (1945) and *1984* (1949). Both these books offer us a critique of Totalitarianism and its politically repressive system of government. His political views were shaped by his personal experience with poverty and oppression and his denunciation of the Soviet Union's anti-democratic communist policies.

Animal Farm is a satirical novella detailing the Russian Revolution through an animal fable. It reveals how the corruption of those in power can harm those they are expected to help. Throughout the fable the slogan, *Four legs good, two legs bad,* was the propaganda slogan used to overthrow the farmers' rule over animals. The sheep in his fable constantly bleat this slogan whenever they are confronted with uncomfortable truths. Do you detect any parallel here with what radical protester shout at their rallies? At the end of the fable, the pigs (those who led the revolution) are dining with Pilkington and other human farmers they sought to overthrow and declare, *Four legs good, two legs better.* The pigs, now walking on two legs, have become the new overlords of evil.

Do some research on the Russian Revolution. Do you believe that the communist elite who led the revolution installed themselves as a new ruling class?

1984, perhaps more than any other book, is quoted as predicting what liberal democracies were in danger of becoming. It presents us with a society dominated by an extremely oppressive government that uses sophistry to twist words into meanings opposite to their original intention. For example, the ever-present slogans, *War is Peace, Freedom is Slavery, Ignorance is Strength* enforced by the existence of a Ministry of Truth that deals in Lies and a Ministry of Peace that deals in War highlight this. Orwell criticised the horrific lengths that totalitarians would go to in order to gain and increase their power. Orwell felt compelled to warn democratic nations of the threat that totalitarian fanatics posed to their liberty. In *1984* the state censors everything that does not align with their doctrine by imposing brutal repression. Thus, eliminating free speech. The party believes that

> *who controls the past controls the future.*

O'Brian, a party faithful, tells Winston, who wants to believe what he sees rather than what the party tells him to see,

> *We, the party, control all records, and we control all memories. Then, we control the past, do we not?*

Do you find any similarities between *1984* and where Australian society is heading today? Do you detect any threats to your free speech that did not exist in the past? What effect might mis/disinformation laws or hate speech laws have on your free speech? What would happen to your understanding of Australia's past if the decolonisation movement carries out the radical reforms it has in mind for our history texts and literature? Do you notice any dissidence between what you see happening in Australia and what you are told is happening? Give a detailed analysis to support what you have discovered.

Here is another debating topic for you –

That what we see happening in Australia today is not what we are told is happening.

Solzhenitsyn points out the importance of maintaining human dignity in times of unbelievable suffering. In his book, *Gulag Archipelago* (1973), for example, he suffers injustice, physical hardship, and horrible abuse while in the custody of Soviet (Communist) authorities, yet he will not allow his tormentors to rob him of his dignity.

Do you think human dignity is worth preserving during times of hardship? Can you find truth in human dignity?

Aleksandr Solzhenitsyn's words, delivered during his Nobel Lecture, are worth mentioning here –

One word of truth shall outweigh the whole world.

Then compare them to the quote from the *Bible* which links truth and freedom and John Keats' words linking truth with beauty. Do these words inspire within you an appreciation of the beauty and power of truth? Do you think this beauty and power of truth can set you free?

Forgive me for not delving further into the works of these, and other, great and influential prophets, philosophers, dramatists, poets and authors but you are probably already tiring of my well-meaning indulgence. Just remember that what we have discussed here is but a tiny fraction of the transcendental truth your ancestors bequeathed you.

The Existential Level

This level of truth starts as far back as ancient Greece with Aristotle and Ptolemy but accelerates dramatically from the eighteenth century with the European Enlightenment, and the Scientific and Industrial Revolutions.

To begin, let's discuss the difference between *deductive* and *inductive* reasoning. The former being the religious and earlier philosophical approach and the latter being the scientific approach.

Conclusions using the deductive approach use syllogistic reasoning containing a conclusion and two or more premises. In this way deductive reasoning uses a specific structure to arrive at a logical conclusion. It is used to go from a general truth to arrive at a specific or individual truth. This is fine if you have a source of general truth, which all religions believe they have in the form of their holy texts. Let's take the example of killing. The *Holy Bible's* 6th commandment tells its believers,

Thou shalt not kill.

This seems pretty clear. War involves killing so war must be sinful. The deductive reasoning is clear here –

Killing is sinful
war involves killing
therefore war is sinful.

But wait, the *Holy Bible* also has examples of wars fought in righteousness and Ecclesiastes 3:8 tells us there is

> *a time to love and a time to hate;*
> *a time for war and a time for peace.*

What are we to make of this? Can you offer an explanation? Is there a distinction between murder and killing that the 6th commandment does not address? This would mean that the first premise is incomplete.

Take this line of deductive reasoning –

> *All cats have four legs*
> *a dog has four legs*
> *therefore a dog is a cat.*

Here the logic is sound but the conclusion is not, because dogs and cats have other distinguishing characteristics besides four legs. The premises of these two syllogistic arguments are not wrong; they are just incomplete and this is the danger when using deductive reasoning to reach conclusions, particularly when we use personal truth as our source of general truth.

Sir Francis Bacon, an English philosopher of the 17th century, is credited with formalising inductive reasoning as a form of scientific reasoning. Inductive reasoning turns deductive reasoning upside down by systematically collecting data, observations and experimentations (individual truths), analysing them to identify patterns, then forming general conclusions or hypotheses.

Can you see how inductive reasoning addresses the problem deductive reasoning has by starting with incomplete premises? Explain Sir Francis Bacon's solution in your own words.

Scholars and scientists, operating on the existential level of truth, use inductive reasoning in an attempt to explain the reality of our earthly existence. The existential level of truth is the domain of scholars and scientists who are guided more by thought than feelings. Scholars and scientists like to separate the Arts and Science by distinguishing between the source of their ideas. The Arts, they claim, comes from preconcepts while Science comes from concepts. That is, a preconcept is a noncognitive apprehension (a feeling) formed before enough facts and information have been established to draw correct conclusions, while concepts come from cognitive experience (reasoning) and are built upon with facts and data.

There is some truth to this since the Arts do operate more on the transcendental level of truth which is arrived at through inspiration and creativity rather than experimentation and data collection. The difference between each being determined by the level of truth each operate on. However, inspiration and creativity, when correctly developed, does involve the participant in observation, contemplation and evaluation.

Do you think that scientists only receive their original inspiration from their minds? Do they start with a sense that something is correct, then gather their data and facts? Is this sense only generated from their minds? Do scientists also have a *feeling* that something is right before they start their research?

However it is arrived at, the existential level of truth is accessible to us through the objective work of scholars and scientists, which is grounded in our earthly existence, and arrived at primarily through Francis Bacon's inductive reasoning. Here we find the great thinkers who apply logic and reason to their observations of the physical reality of our existence, perceived through our five senses (sight, sound, hearing, touch, and taste).

Scholars would include those historians who have articulated advanced theories for ways of viewing our past by collecting and analysing facts and data from the past. There are four such influential historians I would like to cover here. The first is Edward Gibbon (1737-1794 AD) whose 6 volume work on *the Decline and Fall of the Roman Empire* led him to argue that the complex process that led to Rome's decline and fall was primarily driven by a loss of civic virtue and the rise of Christianity. Gibbon's thesis has inspired many current thinkers who see Western Civilisation going through a similar decline today. Next we turn to Thomas Carlyle (1795-1881 AD), who advanced *The Great Man* theory whereby leaders with charisma and strength of character lead us to great things. Another is Arnold Toynbee (1889-1975 AD), who proposed that civilisations rise and fall because of their response to the challenges they face. Finally, there is William H. McNeill (1917-2016 AD), who argued that contact between different civilisation, which he called the ecumene (economic and cultural contact), is the driving force behind their development.

How do these perceptions of history affect your understanding of our history? Do you consider them to be a truthful representation of history?

Let me examine in more detail some factors Gibbon identified as leading to the decline and fall of the Roman Empire. Since Gibbon, others have suggested other factors that produced the same fate for Rome.

First, there was a decline in the birth rate. Rome's parents practised infanticide as recorded by Cicero (106 BC-43 BC), Philo (20 BC-50 AD) and Seneca (4 BC-65 AD), which lowered their birth rate. As Rome's population declined, their enemies, the barbarian tribes, increased, thus putting population pressure on the barbarian lands which led them to invade Rome's Empire and eventually Rome itself.

Second was inflation. Rome's coinage became so debased that it is estimated by some to have suffered an inflation rate of 15,000% between 200-300 AD (Amanda James, *News with a View*, 2022). This happened because the emperors stopped expanding their empire, thereby reducing the revenue raised. To counter this they debased their currency by clipping their coins. Emperors would recall the coins they had previously minted then remint them into more new coins with a lower metallic (gold, silver and bronze) level but with the same value. We have all seen this fact depicted in movies set in this era when characters bite Roman coins. Romans in the past did this to determine the lead content of the coins. Clipping enabled the emperors to increase the number of coins circulating in Rome's economy, leading to higher and higher inflation.

Third was the tribalisation of Rome's population. People came to believe that they were *in* the Empire but not *of* the Empire. In short they no longer had loyalty for the Empire; their loyalty lay with the different tribes within the Empire. What today we would call cultural enclaves within a Nation State. This led to a decline in the desire to defend the Empire. You see, the Romans had for centuries successfully defended their Empire from barbarian invasion, so they had the technology and the skills necessary for Rome's defence. In the end, it was a case of them not having the desire or morale to do what was necessary to defend Rome.

Fourth was a decline in Rome's morality. We are all aware of the notorious Roman orgies. Sexual permissiveness and material gratification became rife in Rome. Having lost their moral virtues, values, and ethics, Rome witnessed a breakdown in family values, and a rise in interpersonal conflict like stealing, prostitution, corruption, and lawlessness (both adult and juvenile).

Fifth, and more recently, is the theory that Romans suffered from lead poisoning (Jerome Nriagu, *New England Journal of Medicine*, 1983). Romans used lead in their coinage, cosmetics, water pipes, pots, and utensils, as well as to line their coffins, to sweeten their wine and later to improve the taste of their food. The theory proports that Romans poisoned themselves, especially the ruling class, making them unhealthy, and more lethargic. Lately, however, more research into this field has concluded that lead poisoning did not contribute significantly to the decline of Roman Civilisation (Penelope.uchicargo.edu).

Finally, Gibbon suggested that Christianity's doctrines of peace and humility discouraged the active virtues necessary for maintaining a powerful empire. He also argued that the church's growing influence and wealth diverted resource away from the state (ebsco.com, 2022).

These are just six factors leading to the decline and fall of the Roman Empire. Examine carefully each factor and compare it with modern day Western Civilisation. How many can you identify as being present in Western Civilisation today? What do you conclude will become of Western Civilisation if it does not make a course correction?

As for scientists, we can start with Aristotle (384-322 BC) and Ptolemy (100-170 AD), who both proposed an earth-centred universe. In the 16th century, Copernicus (1473-1543 AD) revealed his heliocentric universe, which has the sun as the centre of the universe. Among other things, Sir Isaac Newton (1643-1727 AD) articulated the importance of gravity in holding our solar system together. Finally, the 18th century sees Immanuel Kant (1724-1804 AD) discover the existence of Galaxies, which reduces our solar system to a mere speck in the Milky Way, which is just one of countless galaxies.

Two other scientists who influenced our understanding of reality were Charles Darwin (1809-1882) and Albert Einstein (1879-1955). Charles Darwin was a British naturalist and geologist, who established the theory of evolution, in which he proved that earthly species adapt to their environment through a process of natural selection. That is, the fit, strong and flexible species adapting over time and surviving in an ever-changing, hostile environment. Although Darwin's theory offers no proof as to how the species came into being in the first place, many philosophers and scientists after him added the theory of *random chance* to explain the origin of life on earth and evolution as the founding principle for the emergence of life on earth as we know it today.

The concept of Evolution also had negative effects for some societies whose leaders believed in Social Darwinism; a theory that argues that the fittest and strongest societies were the ones that survived. The dangers of Social Darwinism can be found in the pages of Orwell's books.

Albert Einstein, a great scientist who made a tremendous impact on how we think about our place in the universe, proposed his theory of relativity and its famous formula (E=mc²) predicting the interchangeability of matter and energy which made us rethink much of what we had taken for granted for centuries. His theory superseded a 200-year-old theory of mechanics created primarily by Sir Issac Newton. After Einstein had articulated his theory of relativity, our perception of matter, energy, time, and space was forever changed.

Unfortunately, Einstein's theory of relativity was carried over into the social sciences where ethics, moral values and even cultural practices were seen to be relative to the societies giving rise to them. The saying

everything is relative

became widespread, giving rise to moral equivalence and a paralysing uncertainty in Western countries about their values.

I could continue, but it would be impossible to do justice to the discoveries of science and its explosion of theories in our own time. Not to mention the myriad of scientific fields that science has expanded into and the enormous benefits gained from science's growth in the areas of medicine and health.

What I have tried to show with the above observations is that science is never *settled*. It constantly changes and adapts to the new discoveries that observation and experimentation reveal. To that end, the existential level of truth is in a constant state of flux, which is something of a paradox since one would think the physical elements of our existence should be static and plain for all to see.

It would be remiss of me if I did not also point out that new scientific discoveries do not always change existing scientific theories. Some, for example, break new ground and open whole new fields for research and discovery while others confirm and verify existing theories.

Consider this observation – for thousands of years our ancestors believed they were human beings. That is, that they had *being* and did not simply exist, and this separated them from the fauna as well as the flora around them. Today, some refer to *being* as *consciousness* or *sentience*. This line of thought has seen a revival in recent times owing to the invention of AI. Does an AI have consciousness or sentience (is it self-aware)? This is a question of great importance to the scientists today, because of the impact AI might have on human beings.

Today, scientists who accept the theory of chance as the origin of all life on earth and natural selection as the evolution of all life are more likely than not to promote the idea that human beings are merely a part of the animal kingdom, since animals and human beings share a significant portion of their DNA. They claim that there is nothing special about a human being, and so they dropped the *being* from the truth of our existence and refer to us merely as humans. Of course, this belief negates most of what we just covered in our exploration of the transcendental level of truth, because that level of truth leads us into a consideration of things beyond the physical realities of our earthy existence, which we are only able to achieve through our conscious awareness of the transcendental. Although animals may have a limited consciousness, they do not have the capacity for transcendental contemplation.

Do you think this expanded consciousness makes human beings different from all other life forms? Explain your position and why you think what you do.

One final point I would like to make before moving on to the archetypical level of truth is that I find it interesting to observe the emergence of a number of philosophers, scientists and mathematicians today who are advancing the theory of *Intelligent Design* to explain the origin of the universe and all living things rather than the theory of *Chance* and *Evolution*, which had dominated science since Darwin first published his book, *On the Origin of Species* (1859). Those interested in the theory of *Intelligent Design* could begin their research with the microbiologist, Michael Behe (1952 AD-), who first advanced the theory in his book, *Darwin's Black Box*, where he argues the scientific principle of *irreducible complexity*. That is, that microbiological systems are so complicated that they cannot be reduced beyond a certain point and must be present before evolution can begin. This fact, he claims, makes the theory of random chance impossible. He concludes that Darwin's theory correctly illustrates the adaption of living species to their challenging environments but that random chance does not represent how those living species came into existence.

Another scientist advancing the theory of *Intelligent Design* is Stephen Meyer (1958 AD-), Fellow at the Discovery Institute, who in his latest book, *Darwin's Doubt,* 2023, argues that Darwin's theory presupposes the existence of biological life but offers no explanation for how that life began in the first place. He further argues that the fossil evidence shows a sudden appearance of larger categories of animal and plant forms during the Cambrian Period with no discernible connection to ancestorial precursors or intermediates in the lower pre-Cambrian strata. Also, there is his argument about DNA being an information storage, transmission, and processing system which is an automated system for building proteins and protein machines. In short, the existence of DNA makes it virtually impossible to envision how that might have arisen by a series of undirected chemical processes. Therefore, he argues, the existence of DNA is evidence of intelligent design rather than random chance.

John Lennox (1943 AD-), Professor of Mathematics at Oxford, in his book, *Seven Days that Divide the World,* 2011, advances the idea of a top-down infusion of the biosphere. Evolution, in the Darwinian sense being a bottom-up explanation, cannot be responsible for the origin of life for the simple reason that evolution presupposes the existence of life. This presupposition is false because the calculation of the time needed for life to evolve makes it impossible for it to have emerged in this way. John Lennox further argues that the information contained in DNA, for example, is too intricate to have arisen solely through random chance within the timeframe of the universe's existence.

In support of Lennox's conclusions is the recent finding of Grok 4, the most advanced AI yet created. Grok 4 calculated the probability for the origin of life (the emergence of a single functioning gene) forming through random mutations of DNA. Grok 4 calculated the odds at 1 in 10 to the power of 600, highlighting the extreme improbability of such an event happening. A comparison to illustrate these odds would involve finding a specific grain of sand from all the beaches on earth.

> *This aligns with broader discussions on abiogenesis, where the mathematical probability of minimal genomes self-assembling from simple chemicals is considered incredibly low, even over Earth's history.*
>
> (AI Overview 2025)

Of course, if we accept the intelligent design hypothesis, we must also accept the *brutality of nature* as it exists on the existential level of truth. Take, for example, the African parasitic eye worm (loa loa). Once introduced into the eye, if left untreated, it burrows into the eye causing extreme pain, vision impairment and even blindness. It does not discriminate. It attacks all human beings including innocent children and babies. The same can be said for all parasitic, viral, and bacterial infections. What about the fact that to survive some animals must literally eat other animals. This surely is a brutal truth. That is, that this brutality has also been intelligently designed.

Can we find reason for such brutal, natural truth? The first observation we must make when contemplating this is that we have a limited capacity to understand the full dimensions of truth. Since we cannot visualise the full extent of this phenomenon, we must accept its truth. It is, however, accurate to observe that this brutality is found in existential truth, not transcendental truth. Remember, transcendental truth is a utopian ideal, something we admire which drives our aspiration. When artists draw our attention to the pain and suffering found in human existence, it evokes in us feelings of empathy and pathos. Can we find justification for such brutal truth in our empathy and pathos? That is, we all suffer to some degree and, therefore, are capable of empathy for those who suffer.

Do the human feelings of empathy and pathos drive in us a burning desire to alleviate the undeserved suffering of the innocent? Does this not inspire our humanity? Does this make a difference or are we merely avoiding the reality of our existence by claiming this distinction?

Such speculation does, of course, require us to believe in something that is unprovable by using our senses, logic, and reason, in a scientific sense, but is achieved by using our imagination and inspiration. The fact that empathy and pathos exists in all of us, however, gives rise to the truth of its transcendental reality and may go some of the way to help us accept that the brutality of nature may have been the product of intelligent design.

But what of those who suffer? Why should they suffer so we can learn empathy and pathos? These questions do, though, avoid the truth that we all suffer in our lifetimes. Some maybe more than others, but we all suffer. I am reminded of a quote by Hellen Keller (1880-1968), an American author, disability rights advocate, political activist, and lecturer –

I cried because I had no shoes until I met a man who had no feet.

Could it be that we all learn empathy, pathos, courage, and acceptance through the pain and suffering we are expected to observe in others (even the innocent) and endure ourselves?

The universe and nature are physical entities that follow logical patterns and laws that govern their existence. These laws have become apparent to us through our application of mathematics, a purely logical system of understanding. Ask yourself, where logic and laws exist is there not a legislator and designer who invents that logic and laws? Remember, Bill Gates once remarked that –

Human DNA is like a computer programme but far, far more advanced than any software ever created.
(Bill Gates, *The Road Ahead*, 1995)

Gates' statement links computer programming with biology and emphasises the complexity of DNA as a biological information system. Does this suggesting that such complexity might arise from design rather than random chance?

Does science's state of constant flux negate its ability to reveal truth? Or does it reveal the honest reality that, given the limitation of our perception, it is difficult for us to understand how we can ever know the full magnitude of truth? If this is true, are we left only with our own potential and ability to reach a limited understanding of it?

Let us now turn to our final Level of Truth.

The Archetypical Level

This level of truth is accessible to us through our instincts and subconscious drives and passions, which respond to outside stimuli. It is the realm of Psychiatrists and Psychologists. It carries us to a place within our minds that is populated with dark secrets and hidden desires. Of course, I am talking here primarily of the nineteenth century works of Freud (1856-1939 AD) and Jung (1875-1961 AD). To be sure, there are many other great leaders in this field of scientific endeavour, but I am only interested here in highlighting those who were the pathfinders in this field of mental health, and how we can access the Archetypical Level of Truth through their work. This is the reason why I am limiting my survey here to these two early, and more commonly known, scientists of this field.

First on this list is Freud who proposed that human personality is comprised of three elements –

The Id, the Ego, and *the Superego.*

According to Freud, *the Id* is the primitive and instinctual part of our minds, where certain patterns of behaviour, necessary for our survival, are imprinted in our brains. The *hypothalamus* part of our brains produces hormones, and manages our moods, hunger, thirst, and sexual arousal as well as many other functional behaviours. According to Freud, these behaviour patterns include powerful sexual and aggressive drives hidden deep within our memory which continue to influence us today. *The Superego* is the person we want everyone to believe we are. It is our idealistic self, but like all ideals it is difficult for us to live up to its impossible standards. Our poor little *ego* has the unenviable task of trying to mediate between the hidden desires of our *Id* and the impossible standards of our *superego*; between the demon that lurks below and the angel that floats above. No wonder so many of us have mental problems when the behaviour of many of today's cultural icons do not aid our ego with its difficult task.

Can you find any similarities between Freud's construction of our personality and your own experience? Explain in your own words.

Second is Jung. He believed that the human psyche had three parts –

> the *Ego,* the *Personal Unconscious,* and the *Collective Unconsciousness.*

I want to concentrate only on the *Collective Unconsciousness* here, not only because it best illustrates the Archetypical Level of truth, which is the focus of our exploration, but is also Jung's most original contribution to the field of psychoanalysis. At its base, Jung believed that all humanity shares a universal version of mental patterns. These patterns stretch back to our paleolithic ancestors and can be seen in the literature, art, and myths of various cultures. Jung called these mental patterns *archetypes*, and they have been imprinted into our psyche because of our species' need for survival. In short, they are survival instincts that are innate and universal. Jung did identify four *archetypes*, which I won't go into here, but his essential argument was that many of our problems arise from living a modern lifestyle which brings about

> *man's progressive alienation from these archetypes*
> (Carl Jung, *The Undiscovered Self,* 1958)

Do you ever find yourself feeling disconnected from the values and beliefs of your society? If you do, can you see any connection between what you are feeling and Jung's explanation of our archetypes?

What these two great psychiatrists are articulating is, quite simply, the source of our Archetypical Level of Truth, something lurking in the dark recesses of our minds that emerge instinctually when triggered by outside stimuli.

One example of this survival mechanism is the *fight or flight* reaction, as a response to a perceived threat, which triggers in our bodies a series of hormonal changes that increases our heart rate, activates rapid breathing, and provokes muscle tension. It also can lead us into emotional discomfort and anxiety.

Summary

So that ends a limited overview of what I believe are the different levels of truth. What is your first impression of my observations? I hope it has stimulated your curiosity and built in you a desire for further research, and discussion. If I have encouraged you to ponder what I have said and discuss it with others, I will not only have achieved my goal but gained a great deal of joy from our time together.

An interesting experiment for you to conduct would be for you to consider how these three levels of truth interact with one another and attempt to articulate your conclusions, either verbally or in writing. Another question for you to consider is whether or not you think some people live their entire lives functioning primarily on only one of the three levels of truth. Could there be value in trying to explore all three levels of truth to help you live a more meaningful, potentially fulfilling life?

Also, keep in mind that

the whole is greater than the sum of the parts.
(Aristotle, *Metaphysics Book VIII*)

I remember applying this rule to my grading of the essays and assignments of my students, and my adjudication of their debates. When marking, one breaks down arguments into expression and content, ascribing marks to individual elements of an argument, but to arrive at a grade, one needs a holistic assessment. For this, one needs to stand back from the argument and appreciate it as a whole, to ask oneself, "How well does it come together?"; "Is there unity in this argument?"; "Is it complete within itself?"; "Is there harmony in its quality?". This is the central beauty, the truth of an argument, as it is with any work of art. Truth should be appreciated in this way, as a whole, not a part. That is, not partly true or half true.

How would you grade my argument concerning truth so far? Is it easy to follow? Does it jell for you?

Before I close this chapter, let me introduce a completely tangential thought, just so we can encourage lateral thinking as well as vertical thinking. Let me begin by observing that if you were able to travel back to the Middle Ages and were to ask people living in Europe at that time,

What are you?

They would undoubtably reply 'I am a Christian', or they might say 'I am Catholic'. If you were to ask the same question of Europeans today, they would likely reply 'I am an accountant', or an engineer or a doctor or a carpenter or whatever occupation they hold. This clearly demonstrates the secular shift in the time from the Middle Ages to today. However, I think it is more informative than that. Perhaps people want to become something in their lifetime, be that a good Christian or a good professional, tradesman, worker etc. In short, they long for identity by seeking *goodness* in their lives by becoming a better person or a better skilled person. Have you ever listened to men and women talk about the achievements in their lives? Do they try to describe what they learnt from their experiences? Does this suggest they are seeking to become a better person and encouraging you to do the same?

However, are we capable of becoming anything in our lifetime? Could it be that we are incapable of becoming anything in this lifetime because we are all flawed human beings existing in a reality that constrains our ability to achieve perfection? Consequently, are we incapable of perfection? Can it be said that to truly become anything in our lifetime is beyond the scope of our earthly existence? Does this create a dissonance in our existence which highlights a genuine flaw at the root of truth? That is, does our inability to truly become anything in our lifetime highlight the futility of pursuing truth, of achieving goodness?

Well, you might ask, what are we then? Perhaps an answer can be found in that we are all in the process of becoming, but never actually become anything, so when asked the question, 'What are you?' we could answer that we are human beings in a state of becoming. I can suggest this with some authority because of my advanced age, so can confess that even at my stage of life, I am still learning and still making mistakes, which, incidentally, make me feel inadequate and sometimes even very foolish. Thank goodness I have developed the ability to laugh at myself and not beat myself mercilessly over my shortcomings.

I must hasten to add at this juncture that although we may remain in a state of becoming throughout our lives, we will still require structure and discipline to shape our becoming, and that structure and discipline must be guided by the good. Well, why? Why do I have to be good? you might ask. The answer is unequivocal. Without the guiding principle of goodness, we could all become monsters set on tearing each other apart and our society with it. Remember the sexual and violent drives of our Id. What would our world be like if we gave our Id free reign?

Alternatively, we all need a purpose in our lives. Something we strive to achieve. Those who seek purpose through power, money, fame, material gratification, or sexual conquest find they remain unfulfilled and alienated from their true purpose in life: the fulfilment of their potential and the achievement of happiness. A potential and happiness that is made apparent to all of us as we move to discover truth, not self-aggrandisement or temporary gratification.

The structure of our becoming must encourage us to move towards goodness and benevolence and away from evil and malevolence if we want to live in a civilised society, fulfil our potential, and achieve true happiness. Also, the discipline we hold to must insist that we move constantly in the direction of goodness. Without this foundational principle we would doom ourselves to destruction. Of course, you can reply, 'What if I don't want to be good? What if I don't accept the terms of your civilised society?' Let me respond with questions of my own. Do you intend to derive the benefits provided by a civilised society? That is, do you want others to be good so that you can derive the benefits from their goodness? Do you find hypocrisy in such a demand? Let me also point out that those benefits were created by people who adopted laws to protect themselves from the excesses of malevolence and made a commitment to justice that keeps them on the path of goodness.

Consider this. Thomas Jefferson (1743-1826), one of the founding fathers of the American Republic said,

Without virtue, happiness cannot be.

So for Jefferson happiness did not mean feeling good but being good. True happiness, then, is not derived from the pursuit of immediate pleasure but the pursuit of long-term virtue. Does this give you a new understanding of these famous words from the Declaration of Independence,

life, liberty and the pursuit of happiness?

Do you detect a link between being happy and being good or virtuous?

This idea about our becoming is something for you to ponder. Does it hold any value for you? What is that value? Do you have any objections to this idea? What are your objections?

All that we have spoken about in the three levels of truth is the inheritance Australians have received from different cultures, but primarily it is rooted in Western culture. A culture that begins with a Judeo-Christian heritage that is founded on things like the notion of human dignity underpinned by concepts like freedom, equality and humanity. It is further strengthened by a Greco-Roman heritage providing Australians with a wide range of influences including language, cultural, intellectual, and political legacies. Our language is based on phonetics, that is, the use of symbols that represent sounds rather than things. Around 1100 BC the Phoenicians developed this kind of system, which was later extended by the Greeks into the first true alphabet. The Greeks also gave us geometry, a branch of mathematics focused on the study of shapes, sizes and spatial relationships, while arithmetic, a branch of mathematics dealing with numbers and their operation, was first used by the Sumerians as far back as 3,000 BC. Australian culture, then, is not just colonial culture which itself has many antecedents. It is an eclectic synthesis of many different cultures over thousands of years.

Today, Australian culture is being influenced by new cultural elements. However, these elements need evaluation before they are assimilated into Australian culture which promotes individual liberty, equal rights, democracy, prudently regulated capitalism, and social mobility. Remember, your ancestors fought and died for your liberty and liberal democratic way of life. You are the guardians of their truth. Will you protect it or will you allow the decolonialisation movement, radical relativism and post-modernist despair to ravage and annihilate it?

At the start of this discussion, we set ourselves the task of discovering the nature of truth. Do you think the ideas and values expressed in our discussion so far have helped you to better understand the nature of truth? I also linked truth with freedom. From our discussion, in what ways do you think truth and freedom are linked, if at all? Can it be said that the truth shall set you free? Do you think your potential might lie in discovering truth and setting yourself free?

To help us discover truth and fulfill our potential, however, we must maintain mental discipline, emotional control and empathy in our lives.

Chapter 3:
A Disciplined Mind, Controlled Emotions, and Acknowledged Empathy

Consider these three quotes about disciplining your mind, controlling your emotions and acknowledging empathy –

True Freedom is Impossible Without a Mind Made Free by Discipline.
(Mortimer J. Adler (1902-2001), American philosopher, educator, and author)

A real man (or woman) doesn't give way to anger and discontent, and such a person has strength, courage and endurance – unlike the angry and complaining.
(Marcus Aurelius, *Meditations*, 11.18.5b)

Empathy is seeing with the eyes of another, listening with the ears of another, and feeling with the heart of another.
(Alfred Adler (1870-1937), Medical doctor and psychotherapist)

Before you develop empathy, you must first discipline your mind and control your emotions, because you must first learn how to control your bias and prejudice before you can begin to actively listen to others.

Chapter 3: A Disciplined Mind, Controlled Emotions, and Acknowledged Empathy

Let me point out from the start that controlling your emotions is not the same as supressing your emotions. In the first instance you recognise your emotions and only want to control them. In the second instance you are trying to deny your emotions, and this can lead to serious problems for you. When you control your emotions, you still experience them, but you do not derive your life's purpose and meaning from your indulgence in them. Courage/cowardice, calmness/anger, love/hate, generosity/envy, admiration/jealousy, loyalty/treachery, trust/betrayal among many others are all emotions that you will experience in your lifetime. They are emotions that evolved over hundreds of thousands of years which enabled our species to survive, so they all have a purpose in our lives, even the unpleasant ones. It is not the emotions that destroy our ability to live a rich, fulfilling life, it is our inability to control them that does that. In the same way that it is not money that corrupts us but our love of money that does that. Go through each emotion listed here and explain how an obsession with any one of them could prevent someone from achieving a rewarding life.

Can Aristotle's 'golden mean' principle help us not to surrender to the extremes of our emotions? In what way? What about the 'ying and yang' principle of Taoism? The two complimentary yet opposite forces that create the universe and its interconnectedness. These forces are represented by the familiar Taijitu symbol illustrating that these forces are not inherently good or evil but in constant, dynamic balance. The goal being to live in balance with the natural flow of these forces. Does this offer us any insight into controlling our emotions? Explain.

Another point that needs to be made at the outset is that you cannot stop random thoughts from popping into your head at any time. You are particularly vulnerable to this in times of anxiety or when you enter what I call the twilight time, the time just before you drop off to sleep. You see these random thoughts, that usually generate an emotional response like those mentioned above, is the way that our minds attempt to help us solve a problem or remind us of a difficult or shameful thing that occurred in our past so that we do not repeat it in future.

When we are asleep we all dream. Much research has been done on dreams and there are still many questions left unanswered. Dreams seem to be related to our subconscious thoughts, emotions and desires, serving as a means to process our experiences and explore unresolved issues. Some dreams mean very little while others constantly return to events in our lives that caused us great distress, fear and anxiety. Such is the case with PTSD.

There are a number of techniques that psychologists suggest to help in stopping these random thoughts, but the truth is that these techniques only help draw attention to them. Techniques like deep breathing, meditation or distraction exercises are useful relaxation techniques but they cannot stop these thoughts from popping into your mind. When you practise these techniques to stop these thoughts from affecting you, you are only drawing you mind's attention to them. This is why PTSD cannot be cured, it can only be relieved through the use of psychiatric medications and controlled by mindful techniques. Just remember that random thoughts cannot be stopped, so we must learn how to respond to them with the intention of gaining some control over them. We do this by recognising our mind's attempt to warn us and allowing that thought to do its job. Respond by saying,

Yes, I recognise that I was wrong and I will do better in future.

Or that,

I was wronged but I will not obsess over things I cannot change.

It will help you if you remember *The Serenity Prayer*, attributed to the American theologian, Reinhold Niebuhr –

God grant me the serenity to accept the things I cannot change,

Chapter 3: A Disciplined Mind, Controlled Emotions, and Acknowledged Empathy

> *the courage to change the things I can, and the wisdom to know the difference.*

Having dealt with those important caveats, the obvious questions one would ask here are: Why should I discipline my mind and control my emotions? What are the benefits for me if I do? If I decide to do it, how do I go about achieving it? One indisputable answer to these questions is that if you do not discipline your mind and control your emotions, you will have lost control of your free will. This would make you subject to unscrupulous manipulation by others, who could use bias, prejudice, and mob opinion to influence your decision making.

Can you see that none of this would make you a free thinker? Can you see what Mr Adler is advising us about having a disciplined mind in the above quote?

As well as this, uncontrolled emotions inhibit us from achieving a disciplined mind. It has been said in different words by the Hindu sage Vyasa (around 300 BC), the Stoic philosopher Zeno of Citium (around 300 BC), Jesus (4BC-30 AD), and Mohammad (570-632 AD) that

> *those who do not control their emotions will be ruled by them.*

Again, uncontrolled emotions inhibit us from becoming free thinkers. A disciplined mind, however, can aid in controlling our emotions and stop us from making hasty, careless decisions. Decisions that we often later regret. When you feel a sudden powerful surge of emotion, stop, reflect, reason, and say nothing, do nothing until you have calmed your emotional outburst.

One of the things I, as a teacher, was frequently asked by parents whose teenage children I was teaching was

> *Is my child doing the best he or she can?*

On answering this question, I would refer to their child's potential, since my goal was obviously to help my students fulfil their potential. After all, we cannot expect a student to achieve what he/she is incapable of achieving. On the other hand, we should not allow this concept to inhibit us from doing our best to achieve our full potential.

It was my experience that those students who failed in this regard were those who lacked the mental discipline to apply themselves to their studies. Alternatively, some were overwhelmed by the testosterone or oestrogen flooding their system, and this made them unable to control their emotions, leading, once again, to a failure to fulfil their potential.

So, you see, fulfilling one's potential always starts with these two things – discipline your mind and control your emotions. This is another reason why you should do it because it will help you fulfil your potential and fulfilling your potential will enable you to achieve your goals and live a rich, fulfilling, truthful life.

Do you believe that the reasons I have outlined above are sufficient to convince you that it would be a good idea to discipline your mind and control your emotions?

Assuming you have answered the above question in the affirmative and have decided to try to achieve this, we must now turn our attention to the how. How do we go about discipling our minds and controlling our emotions?

A disciplined mind and controlled emotions are interconnected so should be dealt with in a combined manner and not separately. My approach, then, is a holistic one where mind and emotions are melded together. An undisciplined mind will result in uncontrolled emotions, and uncontrolled emotions will lead to an undisciplined mind. Alternatively, a disciplined mind can help to control emotions and controlled emotions can help discipline an undisciplined mind. Now that my approach to this topic is clear, let us begin.

In your daily life I am sure you have heard someone say, or perhaps you have even said it yourself –

Chapter 3: A Disciplined Mind, Controlled Emotions, and Acknowledged Empathy

You're behaving like a child, why don't you grow up?

Or maybe the approach was more direct –

Grow up!

What is meant by this is that the individual under question is being accused of behaving in an immature, childlike (spoilt, privileged) manner, that they are being selfish or narrowly self-absorbed.

'It's not all about you.'

I can hear others say. This habit of taking things personally is often observed in teenagers who have not achieved the ability to see things beyond their own needs. Educators have a word for this. It is called *maturation*, and maturation comes from having a disciplined mind and controlled emotions.

Controlling our emotions leads us to acquiring *empathy* for others. If you can control your emotions you are well on the way to putting yourself in another's place and feeling the disappointment, shame, regret or whatever else they are feeling. Once empathy is acquired, it can also assist you in controlling your emotions. Empathy for others has a way of draining the excess of our emotional outbursts. This reminds me of the saying –

Don't judge another until you have walked in their shoes.
(Ancient Proverb)

Delayed gratification is yet another way of disciplining your mind and controlling your emotions. Accepting that you will have to work hard at your studies today so that you can achieve a higher grade at some time in the future is an example of delayed gratification.

That's how it works. You make a sacrifice now so that you can achieve something you need or want or value in the future.

Do you believe that delayed gratification can help you in disciplining your mind and controlling your emotions? Explain.

The undisciplined and emotional exuberance of the immature has an unsettling effect on those around them. The Germans have a saying for this. They call it the *Storm and Stress* of our teenage years. The English refer to it as our *adolescent years*. The Americans like to call it the *Generation Gap*. Whatever the terms, however, it all adds up to the same thing – an inability on the part of the immature to behave in a disciplined, controlled, and empathetic manner.

The single biggest factor contributing to this shortfall in our personal development is not being able to think in a logical, reasoned, and empathic way. Logic, reason, and empathy are behind almost all the education we receive at school. Let's take English, Maths, Science, History, and Literature, for example. When learning how to write, we are taught the way to structure our sentences by using Simple Sentences, Compound Sentences, Complex Sentences or Compound-Complex Sentences. What we are learning is how to logically construct our thoughts. In Maths we are taught the importance of definitions and how to logically arrive at a correct solution to a problem. Science teaches us to conduct experiments and come to logical, reasonable conclusions from the gathered evidence and raw data. History shows us how to gather historical facts and derive dispassionate but empathetic conclusions about the people of the past. We also seek to understand the guiding principles they lived their lives by and empathise with them for the conditions they had to contend with. As stated previously, Literature teaches us how to understand and empathise with fictional characters.

As well as this, there is our own personal experience that we gain from observations about our own lived experience. If we approach this source of information using logic, reason, and empathy we will develop a goodly portion of wisdom and sharply honed common-sense. If not,

Chapter 3: A Disciplined Mind, Controlled Emotions, and Acknowledged Empathy

we will sink, once again, into a selfish, self-centred, and immature view of life.

In my generation, personal experience was referred to as anecdotal evidence, which was considered as a starting point to any enquiry, requiring much observation and gathering of facts before reaching any conclusion. To jump straight from personal experience, or lived experience, to conclusions about life in general is to go from the particular to the general without any consideration being given to the possibility that our personal experience may have been the exception and not the rule. Much like the conclusion being wrong when the premise of our syllogism is incomplete.

Those who think logically, reasonably, and empathetically have a saying for drawing conclusions from anecdotal evidence –

One sparrow does not a summer make.

Generally, sparrows appear in summer, but one sparrow is not a flock of sparrows and therefore the appearance of one sparrow should not be hailed as the arrival of summer. We need to see a lot more sparrows before reaching that conclusion, and this requires the gathering of data, the examination of evidence and the application of logic, reason, and empathy before reaching any conclusion. To rely on personal experience alone to draw conclusions once again opens the possibility to be swayed by our uncontrolled emotions and undisciplined thinking.

What is your opinion about the importance of logic, reason, and empathy in your life? Do you think they can help you discipline your mind and control your emotions? Explain, drawing on how important they are in your life. Do you think logic, reason and empathy can help you achieve true freedom in your life?

Mature, freethinking people usually set goals for themselves. Setting goals for yourself will help you become an achiever in your life. That is, you won't merely drift through life achieving very little. You may well say that you don't want to set goals for yourself, that you want to be free and just drift through life. You are, of course, entitled to do this. After all, we live in a free society. If you do this, however, should you have the right to be envious of those who do set goals for themselves and achieve a more rewarding life than you? Is it reasonable for you to expect others who have achieved more than you through their goal setting and disciplined, controlled approach to life to sacrifice what they have because you did not set goals for yourself, nor work hard to achieve them? Thankfully, for those who drift through life, achievers are not only guided by their logic but also their reason and empathy. Consequently, they are willing to share some of what they have acquired with those who have little because they are able to empathise with the situation those without find themselves in.

Should those who drift, however, be demanding of, or grateful for, the achievers' generosity? What are some possible goals in life that you would like to set for yourself? Do you want to sacrifice these goals because you would rather drift through life?

You might like to consider some of the following goals for yourself.

1) Try to understand the nature of truth and commit yourself to always advocate for it. This is how you will maintain your integrity.
2) Consistently strive to achieve a disciplined mind, controlled emotions and an empathetic nature. This will enable you to avoid being manipulated by others.
3) Work hard at your studies, chosen job or profession to become the best in what you do. This will maintain your dignity and self-respect.
4) Devote yourself to a fitness program to keep your body in good health. This will maximise you chance for an active old age.
5) Eat a well-balanced diet to avoid becoming emaciated, overweight or obese. This will provide you with a positive

Chapter 3: A Disciplined Mind, Controlled Emotions, and Acknowledged Empathy

      self-image and an alert mind.
6) Maintain a personal hygiene regime. This will assist you in living a disease-free life.
7) Start a savings program to relieve yourself of some of the financial burdens you will face in life.
8) Take on the responsibility of marriage and raising a stable family to achieve lasting happiness in your old age.

These goals will enable you to achieve self-actualisation, enrich your life, and fulfil your potential.

It is often said that we can measure our success in life by those we leave behind when we pass on. Supporting this conclusion are grandparents who continually testify of the joy they experience from visiting with their grandchildren. Can we conclude from this that perhaps the goal of achieving a stable family is the most important of all the goals we can set ourselves? Do you agree? Disagree? Explain your position. How many people do you know who have said that they should have devoted themselves more to their work, or accumulated more wealth during their lifetime? How many wished they had spent more time with their family?

Do you think these are admirable goals to set yourself? If you were able to achieve these goals in your lifetime, do you think you would be able to live a free, happy life? Do you have goals of your own, outside the ones mentioned here that you would like to commit to? Do not take my list to be comprehensive. Your dreams in life must be your own, not someone else's, if you want to maintain your motivation to achieve them. Therefore, accept or modify my list to suit your own needs, but importantly commit to setting goals and acquiring the mental discipline, emotional control, and empathetic understanding to achieve them.

Let us assume that you have decided to set goals for yourself. The next question would be -

How do I go about achieving my goals?

I did some time in the military when I was a young man, and fortunately it taught me self-discipline and the importance of being task-orientated. You see, the military sets itself missions that soldiers must complete to win battles. How did the military teach us to complete our missions? The US marines have a clear statement about this which I think is instructive. They call it *structure and discipline.* That is, you have a mission, or in your case a goal, that you want to achieve, so you must create *a plan* to achieve that goal. Then you need to structure your life, this usually means setting up a specialised timetable and training schedule and exercising the self-discipline to complete the training schedule and carry out the mission to achieve your goal.

Your plan requires setting out the tasks necessary to reach your goal. These tasks are the smaller goals needed to reach the larger, overall goal. The military operates on teamwork, so the smaller tasks are assigned to individuals or groups of individual soldiers, who understand that they must complete each task in the mission if the mission is to be successful. If you set a goal for yourself, much of the effort in achieving that goal will be conducted by yourself. However, that does not mean that you can't get assistance from others. I am sure family members, teachers (or managers in a work environment) and good friends will be willing to help you achieve your goals.

So, what have you learnt so far about achieving your goals in life? Well, first you need a plan broken down into several smaller tasks aimed at achieving your goal. Then you need to structure your life in such a way as to complete these smaller tasks. This will mainly require you to set aside the necessary time to complete your tasks, and that time may require you to do additional research about individual tasks. At school, for example, this may require you to set aside time to read and understand a book which may include some research about the book's background and history, or learning and understanding a maths formula which may include what the mathematician who discovered it was trying to prove, or perhaps a series of historical events that shaped a certain period in history, which may include researching the history behind what led up to these events. As you can see, this requires setting aside the necessary time to achieve these small tasks on the way to achieving your goal of doing the best you can to achieve your desired outcome for your education.

How do we complete these tasks? There is only one way that I know of, and that way is discipline. Remember the US marine motto –

Structure and Discipline.

Having set aside the time and elements you need to complete your task, you now must be determined to complete it. This is hard and will require full commitment on your part. There will be times when your mind will scream at you to stop, that it's not worth the effort, that you'll never understand what you are studying. But wait, you have developed a disciplined mind, so you can exercise discipline over your thoughts.

Tell your mind to grow up and stop bothering you with juvenile thoughts and get on with the task at hand.

At times you will feel the emotional pull to forsake your task and enjoy something more pleasurable. You will tell yourself that you can always come back to it later. Wait, you have learnt to control your emotions. Remember the lesson learnt about delayed gratification and tell yourself that

time off is important, but it should come when I complete a task, not during my attempt to achieve it.

If you exercise mental discipline and emotional control, if you do your best, you will complete each task in your plan and achieve your goal.

Remember to reward yourself as you complete each task, even if it is merely a recognition to yourself that you have completed one small task in your overall goal.

Congratulate yourself on your discipline and control and tick off your completed task.

Take pride in your success and look ahead with eager anticipation to achieving your next task.

Whenever you reach a milestone in your goal, like getting a higher grade in one of your subjects, take some time off. Enjoy a movie or some time with your friends or family. After your reward, recommit yourself to your goal. Tell yourself,

I will achieve my next step and I will reach my desired goal.

What I am encouraging you to achieve in your life is merit. Remember, when merit is watered down we arrive at mediocracy, where the grandeur of our human experience is replaced with a tiresome, uneventful existence. Where the monotonous triumphs over the intriguing.

Have you found our discussion about acquiring a disciplined mind, controlling your emotions and developing an empathic nature helpful? Do you think you could commit yourself to goal setting in your life?

Before I close, let me mention one outstanding item. No doubt, you have heard the saying,

All work and no play makes Jack or Jill a dull boy or girl.

I have already mentioned the importance of congratulating yourself when you complete a task and of celebrating when you achieve a major milestone in your goal. However, there is still more to consider here.

Chapter 3: A Disciplined Mind, Controlled Emotions, and Acknowledged Empathy

Remember to also celebrate or commemorate the important events in your country's and your family's calendar. This is a golden opportunity to develop your empathetic nature. The public holidays set aside by your country for celebration or commemoration are important and should be enjoyed.

Take the time to laugh, relax and enjoy the food and companionship of those you love and hold in high esteem.

Ponder what it is that you are celebrating or commemorating. Appreciate the sacrifice and hardships endured by others who have provided you with the wonderful, successful country you have been given the privilege to be born into.

Do the same for special family events. Birthdays, for example, should be celebrated by the whole family and not just those who have reached a new birthdate.

Remind yourself about the lives of those no longer with you; your ancestors and what they endured to provide you with the life you now enjoy.

Then, there are the times that your family sets aside for a family outing, maybe a picnic or a day at the beach. Do your best to join in and be cheerful about it. Don't spend the day thinking about all you could be doing somewhere else and, by doing so, spoil it for the others.

Why not develop a cultural appreciation for what is on offer. Start with your own district. No doubt there will be theatres and concert halls somewhere near to where you live, where live performances are scheduled. Take time to attend some of them, especially those with guest entertainers who have travelled to your district. They will provide excitement, and their charismatic personalities will lead you to an emotional experience unable to be enjoyed anywhere else. Unfortunately, many modern performers use their platform to deliver political messages. Remember, you are in a vulnerable, emotional state at a live concert, so be circumspect about any ideology delivered to you there. This is also true when you view movies or any live performance; after all, your emotions are being manipulated by others at these times, so be sure to test their messages later against logic, reason, wisdom, common sense, prudence, and empathy. Remember to look for hidden agendas and unintended consequences. Do your research, don't take what they say at face value, even if you admire their acting or musical ability. Remember,

> *What they tell you is only their opinion,*
> *and all opinions need to be verified.*

Their celebrity status does not entitle their opinions to a privileged position. Your own opinion is just a valid as theirs.

Take time to appreciate the timeless quality of Aboriginal culture and its relationship to the natural beauty of the land. Listen while you are told about the importance of traditional Aboriginal dances, cave paintings, and bora rings to Aboriginal culture. Have you gained an appreciation of the values of hunter-gatherer cultures? Remember –

We all had ancestors who lived this way at some time in the past.

The capital city of your state has many centres designed for cultural appreciation, Museums, Art Galleries, Libraries, and Performing Arts Centres. Make sure you include some opera (especially Italian opera) and orchestral performances along with the more frequent performances of musicals, drama and comedy, to name a few.

> *Soak up the cultural experience you will enjoy*
> *by visiting these places.*

Then, there is your nation's capital city. There is so much to see

Chapter 3: A Disciplined Mind, Controlled Emotions, and Acknowledged Empathy

and experience in Canberra, The War Memorial (Australia's cultural heart), for example. What Australian values were these wars fought to protect? Old Parliament House, the new Parliament House, The High Court, Royal Military College Duntroon, the National Art Gallery, The National Library, Science Centre, Royal Australian Mint, and Australian National University only begins your search for

Australian identity reflected through the establishment of these institutions.

Later in life, why not reach out to discover the cultural identities of other countries. When visiting China, take time to climb China's Great Wall – it's steep in places but enjoy the success of your climb. Explore the Forbidden City and Tiananmen Square and discover the significance of these places of interest and what they tell us about China's culture. I remember the time I climbed a particularly steep section of the Great Wall of China. When I reached the top, I was exhausted but I spotted an elderly woman who was there selling cans of coke from an esky full of ice. She had two teenage boys with her, who I assume carried the esky for her, but she must have made the climb on her own and likely did it each and every day. Does this anecdote reveal anything about a possible cultural value of the Chinese?

When you view the Taj Mahal, you will be amazed by its symmetrical beauty, possibly the most beautiful, symmetrical building in the world. It is a mausoleum built by the fifth Mughal emperor, Shah Jahan to house the tomb of his beloved wife, Mumtaz Mahal. His tomb was also interred there after his death. Does this building give you a better understanding of Indian culture?

You can stand in wonder at the Pyramids of Egypt (they're big), the Parthenon in Greece (with its amazing geometric design) and the Colosseum in Rome (the largest ancient amphitheatre ever built). Do these wonderous structures give you a better understanding of the foundational values of Western culture? Why did the Egyptians,

Greeks, and Romans build these functional monuments? What beliefs do they represent?

Why not visit Istanbul where you can look in on the Hagia Sophia Grand Mosque. What is the history of this magnificent structure? Today it is a mosque but originally it was a Christian church, built in the 6th century by the Byzantine emperor, Justinian. What does this tell you about Islamic culture?

If you visit the rich, vibrant cities of Europe and their surprising architecture it will give you pause to consider the values that underpin our modern world. I will not mention all the delights you will discover here, because there are simply too many. Go find them for yourself. Soak up the cultural values expressed in their architecture.

American cities with their smooth, functional, glass, steel, and concrete skyscrapers show us the underlying values of the world we currently inhabit. What are those values? Why do you think that? Before you visit America, look up the works of Frank Lloyd Wright online, and if you get the opportunity to visit some of his architectural wonders, do so.

All this will take a lifetime of dedicated search, evaluation and appreciation but be prudent and circumspect in your evaluation of other cultures.

> *Try to make judgements based on*
> *cultural appreciation and not pride.*

Remember *different from* does not necessarily mean *better than*. Although in some cases we must exercise moral clarity when confronted with malevolent values and practices.

Do you think what I have offered here is sound advice? Do you detect any bias or prejudice in my presentation? Whatever way you answer these questions, I wish you good luck in the adventures your life will bring you. Remember, you are privileged to live at this time in world history where it is possible for you to achieve all the things

I have outlined here. You will, however, need to commit yourself to disciplining your mind, controlling your emotions, developing an empathetic nature, setting personal goals, and dedicating yourself to a structured and disciplined lifestyle.

> *Like all privileges in life, they need to be earned not given, if you are going to reap the satisfaction of self-fulfilment.*

Chapter 4:
Physical Fitness and Healthy Eating Habits

Let me preface this chapter with a disclaimer. I am not a doctor, and I am not a fitness instructor. You need to understand that what I am providing you with here is the motivation to live a healthy lifestyle. I am drawing on my experience from a lifetime of physical fitness and healthy eating habits. Clearly, before you start on any fitness program or healthy eating habit you should consult your doctor as to whether it is appropriate to your needs.

Physical Fitness

The first question you would probably ask when considering whether to embark on this venture is why? Why should I have to worry about physical fitness and healthy eating? I'm healthy and in pretty good shape. Why do I need to worry about physical fitness and what I eat? The answer is that there are many reasons why.

First and foremost is because it promotes discipline. Remember a disciplined mind and controlled emotions are two things needed to fulfil your potential. Also, physical fitness and maintaining a healthy weight influences both mental alertness and emotional stability. Moreover, there are other benefits that physical fitness and healthy eating habits can provide. For example, physical fitness can give you flexibility, muscular and cardiorespiratory endurance, while healthy eating habits may help you live longer, boost your immune system, strengthen your bones, and lower your risk of heart disease. All these benefits should lead you to consider adopting a physical fitness programme and healthy eating habits.

If you want to devote yourself to this venture, the first thing you need to do is think carefully about why you are committing to it. Take your time and be sure about your reasons, then write them down. Next, write a pledge to yourself that you will honour your commitment. Date it and sign it.

In future, if you find yourself waning, or reneging on your pledge, take it out and read it, several times if necessary, until you find the mental and physical strength to re-commit yourself. The first time you re-read your pledge and the reasons for your commitment may not convince you to re-start your healthy lifestyle program. That's all right. It just means that you are not yet in the right frame of mind. However, don't give up on yourself. Come back to your commitment and pledge at some other time when you are in the right frame of mind. The important thing is to never give up on yourself. You are too important and valuable for that.

Since exercise and diet are ways to control depression, a growing problem faced by your generation, it is timely to consider depression at this point in our discussion. You may or may not be suffering from depression. However, the following observations are useful for you or someone else in your life that you care about who might be suffering from depression.

First, there are people in your life who love and need you, and if you do not believe that then look for them. They are there, believe me. If you truly believe that you have no one in your life today, that does not mean you will not have friends in the future. They are there waiting for you to reach out your hand of friendship. If you make the effort, you will find them, and they will support you.

Second, if you suffer from depression, talk to your parents and doctor about it. Then, visit the Australian Government's *Head to Health website*. This will introduce you to apps, online forums, phone supports and much more.

Third, and most important, always remember there is no one else on earth who is exactly like you. You are unique, and that uniqueness makes you important and valuable to the universe you have been gifted with the privilege to inhabit. Look out at the shining stars on a darkened night sky. Are the stars indifferent or benign? Do they fill you with despair, or do they call to you of a truth unmatched by your earthly existence? If you see truth in their beauty, why not submit to the majesty of their mystery. Watch the glory of a glowing sunrise or sunset. Does it call to you of a hidden purpose? Remember that glorious sun has had a sacred duty to perform every day since the formation of our solar system. It is the source of all life on earth, and it goes about its duty without complaint and with compassion for us all. Gifting us freely the life we all enjoy. You included.

Your universe wants you to take up the challenge it has provided for you. Don't let it down. Don't let your family and friends down. Don't let yourself down. Rise each morning with a burning glow of eager anticipation for what this new day will bring to you and with empathy and generosity in your heart for all humanity, all of whom face their own pain and suffering. Why not try to help them in any way you can. Remember every small effort helps, and they will be grateful for your help.

Fourth, perhaps animals are more your calling. There are organisations established to care for and protect suffering animals. Why not join one and volunteer some of your time. Maybe you are more motivated by caring for the environment. See what practical things you can do. Volunteer your service for a clean-up day in your city or a tree-planting day. If you do any of these things, you will feel the burning glow of charity in your heart. Perhaps the greatest of all healing powers you will experience in your lifetime, the gift of giving or service for others.

This is the challenge that the universe has gifted to you. Embrace each new day as the sun does; arise and without complaint perform your sacred duty.

Please understand what I am proposing. I encourage you to engage in activities that lift your spirit, that will fill your heart with charity and your soul with empathy. Therefore, be careful not to let yourself be misguided by those who would use you for their own political purposes. Remember what we said about hidden agendas and unintended consequences. Do you think that joining political rallies where you will be asked to shout slogans or, worse, commit acts promoting inconvenience or violence towards others, or damage to public or private property could lead you into feelings of anger and confrontation rather than promote within yourself feelings of charity or goodwill? Remember, you want to embrace love, charity, and empathy for your fellow human beings, not envy, anger, and hatred.

A good distinction between these two outcomes is the difference between an Anzac Day parade and a political rally. On Anzac Day we march in commemoration of the sacrifice that others have made on our behalf, to protect our liberty and freedom. Political rallies, on the other hand, often become violent and confrontational. There is a place for protest. After all, that is what the Anzacs fought for. However, protest rallies should remain peaceful. They should try to persuade others not confront them, as most modern rallies do. Ignore those radicals who would try to discourage you or lead you away from your sacred duty.

Consider this. Don't get involved in politics until you have made a study of it, and don't study it until you have developed the ability for critical thought. When you do study politics, take a scholarly approach, not a passionate one. Use your logic, reason, wisdom, and common sense to understand the different ideas involving politics. Why do I say this? Because passion leads to bigotry and fanaticism. The religious superstition and bigotry of the Middle Ages took hundreds of years to overcome. In fact, we are still trying to overcome the remaining dregs of it today. Don't get me wrong. I am talking about religious superstition and bigotry, not religion per se. Spiritual inspiration is important, and religion can provide that for us if we do not become obsessed by it to the point of violent opposition. The same can be said for ideology. Those who lack critical thought or spiritual conviction in their lives today seem to have substituted ideology for it. Again, passion can lead to fanaticism here too. There is a place for passion in your life, but religion and politics are two subjects that require a disciplined mind, controlled emotions, wisdom, and common sense to understand, not passionate bigotry or fanaticism.

Do you find my advice helpful or limiting? Let me refer you back to the parable of the blind, wise men, and the elephant in our first chapter. Remember you can still love God or admire a political ideology without resorting to superstition, bigotry, or fanatical violence.

Let's return to our original discussion. Now that you have committed yourself to a physical fitness programme and a healthy eating lifestyle, we need to discuss what this entails. I do not intend to provide you with a fitness programme or a diet. Simply because there is no such thing as a perfect physical fitness programme or a perfect healthy diet that suits everyone. The truth is that we are all unique, and so you must build these for yourself. What I can do, however, is explain what a good fitness programme and a healthy eating lifestyle hopes to achieve and mention some exercises and foods and what they can do for you.

Another thing to consider is that fitness programmes and eating habits will change throughout your life as your needs change. The fitness programme and eating habit I am now following in my advanced age is far removed from those I held to in my youth, my adulthood, and my middle-age, as it will be for you. Just keep in mind what you are trying to achieve and adjust your fitness programme and eating habits accordingly.

The first thing you need to master before even beginning an exercising programme is to be aware of your breathing. This entails recognising that you have two lung organs (left and right) situated in your ribcage. Your right lung has three lobes, while your left has only two. The missing lobe in your left lung makes room for your heart, which is located slightly behind and to the left of your sternum (breastbone), found in the middle of your chest. When you breathe in and fill your lungs with air, oxygen passes into your blood stream (circulating your body via your heartbeats) and exchanges oxygen for carbon dioxide with the cells of your body. It is most important, therefore, to keep breathing when exercising, breathing *out* when your muscles are taking the pressure and *in* when they are releasing the pressure. If you fail to do this, your muscles will become fatigued and stop functioning, and in extreme cases you might faint (pass out) and collapse.

Our bodies make us collapse because the circulation of blood to our brains is easier for our hearts to accomplish in the prone position than in the erect position. When we faint it is because we have a lack of sufficient oxygen in our bloodstream to keep our brains functioning. If you see someone faint, don't panic. First, tap them on the shoulders and ask them if they can hear you. If they are not responsive, check their breathing. Open their airway by placing one hand on their forehead and tilting their head back. With your other hand open their mouth by pulling down on their chin. Put your ear over their mouth with your head turned towards their chest and listen for them breathing while watching if their chest is rising and falling in a regular way. If this is not the case, ask someone to call Emergency while you begin CPR (cardiopulmonary resuscitation) immediately. There are many refresher courses on YouTube for you to view how to perform CPR so I won't go into it here, but I would urge you to regularly view these to keep yourself current. CPR is the action of giving 30 compressions followed by two breaths. Try to achieve 5 sets of 30:2 in about 2 minutes. You must help them to continue breathing and their heart beating until the ambulance arrives otherwise their brains will die, thus ending their life. If they are breathing and their heart is beating, place them in a coma position so they do not swallow their tongue which will block their airway. Now that you know the importance of breathing, let's move on to deep breathing exercises.

The lung organs situated in your rib cage are controlled by your diaphragm muscle sitting below your lungs and heart. It expands when you take in air and contracts when you breath out. The diaphragm allows you to fill the lower section of your lungs, or the upper section of your lungs, or both at the same time. Put your hand over your abdomen and fill only the lower section of your lungs. If you do this correctly, your abdomen should expand and push your hand out while not expanding your chest. Now fill only the upper section of your lungs. This should expand only your chest and not your abdomen. Now fill both sections to their full capacity by breathing in through your nose, hold it for the count of five, then release the air slowly from your lungs through your mouth. Repeat this exercise ten times. This is a deep breathing exercise and will allow you to relax and release tension or anxiety from your body.

If you want to go further and exercise your core muscles, stand with your feet shoulder-width apart, knees bent slightly (locked knees put undue weight on the small of your back); put your hands on your hips and stretch yourself out to your full extent while keeping both feet flat on the ground. Now fill both sections (abdomen and chest) of your lungs while pulling your elbows back. With your lungs fully extended only release the air from the abdomen section while keeping the chest section full. If you do this correctly, you will feel the muscles at the sides of your abdomen tighten. Next pull your diaphragm up as far as you can. Hold this position for the count of ten before releasing the air in your upper lungs and pushing your elbows forward. Repeat this exercise ten times. Your diaphragm and abdomen muscles will have been tightened and strengthened.

Now that you have your breathing under control, let's return to your fitness programme and eating habits. You have probably heard the adage 'calories in, calories out' when referring to a proper balance between fitness and eating habits. Although this is true, if you try to limit your calorie intake because you are not exercising, you will find that you will just get tired and lethargic and unable to perform at your best. The answer, then, lies not in limiting one at the expense of the other, but rather in finding a healthy balance between the two that suits you.

Consider the following. Both physical fitness and weight control rest on spectrums. The physical fitness spectrum starts with those who do no exercises at all, then to some who do moderate exercise for flexibility and cardiorespiratory health, to those who dedicate themselves to muscular strength and endurance, and finally to those who seek bodybuilding through exercise. The last two are for those who exercise for specialised outcomes like sport or bodybuilding competitions. I am not interested in that here, but if you are, then you can go to more specialised publications, both in print and online. I am also not interested here in those who do not exercise at all, because they will suffer from fatigue, lethargy, and a lack of motivation, while those doing moderate exercise for cardiovascular health and flexibility exercises are likely to be better prepared to meet their full potential.

So, I am only interested in those who want to exercise for flexibility and cardiovascular fitness. What does the science tell us about this level of fitness? For moderate exercise to be beneficial it needs to raise the heart rate and cause perspiration. Obviously, the more exercise one does, the better the results will be, but you could start with exercising at least twice a week for a duration of 50 minutes for each session. In time this can be increased to three days a week, giving you the required 150 minutes of exercise a week recommended by professional guidelines. Some of the exercises you might consider would be walking at a rate that raises your heart rate, jogging in places that provide a pleasant outlook and clean air, swimming either in the ocean or your local pool, or bike riding which is less impactful on your body joins than jogging.

Perhaps something completely different is more your style. Dancing requires much strength and endurance, especially when performed with youthful enthusiasm. Why not join a dancing club, where you will learn different styles of dancing, get fit, and enjoy the company of like-minded people.

Maybe you would prefer something involving a sport. Why not join a club of your choosing. There are swimming clubs, tennis clubs, soccer clubs, cricket clubs, basketball clubs, and the contact sports like rugby union, rugby league, and AFL, to name just a few. Whatever your preference, you will be required to train and play, which involves regular exercise and keeping yourself fit. Remember, however, you are engaged in this sport to keep fit, not to become a champion. Unless, of course, you are one of the favoured few who show exceptional potential for any given sport. Also, avoid any temptation to adopt a *win at any cost* approach to sport; it will distance you from your progression towards goodness that we spoke of before. Rather remember Henry Newbolt's famous line in his poem *Vitai Lampada* (The Torch of Life) –

Play up! Play up! and play the game!

His poem tells us that how we play the game is more important than winning. It celebrates the ethics of sportsmanship and fair play, and that courage in the face of adversity is a desirable goal for sport.

I now want to turn to specific exercises designed for flexibility and fitness. Consider this. Since you are exercising your muscles, why not concentrate all your attention on the specific muscles you are exercising. Feel their expansion and contraction and let your mind imagine what they are doing. In this way you will be in tune with your body; your mind and body becoming one. Don't listen to music as you exercise and don't think about things other than your muscles exercising. These are distractions which will take your mind away from what you are doing and sap your enthusiasm for exercising. Enjoy exercising for what it is. Don't try and make it into something it is not. It is not a music session or a mental preview (perhaps even anxiety) of coming events, nor is it a meditation session. It is a coming together of your mind and body.

Before you start any exercise session, always do your stretch and warm-up exercises. Stretch exercises can be used to stretch your calves, thighs, biceps, triceps, chest, neck, and back muscles. Warm-up and cool-down exercises are repeated six times only and could include things like slow marching on the spot (lift your knees as high as you can), slow sidekicks, hip rotations, chest expansions, and arm circles. If you don't know how to perform these stretch exercises, just type their titles into a search engine (e.g., Safari or Google) and you will find illustrations and explanations on how to perform them.

Let's turn now to some muscular strength and fitness exercises you could consider including in your exercise session. This list is meant as examples only and is by no means complete. I encourage you to develop your own set of exercises. Here are some exercises designed to strengthen specific muscles. For upper body strength, you could start with push-ups. Push-ups are great because they exercise so many of your muscles (chest, shoulders, arms, back, stomach, and hips). Now pick up a dumbbell set. Start with a light set and slowly increase the weight as you build strength. Complete dumbbell curls for biceps, dumbbell upright-row for triceps and dumbbell flys for chest expansion. Move now to sit-ups, crunches, leg raises, and arches to strengthening your core muscles. Next do squats and lunges for upper thigh muscles and calf-raisers for strengthening your calf muscles. You could start with sets of 15 and increase the sets to 20 over time. Finish your exercise session with a cool-down period, rehydration and refuelling. During your cool-down period you do light activity and stretching, rehydrate with water or electrolyte drinks, and refuel by consuming a healthy snack. Remember to have a rest day between exercising sessions. Again, use a search engine if you don't know how to perform these exercises.

A good test for your heart health is to time how long it takes for your heart to recover to a normal heartbeat following an exercise session. For a flexibility and fitness exercise session, your heart rate should return to normal after 10-20 minutes, depending on your level of fitness.

Have my words been helpful? Do you now have a better understanding of exercise and how it helps us to keep our minds sharp and focused, and our bodies healthy? Do you think it would be better to focus on one exercise regime (i.e., gym workouts, walking, swimming etc.) or mix them up, so you do not become bored and less inclined to continue?

Fluid Intake

Before we turn to foods, let's first consider the basics of fluid intake for the average human body. The amount of fluid needed by our bodies varies according to what we eat, our age, the temperature, our physical exertion, and whether we have a medical condition. However, on average, men need about 10 cups (2.6 litres) of fluid per day and women 8 cups (2.1 litres). We get approximately one-fifth of our fluids from the food we eat and the rest from drinking fluids.

The fluid we take into our bodies is the biggest contributor to our sugar intake. Water is the only fluid that does not contain some level of sugar content, so water intake, more than any other fluid intake, controls our sugar levels. Sugar intake provides our bodies with energy, stored energy (fat), and is a major contributing factor to sugar diabetes.

Drinking plenty of water every day is important for good health. For example, it moistens our eyes, nose and mouth, regulates our body temperature, helps our bodies absorb nutrients, prevents constipation, lubricates our joints to help us remain mobile, and supports the growth and reproduction of our cells. Between 50% and 80% of our bodies is comprised of water and a lack of adequate water intake can cause kidney stones, constipation, urinary tract infections (UTIs), and headaches through our bodies becoming dehydrated (healthdirect.gov.au).

Do you agree that fluid intake, and particularly water intake, is vital for our body's health? Do you think we should be careful about the amount and type of fluid we consume each day?

Healthy Eating Habits

Turning now to healthy eating habits, let us consider the spectrum. First you have people who do not display any discipline in their eating habits, eating whatever they like whenever they like. These people usually suffer from being overweight or obese which will cause health problems for them as they age. For example, diabetes and heart-related problems are just two problems that will arise as they age. Next you have those who try to create healthy eating habits in their lives. These people usually maintain a healthy, natural weight, and are slim and alert and suffer fewer health problems as they age. Finally, there are those who suffer from an eating disorder like anorexia or bulimia. These people are grossly underweight and must endure constant fatigue and chronic health problems. I am only interested in those who desire to maintain a healthy, natural weight. If you belong to either of the other two groups you will require specialised health care that I am unable to provide for you here. You can still read on and discover for yourself what is required to maintain a healthy, natural weight, but I cannot provide the specialised care you need. For that you will need, in the first instance, to consult your GP, who may refer you to a specialist.

 Before we develop some healthy eating habits let me outline the eating habits of previous generations. My mother and father grew up as children during the Great Depression of the 1930s. Times were hard back then, especially for the poor and working class, so they grew up knowing what it was like to go to bed with hunger in their belly. My Dad told me that in his childhood, at the height of the depression, he ran away from home. At that time his family was living in Toowoomba, Queensland. It took him two days to get from Toowoomba to Gatton (just over 37km away at the bottom of the Great Dividing Range after a steep descent). He had not eaten since running away, so he went to the back of the local bakery and begged the baker for some bread. He was given a half loaf of very stale bread that was too hard for him eat, so he went to Lockyer Creek which flowed nearby Gatton and dipped the bread into the water of the creek to make it soft enough to eat. Luckily for Dad the baker informed the police and they picked up my father and returned him home. Both my mother and father often told me how grateful they were for the secure food supply developed by Australia in the post-WWII era.

As a child growing up in the 1950s, my parents never let me go to bed on an empty stomach. I remember my father saying to me whenever I made the mistake of saying that I was not hungry and didn't want to eat my food,

> *You will eat whatever is put in front of you, young man, and be grateful for it.*

This was followed by a lecture about the children of the world who at that very moment did not have food for their hungry bellies. Let us pray that the days of hungry children will never return to Australia.

Should our political leaders commit themselves to guaranteeing a secure food supply for all of us in the future? Would you like to go to bed without having eaten a dinner, with hunger in your belly? Do you think you should be grateful to live in a country that supplies you with an abundance of food that you can choose from?

I had the good fortune of having my parents live with me for the final years of their lives. My mother was an invalid who suffered great pain from rheumatoid arthritis and breathing problems due to her fluid retention and overweight condition, while my father survived open-heart surgery, suffered from gout, and developed dementia. At times I had to remind him who the people who had come to visit him were, even brothers and sisters. Towards the end he did not even recognise me. It was sad to see a man whose mind had been bright and active having trouble recognising where he was and who he was with. The puzzled, sometimes childlike, fearful look in his eyes still haunts me. Overcoming these sorrow-filled days in our lives requires all our courage and emotional strength, but you do have it within you. All you need to do is cultivate it.

At one time, I was preparing what I thought was a healthy meal for them when my mother said,

Chapter 4: Physical Fitness and Healthy Eating Habits

Ken, we don't do healthy. We eat what we enjoy.

What they enjoyed was a breakfast of bacon and eggs with toast and butter and hot Milo. A lunch of heated baked beans or spaghetti out of a can on toast, or canned corned beef or SPAM covered with a liberal application of tomato sauce on white bread spread thickly with butter. SPAM is brand name for a combination of **sp**ice and **ham**. Mum also liked banana and honey sandwiches for lunch. Dinner consisted of fresh meat (usually steak, mince or sausages) and three vegetables, which always included potatoes or bubble and squeak (potatoes and pumpkin mixed together with a liberal dollop of full cream butter and whole cream milk). Mum and Dad also enjoyed Kentucky Fried Chicken as a dinner treat, and Dad liked seafood, especially oysters, crab, and prawns (which was not helpful for his gout) while Mum's favourite fish was dory cooked in breadcrumbs. They snacked at night, usually on cake (Mum was particularly partial to Pecan Danish) or potato chips, washed down with a cold glass of soft drink. Their diets were not what you would call healthy and their health did suffer as they aged, but they did live long lives. Mum died at age 85 and Dad at age 93. Mum never smoked or drank alcohol throughout her life, and Dad indulged heavily in both until he gave them up completely (cold turkey) when he turned 40 years of age.

Now for developing healthy eating habits. The important thing to focus on here is to lower your insulin resistance. You can achieve this by lowering your intake of sugar, carbohydrates, and saturated fats, together with increasing your intake of unsaturated fats, and decreasing the frequency of meals and snacks. The longer the period of not eating, the lower your insulin resistance will become, so watch your snacking between meals, especially late-night snacks, which should be avoided altogether.

When you eat, don't overeat. Eat until you are satisfied, not until you are full. Don't keep eating, especially if you are bored, anxious or sad. Go outside and exercise. Do some deep breathing exercises and focus on what you are trying to achieve. Don't sit and watch TV or play computer games for long continuous periods while snacking on chips and drinking soft drinks. This only helps you avoid anxiety or depression, it does nothing to help you control it, and you will become overweight and unhealthy.

You could read any of the poems or books listed in the transcendental level of truth above or try reading a challenging book that requires deep concentration. Books like *On Liberty* by John Stewart Mill, *The Communist Manifesto* by Karl Marx, *The Affluent Society* by John Kenneth Galbraith, *Capitalism and Freedom* by Milton Freidman, *The War on the West* by Douglas Murray, *Danger on Our Doorstep* by Jim Molan, and *Colonialism a Moral Reckoning* by Nigel Biggar will get you started.

Alternatively, why not look up a lecturer you are interested in on YouTube. There are many great lecturers on YouTube you can follow. Choose your favourite ones and follow them. May I suggest that you choose those lecturers whose conclusions are data or fact-driven and logically arrived at and not ideologically driven. You could begin with lecturers like Jordan Peterson, Michael Behe, Stephen Meyer, Douglas Murray, Milton Freidman, Thomas Sowell, and Nigel Biggar. Then there are dialogue blogs like *Uncommon Knowledge* presented by the Hoover Institution, *Merit Street Media* presented by Dr. Phil, and *Triggernometry* presented by comedians Konstantin Kisin and Francis Foster, to name just three. For an Australian flavour, why not tune into John Anderson's blog, *Conversations with John Anderson.* John Anderson was Deputy Prime Minister and Leader of the National Party from 1999 to 2005.

Whatever you do, don't get involved with short snippets that push specific ideological ends, and especially get off Tik-Tok altogether. Such short messaging may be entertaining, but it can become addictive and steal not only your valuable time but also your ability for logical and rational thought, not to mention your creativity.

Returning to a healthy diet, eat natural foods and avoid processed foods. Low-fat meats and fresh fruit and vegetables are much better for you than canned, bottled, or packeted foods. Some low-fat meats include silverside, sirloin, porterhouse, T-bone, ribeye steaks, mince with a low-fat content (4%), and extra-lean chicken, pork, and beef sausages. Whenever I grill, I only use extra-virgin olive oil. Growing up, my father liked Worcestershire sauce on his beef and eggs (soft fried, or as the Americans like to call it 'sunny side up'), so I developed the same taste. I also like grilled onions and mushrooms with my beef and mince. You must include fish and/or crustaceans in your diet at least twice a week for its omega-3 content. Among other things, omega-3 lowers blood pressure and triglycerides in the blood, helps reduce joint inflammation in rheumatoid arthritis, and reduces the risk of heart disease and ischemic stroke. Mackerel, snapper, dory, red emperor, and barramundi are my favourites. Make sure you have them grilled, not deep-fried. Canned tuna, sardines and salmon are also healthy (high in omega-3) even though they are canned. My favourite crustaceans are prawns, crab, and Morton Bay bugs. I think lobsters are overrated, but many think otherwise. Oysters are the only molluscs I enjoy and I like them natural. I do not enjoy oyster Kilpatrick although many do and many (my wife included) also enjoy mussels and scallops.

There are a variety of fruit and vegetables to choose from. My cardiologist has put me on a low-carbohydrate, low-sugar and low-fat diet so potatoes, bread, cakes, pastries, pies, ice cream, sugar in my drinks, honey, and some fruits are off limit for me. However, there are other fruit and vegetables, and drinks that I have acquired a taste for. I like all my fruit cold. Apples, mandarins, oranges, passionfruit, kiwifruit, avocadoes, strawberries, blueberries, apricots (especially dried apricots), plums, peaches, olives, and tomatoes are the best for me. Watermelon, mango, banana, and grapes are off limit because of their high fructose (fruit sugar) content. Just remember that all fruit has fructose so be judicious when eating fruit. My favourite vegetables are Brussel sprouts, broccoli, spinach, peas, beans, asparagus, carrots, pumpkin, sweet corn, celery, cucumbers, gherkins, and cabbage.

Remember to steam cook your vegetables to hold in the flavour and vitamins. A handful of roasted almonds daily will provide you with a necessary dose of calcium for bone strength, and roasted cashews are rich in healthy fats like monounsaturated and polyunsaturated fats as well as protein. Nuts also are delicious and make a great snack as do solanato tomatoes. I have a strong preference for mint with icy-cold lemon or lime drinks. I also like hot vegemite and parsley drinks, tea with low-fat milk but no sugar, latte or cappuccino coffee with no sugar or chocolate topping, and hot lemon and ginger tea at night. I use a dash of Ceylon Cinnamon as a topping for my coffee. Ceylon Cinnamon helps to regulate blood sugar, lowers bad cholesterol, and provides strong anti-inflammatory and antioxidant effects. To conclude, have fun getting to know your favourite meats, fish, crustaceans, molluscs, fruit and vegetables, nuts, and drinks as I have.

As far as herbs are concerned, I have only used two long-term: parsley and mint. For a short time in my childhood, I was sent to live with my Nana (my grandmother on my mother's side) and some of my uncles and one aunty. We all lived together in the one three-bedroom home. Nana did all the cooking and I often sat with her while she prepared the meals. Like most country homes there was a leaking tap outside, under which she had placed an old bucket with soil and a parsley plant. The parsley plant thrived, and when she was ready to mash the boiled potatoes she would send me out to get sprigs of parsley, which she diced up and mixed with the mashed potatoes. Since then, I have liked the taste of parsley and used to mix it with mashed potatoes. My cardiologist has taken me off mashed potatoes for my current diet, so I can no longer enjoy this delightful vegetable, although I still appreciate it on rare occasions. I also use parsley in salads or as a garnish with other dishes. I have since discovered that parsley has health benefits. It is rich in vitamin C and antioxidants which help reduce things like diabetes and cancer. It also contains nitrates that relax and dilate the blood vessels, thereby lowering blood pressure and reducing the risk of stroke and heart disease.

Mint is just something that I love the taste of. In my childhood I preferred to chew spearmint chewing gum over Juicy Fruit. Spearmint milk shakes also used to be my favourite. A cold mint drink is most refreshing. I use a sprig of mint and place the leaves in a glass and pour in a small amount of lemon or lime juice (you can buy pure lemon or lime juice in sachets), mix it around so the flavour and goodness of the mint leaves infuse with the juice and then add icy cold water. As I drink, I take a leaf at a time and chew on them. The burst of flavour is delectable and leaves my mouth fresh and my sinuses clear. You can also mix mint with sauces, salads and desserts. Mint contains vitamin A, iron, manganese and folate. Vitamin A is a fat-soluble vitamin critical for eye health and night vision. It is also a potent source of antioxidants which relieve cell stress caused by free radicals.

I heard that camomile helps sleep, so I took a hot drink of camomile at night before going to bed. I tried it for a time but detected no noticeable change to my sleep pattern, so I discontinued its use. My experience should not deter you from trying it though if you are having difficulty sleeping.

I also grow basil which I use with my slow-cooked beef dishes. When slow cooking, rosemary or mint goes well with lamb shanks. Beef ribs taste great with oregano, sage or basil, while dill or lemon verbena enhance the taste of chicken or pork. There are many other herbs, so get to know what they are and choose your favourite way to use them.

Let's talk spices. I like garlic, pepper, curry, and mustard. I use diced garlic for sautés (with diced onions), and stir-fries. You can buy dips, spreads, sauce and even butter mixed with garlic. I use garlic sautés with grilled meat (especially lean mince) and vegetables. Garlic contains allicin which is known for its anti-viral, anti-fungal, and anti-bacterial properties and is often used to fight the common cold and flu. It can also relieve nasal congestion. People also use garlic for high blood pressure, high cholesterol, and hardening of the arteries, although there is no good scientific evidence to support these claims.

Be careful how much garlic you consume daily because it has been linked to a deterioration in liver function. Therefore, restrict your intake to no more than one or two cloves per day.

Black pepper contains piperine, which is a natural alkaloid considered as a type of antioxidant. It is believed to help lower the risk of diseases like atherosclerosis and cardiovascular disease. It helps stimulate hydrochloric acid in your stomach which helps with digestion. Black pepper has been used as a spice to enrich the flavour of food for centuries and is applied to food according to taste. It is best to use whole black pepper and crack it when ready to apply.

Curry is actually a blending of ground spices believed to have originated in India and founded primarily on a mixture of bright yellow turmeric, chilli powder, onion, ginger, and garlic. Curry powder contains an abundance of antioxidants, which reduces oxidative stress, cholesterol, and high blood pressure. Curry powder can be purchased in mild, medium or hot forms, depending on taste. Curry is versatile and can be used in many dishes, beef, lamb, chicken, prawn and vegetables, for example. It also goes well with rice. The best rices to use are those which cook up fluffy such as jasmine, basmati or traditional long grain rice, because they soak up all that curry goodness. Rice is high in carbohydrates so they are off my current diet, but I can still sneak some as a treat.

Mustard has been used as a spice for centuries and is believed to have originated in Ancient Egypt. English mustard is hot while American mustard is mild. Mustard contains antioxidants, glucosinolates, and monounsaturated and polyunsaturated fats, which have many health benefits like relieving muscle spasms, decongesting air passages, balancing cholesterol levels, reducing the risk of cardiovascular diseases, and fighting bladder, cervical, and colon cancers among many others. Mustard is best used with cold or hot meats, chicken, fish or pork. American mustard goes great with hot frankfurters, which you only should eat as a treat. Frankfurters are typically made from a combination of beef and pork, although some may include mutton or veal.

Before going on to salads, there are two items that come with a warning. The first is vinegar which is an acid liquid made by the fermentation of alcoholic liquids like apple cider or red wine. With a Ph between 2.4 and 3.3, it is acidic enough to erode tooth enamel, inflame a digestive tract and stomach, and trigger nausea and acid reflux. That is why it must be used judiciously and mixed with other fluids, like water, juice or oils. Vinegar does have health benefits. It is good for weight management, controlling blood sugar levels, and reducing cholesterol and antimicrobial properties. I prefer white vinegar and use a tablespoon when poaching or steaming eggs and making salad dressings. I don't boil eggs, I steam them; 4-5 minutes for dippy eggs, 6 minutes for soft eggs and 12 minutes for hard eggs.

The second is ginger, which contains gingerol, a powerful anti-inflammatory and antioxidant. Ginger improves your blood sugar levels which helps control insulin production. It also helps control bloating, constipation, and the number of free radicals in your body. Ginger can be eaten raw, ground or cooked. It is used in gingerbread, ginger biscuits, ginger ale and salads. However, ginger can increase the anticoagulant effect of warfarin, possibly leading to warfarin toxicity and bleeding when taken in excess. Therefore, pregnant or breastfeeding women, or those with a bleeding disorder, particularly those taking blood-thinning medication like aspirin should avoid taking ginger.

Let's talk salads. Some great salads are Waldorf, Greek, Italian, and French. Waldorf salad has lettuce, apple and celery cuts, walnuts, 1/2 tablespoon English mustard, 2 tablespoons lemon juice, and olive oil mayonnaise. Greek salad has cut pieces of tomatoes, cucumber, gherkin, red onion, feta cheese, black olives, and green capsicum, dressed with cracked sea salt and black pepper, diced parsley, lemon juice and olive oil. Italian salad has lettuce, solanato tomatoes, red onion or shallots, gherkins, olives, strips of red or green capsicum, and cubed feta cheese, dressed with parsley, mint, white vinegar, olive oil, and cracked sea salt and black pepper. French salad is best arranged on a long plate in separate portions containing olives mixed with cubed feta cheese, quartered tomatoes, tuna, sliced red onion, cucumber, sliced hard steamed eggs, and fresh green beans. French dressing contains white vinegar, Worcestershire sauce, garlic and onion powder, cracked black pepper, and diced parsley. Salads are usually accompanied with cold meats (ham off the bone, or roast beef are best), chicken, pork, prawns or crab. Salads can also accompany hot meats, chicken, pork, or fish.

Then there are the health supplements. My doctor has advised me to avoid supplements because a healthy diet will provide me with all the vitamins etc. that my body needs. However, I have adopted some supplements to my daily intake. When I turned 50 I started to take one 50+ multi-vitamin daily. I don't know if it does me any good but it does provide me with confidence that I am not missing out on any vital vitamins or minerals in my daily intake. When my joints began to ache sometimes, I started to take fish oil. Again, I don't know how helpful this is but I wanted to ensure a good level of omega-3 intake on a daily basis. My aches subsided, my blood thinned and my cholesterol lowered, although this could be owing to other medication prescribed by my doctor.

When I turned 65 I was diagnosed with stage three colon cancer. I underwent an operation to remove over 15cm of my large intestine, had a temporary stoma attached and underwent six months of chemotherapy, which stretched into seven months because I had to suspend transfusion of the drug owing to a lower than acceptable blood count. I lost my appetite, suffered from an abundance of mouth ulcers, went from 88kgs to 60kgs, my immune system was compromised, and I was physically very weak. After treatment, however, I fully recovered, regaining my health and weight. Nevertheless, it did have an effect on my bones. I was diagnosed with osteoporosis, so my doctor has put me on a bone building injection every six months and calcium tablets. I also take vitamin D3 in tablet form. My bone density has improved.

Within a couple of years of my cancer episode and after I had returned to the gym, my trainer noticed that it was taking my heart far too long to recover to a normal heartbeat after a workout. My trainer said it was taking my heart over 20 minutes to recover when, with my level of fitness, it should recover in only 10-15 minutes at most. Visits to my doctor and cardiologist discovered that my coronary artery had positioned itself in the wrong place at birth and was now being squeezed by other organs which had grown larger with age. This was causing an inhibited flow of blood to my heart muscles. The cardiologist said that my condition was an emergency which needed immediate open-heart surgery. He was surprised that I had lived so long with this condition, and told me that a heart attack episode, which could happen at any time, would be fatal, since the only treatment would be open-heart surgery and that could not be done in an emergency situation. My heart surgeon repositioned my coronary artery and replaced one of my heart valves which had a slight leak. During post-operative care he told me that he was able to use my existing artery because it was clean of cholesterol deposits. He further told me that he usually had to transplant an artery from the thigh with this operation. Again, I have fully recovered my fitness, weight, and health, although I did suffer a post-operative complication. I have constrictive pericarditis, which I won't go into here, but I require fluid tablets to relieve my fluid retention. I also require aspirin to thin my blood in case a clot forms and affects my heart. These medications are permanent.

 I tell you these things because I believe that had I not had a healthy diet and a regular fitness regime in place, I doubt I would be with you today, let alone in the good state of health and fitness that I am currently in, fully mobile, engaged in moderate exercise, enjoying healthy foods with family and good friends, and able to enjoy the remaining years of my life. I am also grateful to be living in a country with such excellent medical treatment, a dedicated medical staff, and a government that ensures the best of medical attention for its citizens.

 Have I inspired you to adopt a health and fitness regime for your future? I hope I have. Do you think I have gone too far with some of my suggestions? If you do, which suggestions go too far? Are you sure those suggestions you dislike are unreasonable, or are they just difficult to comply with?

Chapter 5:
Personal Hygiene

Cleanliness is next to godliness. We can no more gain God's blessings with an unclean body than with an unclean mind.
(Mahatma Gandhi, *Guide London*, 1893)

Do you think you have a moral duty to keep yourself and your living space clean? Explain your decision.

Let us examine the reasons for cleanliness. There are trillions of viruses and bacterium germs that we encounter daily. Most of these are harmless. In fact, some are even beneficial, especially those used by our stomach to break down the food we ingest. However, some are detrimental (or even deadly) to our health if they get into our bodies, and these germs have a greater chance of entering our bodies if we do not practise sensible personal hygiene habits. Personal hygiene helps in giving us a healthy and disease-free life.

Do you think this is a good reason for you to adopt personal hygiene habits? Maybe you want to know what these habits are before you commit.

There are two aspects to personal hygiene that we will explore here: cleanliness habits and rest/sleep. What are some good personal hygiene and rest and sleep habits? These lists have been sourced from healthdirect.gov.au.

Cleanliness

This involves keeping your hands and skin clean. In daily life we touch many things, both in public and in private. All the things we touch may carry microscopic organisms like viruses, bacteria, fungi, and protozoa. This is not a problem unless they transfer into our bodies, which can occur when we touch our eyes or our mouths or receive minor cuts and abrasions to our bodies. With this in mind, the following cleanliness habits are recommended –

1) Wash your hands before touching food.
2) Wash your hands after using the toilet or washroom.
3) Shower daily, paying particular attention to areas where skin folds, like armpits, groin, and between toes. This is because there is a high concentration of bacteria in these areas.
4) Change and wash undergarments and handkerchiefs daily. Also, use tissues where possible.
5) Regular washing of your hair not only gives you healthy, radiant hair but also keeps it free from parasites like head lice. Ideally, shampoo your hair once or twice a week, depending on how oily your hair is. This gives your natural oils time to flow.
6) Brushing teeth twice daily (after breakfast and before bed) keeps teeth free from germs, infection, and decay, and helps control halitosis. Try to finish your lunch by eating an apple. Apples stimulate saliva production, which helps wash away food particles and bacteria. Rinsing your mouth with a good mouthwash after brushing your teeth also keeps your mouth free from germs and helps control halitosis. When you rinse your mouth remember to stick your tongue out as far as you can and tilt your head back to get at the build-up of phlegm at the back of your throat. Some people even like to brush or scrape their tongues to remove the white coating caused by a build-up of debris,

bacteria, and dead cells. After snacking or drinking, rinse your mouth with water. It helps remove food particles and bacteria, preventing cavities and gum disease.
7) I also gargle daily with salt water. My dentist tells me it makes my gums healthy and hard, and this is what I have experienced. I also floss between my teeth at night after dinner, my final meal for the day. I do not snack after dinner.
8) When sneezing or coughing always hold a handkerchief in front of your nose and mouth. This helps stop the spread of airborne germs.
9) When washing your face, be sure to wash your eyelids and use eyedrops occasionally to avoid trachoma and conjunctivitis.
10) Don't share personal items with others like handkerchiefs, face washers, undergarments etc.
11) If you receive a minor cut or abrasion to your skin, immediately clean it with a good disinfectant and apply a dressing, e.g. a band-aid.

Rest and Sleep

All organs of our bodies need rest. This is best achieved by adopting regular habits.

1) Sleep at least six hours daily. To help get adequate and sound sleep, go to bed at a set time and wake up at a set time each day. Also take food at regular times. This helps to regulate your digestion, which when unsettled can cause sleep disturbance.
2) Going to bed late or immediately after dinner are not good for your health.
3) Your bowels should be cleared daily. This is usually done after breakfast.
4) Avoid smoking, which is expensive and injurious to health.

It will leave you with short breath and usually leads to cancer. When I was a young man this joke was circulating –

*Kissing a girl who smokes is like licking an ashtray.
I wonder if young women tell the same joke in reverse.*

5) Try to avoid alcohol, but if you must, limit your drinking to special occasions. Be especially vigilant in social settings where excessive drinking can lead not only to bad health but also embarrassment. Avoid binge drinking which causes short- and long-term health complications. Short-term complications include impaired judgement, loss of co-ordination (leading to accidental incidents), and alcohol poisoning. Long-term complications can involve liver damage, increased cancer risks, and mental health issues like anxiety and depression.

6) Keeping your room clean is very important for your self-discipline as well as your health. It can help you relax, feel good about yourself, and enable you to get sound sleep. Make your bed daily. Clean your room regularly. Don't leave clothes or shoes on the floor. Keep your cupboard and dressing table clean and tidy. Keep your room well-ventilated ensuring fresh air and oxygen circulates throughout. This keeps germs in your room at a minimum.

This may sound like a lot of rules, and it might seem overwhelming at first, but if you keep to these suggestions, they will become second nature to you and not seem bothersome at all. Most importantly, however, is that these habits will help you achieve a healthy, disease-free life and encourage your discipline and control. Again, this will help you reach your goals in life and fulfil your potential, so I hope you will commit yourself to these personal hygiene habits. Will you?

Chapter 6:
Financial Security

Annual income twenty pounds, annual expenditure nineteen (pounds) nineteen (shillings) six (pence) – result happiness. Annual income twenty pounds, annual expenditure twenty pounds naught (shillings) and six (pence) – result misery.
Charles Dickens, *David Copperfield*, 1850)

The most important observation to be made from Dickens' quote is that the difference between happiness and misery is because of a six pence surplus in the two equations, and that is the central focus of this chapter –

The importance of a surplus for your financial security.

If you want to achieve financial security, you must produce a surplus from your income. Remember,

*it's not how much you earn that is important,
but rather how much you save from what you earn.*

Before we start our discussion, I want to point out some things that may not have occurred to you yet. The size of your income depends on three things. First, you must acquire a skill or produce a product that someone else is prepared to pay you for. The higher or more difficult the skill you acquire or the more competent you are at performing your skill, the more you will be rewarded for your effort. If you run a business, the demand for and supply of your product will determine the price you can charge for it. Even those who live off their capital must invest in things that other people are willing to pay for. Second, the harder and longer you work the higher your income will become. Finally, the greater your ambition or drive the more your reward will be. So, competency, hard work, and ambition will determine the level of your income.

As far as the type of skill you acquire is concerned, keep this in mind. The lowest level of skill is that of unskilled labour, and therefore, the least rewarded. This group can increase their income, however, by doing dirty or dangerous jobs or working in the heat of the sun that others avoid (e.g. working in the oil or mining industries, on construction sites or in the fishing industry). Next are tradesmen (bricklayers, carpenters, electricians, mechanics etc.). To acquire a trade you need to serve an apprenticeship of between one to four years, have a formal training contract, and undertake training with a Registered Training Organisation (e.g. TAFE). Semi-skilled professional people (draftsmen, legal and accountancy clerks etc.) are also part of this group and acquire a diploma through a TAFE college. This group is better rewarded than unskilled labour, and the more ambitious of this group often upgrade their trade and professional skills which enables them to open their own small business or consultancy firm, which provides them with higher risk and more work but even greater rewards. Finally, the professional class. This group divides into many levels of rewards depending on the demand for their skills. Those with the highest rewards are those with STEM (Science, Technology, English, and Maths), skilled bachelor's degrees, and post-graduate qualifications (e.g. doctors, medical specialists, managers, engineers, lawyers, accountants etc.).

Unless you are fortunate enough to inherit a family fortune, this will apply to you, but even if you do inherit wealth you will need competency, hard work, and ambition if you want to keep your fortune. With this in mind, let's move on to our general discussion about financial security.

I will point out that most of what I say here can be found in greater detail in Noel Whittaker's excellent book, *Making Money Made Simple*. A book that I found very useful in achieving financial security for myself and would recommend as a good starting point for anyone seeking financial security in their lives. His book is easy to read and understand, mainly because it is not full of financial and accounting jargon but rather relies on reason and common sense for understanding.

To help you produce a surplus from your income, you need to set up –

1) a *fixed savings account* (Investment Account) that you do not draw upon;
2) a *fixed expenses account* that you draw on for your fixed expenses;
3) and a *working savings account* that you draw upon for your variable expenses.

The best way to ensure a surplus from your income is just to put a fixed amount from your pay (every payday) into an investment account that you will not draw down on. How much that is will depend upon your circumstances, but it should never fall below 10% of your net income. Remember the golden rule –

> *A tenth of all I earn is mine to keep.*
> (George Samuel Clason, *The Richest Man in Babylon*, 1926)

Remember to deposit a fixed amount into your fixed saving account *first*, before you make the deposits into your other accounts. What you don't see, you won't miss.

Next, work out what your fixed expenses are for a year. Things like rent or mortgage payments, car payments and other credit payments, even things like electricity costs, expected car repairs etc. will go into this account. Then, divide that amount by the period between your pays. Put that amount into your fixed expenses account every payday.

Finally, determine the amount you need to put into your working account. If you are having trouble putting enough into your working account to cover the variable expenses of your spending habits, you can fix this in one of two ways. You must either increase your income or decrease your variable spending habits. Of course, if you want to really increase your investment account, there is no reason why you can't do both.

To increase your income you will need to take stock of what you can do to achieve this. You can either increase your pay or increase your work. You can take on more responsibility by getting a promotion in the firm where you are currently employed. You can achieve this by working hard and showing initiative in your current job while looking around to discover a job you would rather have. Next, talk with your supervisor and ask him what you need to do to get the job. This might require you to enrol in and complete a diploma at a technical college or a post-graduate degree at a university. Alternatively, you can undertake part-time work outside of your full-time job in order to earn more money. There are many opportunities available if you are determined to find something.

To reduce your spending you will have to undertake a careful examination at your spending habits. Look at what you spend in four specific areas –

> *The food you eat, the clothes you wear, the household goods you acquire, and the incidental items you want.*

The Food You Eat

You can start with a stocktake of the food you eat by looking for ways to reduce any purchase of wants over needs. Examine your refrigerator and pantry by looking for food that you haven't eaten or anything that has passed its expiry date. From now on plan what you are going to eat and only buy what you know you will eat. Don't shop for food when you are hungry and don't buy anything just because it looks delicious. If you eat out, ask yourself if you can reduce the number of times you frequent restaurants, and order less expensive dishes on the menu. Do you consume too much tea or coffee? If you reduce your intake of caffeine, it may even improve your health. Two cups a day is fine, more than that is excessive. Besides, try drinking water, it is much healthier for you.

The Clothes You Wear

Examine your wardrobe and determine exactly what you need. From now on plan your wardrobe; only buy those clothes and shoes that you have decided you need. Then there is jewellery; be judicious here. It is better to buy only a few pieces of quality jewellery rather than a drawerful of bling-bling. Don't buy anything on impulse simply because it looks good or cute. In future only buy because you *need* the item, not because you *want* it.

The Household Goods You Acquire

Do you have household goods that sit in your kitchen cabinets and never get used? That's because you succumbed to the temptation of purchasing them on a whim, believing that you needed them because an advertisement told you that you did. Here you must exercise self-restraint and only purchase those household goods that you know you will use, not what you desire to use.

The Incidental Items You Want

Do you like to party, or visit restaurants? Why not reduce the number of times you go out and how much you spend when you do. Then comes your desire to own a new car, a new mobile phone, or a new computer. Put off buying them until you can afford them. Also, be responsible when it comes to holidays, by searching for the best deals and reducing your expenses when holidaying. Why not consider holidaying with family or friends.

If you really want these things,

> *you will need to start a separate special purpose savings account and save for them.*

Do not fund them with credit or drawing down on your investment or fixed expense account. All these suggestions are worthy of your consideration.

If you plan your pantry, your refrigerator, your wardrobe, your household goods, and your incidental items, you will not waste and you will cut back on your spending. In this way your savings will grow.

I remember my mother saying to me,

> *Waste not, want not.*

However you do it, you must produce a surplus from your income, if you are going to achieve financial security in your lifetime. This point cannot be stressed enough; you must produce a surplus to your spending, regardless of what your income happens to be.

Do you think you can commit yourself to a disciplined saving habit? The key theory behind this commitment is

> *delayed gratification.*

This is a concept we have already visited in Chapter 2. Is your future financial security worth the discipline necessary to create a surplus in your spending habits today? I hope it is. Remember it is the difference between your future happiness or misery. Having ensured that you produce a surplus, the next question for you to answer is

Chapter 6: Financial Security

what do I do with my surplus?

There are two ways you can spend your surplus –

Either on things that depreciate in value or things that appreciate in value.

Since you are trying to accumulate value for your investment account, you should only purchase things that have the potential to appreciate in value.

There is a spectrum of things to invest in which accumulate in value, starting with a savings account with a bank, which is the safest form of investment, all the way to investing in cryptocurrency. Each investment platform carries with it different levels of risk. Some investment platforms include –

1) Savings accounts
2) Cash deposits and government, corporate, or insurance bonds
3) Debentures
4) Real estate
5) Equity (shares)
6) Commodities
7) Currencies
8) Collectibles
9) Investment funds
10) Cryptocurrency

Before we look at each of these investment platforms, let me inform you that I am not a financial advisor, nor am I suggesting that I have covered all the investment platforms here or that I am suggesting any one platform over another. These are decisions that you must make for yourself independently. What I hope to achieve with this review is to make you aware of the variety of investment platforms available to you and encourage you to save and to think seriously about your investments. This is merely a starting point for you. As you accumulate wealth, you should seek the advice of professionals in their own fields.

> *Try not to be influenced by tips and salespersons who contact you through the phone or doorknocking.*

They generally are paid by commission and therefore have a stake in selling a certain type of investment, or they may even be trying to scam you out of your hard-earned money.

The Financial Advisor Standards and Ethical Authority (FASEA) has been established by the government to set the education, training and ethical standards of the financial advisor industry in Australia. Further to this is the Financial Conduct Authority (FCA), which is the governing body of financial advisors. If at some stage of your saving initiative you decide to consult a financial advisor, check out the financial advisor of your choice to see that he/she adheres to these checks and balances. You can generally get an interview with a financial advisor before you decide to engage his/her services. This will cost you a nominal fee. You can shop around before deciding to go with any one advisor, but once you have decided on one, the normal fee charged by financial advisors ranges from 0.5% to 1.5% of your assets under management (AUM).

Next, you will need to take taxation advice. The difference between a tax agent and an accountant is that a tax agent can handle tax returns for businesses and individuals, while accountants can analyse your financial reports and identify areas for improvement. A tax agent, for example, does not interpret the taxation law and offer advice as to their clients' personal circumstances. The Tax Practitioners Board (TPS) is responsible for the registration and regulation of tax agents, while the Australian Accounting Standards Board (AASB) is the

Australian Government's agency responsible for developing, issuing and maintaining accounting standards. There are three professional accounting organisations in Australia – Certified Public Accountant (CPA), Chartered Accountants Australia and New Zealand (CA ANZ), and the Institute of Public Accountants (IPA).

When the time comes for you to seek the advice of professionals, keep these organisations in mind and ensure their membership and adherence to these organisations' rules and regulations.

Savings Accounts

Most people start with a simple savings account with a trustworthy bank which pays the highest interest rate. Savings accounts, however, offer the lowest interest of all forms of investment, and enable you to withdraw your money at any time you want, which is a temptation you must overcome. Despite this, bank deposits are a safe way to invest because banks in Australia are highly regulated and their deposits are generally insured. In the last economic crisis (2007-09) the Australian Government even guaranteed bank deposits. Because the interest paid on these deposits is low, once depositors accumulate a thousand dollars, they tend to look for better returns on their money.

Cash Deposits and Government, Corporate, or Insurance Bonds

Cash Deposits, and Government and Corporate Bonds are also a safe form of investment. When you invest in these, you place your money in a fixed term deposit. That is, you agree that you will not withdraw your money for the term of the fixed deposit. Because the bank or the government or corporation can be sure about how long they have the use of your money for, they are willing to pay a higher interest rate on these fixed deposits than you can get on savings accounts. The amount of interest that a bank or government or corporation is willing to pay will depend on the time and size of the deposit. Generally, you can invest a minimum of $1,000 to $5,000 over time spans ranging from one month to five years.

Your main consideration should be how much interest you will be paid and the amount of time you are prepared to leave your money in the fixed deposit. If interest rates are high and likely to fall, it is best to invest in longer term deposits. The opposite is true if interest rates are likely to rise. Be aware that if you decide to terminate your term deposit before the fixed term has expired, you will pay a penalty, but this should not worry you since this is your investment money and you don't intend to withdraw it. Remember to ensure that you

reinvest all the interest you are paid from your fixed savings account or fixed deposits.

This way any money you earn from your investments will earn even more money for you. Isn't it nice to realise that you didn't have to work for that interest payment; your investment money earned it for you.

This rule should apply to all your investment choices. Reinvest any money earned to make even more money for you. If you do this you will be earning *compound interest* instead of *simple interest*. Simple interest is paid on the original principal amount only; compound interest is paid on both the principal amount and the interest amount invested.

It is the interest you earn on interest that makes compound interest increase your savings faster than simple interest.

Consider this –

Passive investment is a long-term investment strategy that focuses on buying and holding investments for the long term... Examples of passive investment are rental income from investment properties, investing in dividend stocks, or earning interest through a high-yield savings account.

(td.com, *Passive investing 101*, 2025)

You can add to this government, corporate, and insurance bonds. If you reinvest the rental, interest, dividends or bonuses paid on your investments you will accelerate the value of your portfolio quicker. Brokers have a service called DRIP (Direct Reinvestment Plan) which allows them to reinvest your dividends back into the shares that paid your dividend without you having to worry about it. However, rental and interest income reinvestment must be handled by yourself. Bonuses paid by insurance companies are automatically reinvested and the principle investment along with all the bonuses earned over the lifetime of the bond is paid out on the bond's maturity.

Insurance bonds are different from cash deposits, or government and corporate bonds in that they do not pay an interest rate. They are sometimes known as investment or growth bonds because they do not distribute income like rents, dividends, interest or realised capital gains. Insurance bonds carry a whole or term life insurance policy and are a long-term investment platform where investors' money is pooled and invested according to the investment option chosen.

Insurance bonds receive regular bonus payments that are reinvested.

Withdrawing money from the insurance bond or cashing it in before it matures attracts penalties. If the bond is held for 10 years it is tax free when cashed in, since the insurance company or friendly society issuing the bond has already paid 30% tax on all income.

Before I move on to debentures, I need to mention the existence of *credit ratings* by agencies like S&P Global and Moody's. The credit ratings published by these companies tell you the *amount of risk* you are taking on when you loan money to a corporation or government. I will limit our discussion to government bonds but the same principles apply to corporations and bank cash deposits. The credit rating tells the investor what the likelihood is of a government paying back its bond. Credit ratings are determined by examining things like a government's payment history (any government with a history of default will have a very low rating), the amount of debt carried by the government issuing the bond, and their ability to pay back their debt. So things like *debt to income* (revenue), or *debt to GDP* are considered.

The credit ratings for Moody's range from Aaa to Caa3. The higher the rating the less risk you are taking by buying that particular bond, while the lower the rating the more risk you are taking. Also, the higher the credit rating is for a government wanting to sell bonds on the open market the lower the interest rate that government will offer to pay to attract investors, while the lower a credit rating for a government bond is the higher the interest rate that government has to pay investors to attract their investment.

If you draw a line under Moody's Baa3 rating, the ratings above the line are considered good investment ratings by investors while those below the line are considered non-investment bonds or junk bonds.

Junk bonds provide the investor with high returns, but much higher risk and even a risk of default.

Currently the Australian Government has a credit rating of Aaa, although Moody's has stated that unless our Federal Government gets its debt under control Moody's will downgrade Australia's credit rating. State Governments also have credit ratings. Victoria recently received a downgrade in its long-term corporate family rating (CFR) and its senior secured notes from B3 to Caa1. The downgrade was owing to the heightened risk of refinancing (au.investing.com, 2025).

Governments that receive a downgrading in their credit rating face a major financial problem. A higher interest rate on a high debt means it becomes even harder for the government to pay off the debt, and this can lead to a country's economy going into a debt spiral, where the debt keeps getting bigger and bigger and the interest on the debt higher and higher until the government can no longer fund the debt. There is also the temptation for a government to pay the interest by borrowing more, thereby raising their debt level even further. This can lead to hyper-inflation and a total collapse in a country's economy. Such a situation is very painful for all citizens of such a country, because they lose all their savings to inflation and, at the same time, the government is forced to adopt severe austerity measures to correct the situation and get their country's economy back on a more sustainable level. Such a situation is, of course, extremely painful for all citizens.

I might also add that credit companies and banks carry a *credit score* (ranging from 300 to 850) for people seeking to take out personal loans with them. A high credit score indicates that the borrower has a high probability of paying back the loan, while a low credit score indicates that the borrower has had trouble paying back loans in the past and might follow the same pattern in the future. Obviously, the lower your credit rating the less likely you are to secure a loan. At this stage of your investment strategy, however, you should not be concerned with that. If you were thinking of leveraging (borrowing money to invest) your investments, this would be of concern to you, but leveraging takes you into a whole new avenue of investment that I am not going to consider here, because of the higher level of risk involved and the fact that I am only trying to illustrate the range of investment opportunities open to you. Whether you choose to leverage or not is a decision that requires a lot of consideration on your part, a decision that I would not want to influence. Obviously, when you take out a loan to buy property either to live in or invest in you are leveraging, but the existence of an appealing negative gearing tax concession and the higher security level involved in property purchases makes this type of leverage more attractive. That is not to say that property investment does not come with risk, especially if you purchase during a real estate bubble.

Debentures

Debentures are loans issued by companies and the government. These investments are less secure than term deposits with banks or government or corporate bonds because they are only backed by the credit worthiness and reputation of the borrower and usually have an investment term greater than 10 years. Of course, interest rates can, and do, vary greatly over a 10-year period. Therefore, investors are usually only interested in this form of investment when interest rates are high. Naturally, if interest rates decline below your interest rate, you are a winner; if they increase beyond your interest rate, you are a loser.

Real Estate

I recognise that some investors today are turning away from real estate investment, because of the taxes and regulations imposed by the government on this sector. I am also aware that our current government intends to introduce a tax on unrealised capital gains which will make real estate investment even less attractive for some investors. I hope this will change in the future, because it is currently having a negative effect on the rental accommodation market.

Economists Professor Peter Siminski (University of Technology Sydney) and Professor Roger Wilkins (University of Melbourne) use the term

Homeowners' welfare state

to describe Australia's economy. They argue that Australian homeowners enjoy a lack of taxation on imputed rent and capital gains, providing them with a form of welfare and potentially exacerbating income inequality. They further argue that a capital gains tax alone on homeowners would deliver the government $50 billion annually. This concept was also raised in the government's economic summit held in Parliament House in August 2025.

Unfortunately, some governments spend so prolifically that they are constantly looking for sources of money that they can tax. A move such as this would lead to a depletion of citizen aspiration and national wealth creation generally. I am reminded of a quote by Margret Thatcher (1925-2013. Prime Minister of Great Britain, 1979-90) –

> *The problem with socialism is that you eventually run out of other people's money.*
> (Interview, *This Week,* Thames TV, 5 Feb 1976)

A terse reminder that while government handouts may sound good, someone still has to pay the bill. Of course, overtaxing the prudent only leads to widespread extravagant behaviour, which is detrimental not only to the individual citizen but also to the national economy.

In the past, most people turned to real estate as their next investment. There are two types of real estate investments. Firstly, you can buy *a home where you will reside,* or an *investment property* where you do not reside but rent out to others. Since there are taxation considerations with these types of investments (Capital Gains Tax, Negative Gearing etc.), I would advise you, once you reach this level of investment, to seek the advice of a taxation accountant or trustworthy financial adviser.

There are a couple of pieces of general advice I can offer, however. When buying a home, remember you will probably need at least three homes in your lifetime.

> *The first home is the one you can afford.*
> *The second is the one you will raise your family in.*
> *The third is the one you will retire to after you end your working life.*

Each home has different priorities and needs, so you need to be flexible and prepared to move up and down in size and luxury when it comes to obtaining the right home for your needs.

Investment properties are different. The income generated from these properties ranges from *rent* to *capital appreciation* (your equity in the property) to *taxation considerations* (especially if you are married and both spouses work). If you decide to enter this field of investment, and the rewards are there if you do, remember two things –

Real estate investment is the same as any other type of investment; it can appreciate or depreciate in value.

Real estate goes through cycles like any other investment. That is, there are real estate booms and busts, so there are risks involved. I know that Australia has had a long boom period in its real estate market, but this can change at any time. Evidence of this can be found in the decline in Australia's real estate value of 0.1% in December of 2024. Also, the New Zealand residential property market has experienced a sharp decline recently. For example, Auckland's median house price fell by 3.4% year-on-year (Q1, 2025). The last crash in Australia's real estate market was in the early 1990s when the property market in Melbourne fell by 19% and the commercial property market experienced declines of up to 40%.

The second thing relates to which house you decide to buy. These are a few general rules to get you started with your real estate investigation, but they are by no means a complete list. The old, but true, adage to keep in mind here is that the best house to buy as an investment is

the worst house in the best neighbourhood.

Remember, any repairs carried out prior to renting are tax deductable, while improvements (not maintenance) you make to your rental property after renting can be deducted from the capital gains tax you will be required to pay once you sell your investment property, so be sure to keep all receipts for any of these expenses, and seek professional taxation advice. Another tip is that

> *you can sometimes get a good discount from someone who needs to sell his/her property quickly.*

Additionally, there are some things to look for, like how close the property is to *schools* (most renters have children), *shops* (most renters want shops handy to their property), *transport* (those working will need this facility) and *medical centres or a hospital* (in cases of emergency).

To help you better understand the Australian real estate market, you can research it on websites like domain.com.au or realestate.com.au. The Australian Government also has a website dedicated to this topic – moneysmart.gov.au/property-investment. There are also a couple of books you should read before you invest in real estate. *Safe as Houses* by George Poray, and The *Beginner's Guide to Real Estate Investing* by Gary W. Eldred, PhD are a good place to start.

Congratulations if you have reached this level of investment; you are in a minority of the population. Your disciplined commitment to your savings initiative has paid off handsomely. You should now be working towards owning your own home and buying one or more investment properties. Any alternative investment beyond this stage requires more than just discipline, however. It is fraught with risks that you have not yet encountered. To go beyond real estate investment will require you to acquire *specialised knowledge* beyond what I can give. Again, I can offer you *general advice*, but you really do need more knowledge about specific investments than what I can offer you here. Acquiring this knowledge will also take up more of your time if you are to make informed decisions about your investments. If you are unable or not prepared to spend the time in acquiring this specialised knowledge, you can always invest in *funds*, but make sure you do due diligence in selecting the fund you finally decide to invest in. There are four different kinds of funds that I will explain later.

Shares (Equity)

Investing in shares requires the consideration of several crucial factors.

First, *equity is fluid*. That is, shares can be bought and sold instantaneously, depending on the emotions of the owner. For example, *greedy speculators* seeking quick profits can buy and sell shares at short intervals. This is known as *pump and dump*. Although this activity is illegal, it does happen and can temporally drive up share prices, only to see them fall later. Other greedy investors who see stocks rising quickly and want to get in for the ride are participating in what is known as the *greater fool* investment strategy. These investors buy shares believing that they will rise in value and a greater fool will come along and buy them at a higher price. There is usually some reason for this speculation to occur. It may be, for example, that the market anticipates that a corporation's profit will increase dramatically owing to some new technology becoming available or some new product being in high demand or the acquiring of a large contract, especially government contracts.

These activities, *pump and dump* and *greater fool*, create speculation bubbles that will inevitably burst at some future time when the expected corporation profit either does not materialise or the share price has been driven up far beyond its *intrinsic* (actual) *value*.

The opposite of the greedy investors are the *fearful investors* who, believing that the share price has gone too high and will soon fall in price, *dump their shares* at any price trying to sell before others and thereby minimise their loss. This causes the price of the shares to drop swiftly and dramatically, and leads to problems for all investors in the share market, simply because a lot of people lose a lot of money when a speculation bubble bursts. Consequently, a number of investors lose faith in shares as a form of investment, causing a drop in investment and a slower rise in the value of shares. In worst case scenarios it can, and does, lead to greater problems for the economy more generally, because it usually creates an economic recession.

Second, the *strength of a nation's economy* can determine if its stock market experiences a *bull* (a period when shares are in high demand) or a *bear* (a period of low demand for shares) sentiment from investors. What is true for a nation's economy is also true for the *world economy*. A recent example of the whole world being affected in this way was during the financial crisis of 2007-09, when financial firms became stressed owing to the poor lending management of their funds, the bundling of junk bonds with good bonds. This financial crisis resulted in US house prices falling and a number of borrowers being unable or unwilling to meet their mortgage payments. Some firms were bailed out by governments around the world, while others were left to crash and go into receivership. Some financial firms and even some corporations affected by the crisis were deemed by governments to be *too big to fail* (TBTF), so they were bailed out with public loans or grants.

Third, *world-wide superannuation funds and investment companies* (like BlackRock, Vanguard Group and Fidelity Investments) have billions of dollars to invest daily. The managers of these funds and investment companies are constantly seeking ways to achieve higher returns for their members than what the market average provides and what other funds achieve. Markets can be, and are, manipulated by these managers to ensure a higher dividend for their funds. More recently we also have seen the introduction of *ESG* (environment, social and governance) *point scores* assigned by fund and investment company management to private corporations listed on the share market, according to their compliance with ESG. The ESG score controls the funds' and investment companies' investment in these private corporations. So corporate CEOs must now consider these point scores along with their *profit motive* when running their corporations. What does this mean? Well, for example, this can lead CEOs to invest in renewable energy rather than fossil fuel energy, even though the fossil fuel option would be more profitable, or CEOs might employ staff on the grounds of diversity, equity, and inclusion (DEI) rather than employing the best person for the job. This is done to ensure the funds continue holding or increasing the purchase of their shares, thereby maintaining, or increasing their share price on the market.

Fourth, consider the *long-term chart* (5 year and 10 year) for the stock price of the company you are interested in. Ask these questions: in general, has the stock been moving upwards, downwards or sidewards? Are there any major drops or spikes in the chart? If there were sharp drops, did the stock bounce back or take a long time to recover? Does the stock show steady or long-term growth? The answer to these questions will determine whether you should consider the stock worthwhile exploring further.

Fifth, consider the *market capitalisation* of the company you are interested in. This simply tells you how big the company is. Companies with a market capitalisation above $10 billion in today's money are considered blue chip companies because they are large, stable, and financially reliable. Companies with a market capitalisation below $10 billion are considered penny stock companies, or, in some cases a potential growth stock company. If you are a passive investor you would only be interested in blue chip companies.

Sixth, the *P/E ratio* has been used as a good measure of a stock's value over a long period of time, but remember there are other factors now at play which determine the price of shares. The value of a share can be determined by the relationship between a corporation's *stock price and its earnings per share*. This is the P/E ratio, which only measures past performance. To determine a more reliable value for a corporation's share price, one must also consider the *potential future earnings* of the corporation. If it is a mining corporation, for example, ask if the mining corporation is likely to increase its mineral deposits or, if it is a manufacturing corporation, is it likely to acquire a new contract in the future?

P/E ratios are divided into one of two categories, Low P/E or High P/E. Different sectors of the share market have different P/E ratios determining what is a high or low ratio. As you can see, many things determine which shares are best to invest in. Also, it is not simply a case of a corporation having a Low P/E being better to invest in than a corporation with a High P/E. I have already mentioned two of the factors determining this – potential future earnings, and high or low ESG scores – which will affect the profitability of the corporation and the price of its shares.

As a general rule of thumb, however, a P/E ratio of 15-25 is considered normal. P/E ratios above the average might have been determined by some of the factors listed above, but this means that the value of the share has already been realised by the shareholders. This does not mean that the shares are not worth consideration; it just means that investors are expecting the company to grow significantly in future. P/E ratios below 15 are considered cheap. There could be a good reason for this, but it could also mean that the share price is undervalued. This is especially true during a bear market.

Seventh, consider the *52-week price range* of the stock you are interested in. Look for the lowest and highest prices for the stock. If the current price is close to the highest price, it might be expensive. If it's closer to the lowest price it might be undesirable.

Eighth, consider the *dividend yield* (DY). The DY shows the dividend paid as a percentage of the share price. A DY of 5% or more is a good DY. A DY of 10% would mean that the company has had an exceptional year of trading and can afford a high DY, or it could mean that the company has an issue with its stock price and is trying to attract investors. Remember, a company should consider reinvesting more of its profits into growth.

Keep in mind that *Dividend Aristocrats* are companies that have been paying and growing their dividends for 25 consecutive years. *Dividend Kings* are companies that have been paying and growing their dividends for at least 50 consecutive years.

Eighth, consider the *ability of management* to achieve the corporation's future earnings, either established or potential. Management considerations include if the management is stable or undergoing change. If it is undergoing change, what are the reasons for the change? Is the new CEO being promoted from within the company or is an outsider being brought in? If the new CEO is being brought in from outside, what is the reason for this? Will the future management be able to provide the necessary support and guidance for their teams to achieve their goals? What is the management's past success rate? Is management responsible? Does it have good industry knowledge? How committed is management to achieving its goals? How hardworking is management? Is management positively or negatively orientated? Is management honest and truthful? Is management able to organise its workforce in the most efficient manner? Is it decisive enough to make any necessary adjustments?

Ninth, consider the *impact of technology*, which is constantly changing and threatening the market share of corporations, or even destroying them. Automobiles replaced the horse and carriage industry; old style film corporations were replaced by digital camera corporations, which in turn were replaced by mobile phone corporations when digital cameras were included in mobile phones, and mobile phone corporations themselves are subject to rapidly changing technology. Apple is now the top selling mobile phone on the world market, but in the past companies like Blackberry and Nokia held that position. Blackberry were able to reinvent themselves by moving into cybersecurity, embedded systems, software-defined vehicles, and secure management to name only some of their current products; and Kodak moved into the areas of commercial print, packaging, publishing, manufacturing, and entertainment. These are good examples of management being decisive and making the necessary adjustments to ensure their corporation's survival. The size of their corporations may have suffered, but they did survive the impact that technology had on them.

The big technological change about to hit the marketplace in the future is that being generated by *AI* and *Robotics*. Clearly, robotics will have a profound effect on manufacturing productivity and employment. Will there be any need for a manufacturing workforce in the future? What will this mean for the profit of manufacturing companies? AI will hit the decision-making aspect of companies, which will see AI contributing to, or even making, all management decisions. What effect will this have on the management costs of corporations? Couple this with AI's impact in the arts. We have already seen the ability of AI to create paintings, AI-generated images, films, and AI-generated creative writing which can even emulate writers both past and present. Will we see the return of dead film stars from the past on our screens? Will there be anything left for human beings to do, particularly if AI and robotics are able to *maintain themselves, self-improve, and reproduce*? Will this shrink the workforce and consequently the consumer base of countries? If so, how will governments ensure that people will be able to purchase future corporation products? Understand that a consumer base is vital for corporations' profits. You might also like to consider the *potential dangers* regarding possible future developments in AI.

There are seven types of AI; some are currently in operation, others are still being developed, while others are theoretical or hypothetical. Three types are based on *Capabilities* – Narrow or Weak AI (current), General AI (being developed), and Superintelligent AI (theoretical). There are four types that are based on *Functionality* – Reactive Machines (current), Limited Memory AI (current), Theory of Mind AI (theoretical), and Self-aware AI (hypothetical). Each type of AI has a specific practical application for our daily lives. Remember AI can contribute to our quality of life but can result in dangerous application. Please go online and look up ebsedu.org, *Understanding 7 types of AI (artificial intelligence) with examples*, 2025.

What are some of the dangers if AI outstrips our intellectual and creative capacity? How might unscrupulous individuals utilise AI to control future societies? Discuss.

On Monday 19 October 1983 the Dow Jones Industrial Average (DJIA) plunged 22%, making this the largest trading day loss in a single day of DJIA history. To this day stock market traders refer to this day as *Black Monday*. What happened? Why did this occur? The first half of 1983 saw the stock market trading in a bull market. But when the mid-year company profits were announced, many investors were disappointed. When they sold their shares, it led to prices falling below the *stop loss* levels of other investors, so their brokers sold off their stocks as well. This drove the price of shares even further down, which triggered more and more stop loss selling. This selling contagion spread around the world.

What is *stop loss* selling? Stop loss orders can be placed with your broker to limit the amount of loss you might suffer if there is a run on your stock. This means that the broker will *buy or sell* on your behalf whenever a particular stock reaches your *set price*. Stop loss orders can be used in other investment markets, like the commodities and currency markets. What made Black Monday so bad was that computers had automated many stockbroker activities, so stocks were automatically sold. Panic set in and shares were sold in record numbers. When calm returned to the stock market, brokers and buyers recognised that prices had fallen well below the intrinsic value of most shares. This triggered a bull market run and the DJIA recovered in a relatively short time. Unfortunately, many fortunes had been lost and gained over this short period of trading.

Governments around the world have now introduced *trading circuit breakers* to partially overcome this problem. A circuit breaker is a compulsory halt to trading for a set period of time. This allows brokers and traders time to reassess the market before trading recommences. The US government, for example, has set circuit breakers to halt trading when the S&P 500 Index drops 7%, 13%, and 29%.

Finally, consideration must be given to *the cost of investing in shares*. To buy and sell shares you will need to open a brokerage account with a brokerage firm. There are a number of these, and you can go online and discover for yourself which ones you are interested in opening an account with. You can investigate CommSec, nabtrade, ASX:SWF and CMC Markets to get you started but there are many others. Remember, however, brokerage firms charge fees for the purchase and selling of shares.

As well as this, any income generated from your ownership of shares is subject to tax. Income from your shares may be in the form of *dividends* (both franked and unfranked), *capital gains*, or the *granting of shares* by the company itself (two-for-one deals, for example). Another form of income from holding shares is when one corporation or company (the acquirer) wishes to *take over* another corporation or company (the target). The acquirer will approach shareholders in the target and offer to purchase their shares at a premium price, with the offer available for a limited time. So you can see that the income from shares has a large source and must be kept track of by the shareholder. As well as this, the taxation on shares is very complicated, including income tax and capital gains tax. The amount of tax you will pay is determined by things like your marginal tax rate, what income you received from your shares, whether your dividends are franked or not; and with regards to capital gains, how long you held the shares for. These are just some of the considerations you need to be aware of before selling your shares. Given all this, you should consider employing a competent and trustworthy tax accountant, if you have reached this point of investing.

As a closing remark to this section, may I point out that you will, no doubt, read many books on investing in shares. Some of these books will provide you with ideas or even schemes to follow when investing in equity. Here are some strategies I discovered in my reading.

The *chartists* are investors who believe that future price trends can be predicted through a study of past trends. They plot charts which display these trends, then make their purchasing decisions based on the projected movement of the line on their charts. Of course, past trends may, or may not, be a predictor of future trends. Two good books for you to consult if you are interested in studying this type of investment strategy are Thomas Bulkowski's books, *Getting Started in Chart Patterns,* and *Encyclopedia of Chart Patterns*. Remember, if you are investing in shares, these books are tax deductable.

Conservative investors believe that investors should *spread their risk* across as many sectors of the stock market as possible. Some sectors of the share market are the financial sector, the energy sector, the mining sector, the transport sector, the health care sector, the industrial sector, the farming sector, the consumer staples sector, the manufacturing sector, and the utilities sector. This is by no means a complete list of the different sectors of the stock market, but it certainly is enough to keep you busy for a while. They advise this because your investment is protected if one or more sectors suffer a setback while other sectors improve in value. On the other hand, aggressive investors believe in taking risks by investing heavily in shares they consider have *the greatest potential for rising value*, regardless of whether they limit their investment to only one or a few sectors. They claim that spreading your risk increases the chance of one sector's loss cancelling out another sector's gain so that you end up with a much lower gain than you would have by investing in only a few sectors.

Other investors take a more practical approach. They simply observe *what people are buying*. Where are the crowds? What is exciting consumers? I remember when Kentucky Fried Chicken opened their first store in Australia. It was on the Gold Coast, and it was always crowded. The same can be said for McDonalds when they first opened their shops. Hungry Jacks, on the other hand, is a wholly owned subsidiary of Competitive Foods Australia, a privately held company owned by Jack Cowin, so no shares are available for trading in this company. When Just Jeans first opened their shops, young people flocked to their stores. Just Jeans was delisted from the ASX in 2008 and is now part of the privately owned Myer Holdings Limited. Buying shares in these companies at that time would have generated a profit for anyone.

One piece of advice that John Paul Getty (1892-1976), at one time the richest man in the world and a seasoned investor in stocks, made was –

The best time to buy is when everyone else is selling.
(novelinvestor.com, 2025)

You see, John Paul Getty bought shares during the depression when everyone else was selling (so the prices were low) and sold them when everyone else was buying (so the prices were high). If you are interested in John Paul Getty you can read his book, *How to be Rich*. This spawned a whole theory of investment called the *contrarian theory of investment*. That is, always buy when others are selling and always sell when others are buying. The trick to this theory of investment is *timing*. You see, it is best to buy shares when the market hits the bottom and sell them when it reaches its peak. The trouble with this theory of investment is one of human nature, *greed*. Greed makes some investors buy too early, thinking that the market will recover so they need to get in before everyone else, only to find it continues to decline. Greed also makes investors wait too long before selling, thinking that they will make more money if they hold on to their shares, only to find that the market has reached its peak and starts to decline. One way to overcome this problem is to decide what *profit* you want to make from a share purchase and sell when you achieve it. Following this strategy means it doesn't really matter so much when you buy or sell, so long as you make a profit.

A second consideration about when to sell is the 7% rule. According to this rule,

If a stock falls below 7-8% below your purchase price, you should sell it immediately – no exceptions.
(William J. O'Neil, *How to Make Money in Stocks*, 1988)

Another famous contrarian investor was Baron Rothschild, an 18th century nobleman and member of the Rothschild banking family who is believed to have said,

> *The time to buy is when there's blood in the street.*
> (Investopedia.com, 2025)

A little dramatic, but you get the point. This quote emphasises an important truth about betting against market psychology.

During a bear market, stock investors turn to the more *defensive sectors* of the stock market because they remain stable, may increase in value, and might even pay dividends. These sectors provide *essential goods and ser*vices that consumers continue to buy. The sectors of the stock market that fall into this category are, for example, healthcare, consumer staples, and utilities. Healthcare companies are involved in providing pharmaceuticals, medical equipment, and healthcare services. Consumer staples companies sell things like food, beverages, and household products. Utilities companies provide essential services like electricity, oil, gas, and water. Some investors, however, leave the stock market altogether and invest in real estate, bonds, and debentures.

Berkshire Hathaway Inc. is an American multinational conglomerate holding company established in 1965 under the management of Chairman and CEO Warren Buffett and Vice Chairman Charlie Munger. Charlie Munger died in 2023 and Warren Buffett will step down as CEO at the end of 2025. Greg Able, the current vice chairman will take over as CEO on 1st Jan 2026.

You might like to consider reading up on Charlie Monger (1924-2023), an American businessman, investor, attorney, and philanthropist and Warren Buffett (1930-) an American investor and philanthropist, two of the leading equity traders in recent times.

Charlie Monger's most famous quote was,

> *Spend each day trying to be a little wiser than you were when you woke up. Discharge your duties faithfully and well.*
> (goodreads.com/quotes, 2025)

He wrote two books, *Poor Charlie's Almanack* (2005) and *On Success* (2009). His major advice to investors can be found in this quote –

> *If you have a standing start at zero, getting together $100,000 is a long struggle for most people ... people who get there relatively quickly are helped if they are **passionate about being rational, very eager and optimistic, and steadily underspend their income grossly**. I think those three factors are very helpful.*
> (Berkshire Hathaway shareholder meeting, 1998)

A famous quote from Warren Buffett, one of the most successful investors of all time, is

> *You should think twice before mimicking the investments of billionaires and cash is always a bad investment.*
> (inverstopedia.com, 2025)

His main advice to investors is found in this quote –

> *It is better to invest in a company with **a proven track record of success, a durable competitive edge, and strong growth potential** even if it means paying a fair price, than to invest in a company with a lower price but weaker fundamentals.*
> (investing.com, 2025)

He wrote many books, but two that will get you started are *Buffetology* (1999) and *Warren Buffett on Business* (2009).

These are just some important issues and questions you need to consider before buying shares. Evidently, this form of investment is very different from anything you have undertaken to date. If you decide to invest in shares, be prudent, be careful, and accept that you are investing in a more volatile form of investment than you have experienced in the past. The *rewards* are there, but so too are the *risks*. Remember, any profit (after tax) you receive from your share trading must be re-invested and not spent if you want to watch your investment account grow. Actually, you can now call your investment account your *investment portfolio* because you might have now diversified into up to five categories of investment. Namely, savings account; cash deposits; government, corporate, or insurance bonds; debentures; real estate; and shares. However, there are still other categories of investment to consider.

Commodities

Commodities are tangible items that people buy and sell. They can be items needed for manufacturing or consumption. They are often divided into four types –

1) *Precious metals and gems*
2) *Agriculture*
3) *Energy*
4) *Meat and livestock.*

Some examples of precious metals and gems include things like gold, silver, platinum, copper, diamonds, rubies, opals, and emeralds. The demand for precious metals and gems remains relatively stable, so they provide protection against inflation because they retain their monetary value over time. Some people believe that investing in precious metals and gems is a slow way to make money. However, they do hold their value and they do make money over time. For these reasons investors often will buy precious metals or gems to *underwrite* their investment portfolios. They are a guarantee that investors will not lose all their money during a period of serious downturn. There is a saying that combines two different investment strategies, the contrarian strategy and the strategy deeming, that in times of panic and crisis, tangible assets will retain their value –

When there is blood in the streets, gold is king.
                                          (anonymous)

Since precious metals and gems make money over time, some investors adopt a strategy of buying them over time. For example, they might buy a *set amount* (in dollar terms) of gold at *set times*, say every six to twelve months and build up their reserve of gold in this way. This ensures that they will buy at the average price of gold regardless of fluctuations in the marketplace.

One problem with purchasing gold is that it must be *stored*. This means you will have to pay a storage fee to keep it safe. Banks offer deposit boxes for this purpose. Some investors prefer to buy jewellery and wear their gold and precious gems. For example, rings, necklaces bangles, and gold watches with inlaid gemstones are good examples of this type of investment. If you are interested in this type of investment,

only buy 22 carat (916) gold pieces, and buy from countries with developing economies.

Jewellery does have the added cost of the labour used to produce it, which is cheaper in countries with developing economies. However, wearing jewellery can make you a target for thieves. Nevertheless, this investment strategy ensures that you always have your gold on hand, and it does keep the ladies happy. Remember to *insure* your precious jewellery against theft or loss. Another way of holding precious metals and gems is to buy stock in mining companies with large reserves of precious metals or gems. This way you avoid the storage fees and danger of wearing your gold. Remember though, if you do this, you will still be subject to all the risks associated with share market investment explained previously.

If you are interested in investing in gold, a good book to get you started is *The Beginners Guide to Investing in Gold*, by Maxwell Aldrow. *How to Invest in Gems: Everyone's Guide to Buying Rubies, Sapphires,*

Emeralds, and Diamonds by Benjamin Zucker will help you if you decide to invest in gemstones.

Here's a little aside. When your financial security permits, consider taking a holiday to the Columbian city of Cartagena on the shores of the Caribbean. It was the city where the Spanish used to store their gold before shipping it off to Spain. There is a Spanish fort there which you can tour. It will enlighten you as to the value of gold and the lengths Spain went to in order to preserve it. The people of Cartagena are gracious and very friendly, and they have also preserved the old colonial section of the city. Going there is like stepping back in time. People still live in this colonial section, and it is not just a few buildings but a whole suburb of the city. One of the *Pirates of the Caribbean* films was shot there. Columbia is also the emerald capital of the world, so you can learn a lot about emeralds and pick up a bargain while you are there.

Agricultural commodities include things like wheat, rice, corn, cocoa, and soybeans. Farmers sell their crops both domestically and internationally, so there is a huge market for agricultural commodities and people must eat to survive, so the demand is fairly constant. The agricultural commodities market, however, is subject to fluctuations. *Oversupply* (or gluts) of any given crop can lead to a reduction in price, while *undersupply* coupled with *high demand* for the same crop can lead to a spike in prices. An example of this is the war in Ukraine which created a shortage in wheat supply to the world since Ukraine is a major supplier of wheat to the world market.

Floods, fires, and droughts create shortages of food supplies while good seasons of rain create abundance. Floods destroy farmers' crops as do locust and mice infestations. Those investing in agricultural commodities usually do so by buying *futures*. That is, they buy at a price now that they believe will increase in the future. This form of investment is speculative. One can make a lot of money, but one can also lose a lot of money. Think carefully before you venture into this form of investment. Because food is perishable, the buying and selling of food stocks must be completed in set time frames, and prices for food stocks depend on its quality and the amount being bought and sold.

Here is an interesting insight into investment in the time of ancient Greece. The Greek philosopher, Thales of Miletus, predicted an abundant olive harvest so he secured all the olive presses in Miletus by buying or renting them. When the harvest came in the farmers were forced to pay higher prices for pressing their olives since Thales had created a monopoly of the presses. Of course, most countries today have laws prohibiting monopolies for this very reason. International cartels, however, do exist that try to create monopolies in which companies or countries collude with one another to limit the supply of commodities on some sections of the international commodities market. International cartels that have existed or do exist in the commodities market are the Organisation of the Petroleum Exporting Countries (OPEC), the International Rubber Regulation Agreement, the International Coffee Agreement, and cartels in bauxite, copper, uranium, mercury, and tin. In recent times, China has created a monopoly on critical minerals which America is now trying to alleviate by entering critical mineral deals with several countries, including Australia.

To overcome the possibility of losing too much money due to a drop in the price of a commodity some investors will *short* some of their investment. This is achieved simply by borrowing shares from a broker and immediately selling them. If the shares drop in price the investor buys back the shares at the lower price and returns them to the broker while pocketing the difference. If the shares increase in value the investor has lost money, so most investors hold some shares and sell some. Shorting is often done to limit an investor's loss, but some investors use shorting as a major part of their investment strategy. That is, they look for stock that they think will decline in value, and then short it.

A good book for understanding the workings of the agricultural commodities market is *Agricultural Commodity Markets* by Michael Atkin.

Energy commodities are used to power the world's countries and their economies. Some energy commodities include coal, natural gas, crude oil, and uranium. Since energy is necessary to keep things running its demand is pretty constant. Prices do rise and fall, however, and price fluctuations usually relate to factors of supply.

Fossil fuel prices are affected by many factors. For example, wars may break out causing a drop in oil production or a threat to oil supply lines. Another factor is the Organization of the Petroleum Exporting Countries (OPEC) which controls most of the world's crude oil supply; the amount they produce will determine the price of crude oil on the world market, which in turn determines the price of diesel and petrol. OPEC does adjust its supply of crude oil to determine the price for this commodity on the world market. Under Trump's presidency, America is about to produce huge amounts of fossil fuels. This will obviously affect the future price of this energy source. Once again, investors in this market buy quantities of these commodities to sell at a later price. What they get for their investment in the future will depend on the supply of those commodities to the world market and the demand for it.

Currently, many governments around the world are trying to move away from fossil fuels by converting to renewable energy. As they do so one would think that this would create a decrease in demand for fossil fuels, but the opposite has occurred. Why? You see renewable energy sources (wind turbines and solar panels) require fossil fuels to manufacture them and they produce unreliable energy (renewable energy needs wind and sunshine for its production). So renewable energy requires a backup energy source for those times when the wind does not blow, and the sun does not shine. This is called baseload power, and currently fossil fuels provide the majority of this baseload power in the form of coal and gas. There are future plans for batteries, hydropower, and hydrogen to supply this. However, all these plans have run into serious technical and economic problems in Australia so replacing fossil fuels with these alternatives is still a long way off, if it can be achieved at all. Renewable energy is also proving to be very expensive. Those countries which have decided to adopt this form of energy source have the most expensive energy costs in the world today, Australia included.

This has led many countries that pursue net zero by 2050 to turn to nuclear power as a baseload source for renewable energy or as an energy alternative. Nuclear power is the most energy dense source of electricity currently available. It can produce a large amount of power from a relatively small amount of fuel, which makes it efficient and cost effective, which is vital for the development of AI, since AIs consume large amount of electric power. In the past, people were frightened by the thought of nuclear power, and the Australian Government even passed legislation that created a moratorium on its use out of this fear. People were afraid of nuclear power plants melting down owing to a lack of cooling. This would obviously be catastrophic. They also feared having to store the waste from nuclear plants for thousands of years. These problems have been addressed by using coolants other than water and the development of breeder reactors which has reduced the amount of nuclear waste to a large extent.

Korea Hydro Nuclear Power (KHNP), a subsidiary company of Korea Electric Power Corporation (KEPC), has built and operated large scale nuclear power plants in South Korea and has expanded sales outside of South Korea (world-nuclear.org, 2024). In 2025, the South Korean Government invested $100 million in KHNP (nucnet.org). The advantage KHNP has over its competitors is the time it takes to build their reactors (56 months) which is more than three times faster than other countries (koreatimes.co.kr). Large scale nuclear reactors produce zero carbon dioxide gas and other greenhouse gas emissions during operation.

Small Modular Reactors (SMRs) are smaller, prefabricated nuclear reactors that can be deployed more flexibly (they take up a small area and can be placed in parallel to make any sized generator) and cost much less than large-scale nuclear reactors. They can also be integrated with renewable energy sources to create hybrid systems. Currently, SMRs use coolants like gas, liquid metal or molten salt making it almost impossible for a SMR to melt down. The British and American navies have operated SMRs in their ships for many decades without mishap. As of 2024 only China and Russia have operational SMRs (wikipedia.org). Rolls Royce claims its new SMR will have a lifespan of 60 years and produce roughly a tennis court size of waste during its lifetime (gda.rolls-royce-smr.com).

Breeder reactors can now recycle most nuclear waste allowing the fuel to last a lot longer and produce less waste over a plant's lifespan. Breeder reactors can also transmute some long-lived radioactive material into short-lived ones, but they also produce plutonium-239, which has a long half-life and is suitable for producing nuclear weapons. Today, large-scale nuclear power plants have a lifetime lasting for up to 40-60 years (world-nuclear.org). The Beznau nuclear power plant (in Switzerland) is the oldest currently in use and became operational in 1969 (power-technology.com). Nuclear power plants produce less waste and environmental damage than any other form of power production, including renewable energy. Currently, there are 440 nuclear reactors operating in 32 countries worldwide. Another 30 countries are considering, planning or starting nuclear power programmes (world-nuclear.org, 2025).

Clearly, as large-scale nuclear power plants and SMRs are adopted by more countries around the world, an increase in the demand for uranium will occur, which may drive up the future price of uranium. Let's hope that by the time Australia gets around to using SMRs or large nuclear reactors, our uranium will not be tied up in contracts from overseas, as is the case with our gas supplies today.

One thing that should be clear about investing in the energy market is that it is heavily influenced by politics and therefore highly unpredictable.

The meat and livestock commodity market controls our food supply and provides us with a balanced diet. Farming businesses also use livestock production to help with land maintenance. Animal waste and blood and bone can be used as fertilisers, for example. Meat and livestock commodities include meat like beef, lamb, pork, and poultry, and live cattle, sheep, and pigs. Once again, most people eat meat, so demand for this commodity is pretty stable, but supply can be disrupted for a number of factors. Take drought, for example. One would think that drought would drive the cost of meat up in price because of scarcity, but initially it actually drives it down. On the other hand, when the drought ends prices rise. Why is this? Well, livestock producers actually sell their herds and flocks in greater numbers during times of drought, because they can't afford to feed them, thereby driving the cost of meat down. When a drought ends, however, livestock producers restock their herds and flocks, thereby driving the cost of livestock up.

Live exports are also subject to sudden government regulation changes which affect the demand for this commodity. In the past, Australian governments have halted the live export of cattle and sheep, and some overseas governments have halted their import.

Again, meat and livestock are bought and sold on the domestic and world markets, so buyers who buy with the intention of selling for a profit in the future need to recognise that the sale of livestock and meat commodities are subject to many variables, so be cautious when venturing into this market.

Once again, the meat and livestock market is heavily influenced by natural disasters and politics which makes it subject to sudden and unpredictable changes.

Currencies

I hesitate to mention this form of investment because it so *volatile*. The swings in currency markets can be sudden, substantial, and long lasting. Depending on how much you invest, you can make a fortune, or you can lose everything, particularly if you leverage your investment.

A nation's currency value is determined either by the foreign exchange market, Forex (FX) or it is set by a nation's government. Exchange rates arrived at by the FX are referred to as *floating exchange rates*. Australia has had a floating exchange rate since 1983. When exchange rates are set by a nation's government it is referred to as a *pegged or fixed currency* and is tied to another nation's currency, usually the $US. The value of a nation's currency is important because it affects that nation's economic activity, inflation, and the nation's balance of payments. A nation's currency exchange rate is expressed in terms of its value against another nation's currency.

The FX is the largest and most liquid market in the world. Trillions of dollars are exchanged daily and continue over 24 hours every day, because trading centres around the world change as daylight drifts into different time zones.

The goal of trading FX is to make a profit from the changes in exchange rates between any two currencies. To trade FX you must open a trading account with a broker. You need to do your research here, taking into consideration things like the terms of the trading platform, fees, margin rates, and customer support. Again, you must beware of scammers.

Once you have opened your account and made your trading deposit, you can trade currencies by placing buy or sell orders. Many variables move the trading market like

- *economic indicators,* (GDP, unemployment rates, inflation rates, interest rates, and trade balance, to name just five),
- *market sentiment* (investor confidence and news and media sentiment etc.),
- *geopolitical events* (government policies, international relations, political instability etc.),
- *technical factors* (based on things like price charts and trading patterns).

Remember currency trading continues throughout a 24-hour period, even when you are sleeping, and currency changes can happen suddenly and profoundly. I would advise anyone entering this market to instruct your broker to place a stop loss order on your specific buy or sell orders.

If you place a buy order in USD/AUD, you are *betting* on the USD appreciating against the AUD. If you place a sell order, you are betting that the AUD will appreciate against the USD. The first country's dollar in the trading pair is known as the base currency. Trades are sized in lots. The standard lot is 100,000 of the base currency. If you placed a buy order in USD/AUD, for example, you would be buying $100,000 USD, and betting that it will increase in value against the AUD.

As you can see, currency trading requires *large amounts of cash*, so is usually the preferred investment option of the very wealthy. Commercial and National Reserve Banks are big traders, as are Hedge Funds. As stated before, the small investor can get into currency trading by buying into a *hedge fund*.

Here is a true story. In 1995 the Barings Bank scandal broke on the news. Barings Bank was the oldest merchant bank in England (established in 1762). Nick Leeson was the Barings Bank currency trader in Singapore. He carried out risky trades (bets?) which he concealed from Barings and even raised fraudulent loans to leverage his trades. In 1995 values, his losses exceeded 827 million pounds Sterling (approximately $1,695,350,000 AUD), ultimately leading to Barings' insolvency. I was living in Singapore at the time and this incident cured me of any thought I might have had about entering the currency market. Nick Leeson was sentenced to six and a half years in Changi Prison in Singapore for his role in the collapse of Barings Bank. He served four years and four months before being released owing to his good behaviour and a diagnosis of colon cancer. He lost his wife, who remarried, his career, and all his assets and money. People claimed that he must have hidden away some of the money he had lost, but he claimed that he wished he had. He survived his colon cancer and now lives in Ireland with his second wife and three children. He is a much sought-after speaker and advisor on matters pertaining to corporate intelligence work and financial misconduct.

National currencies can be, and are, manipulated by national governments and large fund managers. We have all heard about the activities of George Soros, a billionaire currency trader, and how he was accused (by Malaysian PM, Mahathir Mohamad) of manipulating the currency of Malaysia by his short-selling speculation of the Malaysian ringgit in 1997. This led to the Asian financial crisis and it took many years for the currencies of the Asian Tiger economies to recover. The crisis began with the Thai baht, which lost approximately half its value against the $US. It then spread quickly to the other Asian currencies; the Malaysian ringgit lost approximately half its value, the Indonesian rupiah lost approximately 75% of its value, the Philippine pesos lost around 37% of its value, while the South Korean won lost about half its value. George Soros, who founded Quantum Fund in 1970, which was one of the first hedge funds in the world, denies his trading activity had anything to do with the currency collapse of the Thai and Malaysian currencies, the two currencies in which he invested billions in short-selling. He is on record as saying,

> *I cannot and do not look at the social consequences of what I do.*
> (wikiquote.org)

Keep in mind that many currency investors at this time followed George Soros' lead and this compounded the pressure on these Asian currencies. The Malaysian and Philippines currencies recovered by 1999, while it took until 2003 for the Indonesian and Thailand currencies to recover.

I started my explanation of currency trading by saying that I was reluctant to mention it, but I have included it for the sake of completeness. It is my personal opinion that trading in the FX, for the average investor, is *gambling*. In fact, I have deliberately used the word *bet* when describing the placing of a buy or sell order. I did this for good reason. Nevertheless, the more risk-accepting investor may be attracted to this form of investment, so I had to cover it. A few people have made a lot of money out of currency trading, the majority have lost money and some, even large banks, have lost everything.

Collectibles

Some people refer to this form of investment as a *hobby* rather than an investment because people derive so much pleasure from it. Some collectibles you might be interested in are things like wine, stamps, coins, books, antique or classic furniture, antique or classic cars, and art works like paintings, sculptures, and stencils. Some people even collect things like sports cards, old records, magazines, comics, and toys. While it is true that these items do appreciate in value over time, it is difficult to know just which ones will and which ones won't and by how much. Furthermore, if they are not stored and maintained properly, they may be stolen or deteriorate.

Also, you run the risk of getting too emotionally attached to these items and find yourself investing far too much in them. No doubt the collectibles that already have value today will appreciate more in the future but how long will you have to hold them for? Nevertheless, collectibles do make up a *valuable asset base* for your investments, and you can buy part ownership in them through a *Collectible Fund*, which is capable of buying items beyond your price range. Just remember, do not get carried away and spend too much on any one item, especially cars which seem to run up costs through their storage and maintenance.

In the 1980's I bought a Triumph TR7 sports car with a moon roof (glass insert that could be popped up). It was in poor condition so I got it for a good price. It was the first car in the world that was built using computer-aided design (CAD). It was the first wedge-shaped car with pop-up headlights. For these reasons, I thought it would be a good investment. The oil crisis was in full swing when it was built, so it had a fuel-efficient engine which made it a little underpowered for a sports car. I spent a lot of money restoring it to a safe, drivable condition (suspension, breaks, engine, etc.). All that was left to do were the aesthetics, like new paint, new seat covers, etc. I kept all the receipts for the work I had done on it. If you invest in a collectible you must do this. Otherwise you will never know what return you will make on your money. My ex-wife and I enjoyed outings in it. Sunday drives in the countryside highlighted by malted milk shakes in quaint country cafes, evening drives after visiting restaurants some distance from our home. Unfortunately, my career took me to Singapore so I had to sell my collectible investment. The price I got for it was exactly what I had invested in it. I had made no profit on my investment. However, that special car gave me many memorable experiences, so it did make a return for me, only not in a monetary sense.

Funds

All funds pool the money of many investors and then invest the money on their behalf. There are four types of funds you can invest in –

1) *Index Funds*
2) *Mutual Funds*
3) *Hedge Funds*
4) *ETF's* (Exchange Traded Funds).

Each of these funds is designed for different types of investment and, therefore, cater for different types of investors.

1. Index Funds

> *Index funds are investment funds that aim to match the performance of a specific market index, like the S&P 500 or the AXS 200.*
>
> (AI Overview, 2025)

Index funds, therefore, hold stocks or bonds in what they believe mirrors the index composition. Key features of index funds are –

Passive management – they don't try to outperform the market; they only attempt to match it.

Low fees – because they don't require active management and may even rely on machine-driven investment. Therefore, their management fees are much lower than actively managed funds. Fees generally range from 0.02% to 0.20% of the annual percentage of the net assets under management (AUM).

Diversification – because they invest in company stocks across a wide range of market sectors.

Tracking indices – because they track various market indices, for example, the ASX 200 index fund that tracks the performance of the 200 largest companies listed on the Australian Stock Exchange or the S&P 500 index fund that tracks the performance of the 500 largest publicly traded companies in the United States.

Accessibility – Index funds can only be purchased at the end of the trading day. The price for the funds is calculated using a simple formula: (the total value of assets – expenses) divided by the total number of shares. You may place a buy order during the day's trading but the cost of the shares will not be determined until the end of the trading day, usually at 4.00 pm. The Australian Stock Exchange, for example, operates between 10.00 am and 4.00 pm Monday to Friday. This excludes weekends and national public holidays. This gives Index Funds the same accessibility as Mutual or Hedge Funds, but less accessibility than ETFs whose shares can be bought and sold at the market price at the time of the trade.

Also, you do not have to become a member of an Index Fund, instead you purchase shares in the fund through a brokerage firm or retirement fund.

These features of Index Funds make them an attractive form of investment for beginners since they are easy to understand and invest in. Their diversification means they are less vulnerable to the impact of change to only one or a few individual stocks, and their lower management fees means small investors do not lose too much of their returns on management fees. Since Index Funds track the performance of the market they have invested in, their returns are also consistent and predictable.

2. Mutual Funds

Mutual funds are a way to

> *venture into different markets without having to make decisions about what to buy, when to buy, and when to sell.*

There are many different types of Mutual Funds. For example, there are funds which specialise by investing only in bonds and debentures, or real estate, or shares, or energy, or commodities, or currencies, or collectibles or cryptocurrency. Other funds offer a balanced approach to the different markets in their investment strategy. You can usually decide what markets the account with your mutual fund invests in, giving you a choice between the *conservative approach*, the *riskier approach*, or a *balanced approach*. Obviously, the higher the risk, the higher the return or loss.

To invest in a Mutual Fund you first need to become a member of the fund. This will entail filling out an application form and providing personal details to the fund, like your bank details, so ensure you are dealing with a respectable, well established, and trustworthy fund and not some dubious one or even a scammer. Next you need to decide how much you will invest in the fund. Mutual Funds require a minimum deposit of somewhere between $1,000 and $5,000. You can invest for 3-5 or 10-year periods. You can make deposits like these on a continuing basis. For example, you may want to deposit $1,000 for a 3-year period every 3 months. All funds level fees and charges on investors so be aware of this when investing in this way. Before investing discover how much these fees and charges are. Also, look at the past performance of the fund. Be careful here, because funds will try and inflate their performance by stating investment periods which provide evidence of their highest returns.

You may, or may not, know that your *Superannuation* is in a Mutual Fund. You and your employer makes regular deposits into your Superannuation Fund, and because you can't touch your superannuation until you retire, it grows at compound interest over the period of your working life, thereby providing you with a handsome return on your investment. The Australian Government also has granted generous tax concessions to Superannuation Funds. Concessions you would not be entitled to for your private investments. The Australian Government also allows you to top up your Superannuation Fund. That is, you may want to increase your deposits beyond the compulsory level. After tax, you can contribute up to $110,000 each year. If you receive a windfall, like an inheritance, you may be eligible to add up to $330,000 in the one deposit, but you won't be able to make any more voluntary deposits into your Superannuation Fund for three years. As I have stated, Superannuation Funds have good tax concessions, so many investors add as much to their Superannuation Funds as they can.

One word of caution though – successive Australian governments have made many changes to the laws governing Superannuation Funds. Over the years, many of the big taxation benefits have been eliminated, but they are still a better investment than most other funds. Currently, the Australian Government intends to introduce a tax on unrealised capital gains against Superannuation Funds of more than $3 million. If this is carried through, when it reaches the Senate the Green Party have stated that they want the limit placed on $2 million. The Labor Party must have Green Party support to pass legislation through the Senate. The Australian Government has scrapped its proposed tax on unrealised capital gains and replaced it with a proposed additional 15% tax on 'realised earnings' on the proportion of the total super balance above $3 million AUD. As you can see Australian Governments make changes to the tax on Superannuation Funds to meet the interest payments on Australia's accumulated debt and the government's deficit spending.

As of June 2025, Australian Superannuation Funds hold approximately $4.33 AUD trillion in assets. The appointment of Superannuation Fund directors varies by fund type but generally involves the fund's shareholders or sponsoring organisations, such as industry bodies and unions. The directors of some government-related funds are appointed by the Minister for Finance. Some investors in Superannuation Funds are worried that future renewable energy projects will be funded increasingly by Superannuation Funds rather than government.

Remember, you don't get access to the money in your Superannuation Fund until after you retire, so you have a long wait.

3. Hedge Funds

Hedge Funds are funds that pool money from investors to invest in complex trading which aims to maximise investment performance by taking significant risk. Among some of the techniques used by Hedge Funds are

short selling, the use of leverage and derivative instruments.

Hedge Funds are for large investors. It is not uncommon for a Hedge Fund to require at least $100,000 or even $1 million to participate.

Hedge Funds also charge higher fees than other investment funds, and funds are usually locked up for a year before shares can be sold. Today, Hedge Funds employ a "2 and 20" fee system. That is, a 2% management fee and a 20% performance fee. The 2% management fee is based on the net asset value of each investor's shares, while the 20% performance fee is based on the profits.

Some things to consider before investing in a Hedge Fund –

1) Read the Hedge Fund's documents and agreements which contain information about investing in the fund, the strategies of the fund, the location of the fund, and the risks anticipated by the investment.
2) Does the anticipated level of risk involved with the Hedge Fund match your own investment goals and risk management?
3) Check the management's background and past performance and evaluate any potential conflict of interest.
4) Understand how the fund's assets are valued. Some funds invest highly in illiquid securities and evaluation of these securities will determine your management fees and performance fees.
5) Make sure you understand any limitations to time restrictions imposed to redeem shares.

The largest four Hedge Fund firms are –
- Bridgewater Associates located in Westport, CT;
- Man Group located in London, UK;
- Elliott Investment Management located in West Palm Beach, Florida; and
- Millennium Management, LLC located in New York, NY.

According to a Capco (a global management consulting company) study, 50% of Hedge Funds shut down because of operational failures. Some Hedge Funds have even defrauded investors of billions. The more infamous Hedge Funds that were found to have defrauded their investors were Madoff Investment, SAC Capital, the Galleon Group, Long-Term Capital Management, Pequot Capital Management, Amaranth Advisors, Tiger Funds, and Aman Capital. Two infamous crypto investment platforms that operated Ponzi schemes before their collapse was FTX in 2022 and CBEX in 2025.

As you can see, investing in Hedge Funds requires a large capital outlay, higher than usual risk and higher than usual fees. It is not for the average investor, but I have included it for the same reason I included currency trading, that is, completeness.

ETFs

An ETF (exchange traded fund) pools a group of investments (stocks, bonds etc.) into a fund that allows an investor to trade them like an individual stock on the stock exchange. This allows a small investor to invest in many securities at once. Many more than he/she is likely to invest in alone. The amount of cash invested in ETFs has expanded into the trillions since the turn of the century.

Some important facts about ETFs are –
1) An ETF is an exchange traded fund containing a basket of securities that trades on an exchange just like a stock.
2) ETF prices fluctuate throughout the trading day, just like stocks.
3) ETFs offer lower fees and fewer brokerage fees than buying stocks individually.
4) Volatility is limited with ETFs because their holdings are diversified and can be used to rotate in and out of market sectors during market cycles.
5) There are a variety of ETFs designed to match an individual investor's portfolio. For example, passive ETFs, actively managed ETFs, Bond ETFs, sector ETFs, commodity ETFs, currency ETFs, Bitcoin ETFs, inverse ETFs (that operate on more risk-adverse investment like short stocks, derivates and exchange traded notes (ETN), and leveraged ETFs, to name some that are available to the investor.

The biggest ETFs in terms of assets under management (AUM) are – SPDR S&P 500 ETF Trust (SPY) that tracks the S&P 500 index. It is one of the most popular and liquid ETFs available.

iShares Core S&P 500 ETF (IVV) also tracks the S&P 500. It is known for its low expense ratio.

Vanguard Total Stock Market EFT (VTI) is the most diversified ETF on the US stock market including large, mid and small-cap companies.

Vanguard's Australian Shares Index ETF (ASX:VAS) is the largest Australian ETF on the Australian stock exchange with over $20 billion in assets.

As can be seen, most average investors in Australian shares favour ETFs over the other fund investment packages and for good reason.

Cryptocurrency

This is a relatively new form of investment which investors find puzzling and, consequently, shy away from. There is nothing to be puzzled about cryptocurrency, but there is much to be aware of.

> *Cryptocurrency is a digital currency in which transactions are verified and records maintained by a decentralised system using cryptography, rather than a centralized authority .... Decentralised cryptocurrencies such as bitcoin now provide an outlet for personal wealth that is beyond restriction and confiscation.*
>
> (Oxford Languages, 2025)

Cryptocurrency is protected by a *cryptography technology* and a function called *blockchains* where all transactions are permanently recorded and immutable. Blockchains operate as a decentralised distributed database, with data shared across computers, making it resistant to tampering or hacking. For example, any change to a cryptocurrency account must be able to be verified on a multitude of computers, not just one computer, hence the blockchain.

> *In cryptocurrency, miners (those who earn rewards for their work) are participants who use their computer power to validate transactions and create new blocks on a blockchain .... This process is crucial for maintaining the security and integrity of the blockchain network.*
>
> (AI Overview, 2025)

The three biggest cryptocurrencies are –

- *Bitcoin* (BTC) with a market capitalisation of $2.35 trillion and a current price of $118,290.79.
- *Ethereum* (ETH) with a market capitalisation of $403.52 billion and a current price of $3,344.52 and
- *BNB* (BNB) with a market capitalisation of $98.64 billion and a current price of $708.21.

All money quoted above is in $USD and is current as of July 2025. When you invest in cryptocurrency you do not need to purchase a whole digital coin at its current value. You generally purchase a fraction of a coin, but once you do, your money becomes cryptocurrency and it is no longer cash money.

Cryptocurrency grows in value for two reasons. The first is that there are a *fixed number* of bitcoins (digital not cash) available on the market and that number will never increase, thereby being an effective hedge against inflation. The second is *market speculation* (driven by supply and demand). As long as bitcoin maintains its users' demand, driven by its means of exchange (like cash money) and its store of value, it will maintain its attractiveness as a source of speculation regardless of its monetary value. For example, today bitcoin can be used to purchase many items like cars, fashion garments, real estate, electronic goods, and luxury watches, to name just a few. It can also be used for online shopping. Another driving factor of cryptocurrency's value is when *interest rates* are low, which in the past have coincided with bull runs on bitcoin.

The past success of cryptocurrencies has led some countries to integrate them into their economy by recognising them as legal tender and holding them in reserves, while some other countries ban them altogether. Some countries, America included, are considering introducing their own digital currency in the form of a central bank digital currency (CBDC) which would provide users with the speed and other benefits of cryptocurrency without the associated risks.

There are a number of risks associated with cryptocurrencies. These include the *high volatility* of their value, which can change suddenly and unpredictably; the *potential for hacking and fraud* with no recourse for recovering lost funds; and the *lack of regulation* on cryptocurrencies, because they operate outside of traditional financial systems. Other risks involve the nature of *irreversible transactions* which means they cannot be reversed and can be a problem if you make a mistake or are scammed; *Market manipulation* which can be used by large investors and lead to artificial price swings; and *Regulation uncertainty* because it is likely that new, stricter regulations will be introduced by governments in the future. There are other risks involved with cryptocurrencies, but these are the main ones.

Over 50% of all cryptocurrencies have failed. Of the nearly 7 million cryptocurrencies listed on Gecko Terminal since 2021, 3.7 million have ceased trading and are considered failed.

Now that you know what cryptocurrency is, how it works, what the major cryptocurrencies are and what some of the risks are involved in their trading, what is your conclusion? Are you ready to trade in cryptocurrency?

A General Observation

All that we have covered here was available to me in my lifetime and is available to you now. There is no guarantee that this will continue in the future. What is needed for this to continue is a capitalist economy operating in a free or regulated market. Obviously, the regulations on a capitalist economy and the taxes imposed by governments on the companies and individuals operating within the market will determine their profitability and individual aspiration. Regulations on national, capitalist markets in liberal democracies can be too restrictive or too relaxed. When regulations are too restrictive they impede investment, entrepreneurship, and aspirational citizens. When they are too relaxed they create economic corruption, market volatility, environmental degradation, and worker exploitation.

People refer to red tape, green tape, and black tape as being the regulation mechanisms affecting Australia's capitalist market. Red tape refers to bureaucratic regulation of the economy. Red tape can provide necessary checks and balances, accountability and compliance. However, when radicalised it stifles an economy by creating delays, increasing costs and suppressing innovation and productivity. Green tape refers to environmental controls on the economy. Green tape can limit the impact businesses have on the quality of our air, water and ecosystems. On the other hand, radical green tape deliberately inhibits growth in the economy. Black tape refers to Aboriginally related legislation. Black tape can empower Aboriginal communities through Native Title, Land Rights and protection of their sacred sites. At the same time, it can limit access to natural resources and impede sustainable economic development.

Governments can also become over-reliant on expert advice in drafting the economic regulation of their economy. When governments do this they ignore the will of the people and take the advice of the experts in their bureaucracy. Of course, this defeats the very purpose of a democracy. Although Australia is a democracy, it operates under a two-party system of government, so whenever there is bi-partisan support for any piece of legislation, it passes, regardless of the will of the people. For example, in recent years there has been bi-partisan support for mass immigration which the majority of Australian people have never supported. In this case, the experts advised the government that mass immigration would guarantee a continuous increase in Australia's GDP, thereby providing the government with an ever-increasing revenue stream which both political parties needed owing to the huge debt incurred by their excessive spending. For the Australian people, however, this policy has delivered them with an ever–shrinking individual GDP (standard of living), a higher cost of living (inflation created by the increased demand on limited goods and services), a housing crisis, and a decline in the availability of services like hospitals, schools, traffic flow etc.

The economy of a liberal democracy is also governed by how much a government is involved in the capitalist marketplace. You see the *marketplace* is divided into the *government sector* and the *private sector*. The larger the government sector grows the smaller the private sector becomes, because the larger the amount of money in the marketplace controlled by the government becomes the less there is for the private sector. This can have a debilitating effect on the marketplace, because there is less money for the private sector to invest. Since the *private sector creates the wealth* of a nation while the *government sector distributes its wealth*, this can create a dwindling revenue base for the government and a consequent rise in taxes.

Likewise, a government can become so large that it keeps employing more and more public servants. This reduces the size of the workforce available to the private sector. Consequently, more and more of the workforce is engaged in distributing the wealth of a nation rather than creating it in the first place. Currently, one million Australians are employed as public servants (smh.com.au, 2025). This does not include those in the healthcare industry, educators, emergency service personnel, the defence force or those in government-owned businesses, various agencies and those granted consultancy or other contracts. With a workforce of 14 million and a current unemployment rate of 4.3% (abs.gov.au, July 2025), do you think too many people are employed either in the public service or working for the government?

When I started out many decades ago, the government was small compared to today. We did not have the services that the Australian Government provides for its citizens today, but we also did not have the taxes that citizens have today, nor the number of regulations governing our behaviour. I make no judgement about this; I am just pointing out the reality of how a regulated capitalist marketplace in a liberal democratic country operates.

I would, however, like to point out that your ancestors have gifted you with a sophisticated, resilient, mixed economy that provides you with food security and a high standard of living. However, a once reliable, cheap energy source has now been converted into an energy source that is among the most expensive in the world and has become less reliable. So much so, that it has become an incentive for industry and commerce to move offshore from Australia. Some examples of this are –

Morgan Engineering is considering relocating owing to energy bills of $250,000 to $300,000. *Food and grocery manufacturers* and steel producers like *BlueScope* who are facing the same problem are also considering relocating. Two of Australia's biggest aluminium smelters, *Portland Aluminium* in Victoria and *Tomago Aluminium* in New South Wales, are considering relocating because of high energy costs. As well as this *Nyrstar* will receive a $135 million bailout to keep their steel smelters going in Tasmania and South Australia.

On October 8, 2025, the Albanese and Crisafulli governments announced up to $600 million AUD over three years in financial bridging support to Glencore's Mount Isa copper smelter and Townsville refinery to protect jobs and Australia's copper supply.

Net Zero by 2050 and the government's commitment to renewable energy are also impacting our farmers and graziers by putting a future limit on their food production and herd sizes and turning their land over to solar factories, wind generators, and transmission lines. Australians need to think carefully before they make any changes to Australia's economy which will involve them in a trade-off. Australians need to ask themselves what sacrifices they are prepared to make to accommodate these changes.

Furthermore, Australians have a golden opportunity to take Australia's economy to even greater heights through the development and production of AI and robotics. This will not materialise with renewable energy because it cannot guarantee the supply, the reliability, nor the affordability of energy vital to the development of AI and robotics. This is Australia's inheritance and challenge for the future. I am confident Australians have the education, skills and ambition necessary to make a difference towards building an even greater Australia than what their ancestors built for them.

Warning

Did you learn anything from your reading of this chapter on financial security? I hope you did, because I am hopeful that you are now convinced to start a disciplined savings programme and watch your investments grow. Before I end this discussion with you, I would like to highlight it with a warning. Please indulge me.

First, *don't compare yourself to others*. Rather, concentrate on your own ambition and achievements. If you are tempted to compare yourself with others reflect on these words —

> *If you compare yourself with others,*
> *you may become vain and bitter;*
> *for always there will be greater and lesser persons than yourself.*
> *Enjoy your achievements as well as your plans.*
> (Max Ehrmann, *Desiderata*, 1927)

I have mentioned that you will need ambition to acquire financial security. Don't let your ambition lead you into *envy* or *revenge*. You will encounter many people who have achieved more than you in their lifetime. Be happy for them. Allow them to enjoy their success and use their ambition, determination and achievement to encourage you to fulfil your own ambition. You will also encounter people who receive undeserved rewards. Do not let this make you bitter and lead you into radical politics or allow your ambition to tempt you into doing anything that would *compromise your integrity*. If you allow your ambition to lead you into a campaign of revenge when you are wronged or suffer an injustice, you will only be destroying your chance at achieving inner peace and happiness. Such self-centred, spiteful indulgence will lead you into a life of hateful, evil plotting. Let the truth come out; don't engage in wrongful behaviour that will compromise your integrity.

Second, as you become more and more financially secure *do not allow this to affect your relationship with others*. It is possible that you may start to adopt a boastful or *arrogant*, condescending, sarcastic attitude towards those who do not have as much as you. This is fatal for your happiness and well-being, for it will drive others away from you who could have become genuinely friendly with you, and it could lead you further into pride and narcissism. The kind of person others not only dislike but, in some cases, even despise. Do not boast of your good fortune and only offer advice to those who seek it. Always remember to be respectful to others and give due regard to their dignity, regardless of their position in society. Above all else, be courteous and *polite* to all. You never know what you can learn from them.

> *It is impossible for a man to learn what he thinks*
> *he already knows.*
> (Epictetus, Stoic philosopher, 55-135 AD)

Here is a research topic for you. Look up the Stoic virtue of justice. In your own words explain what the Stoics meant by justice. How does it differ from our view of justice today? Can you identify any similarity to the Stoic virtue of justice reflected in my paragraph above?

Arrogance is one possible pitfall to wealth accumulation; *miserly behaviour* is another. Midas was a mythical king of ancient Greece. He was considered the wealthiest man of his time, and believed to have gained the Midas touch, which enabled him to turn everything he touched into gold. This touch was appreciated by Midas when he touched inert objects like stones, bricks etc. and they turned into gold. But his Midas touch (a term in common use today) also turned living things into gold as well. Not so much appreciated, especially after he touched his daughter. Clearly, the moral of this story is not to become obsessed with gold (money) or it will corrupt everything you touch, even your relationship with family members.

The Australian gold rush (1851-1893) spread all around Australia. Starting in Bathurst, New South Wales, and Ballarat, Victoria, it travelled up the east coast of Australia, across the top end and down the west coast where it ended in Kalgoorlie Western Australia. It attracted thousands of gold diggers from around the world in search of alluvial gold and a quick fortune. There was a big gap between their expectations and realisations, but they kept chasing that wonderous precious metal. Their excitement for gold discovery became known as *gold fever*.

As you watch your money grow, it is possible that you too will be struck with the Midas touch or gold fever and become preoccupied with *the love of money*, which will inhibit your ability to reach a truly fulfilling life. There is a big difference between being prudent and being miserly. My advice to help you avoid this fate is to develop a capacity for *charity*. As your wealth grows become a more charitable person, because giving your money away will help you overcome any obsession you may develop towards it, and charity will fill your soul with contentment. Without charity you might become greedy and develop miserly habits.

Consider this. Charity is a two-sided coin; it has a good side and a bad side. The good side involves giving to those who are willing to help themselves, those who are incapable of helping themselves or those who find themselves in an emergency (either a natural or economic disaster) through no fault of their own. There is an old saying, *Charity begins at home*, so make sure your family is properly provided for before you offer charity to others. Charity works best when we help others to fulfil their potential and realise their dreams. It works worse when it enables others to sustain the bad choices they have made. In these cases, charity becomes an *enabler*. Charity can also lead to corruption in those responsible for administering it, so do your due diligence and be judicious in your donations.

The Australian Government even allows tax deductions for some forms of charitable donations. They do this to encourage charitable habits in their citizens. A commendable aim of government. Remember the only people misers help are those who inherit their wealth after they die. We all die at some point in our lives, and we can't take our wealth with us.

When one is young, money is important to acquire. As one grows older, and hopefully wealthier, one looks for other avenues for personal joy and fulfilment. At this point in life, a genuine smile on the face of someone you love becomes more important to you than the money you possess. I am not suggesting that you try to buy someone's happiness. What I am suggesting is getting more involved with those you love. Spend more time with them, encourage them, and when asked, advise them. Relate to them the lessons you have learned from your successes and failures in your own life. You might be surprised at how grateful you will be for their allowing you to spend more time with them. Especially, help the young to help themselves in fulfilling their dreams.

What is your assessment of my advice? Do you think there are pitfalls to acquiring wealth? Have you gained an insight into how your country's economy operates and what opportunities it offers you? Do you think envy and greed can prevent you from fulfilling your potential and, by extension, achieving happiness during your lifetime?

Remember: This all begins with you acquiring a skill that someone else is willing to employ you to use, or starting a business that someone else wants to buy products from; employing hard work, ambition, and initiative in your chosen field of work; and starting and committing yourself to a savings programme. Of course, this is only available to those who live in a country that upholds their liberty (especially the right to own private property) and operates a prudently regulated capitalistic economy. None of this is available in an over-regulated or over-taxed economy or a communist country, because the stated goal of socialism and communism is the abolition of private property and inheritance.

Chapter 7:
Love, Marriage, and Family

I recognise that this chapter may infringe on the proprietary rights (not to be confused with property rights) of parents. Property rights pertain to the ownership of something while proprietary rights define how property may be used and the rights of exclusion to prevent others from access to the property. Therefore, may I respectfully suggest that the following approach be adopted. First, I encourage parents to read the chapter for themselves. If they find it is age-appropriate for their teenage children, they could have them read it or read it together, then follow it up with a discussion of the ideas raised. I consider all the points raised here to be valuable for the maturation of Australia's youth and their gaining a fulfilling and rewarding life, so I hope parents will not censor this chapter merely because it offends them. Remember, the purpose here is to allow our teenage children to grow into mature, critical-thinking adults who can arrive at decisions for themselves. Any disagreement parents have with the material covered here could be explained and alternative views/ideas given to their children.

Before beginning this discussion, I need to explain that I will approach this topic from the conservative and reformist points of view. I will ask you to consider if some of the changes to these cultural cornerstones are actually radical rather than reformist. I do not intend to make value judgements but merely present both sides and allow my readers to draw their own conclusions.

Love

> *And the Lord God said, 'It is not good that the man should be alone: I will make him an help meet (helper, helpmate) for him.'*
> (Holy Bible, Genesis 2:18)

I know that it is provocative to start this chapter with a quote from the *Bible*, but as you read on you will understand why this is important. Please be patient and bear with me. Assume for the purpose of argument that there is a God. Why would God think that it is not good for someone to be alone? In what way could Eve be a 'helpmate'?

So we have established that God wanted two people to share their lives with one another because it is good that they do so. Why would God think it is good? Could it have something to do with procreation and the survival of our species? If this is so, would it not follow that there needs to be an attraction that brings two people together? That attraction we call love, and it can be observed on the transcendental, existential, and archetypical levels of truth. Let's look first at the existential (scientific) level.

> *Falling in love causes our body to release a flood of feel-good chemicals that trigger specific chemical reactions. This internal elixir of love is responsible for making our cheeks flush, our palms sweat and our hearts race.*
> Pat Mumby (PhD). (**Science Daily**, *What Falling in Love does to your heart and brain*, 2014)

The religious and scientific quotes listed above operate on two differing levels of truth: the *Holy Bible* on the transcendental level and Pat Mumby on the existential. Both reveal different aspects about how we view love. Let's now examine what the science tells us about the existential reality of love.

Pat Mumby's article includes more specific information which is relevant to our discussion if we want to get the science settled. The *love elixir*, mentioned in her quote, is comprised of substances like dopamine, adrenaline, and norepinephrine, which all increase when we fall in love with someone. These are feel-good drugs which put us into a state of euphoria.

She goes on to explain that the pleasure centre of our brains light up, blood flow increases, and we experience lower levels of serotonin. Our hormone levels rise and drive within us a passionate hunger toward the object of our desire. These activities are also common with people who experience obsessive-compulsive behaviour. This helps explain the early stages of a love relationship where the person in love is fixated on the person he/she loves.

When our bodies develop a tolerance for the love elixir and our hormone levels drop, we move out of this obsessive-compulsive phase in our love relationship and into a phase of attraction. During this phase our bodies are flooded with endorphins, hormones vasopressin, and oxytocin, which creates within us a sense of well-being and security. We continue to love that person and desire to keep him/her in our life. Because we remain attracted to that special person, we eventually move into a longer lasting relationship based on the continued feelings of well-being and security that we feel towards our partner. Our love remains but is no longer an obsessive-compulsive love, but rather one of commitment and loyalty.

So that's the science. I must say it makes logical sense to me and seems to fit the pattern of my experience. What do you think? Do you think Pat Mumby is onto something? Does her explanation match your experience? Assuming, of course, that you have already experienced a loving relationship with someone. Or maybe you don't believe in love at all. Maybe you think love is all an illusion and not real. That we just temporarily desire someone in a passionate way and then, after some suffering, get over it altogether. That the concept of moving on to a more lasting relationship is just a fiction that you are not interested in.

If you do think that, ask yourself why do you experience a period of suffering after separation? Could this period of suffering we feel after breaking up with someone while in the passionate stage of our relationship be related to an unfulfilled desire to move on to a more mature loving relationship? Could it be that we suffer because we suspect that we might be missing out on a potentially life fulfilling experience? Could the same be said about partners who break up during a commitment/loyalty period of love?

Dr. Mumby seems to be suggesting the existence of two different types of love namely, a *romantic* (obsessive/compulsive) love and a *mature* (committed/loyal) love. One involves desire, passion, and obsessive/compulsive behaviour while the other creates within us a yearning for commitment and loyalty. Our being in love, then, takes us on a journey where we experience both types of love, moving from one to the other in a smooth, ordered way. If this is true, why do homo sapiens experience this? To answer this question we have to leave the existential level of truth and migrate to the archetypical.

All forms of fauna and marine life on earth develop species-related survival habits. Fish, for example, know how to swim from the moment they hatch. Turtles know how to dig themselves out of their sand entombments and crawl to the sea. Notice that they know how to crawl and which direction to go in. On entering the water they also know how to swim. Within minutes of birth, the gazelle, an African plains animal, is on its feet and running with the herd, because the incredible speed and agility of the gazelle is its only defence against predators. All these actions are driven by instinct, these creatures know what to do from the moment of their birth. They do not have to be taught what to do, it comes to them via instinct.

Is it reasonable to believe that modern homo sapiens have also developed survival instincts over the roughly 300,000 years of our existence? If we have, we need to look at the realities of homo sapien existence if we want to discover what these survival instincts are. Human beings have the largest brains of all the species on earth, and after birth need many years of care and attention before reaching self-sufficiency, but for these characteristics we pay a high price.

Because of our large brains, our heads are also large and must pass through the birth canal of the female of our species. This puts a physical toll on them. The pelvic bone in females must be wide enough to accommodate our birth and their bones need to be soft and capable of expansion. This puts a limit on their ability to run, for example. Also, when born, homo sapiens are babies and remain totally dependent on an adult to care for them. For hundreds of thousands of years their food supply during babyhood was gained from their mother's milk, so this baby dependency was borne by the female of our species. Infants also depend on adults to feed, clothe and shelter them. This caretaker role was largely filled by the female of our species and meant that the female of our species was more capable of expressing empathy and compassion for her offspring and less capable of violent aggression and defending herself.

Enter the male of our species, who over hundreds of thousands of years provided that protection. On average, males are taller than females, have stronger upper body and thigh strength, and are more aggressive and competitive than females. Our ancestors dwelt in caves. Males had to clear the caves of any competitors, including sabretooth tigers, bears, snakes etc. This took aggression and courage. Males also hunted for food for the tribe. In Europe, their early food source was mammoths, a huge hairy type of elephant. Male homo sapiens hunted in groups and invented a thrusting spear to kill the mammoths. This meant team cooperation and close quarter fighting, where males were subject to injury (broken bones, etc.) or death. Once injured, the male had to be cared for by the tribe if he was to survive. The hides of the mammoths were also used to create clothing, so after death the beasts had to be skinned, and the meat cut into pieces suitable for cooking, smoking, and drying. These tasks mainly would have been performed by males, as it can be observed in palaeolithic, hunter-gatherer tribes today.

I mention this in order to understand what some of the survival instincts for human beings might be. The female survival instincts appear to be that of caregivers, while the males that of a provider/protector. But the important point for our discussion here is that for our species to survive we needed the commitment and co-operation of both females and males to the common cause of species survival.

This brings us back to how the love pattern of our species is instinctually played out. We need the elixir chemicals of love to create the romantic desire within us which drives males and females to procreate; and the mature aspects of a mature love to care for, protect, and provide for the survival of our species, from babyhood to childhood to the teenage years to adulthood to old age. My point is that the type of love pattern that Dr Pat Mumby describes appears to be instinctual to our species and fulfils a deep desire within us to follow a survival pattern of behaviour.

Before leaving our discussion of the evolutionary effects on sexual behaviour, I would like to raise a different issue for purely interest's sake. Have you ever wondered why men are more territorial about sexual behaviour than women? That is, why are men more demanding about sexual fidelity than women? Women are also sexually territorial, but men can go into homicidal rages over it. Basically, men have evolved that particular response because they want to be sure about their parental certainty. We are a bi-parental species and women have parental certainty while men do not, and men want to be sure about the fatherhood of a child for hereditary reasons (Daly et al., 1982; Buss, 1988). This is another way in which evolution has affected our instinctual sexual behaviour.

Yet another way is how women are more particular about the material circumstances of their partner than what men are. Generally speaking, women want to be assured that their man can provide for and protect them and their offspring. Therefore, women are more selective in their choice of partner than men. An old, anonymous lyrical ballad, *Scarborough Fair*, tells the story of a young maiden who goes to Scarborough Fair and falls in love with a young man. She places impossible material requirements on him before she will marry him. Now she regrets her lost love. Perhaps this conflict between romantic and mature love is a timeless consideration for women.

When I was lecturing in Singapore I had conversations with many young adults from both sexes, and they told me that Singaporean women looked for the 5C's (career, cash, credit card, car, and condominium) in prospective husbands. I wonder if this has become a requirement for many women in countries with developed economies today before they are prepared to fall in love. Could this be an instinctual, species survival behaviour that young women follow?

Now that the existential and archetypical truth of love is understood, we can move back to the transcendental level. Much of our art, since recorded history began, has been preoccupied with love. Love is recorded in our paintings, sculptures, songs, poems, and stories. Most of these representations depict moments of desire, intense passion, fatal attraction, despair, or tragedy while others depict beauty, contentment, serenity, harmony or the love of both a mother and a father towards their offspring. Much of our art, therefore, represents both types of love (romantic and mature) mentioned before.

> *The greatest thing you will ever learn*
> *Is just to love and be loved in return.*
> (Nat "King" Cole, *Nature Boy*, 1948.)

This was a sentiment commonly expressed in the 1940-50s. Do you think it is still popular today? Explain your opinion.

Perhaps the greatest of all love stories is the love portrayed in Shakespeare's play, *Romeo and Juliet*. The first thing of note about his play is that the two main characters in it are teenagers and therefore highly motivated by their emotions. All teenagers go through an intense period of change when their hormone levels rise and affect dramatic changes in their bodies and emotions. These changes are due to the increased levels of eostrogen in the bodies of young girls and testosterone in boys. These increased levels of hormones in the bodies of teenagers drive their sexual attraction for each other.

Such is the case with Romeo and Juliet, who display all the behaviour of romantic love most often observed in teenagers. Romeo and Juliet's love is driven by desire and obsession, and moves fast from intense passion to despair and ultimately suicide. The intensity of their love touches us deeply, and we experience profound sorrow over their tragic demise. A rewarding play with valuable insights into the way teenagers love each other during the romantic (some would say irrational) phase.

Another example is found in a line of dialogue from a classic Hollywood movie, *Midnight to Dawn* (1950). A mother and daughter are talking about a policeman ('Rocky' Barnes) that the daughter likes. The daughter tells her mother that she will never marry a policeman because of the danger to his life every time he goes to work.

> *'Oh, Kate,' her mother replies,*
> *'you love with your heart not your head.'*

That was a sentiment commonly held by my mother's generation and is based on a romantic notion about love. In this movie, the mother's view is the same as that found in Romeo and Juliet's love for each other. After all, Romeo and Juliet fall in love despite coming from the opposite sides of feuding families, the Montagues and the Capulets.

The 1964 musical *Fiddler on the Roof* is a fine artistic depiction of mature love as it existed in Imperial Russia around 1905. The story centres on Tevye, a poor Jewish milkman and his wife, Golde, and the raising of their daughters who are strong-willed and want to marry for love rather than arrangement by a matchmaker. Tevye's daughters' insistence on marrying for love leads him to question the nature of his own marriage to Golde. Is the modern insistence of love before marriage better than their arranged marriage, which began with the first sighting of each other on their wedding day? Do they love each other? He wonders. One of the great songs arising from the musical is *Do You Love Me?* In the song both Tevye and Golde examine the life they have spent together. Golde reflects on the struggles and setbacks they have endured, and the 25 years of hard work and living as one to make their marriage work. She asks Tevye,

> *'If that's not love, what is?'*

They both conclude that after 25 years it's nice to know that they do love each other and are not living together simply because their parents and a matchmaker deemed it so. This story is an affirmation of mature love as well as an insightful musical, well worth watching.

So romantic and mature love is portrayed in our arts, defined in our science and explained by our instinctual drives. In short, our transcendental, existential and archetypical levels of truth confirm it. Are you convinced by this explanation of what love is? Do you accept that this description of love has links with our survival instincts? If you do accept this, would it not also follow that to feel a sense of fulfilment in our lives we would need to participate in long-term, mature love?

The difficulty arises, however, from the ecstasy experienced during the romantic phase of love. Some individuals become addicted to this euphoric feeling and decline to move on to the mature phase, preferring instead to move on to another partner where they can experience the extreme delights of a simple short-time relationship. Alternatively, for those who do move on to a mature relationship, in later life (particularly during middle age and the 'empty nest' phase of their marriage) they develop a longing for the long-absent intensity of the romantic love they have preserved in their memory. They often think,

> *Where did the love go that I once knew?*

This thought leads them to rediscover it with their spouse, but if this fails they are tempted to fall into an affair. Such behaviour is, of course, frowned upon by society who want their citizens to engage in long-term relationships in order to procreate and care for their children. This brings us to an examination of the conservative and reformist views of love.

What is the conservative view?

> *Love is patient and kind; love does not envy or boast; it is not arrogant or rude. It does not insist on its own way; it is not irritable or resentful; it does not rejoice at wrongdoing but rejoices with the truth.*
>
> (New Testament, 1 Corinthians 13:4)

In this passage, what are the qualities that love consists of and what are the qualities it does not consist of? If you were in a loving relationship that upheld these positive qualities, do you think you would be happy? Do you think you would be happy in a loving relationship displaying the negative qualities of love listed in this passage? Explain your position on these qualities in detail. Could it be said that the positive qualities listed here are more empathetic towards one's partner than are the negative qualities?

> *In everything, then, do unto others as you would have them do unto you.*
>
> (New Testament, Matthew 7:12)

This is commonly known as *The Golden Rule,* or the ethical principle of reciprocity. My mother once said to me regarding what to expect from a loving relationship,

> *Ken, when it comes to love, you get what you give.*

This was her way of explaining this principle to me.

If you and your partner followed this ethical principle in a loving relationship, do you think you both would find a lasting treasure in each other's company?

What we have established here are the conservative views of why we should fall in love and what that love should and should not consist of.

Let's turn now to the reformist view of love before moving on to marriage.

Essentially, reformists view conservative concepts of love as being a part of the male domination of society. So they see the conservative view of love where romantic love leads to commitment as establishing an oppressor/oppressed relationship, and they call for women to liberate themselves from this oppression. They claim, women should enjoy sexual freedom and not be locked into one single loving relationship. There is plenty of time to commit after a woman has established a career for herself, and she should not be locked into the role of caregiver/homemaker if she commits to a relationship. They do not seek a 'significant other'. Instead, they seek to learn more about themselves by looking inward rather than outward.

I want to find myself.

This is a sentiment often used by reformists. Both men and women today lay claim to the same liberation from their conservative roles.

How would you classify the reformists' views? As reformist or radical? Do they wish to reform our experience of love or overthrow it?

As we have seen, this runs counter to the archetypical behaviour evolved over thousands of years. However, this approach by reformist men and women is facilitated today because of the long lifespan and low death rate of modern society. The average lifespan of stone age people was just 20-25 years while bronze and iron age adults got to be 30-35 years old (https://exarc.net). The death rate was also staggeringly high. Nearly half of all babies born in prehistoric times, for example, died in the first year of life (anu.edu.au). Also, more than 30% of women in ancient Greece died in childbirth (brandeis.edu). This meant two things – women in prehistoric and ancient times had to conceive very young and have as many children as possible before they died, if our species was to survive. The opposite is obviously the case today. Also, the invention of contraceptive pills and the practice of abortion in modern societies means modern women are not restricted by their biology as much as they were in the past.

Do you think the reformist view of love is more suited to a modern lifestyle? Do you think conservative values still play a role in fulfilling the needs of modern women? How fulfilling do you think the reformist view of love is likely to provide for those who follow the path of their liberation rather than those of conservative values?

What effect do you think this modern reality and reformist approach is having on marriage and the raising of children? Here are some statistics for your consideration. Different sources offer differing figures over different time spans for totals for youth crime (aged between 14-17). For example, 38,621 between 2022-23 (ABS) and 52,742 to 30th Oct 2023 (bond.edu.au). Clearly youth crime is rising. Do you think this could be related to rising divorce rates? For instance, divorce rates in Australia are at 30% (ABS), and almost 50% (separation or divorce) in America (wf-lawyers.com).

Obviously, societies around the world prefer a stable family environment for the raising of children. You can find examples of the encouragement that societies give their citizens to choose the more mature approach to love from the customs and rituals they adopt, which are found in the marriage and family traditions and responsibilities they enforce.

Marriage

Marriage is the coming together and bonding between two individuals. This bonding can be conservative-based (cultural/religious) or reformist-based (secular/legally). It tries to establish what each person engaged in the union can expect from one another in terms of rights and obligations. Marriage is found universally in all cultures around the world and involves similar bonding ceremonies. Some cultures emphasise the religious/cultural nature of marriage, while Western marriage ceremonies have seen an increasing emphasis being placed on the secular/legal aspects of the bonding. One important aspect to marriage is formalising the physical, sexual intimacy of two individuals, and the boundaries pertaining to these activities.

Since a healthy sexual relationship is so important in a marriage and involves issues of not just personal satisfaction but also trust and loyalty, is it important for couples to remain committed to the bond each has established throughout their marriage?

Therefore a man shall leave his mother and his father and hold fast to his wife, and they shall become one flesh.
(*Holy Bible*, Genesis, 2:24)

Do you think a man should put his wife before his father and mother? Why do you think that? In what way can a man and woman become one flesh?

So they are no longer two but one flesh. What therefore God has joined together, let no man separate.
(*New Testament*, Matthew 19:6)

What do you think Jesus is referring to when he says, 'let no man separate'? Do you agree or disagree? Explain your position.

However, let each one of you love his wife as himself, and let the wife see that she respects her husband.
(*New Testament*, Ephesians, 5:33)

How can a man love his wife as himself? Why should a wife be respectful to her husband?

The Biblical quotes above are just three of many quotes dealing with conservative (religious) marriage, which formalises the bond between two individuals, usually by having them publicly swear established oaths to one another in the presence of God. This is a highly spiritual bonding and has a divine purpose (to procreate and keep each other on a moral path), not just a legal one. In terms of our three levels of truth, it is an invocation to enter into a loving relationship based more on the moral/ethical transcendental level than the legalistic/secular existential level, or the base instincts of the archetypical level.

At this point in our discussion on marriages, it is appropriate to review some of the statistics regarding a comparison between conservative (religious-based) marriages and the reformist (secular/legalistic-based) marriages. Conservatives marry younger, and do not cohabit before marriage and have a lower divorce rate than reformist marriages.

> ...we also have evidence suggesting that religious Americans are less likely to divorce even as they are more likely to marry younger than 30.

> ...women who grew up religious are about 20% less likely to begin a cohabiting union in any given year than their non-religious peers.

> ...the annual divorce rate among married women with a non-religious upbringing is around 5%. For religious women it is around 4.5%.
> (ifstudies.org, *The Religious Marriage Paradox: Younger Marriage, Less Divorce*, 2021)

Clearly, both conservative and reformist women can find themselves divorced while having to support children. We should show empathy for these women who are placed in a desperate situation where they may try to find a second husband or support themselves.

Let us turn our attention to reformist marriages, which emphasise the voluntary nature of the marriage, a commitment to live together and an acceptance of divorce if the marriage breaks down. In a reformists' ceremony, marriage vows made to each other are most often written by the individuals involved, which has little to do with a spiritual connection and more with a secular/legal commitment.

Sometimes legal documents in the form of prenuptials are signed to protect the property rights of individuals within the marriage. Owing to the sexual bias exhibited in the custody of children and subsequent distribution of wealth following a divorce, this can happen before both conservative and reformist marriages are entered into.

Regardless of the type of commitment one makes, the purpose of marriage, in terms of societal expectation, is the establishment of a stable environment for the raising of children; the very future of the society itself depends on this. Since society does not see marriage as a purely selfish pursuit of either partner, the legal penalties involved in the dissolution of a marriage can be severe. This has given rise to much dissatisfaction in Western culture when marriages end in divorce settlements. So much so, that many men and women in Western societies are turning away from marriage altogether, preferring instead to engage in a series of sexual partners. This may be in the form of serial monogamy or multiple concurrent partners. This has had a profound effect, not only on the relationship between men and women but also on the birth rate in Western societies, which is now well below replacement level. In Australia the current birth rate is 1.5 (ABS, 2025). The replacement rate is 2.1. This change cannot be seen as anything other than radical, because it radically changes the cultural and societal norms of Australia's previous society.

One can clearly see the difference in conservative and reformist values from their attitude towards marriage. People upholding conservative values are committed to long-established cultural norms passed down through the generations of the society they live in. It involves a commitment to the time-tested moral, ethical, and religious beliefs of their society. Reformist values, by contrast, centre more around the pursuit of self-interest, personal accomplishment and personal happiness.

I need to find (discover) myself.
I am not happy in my marriage.
I only get one life; and life is not a dress rehearsal.

These are sentiments often expressed by either reformist partner when contemplating divorce or engaging in an affair. Communities with reformist values are more understanding and accommodating towards this behaviour than conservatives.

Of course, some individuals espousing conservative values also engage in extra-marital behaviour, but in doing so they isolate themselves from their conservative community. Some conservatives, however, are more accommodating towards this behaviour than others. Despite the dominance of Catholicism in their culture, for example, the French have a reputation for being sophisticated about taking on lovers and mistresses and do not allow this to interfere in their family life.

From our earlier discussion about romantic and mature love, can you see any connection between conservative and reformist types of love and marriage? Can it be said that those expressing reformist values are more likely to seek fulfilment through romantic love, while those upholding traditional values would be more likely to seek it through mature love? Keeping in mind what we discovered about instinctual behaviour, which of these values do you think is more suitable for the raising of children and more likely to provide individuals with a sense of self-fulfilment?

Family

A family is a group of people related to each other through birth, marriage, or adoption. The purpose of a family is to provide its members and society with stability and well-being.

Conservative families follow a long-established relationship whereby the male partner works outside the family and takes on the role of provider and protector of his family while the female partner manages the home and children. The conservative view of family is that parents have proprietary rights over their children.

When it comes to marriage and family today, however, many women, because of financial necessity, are expected to balance the roles of career, mother, and wife. Is this possible? Feminists and Hollywood argue that

women can have it all

while others like Michelle Obama and Oprah Winfrey (interview with Oprah at 'The United State of Women Summit', 2016) and Indra Nooyi, former CEO of PepsiCo (CBS News interview with Margaret Brennan, 2019), believe

women can have it all, but not at the same time.

This seems to suggest that reformist values involve a *trade-off* between career, motherhood, and wifehood for the reformist woman. The priority suggested is usually in that order. This is, of course, a precise inversion of the values found in conservative families, which starts with the husband and wife becoming one in their struggles with life. Again, decide for yourself if this is a reformist or radical approach to change.

What, then, are the choices that women are asked to make in today's society? First there is the choice which involves putting their *career* above everything else. This would involve a single lifestyle or a childless marriage or partnership. Alternatively, they could choose a *family* above everything else. This would involve them in giving up their career and devoting themselves to the conservative lifestyle of wife and mother. Third is a choice involving a *compromise* between these two lifestyles. By definition, this third choice must result in sacrifice, choices and trade-offs, and this, by necessity, must involve a priority of some sort involving the roles of career, mother and wife having to be made by the women who choose this lifestyle.

Look at the female lifestyles found in Western countries today. Is it likely that young adults (18 to 34) will be attracted to reformist values while those older adults (35+) will be more desirous of finding a partner who upholds conservative values? Today, the conservative and reformist approaches are both faced with the same problem. Those who seek fulfilment through creating and raising a family need to find each other, get married and start a family before the woman enters the 35+ period of her life, because this is the reality of a woman's biological clock. It is also a more natural, instinctual approach to life, as well as the time when women are at their most fertile and better able not only to produce healthy offspring but also care for them, being fitter and stronger in their youth.

Can you find evidence of this by observing your society? Can it be said that only those who adhere to mature love should start a family, since that love is more likely to provide children with the stable family environment needed for their education and maturation? Alternatively, do you believe that women should seek to have a career, children and a husband, either concurrently or at different times of their lives? Which would be the best time for a woman to have children – before they pursue a career, after they have established one, or concurrently?

The Institute of Family Studies (IFS) in America did an analysis of a General Social Survey in 2021 and concluded that the majority of women in the 18-34 range were happy about not having children, while the majority of women in the 35+ range were unhappy about not having children. This fact runs counter to the smooth path from romantic to mature love and the biological demands of starting a family.

Since families form the foundation of a society, much attention is given to them by their governments. In the past, it was accepted that parents held the proprietary rights over their children. That is, it was up to parents to teach their children the socially, morally, and ethically acceptable behaviour of a good citizen. It is this right that provides parents with the greatest satisfaction for establishing a family in the first place. Parents and grandparents derive great pleasure and happiness from watching their descendants grow into mature and independent adults, through their guidance, care and oversight.

However, much of this has come under challenge today, and Western Governments have been met with increasing dissatisfaction from parents with conservative values who believe that their governments have encroached too far onto their proprietary rights. At the moment this conflict is polarising Western societies, between those who want greater government control over the education of children and those who believe that it is the parents' right to oversee the education of their own children. This becomes heated when the values and standards espoused by governments clash with those held by parents with conservative values. Much of this conflict centres around preferred sexual behaviour and the conservative and reformist values held by each group. Where this will lead to in the future is uncertain, but governments will have to become involved in settling these differing opinions or face increasing levels of social unrest and instability.

One factor that has led to this unrest has been the emergence of feminism, which has evolved through three stages (some now say four), and each stage challenged the conservative family values and standards of the society at that time. I recognise that our discussion has now entered into an area of high emotional commitment on the part of the advocates of both sides of this debate, but I feel the need to explain the claims of both sides and let you decide for yourself where you stand. It is impossible to present a study on family without mentioning the changes that feminism has brought to it over the years.

Feminism, as it is understood today, first emerged in Western societies with the suffragette movement of the late 19th and early 20th centuries. At that time women were fighting for the right to vote and protested under the banner, *Votes for Women*. After a struggle of some proportions and duration, women were given the vote in Western societies, and over time most people accepted that women did indeed have a right to vote. What is less well known about this movement, however, is that it also supported the concept of free love and contraception (at this time limited to unreliable methods).

Free love is a social movement that believes the state should not play a role in sexual matters like sexual behaviour, birth control, marriage, and adultery. The best-known British advocates of free love during this time was the philosopher Bertrand Russell (1872-1970), and Mary Gove Nichols (1810-1884) a well know suffragette who described marriage as

> *the annihilation of woman.*
> (www.connexions.org, 2025)

You see, working class women at that time usually had large families, ranging from 6 to 12 children, and the suffragettes saw this as keeping women bonded to their families as they struggled to keep them fed, housed, and clothed. They also argued that marriage made women the property of men in law and public sentiment, thereby allowing tyrannical men to deprive their women of their freedom. The suffragettes wanted women to be free to live what they claimed was a more fulfilling life, believing women were incapable of achieving this through their families alone. It was these values (free love, contraception, and equality in marriage) that would be taken up by later feminist movements.

The second-wave feminists emerged during the 1960s after the invention of the contraceptive pill and the enormous economic growth of Western economies. They demanded that women have the right, if they so choose, to work for

equal pay for work of equal value

which they did not have at that time. Again, most reasonable people saw this as a justifiable request and supported it. However, it was the choice between work and family that became the most contentious issue for second-wave feminism. In an interview with Betty Friedan in 1975, for example, Simone de Beauvoir said,

No woman should be authorised to stay at home and raise her children. Society should be totally different. Women should not have that choice precisely because if there is that choice, too many women will make that one.
(https://en.rattibha.com/thread)

Do you agree with Simone de Beauvoir? If given a viable, financial choice would most women prefer to stay at home with their children? Do you think second-wave feminists wanted women to devote themselves to a career by deliberately encouraging them to undervalue motherhood? Would you consider this goal on the part of second-wave feminism to be reformist or radical?

What also went with this second-wave feminism was the re-emergence of free-love thinking. Second-wave feminism advocated for the removal of any stigma that might exist about women engaging in pre-marital sex, as the emergence of the contraceptive pill meant that women could now control their conception. They claimed that men engaged in pre-marital sex (a double standard), so women should have the right to do so as well. This argument is based on a logical fallacy, *tu quoque* (Latin for 'you too' or 'you also') or an appeal to hypocrisy. Just because someone else does not live up to a certain standard that does not give you the right to not live up to it.

A double standard did exist at that time, but those with conservative values frowned upon it. In fact, a man who engaged in this activity in British society was called a *cad* (a negative British slang word). In a more religious context *fornicator* is the word used. This is where the first substantial clash with conservative values occurred. You see, conservative values hold that both men and women should abstain from pre-marital sex. Promiscuous sex by either men or women is vilified as dishonourable behaviour by conservatives who believe this, not just because of conception reasons but also to avoid the possibility of being infected with an STD, which could affect not just the active party but also their future partner and offspring. They also believe that pre-marital sex erodes the value and commitment that women and men make to their marriages and families. That men and women who engaged in pre-marital sex are more likely to divorce their spouses and leave their families for another man or woman championing free-love thinking. Both men and women who take married partners from a marriage are looked on by conservatives as home wreckers.

Reformists, on the other hand, claimed that men and women living in a loveless marriage for the sole purpose of raising their children would be damaging for them and their children. The dissatisfaction each would feel for the other would not be conducive to a healthy environment for their children to be raised in. That is, the likelihood of arguments and potential violence of both partners towards each other would inhibit their children from developing their own loving relationships.

What does the scientific evidence tell us about how children fare in an intact marriage versus a divorced marriage?

> *Nearly three decades of research evaluating the impact of family structure on the health and well-being of children demonstrates that children living with their married, biological parents consistently have better physical, emotional and academic*

> well-being... *The scientific literature to date suggests that, with the exception of parents faced with unresolvable marital violence, children fare better when parents work at maintaining their marriage. Consequently, society should make every effort to support healthy marriages and discourage married couples from divorcing.*
>
> (pcm.ncbi.nlm.nih.gov, The Linacre Quarterly, *The Impact of Family Structure on the Health of Children: Effects of Divorce, 2014*)

The issues of free love and divorce created a divide between those espousing conservative values and those championing reformist values. A divide which would become a chasm after third-wave feminism emerged.

Do you think attitudes towards pre-marital sex by conservatives is pompous or are reformists too promiscuous?

Third-wave feminism has so many fronts to it that it is difficult to remember them all, so please excuse me if I miss some. Before we start our discussion, however, it must be pointed out that third-wave feminists view society through the eyes of Marxist ideology, i.e., a struggle between the oppressed and the oppressors. Second-wave feminism also highlighted this belief, but it became more pronounced during third-wave feminism and migrated into other groups in society who accepted the oppressed/oppressor model of societal hierarchy. These other groups are supported by third-wave feminists. Third-wave feminists see society as a hierarchy dominated by a patriarchy which largely excludes women. They claim that men in general maintain this hierarchy through oppression. They believe women are oppressed and men are their oppressors.

First, third-wave feminists claim that women and men are not paid the same. Remember that the initial claim of second-wave feminists was for *equal pay for work of equal value*. It was never expected that women would receive the same pay if they did work of *unequal value*.

This is a hotly contested issue today. Men claim that they do more overtime, work dirtier and more dangerous jobs, and generally work in higher paying (STEM) jobs than women, so overall are paid more. This argument has some validity, because it is now illegal for employers to pay different hourly rates of pay for men and women doing the same work. The hourly pay rate is, of course, different for different jobs. For instance, men and women who risk their lives in jobs which protect the public (police, firefighters, and soldiers) are generally paid more, because there is more personal danger in those jobs. It's just that fewer women than men take up these occupations. Sporting women claim that they should be paid the same as men playing in the same sport, regardless of how popular their sport is. Men argue that sportswomen should be paid what their sport can afford. If their sport raises more than men's sport they should be paid more, if it raises less they should be paid less. Sportsmen, generally, reject the argument that requires their sport to subsidise sportswomen, because it leads to less money being offered to sportsmen in their contracts.

Second, third-wave feminists want to hold the same number of jobs in higher fields of employment that are currently occupied predominately by men. To achieve this, governments and companies have introduced affirmative action (DEI) programmes designed to achieve the same number of men and women working in these fields of employment. Remember, second-wave feminists were against discrimination, because they believed it favoured men, now third-wave feminists are arguing in favour of discrimination because it favours women. Men argue that women can now enter these fields of employment if they have the same merit (qualifications, experience, and competency) as men, so why does society need to discriminate to achieve something many women generally don't want or are not as competent at as men? Men also want to know if women want the same number of jobs in the dirty and dangerous fields of work. Men ask if women want to break into society's cellar as well as its ceiling. Men are also arguing that women should now be subjected to conscription since they are calling for equality with men. Men believe that third-wave feminists want women to be liberated from their conservative values (homemaker and family caregiver), but for men to remain bound by their traditional values (provider and protector) because the child custody and divorce settlements favour women over men.

What do you think? If women can be liberated from their conservative roles should men also be entitled to the same liberation?

Conservatives see all this as an attack on their values. Conservative women, in particular, want their husbands to work hard for their families and see all this as sapping their husbands' work ethic and eroding the chances of promotion for their husbands and sons, and they definitely do not want female conscription which would take them from their families.

Third, third-wave feminists tell women that family commitment should be secondary to career ambition. For example, they encourage women to put off having children until they have climbed the corporate ladder. This usually means putting off having children until women are in their late 30s, beyond the ideal time for childbearing. This leads the majority of women who are without children in their late 30s feeling they have missed out on something important in their lives. This is not surprising given our earlier discussion about the biological reality of women and homo sapiens' survival instincts.

Conservative women, on the other hand, want to start their families at the time when they are most fertile, fit and strong, and put off their careers (work) while they have children and care for them until their children start school. Owing to the inability of most men to be the sole providers in today's economy, most women support government subsidies for child-minding and pre-school centres, so they can place their children in these centres while they go back to work. This can, and most often does, cause women with conservative values to feel guilty about sharing the care of their infants with outsiders. The majority of conservative women today also feel that these centres are teaching their children values that they do not ascribe to.

Conservative men want to maintain their conservative role as provider and protector for their families but find it difficult to maintain this position in a society economically geared for two income families. Many find the wants and needs of their families beyond their earning capacity. Having to see their wives working, when their wives would rather be at home with their children, leaves conservative men feeling shame and guilt at their inadequacy to live up to their preferred conservative values.

Do you think these problems create an unfair hinderance for those couples espousing conservative values?

Fourth, third-wave feminists make the claim that abortion is a human right of women, some even arguing in favour of abortion up to the moment of birth. Conservatives claim that life begins at the moment of conception (DNA and sex having been established) and therefore that abortion at any stage of pregnancy is taking the potential life of a future human being. The emergence of family planning clinics has also caused much contention. Third-wave feminists claim that these clinics should be government funded since abortion is a women's health issue, while conservatives argue that their taxes should not be used in the taking of a potential human being's life. The same arguments are made over the cost of contraception, which third-wave feminists see as a women's health issue, while conservatives argue that the use of contraception is an individual choice, and, as such, should be paid for by the individuals engaging in pre-marital sexual activity, married couples who do not want to have children, or those engaged in adulterous behaviour.

We have also witnessed the emergence of a men's rights movement, where men are calling for the right to a financial abortion from their offspring when in their mother's womb. They argue that if a woman can claim an abortion on the grounds of lifestyle choice, why can't men claim the same thing? They are also calling for DNA testing on all newborn babies, because DNA challenges in court have resulted in 30% being found not to belong to the father claimed by women (dnatesting.com/paternity-fraud). The state of Tennessee in America has now passed legislation making it compulsory for DNA tests to be done on a potential father and the baby before he signs a form accepting that he is the father. As stated before, the men's rights movement is also calling for female conscription.

Men are also claiming that they should have equal custody of their children following a divorce. More than 90% of the time, the Family Law Court grants the mother primary custody (melbournefamilylawyers.com.au, 2023). Men argue that the current custody decisions by the Family Law Court discriminates in favour of women. They assert that since men and women have now been liberated from their conservative roles in society, why should such discrimination continue.

What are the statistics regarding who typically makes the better parent in single parent families, men or women –

> *Studies have found that children from single mother households are 5 times more likely to commit suicide than both unbroken and single father households, 9 times more likely to drop out of high school, 10 times more likely to abuse chemical substances, 14 times more likely to commit rape, 20 times more likely to end up in prison and 32 times more likely to run away from home…. Single mother households also account for 70% of all teenage pregnancies, 70% of all child murders, and they account for the majority of filicide cases (a parent killing their own child)…*
> (medium.com, *Single Father Households Do Vastly Better Than Single Mother – Here's The Reason Why*, April 9, 2023)

These statistics can be attributed to differences in family structure, socioeconomic factors, and potential outcomes. Although the outcomes are evidently different, it should be recognised that these outcomes are not present in all single mother households. Many single mothers struggle to provide the best outcomes for their children and many succeed. However, it cannot be denied that the statistics clearly show that, generally speaking, single father households provide better outcomes for their children than do single mother households.

Fifth concerns the education of children. Here third-wave feminists (using intersectional feminist ideology) demand the right of government to provide sex education for children, even at pre-school level. Much tension has arisen over the issue of gender dysphoria, with kindergarten children being taught that gender is fluid. Conservatives argue that this educational responsibility falls under their proprietary domain and not that of government, while third-wave feminists contend that they want to create safe environments for children who believe they are not the gender they were born with. Conservatives counter that children are not capable of understanding what adult teachers are telling them during these sessions, and that the teachers are instead indoctrinating their children into believing things that will create confusion and uncertainty in their children's lives and potentially lead to future unhappiness.

Add to this the fact that children are naturally inclined to believe what they are told, because their trust levels are designed to alleviate the necessity of constant evaluation of everything they hear (Vikram Jaswal, *Young children have a specific, highly robust bias to trust testimony*, National Library of Medicine, 2010) and you have another anxiety factor for mothers to handle.

Is my child being told the same things that I value?

This would be a question that would constantly play on the mind of a conservative mother, if her child was being taught by someone she suspected of holding third-wave feminist values.

Third-wave feminists argue that they want to reduce the suicide rate among transsexuals. They claim short-term studies support this claim but conservatives oppose this with long-term studies which they claim do not. Conservatives also point to an increasing number of transexuals who had transitioned now wanting to de-transition, only to find they have inflicted irreversible damage on their bodies. Once this spills over into gender affirmation treatments like hormone blockers and even sex-altering surgery on minors, sometimes without the consent of parents, there seems little room for conservatives to move except into open defiance of authority. Where this will lead to in future should be of concern to all citizens of Western societies.

Six, third-wave feminists argue for the inclusion of transgender females into female sports. They view this as an integral part of intersectional feminism. They claim that transgender women are women and therefore entitled to compete in women's sport. Conservatives point out the disparity in the physical ability of biological women to compete with transexual women. With so many transexual women winning women's competitions, conservatives argue, it is only a matter of time before transexual women will hold all the women's records of achievements. Obviously, this becomes a serious problem for biological women wanting to gain scholarships, and who have dedicated their life to training for such an opportunity.

Conservatives and young biological women also object to sharing ablutions with transgender women for modesty and safety reasons. Third-wave feminists argue that transexual women are afraid for their safety when forced to use male ablutions, while conservatives argue the same point for women, pointing out that teenage girls at schools have been sexually assaulted by teenage boys claiming to be transexual girls, and women in women's prisons have become pregnant after transexual women were incarcerated in their prisons. Some transexual women now claim that they are lesbian women. Conservatives ask, is she a heterosexual male?

Many of these ideas and demands of third-wave feminists have been taken up by other reformist minority groups in Western societies who perceive themselves to be oppressed. For example, reformist individuals increasingly identify with groups based on sex, race, and gender. Also, reformists now maintain that intersectional groups, that is groups that believe they intersect with one or more of the other disadvantaged groups, should be given priority over those claiming single group identity. Members of these intersectional groups now demand priority over the other singularly disadvantaged groups. This victim mentality, involving perceived oppression, discrimination, and disadvantage, seems to have embarked on an endless process of metastasis, which will make it impractical for Western governments and society generally to accommodate all its demands. Naturally, reformists support these claims, while conservatives reject them.

It has been said that —

> *Third-wave feminists often engaged in "micro-politics" and challenged the second-wave paradigm as to what was good for women.*
>
> (wikipedia.org)

Do you think third-wave feminism is a reformist or radical movement?

This situation in Western societies has arisen since the Industrial Revolution. Why is this? Let's look back on what we discovered previously about the instinctual habits of homo sapiens. For our species to survive thousands of years ago the birth rate had to be high, because the death rate was also high. Women often died in childbirth while the majority of their offspring died either during childbirth or as a result of the harsh conditions of their lives which were much shorter than today. For these reasons women usually started to menstruate in their early teens and were most fertile up to their mid-30s. (Remember that a 40-year-old was rare at this time.) This is still the biological reality of women's ability to conceive today, but the death rate has dropped dramatically since the beginning of the

Industrial Revolution. This is due to the astonishing improvements in things like food production, medicine, hygiene, and education, fewer women dying in childbirth, fewer offspring dying in childbirth, and fewer children dying as they grew into adulthood. As well as this, contraception and abortion are available for women to determine how many children they have.

The point is that women no longer need to spend their entire lives producing the next generation. Consequently, an increasing number of women want to limit (or eliminate altogether) the number of children they have during their lives, and spend more of their lives educating themselves and pursuing careers. One thing is clear, those countries where women are better educated are experiencing a dramatically declining birth rate. In most rich countries today the birth rate is below the level needed for sustainability. Just as the high birth rate increased population growth exponentially, so the birth rate below replacement does the reverse.

This is of major concern for the governments of countries with developed economies, because a country's economy cannot sustain itself at these low birth rates. Eventually, there will come a time when there are more older people in these countries than young ones needed to support them. Most developed countries have addressed this problem with immigration, but this will only last while there is an economic incentive for people to migrate. If the economies of developed countries decline, or emerging economies grow to levels where it is no longer attractive for their people to emigrate, or the women of emerging economies lower their countries' birth rate, today's developed countries will fall into an existential crisis. Increased immigration also disregards the fact that today's immigrants will one day be tomorrow's elderly much faster than the natural cycle, which creates a never-ending need for more and more immigration.

At some point in the future it will be necessary for governments to encourage women to recognise that they need to change their desire for 1-2 children to that of 2-3 or even 4. In Poland, for example, women who have four or more children have a lifetime exemption from paying tax (politico.eu 2023). This type of government action might encourage women with conservative values to have more children and devote themselves to their families, but they will still need to work if they want to receive the tax exemption. Perhaps a scale of tax exemptions for couples with three or more children might be more effective.

Unfortunately, it seems Western societies are rapidly dividing into two irreconcilable camps. Conservatives in the past were content to stick together while espousing a *live and let live* approach to these changes by accepting that reformists have the same right as them to live their lives according to their reformist values. Conservatives also believe that reformists also have the right to express their opinions but not the right to impose them on others. This leads conservatives to conclude that reformists not only want to live according to their values but are trying to enforce, through government legislation and economic necessity, what conservatives now view as radical values on others.

Consequently, conservatives have begun to fight back. They have invented the term *lawfare* to describe the actions of government to enforce radical values on them and are calling for an end to this practice. They are also calling for economic changes that will enable families to thrive on a single income. They now believe that they are involved in a legal and economic battle over the continued existence of their conservative lifestyle.

Can this continue? That is difficult to determine given the potential changes owing to AI and robotics. Whatever the outcome, we are seeing an increasing number of women who followed third-wave feminist and reformist values regretting their decision in their late 30s and beyond, because the men who were once sexually attracted to them have now turned their attention to younger women. Having spent their youth upholding reformist values by engaging in long-term career commitments and short-term relationships with men, women with previously reformist values now want to marry and start a family. The realisation that they may end their lives alone without children or grandchildren to comfort them in their old age frightens them.

Alternatively, they may have tried to 'have it all at the same time' and so alienated their husbands that their marriages ended in divorce. Many 35+ women now ask where all the good men have gone. Whenever we hear stories like this, we obviously empathise with the situation these women find themselves in. Their plight seems to fit the two types of love we discovered before. Whereas they were once happy to engage in a succession of men offering them romantic love, or putting their career before their marriage and family which led to their divorce, they now feel a deep desire to move on to a man who will show a genuine interest in them and is willing to commit to them and show loyalty towards their families. One wonders what these women mean when they now say there are no longer any *good men* to be found. If by that they mean men with conservative values, those men have all married and committed themselves to traditional women and the families they have created.

Consider this. What if the Western hierarchy is not male dominated but rather *apex* dominated? What if this apex is comprised of both males and females who dominate our society by manipulating our economy through the ownership of its powerful elements like technology, finance and media, and our politics through the use of money and power to corrupt our democratic process? What if this apex uses greed and fear to manipulate us and has established organisations like the UN and WEF to achieve their goals, like globalisation, mass immigration, open borders, and an end of liberty, democracy, and nation states? What if these organisations use envy, jealously, and hatred generated from theories like socialism, sexism, racism, war, climate emergency, pandemics, and global financial collapse to gain hierarchical control and domination over societies? What if our apex elites are using Post-Modernist theories about social engineering to manipulate and control us into creating a New World Order they so forcefully inflict on our society? Of course, all this could be nothing more than just another conspiracy theory, but what if this hierarchy's apex uses the accusation of conspiracy theory to hide their agenda? I know that such speculation seems fanciful, but is it worth consideration?

Alternatively, what if life is not that complicated? What if all this talk about hierarchies and dominance and all its theories of socialism, sexism, gender, racism, climate emergency, globalisation etc. is nothing more than the indulgence of overeducated imaginations with nothing better to do with the abundance of free time in their lives? What if the reality is simply that individuals struggle to find a better way to survive? What if they merely want to be better people by maintaining their integrity, by always telling the truth without the corrupting influence of greed, envy or fear. What if they co-operate with other individuals through marriage, family, friendships, and associations for no other reason than simply to survive in a hostile, indifferent environment? What if the only ones to achieve true happiness in their lives are the ones who put the maximum effort, devotion and passion into this rudimentary philosophy and these four human relationships encountered in their lives? Could this be closer to the truth?

Before closing this chapter, allow me to indulge myself by offering parents some advice. Whatever values and standards you decide to encourage your children to follow, make sure you live by them yourself. No doubt you have heard the saying,

Do as I say, not as I do.

This is the creed of hypocrites, and teenagers are just as sensitive to hypocrisy as we are to it in our leaders. Don't expect your teenage children to live by standards and values you are not prepared to live by yourself. If you live the values and standards you preach, your children will respect you for it. You will not be immune from the storm and stress of their teenage years, because free-thinking teenagers will always test the boundaries, but their respect for you will help them mature into adulthood.

I am reminded of a joke I once heard. Two young men were talking. One said to the other, 'When I was 18 I couldn't believe how ignorant my father was. When I turned 21, I couldn't believe how much he had learned in just 3 short years.'

I have thrown a lot of facts and ideas at you in this chapter. What is your opinion about them? Do you find any validity in what we have shared? Do you have alternative views? Whichever way you answer these questions, I hope you have found value in giving these ideas consideration. Have you?

One piece of advice in closing this chapter, be discerning about who you fall in love with, who you marry, and who you start a family with. It can mean the difference in your life between success and failure, happiness or misery.

First be cognisant about the difference between passionate, romantic love and the commitment necessary for mature love.

Ask yourself,

Am I prepared to share the rest of my life with this person?
Am I prepared to create and raise children with this person?

Since financial stress is a major contributing factor in marriage breakdown, be sure you know how much debt your prospective partner carries before you marry. It is no good discovering this after you are married. You could begin by making sure you know the answer to this question –

Does this person share the same financial goals as me?

Keep in mind that –

Some people are happy with less, others want more, and some are never happy no matter how much they have.

When I wrote the first draft of this book, I had intended to stop at this point, but I felt something was missing. That something was an examination and evaluation of the malignant, post-modernist nightmare Australia now struggles to awaken from.

As I present my opinion about this struggle, please forgive me if I repeat some of the evidence I have already used in my previous examination of important Australian values, because I am now investigating a very different issue, but some of the evidence may remain the same even though it proves different points.

I know some Australians will be challenged by my opinions, but no offence is intended; my only focus is on a factual examination of the current attack on Australia's culture, not any individual or group.

For me, two iconic Australian images spotlight the nightmare that is gripping Australia. The rugged, practical beauty of the Sydney Harbour Bridge, once a symbol for Australia's unity linking its past with its future, and the symmetrical beauty of the Sydney Opera House, once a symbol of Australia's arrival into a New World, both now forever stained with the bile of antisemitic hatred of Israel.

Oh, Australia, where is your moral clarity?

Chapter 8:
New World Issues

This chapter contains my own opinions about some current Australian issues. It is not a comprehensive list and I believe you will find some social, political, and economic issues yourself that remain unsolved. Hopefully, you will be able to apply the definitions and critical thinking skills we have developed here to analyse and evaluate problems and arrive at solutions for yourself. Earlier, I told you that you should not study politics until you are ready to explore the issues dispassionately and objectively. The remaining part of this book is for those of you who feel you have reached a level of understanding and maturity that will enable you to take this approach.

I hope to apply some of the *truths* we have discovered so far to this topic. Many of the new world issues found here did not exist during my generation and seem to be bringing an end to the world I experienced in my lifetime, so be careful before accepting my opinions at face value; they may be tinged with nostalgia and cynicism. All that we have shared here so far tells you not to accept my conclusions without testing my assumptions and facts, checking for logical fallacies, then asking, are my opinions logical? Are they reasonable? Are they wise? Do they make common sense? Are they empathetic to those of the past and present? So here goes, sharpen your critical pens.

Arthur Bloch (1922-2005), author of *Murphy's Law*, once said,

> Friends come and go but enemies accumulate.

After reading this difficult yet intriguing section on Australian's current problems, I trust you will appreciate just how much this expression applies to the New World you are about to inherit. In speaking my truth about these problems, I hope I will not accumulate too many enemies, and that those who are my friends will stand by me.

Many Australians today accept that

the current generation is less likely to be as prosperous as the previous one.

They believe this based primarily on their observation of a widening wealth gap between not only the rich and poor but also the older and younger generations; stagnant living standards for younger people; increasing costs like housing, energy, and food; and a dividing of Australian society into groups consumed with envy, greed, and even hatred. It is my belief that this trend can be reversed, first by identifying the underlying causes of these problems, then analysing them, and finally creating practical and prudent solution for them.

To this end, I have divided Australia's current problems into five categories: *Moral Integrity*, *Political Integrity*, *Economic Integrity*, *Cultural Integrity*, and *National Integrity*. I will look at each problem separately, define the problem as I see it, and provide probable solutions for your consideration. Again, I do not profess to be the harbinger of absolute truth, nor the provider of correct solutions. Hopefully, however, my suggestions may be given due consideration, and if implemented, prove to be effective.

As you read on, keep in mind one overarching principle –

As goes the individual citizen, so goes the nation.

Moral Integrity

Moral integrity constitutes the consistent, honest adherence to a personal and societal set of deeply held moral principles and values, even when faced with pressure, temptation, or difficult situations.

Liberal democratic societies base their morals on liberty, equality, democracy, citizen rights, community involvement, and environmental stewardship. This sense of freedom and individualism can produce a rich society, both in terms of culture and wealth. However, that same sense of freedom and individualism can lead liberal democratic societies into atomisation, where a state breaks down from unity into self-interest, individual isolation, and hedonistic materialism. Once lost, the only way for a liberal democracy to regain its social cohesion is to reassert its commitment to moral integrity. To this end, I will examine three moral choices available to citizens of liberal democracies, examine their strengths and weaknesses, and give reasons why I choose one over the other two. The three moral choices I will examine are *moral certainty*, *moral equivalence*, and *moral clarity*. Although I use the word 'moral' in this analysis, it should be understood that 'moral', in this instance, also embraces *ethical* behaviour.

Moral Certainty

Moral certainty is a state of subjective certainty leaving no real doubt about a matter.

(Merriam-Webster)

Those who use moral certainty in their lives have an absolute conviction that their moral judgement is right and therefore better than all others. They operate on a level of morality that leaves no doubt in their minds as to the righteousness of their convictions. Unfortunately, such conviction can and does lead to religious intolerance and, in modern times, to ideological fanaticism. Both religious intolerance and ideological fanaticism lead their devoted believers into prejudice against those who do not believe. It becomes the justification for replacing liberty with religious intolerance or ideological fanaticism, replacing democracy with authoritarianism or totalitarianism.

A major problem with moral certainty is that each religion or ideology claims exclusive rights for their interpretation of transcendental truth, when this level of truth is, in fact, accessible to everyone. Does this mean that the interpretation of transcendental truth is limited only by the imagination of every individual human being who exercises their personal interpretation of transcendental truth? Well no, because we all have a light of understanding, of recognition of the beautiful and the good, and this light is what leads us to accept the good and reject the evil, of endorsing the beneficent and rejecting the malevolent. This light of understanding within us all is what has been known throughout the ages as God; the *Ipsum Esse Subsistens,* the ultimate, foundational reality (St. Thomas Aquinas, *Summa Theologiae,* 1846.) who directs our understanding, our consciousness towards the good and the beautiful. This Godly concept is found in all cultures and civilisations across time. It is universal and timeless. The accepting of good and the rejection of evil is what makes culture and civilisation possible, so if we want to live in a cultured, civilised way this fundamental principle must be central to our understanding of transcendental truth. Those who claim exclusive right to God, however, promote their moral certainty at the expense of all others.

When religious intolerance rules countries, it results in malevolent theocracy, where the immoral, according to the judgement of its moral certainty, are punished in the most inhumane ways. Stoning to death for adulterers, burning to death at the stake for heretics, and beheadings for homosexuals and infidels, for example, are just some of the punishments administrated by the morally certain theocrats, both past and present. Such punishments are viewed as just by those who are certain about their moral convictions. What can be just as bad is the enforcement of boundless compassion by the morally certain believers. The stealing of wealth from the next generation, or even from those (without their consent) who have *justly* accumulated wealth, to satisfy the morally certain believer's commitment to boundless compassion is itself morally wrong, not to mention impractical.

At the same time, it needs recognising that religious moral certainty needed a warrior class to protect and spread its influence. Before Christianity was adopted by the Romans as their Imperial religion, for example, it was a small offshoot of the Hebraic religion. True it was growing by the example of early Christian martyrs, but it still had a long way to go before becoming the influential religion it is today. When Mohammad left Mecca for Medina he was a humble preacher. Later he built a conquering warrior class of Muslims who returned to Mecca, subdued it, and spread Islam across Arabia. Later, after Mohommad's death, that same warrior class invaded and conquered north Africa, and temporally invaded Christian Europe.

Christianity and Islam became so influential because of the hero narrative of their founders. Joseph Campbell describes the elements of a hero narrative in his book, *The Hero With a Thousand Faces*, in which he reveals the hero narrative found in ancient mythology and modern literature. The hero narrative fills us with inspiration, hope, and cultural identity by portraying courageous characters who overcome obstacles by exhibiting ethical behaviour and integrity. What is true for the heroes found in mythology and literature is also true for the founders of Christianity and Islam.

The appeal of Christianity can be found in the heroic nature of Jesus' biography. Jesus is a man born into an ordinary existence who is called by God into a *divine mission*. Angels appear to him as *mentors* to school and strengthen him during a time of *trial*. Later he performs his *quest* in the form of his ministry, teaching and performing miracles. Finally, he must face the *supreme ordeal*: his crucifixion, where his death and subsequent resurrection reconciles humanity with God by atoning for their sins and defeating the power of sin, death, and Satan. There can be no doubt that this hero narrative is central to the appeal of Christianity for everyone, especially the early Christian martyrs and next the warrior class who were prepared to surrender their lives in its cause. Jesus' life reflects His hero narrative in that He becomes the incarnate Word of God, embodying divine perfection, grace, and truth.

Just as Jesus' life fulfils the hero narrative for Christians, so too does the Sirah (Muslim term for biography, specifically Mohammad's biography) for Muslims. Although Mohammad was born into the powerful Quaraysh tribe of Mecca, he adopted a selfless lifestyle of humility, self-reliance, and compassion for the poor throughout his life. Growing up Mohammad often secluded himself in a mountain cave for several nights of prayer, eventually leading to his visitation by Gabriel (a prominent archangel and messenger of God in the Judeo-Christian and Islamic traditions) who delivers his first revelation from God. In heroic narrative tradition, Mohammad is mentored and given his quest, which leads him to preach his revelations publicly, calling on Arabs to surrender their will to Allah, that 'Allah is one' and that he, Mohammad, is a prophet of Islam. For this message Mohammad suffers persecution at the hands of the Meccan polytheists for 13 years. In 622 AD he migrates from Mecca to Medina where he unites the Medina tribes under the Constitution of Medina. This event is known by Muslims as the Hijrah, which marks the beginning of the Islamic calendar. This is his supreme ordeal in heroic terms. However, Mohammad's Sirah ends with him returning to Mecca with a conquering army and subduing it. By the time of his death in 632 AD, most of the Arabian Peninsula had united under Islam.

The Muslim warriors then went on to conquer all of North Africa and the Christian Holy Land Including Jerusalem and Lebanon in the 7th and 8th centuries. It is difficult for us to appreciate how influential Christianity was in these regions before the conquest by Muslim warriors, because it has so little influence there today. The Christian Byzantine warriors briefly regained control of the Holy Land until the Seljuk Turks, a Sunni Muslim Dynasty, retook it in the battle of Manzikert in 1071. The First Crusade occurred in 1095 AD largely in response to the attack of Seljuk Turks on the Christian

Byzantine Empire. The Fourth Crusade, along with their Venetian allies, sacked Constantinople in 1204 AD, causing widespread destruction and looting. In 1453 AD the Muslim warriors, led by the Ottoman Sultan Mehmed II, with the aid of cannons manufactured by Orban, a Hungarian engineer and cannon maker, attacked and took Constantinople, the capital and cultural heart of the Byzantine Empire, changed its name to Istanbul, and established the Ottoman Empire (1299-1922) until it was superseded by Muslim Turkey.

These are the two heroic narratives underpinning Christianity and Islam. One narrative ends with the martyrdom of its divine founder, while the other ends in his conquering glory. Both Christians and Muslims attempt to achieve salvation through emulating the hero narrative found in the lives of Jesus and Mohammad.

From its humble beginnings, Christianity was granted religious tolerance by the Edict of Milan (313 AD) issued by Emperors Constantine and Licinius. Christianity, which had spread significantly, was heavily favoured by Emperor Constantine after he became sole Emperor in 324 AD, and Nicene Christianity was formally established as the official state religion of the Roman Empire following the signing of the Edict of Thessalonica (380AD) by Emperor Theodosius.

Throughout the 3rd and 4th centuries, urban bishops gained increasing influence and power, relying on Imperial support for their roles in administration and justice. The Roman Empire fell when the last Roman Emperor, Romulus Augustulus was deposed by the Germanic chieftain Odoacer in 476 AD. From the 6th century onwards the bishop of Rome's power and prestige increased so dramatically that the title of 'Pope' (from the Greek 'pappas', meaning 'father') evolved over time, granting the bishop of Rome leadership of the Roman Catholic Church. The warriors of Charles Martel, grandfather of Charlemagne, Emperor of Europe, defeated the Muslim warriors of Abd al-Rahman al-Ghafiqi at the battle of Tours in 732 AD, thus ending the Muslim invasion of Christian Western Europe.

Christianity had survived but became divided following the

Great Schism of 1054 AD into the Roman Catholic faith of Western Europe and the Orthodox Christian faith of Eastern Byzantium. The underlying cause of this split was a mix of long-standing doctrinal, political, and cultural disputes, including the papacy's claim to universal authority. This solidified into a formal break following the excommunication between the Papal Legates and the Patriarch of Constantinople in 1054, and the Fourth Crusade's sacking of Constantinople in 1204. Both Christian faiths were protected by the warrior classes of both empires. The Byzantium Empire eventually fell in 1453 AD, which installed Islam as the dominant religion over what had been Eastern Christendom.

During The Protestant Reformation (1517 AD-1648 AD), Western Christianity was further divided into the Catholic and Protestant Christian religions and protected by the warrior classes of the Kings and Queens of Europe, who used the Christian religion to guarantee the authority of their sovereignty. A coalition of allied Christian warriors defeated the Muslim warriors of Kara Mustafa Pasha in the battle for Vienna in 1683 AD, thus ending the Muslim conquest of Eastern Christianity. Clearly, Christianity in Europe survived by being defended by a strong, united warrior class who were willing to sacrifice themselves to protect Christianity and keep the conquering Muslim warriors out of Christian Europe.

In 1184 AD, Pope Lucius III created the Episcopal Inquisition to combat Catharism in southern France. The word 'inquisition' comes from the Latin verb *inquiro,* meaning 'inquire into'. Later, inquisitions were established by succeeding Popes and sometimes by secular governments to combat heresy. In 1252 AD, Pope Innocent IV licensed inquisitors to allow heretics, who stubbornly refused to admit their guilt, to be tortured by lay henchmen. I will not explain the inhuman treatment that 'heretics' were subjected to during their torture because it is disconcerting, to say the least. From the 15th to 19th centuries, inquisitions were permanently established, and bureaucratically organised, appointed, and supervised. Heretics were denounced by religious and secular authorities, including church councils, popes, inquisitors, and in some societies civil authorities and religious leaders, and once having been found guilty had their property confiscated and were executed by public burning at the stake to 'purify' their souls.

On Friday, 13th October 1307 AD (Black Friday), King Philip IV of France (who had significant debts to the Templars), ordered a mass arrest of the Knights Templar, a military-religious order with vows of poverty, chastity, and obedience to their Grand Master in defence of the Christian faith against infidels. The Knights Templar had amassed landholdings and wealth which were confiscated by the king, although the legendary treasure was never found. Pope Clement V initially was reluctant to persecute the Knights Templar but later issued the bill *Pastoralis Praeeminentiae* to arrest members of the Knights Templar and seize their lands and wealth. This led to the widespread persecution of the Templars across Europe and eventually England.

What had started out as an enquiry into heresy was corrupted into the most infamous persecution conducted by the Roman Catholic Church. A persecution based more on money and power than spiritual 'cleansing'. Such is the result when moral certainty is coupled with absolute power, especially when it is managed by secular bureaucracy.

As well as this, wars in Europe occurred between Catholic and Protestant warriors from the 16th century into the early 18th century. These wars were sparked by the Protestant Reformation beginning in 1517, involving religious, territorial, dynastic, and commercial motives across Europe. These wars included, but were not limited to, the French Wars of Religion (1562-1598), The Eighty Years' War (1568-1648), the Thirty Years' War (1618-1648), and the Wars of the Three Kingdoms (1639-1653).

During the Age of European Imperialism (15th century to the early 20th century) Christianity followed in the wake of courageous explorers, conquering warriors, brave merchants, and resilient settlers, who established Christianity world-wide. Now that the European warrior class no longer provides protection for Christians worldwide, we have witnessed the slaughter of thousands of Christians, particularly in Africa and the Middle East where they compete for believers with the Muslim religion. Within European countries today, Christianity is currently under threat from the general loss of faith by its believers, and the illegal mass immigration of Muslims leaving their countries and establishing ethno-centric enclaves within the European nations who harbour them.

For Muslims it was the warrior class of the Islamic leaders that performed the same duty for the Islamic religion and the moral certainty of its leaders as it did for Christianity. Early Muslim conquests in the 7th and 8th centuries by Arab armies from Arabia established Islamic rule across the Middle East, North Africa, and temporarily into Spain. The major battles that led to the spread of Islam were Badr (624 AD), Uhud (625AD), Khandaq (627 AD), Khaybar (628 AD), Mecca (630 AD), and Hunayn (630 AD). The *Quran* states that Allah sent an 'unseen army of angels' that helped the Muslim warriors defeat the Meccans.

Shortly after Mohammad's death in 632 AD, Islam divided into the Sunni and Shia factions. The Sunni believe that the successor to Mohammad must be a member of Mohammad's family, while the Shia believe that a new leader should be chosen by consensus. Over time these factions have established differences in theology, law, religious texts, and spiritual practices. While both groups have been involved in conflicts, violence between them is mainly rooted in power imbalances and geopolitical conflicts. However, the decentralised nature of Sunni allows extremist groups like ISIS and Hamas to operate more autonomously.

The Sunni Almohad Muslim Dynasty conquered all of North Africa as far as Libya. Muslim wars against Christians had been raging in the Iberian Peninsula since the 8th century, but the Almohads temporarily conquered all of Al-Andalus (Moorish Iberian Peninsula) in the 12th century, making Seville their capital. The fundamentalist Almohads declared an everlasting Jihad against Christians, and gave infidels the choice between death or conversion, resulting in many Jews and Christians emigrating. Almohad dominance on the peninsula was eventually broken by the Battle of Las Navas de Tolosa in 1212 AD.

The Byzantine warrior class failed to protect their empire and it fell to the Sunni Ottoman Turks. Today, a mosque now stands in the Hagia Sophia, once the most beautiful of Christian churches in the world and the cultural heart of the once mighty Byzantine Empire. The temple mound in Jerusalem is a sight of great religious significance for Jews, Christians, and Muslims alike. Today the Al-Aqsa Mosque, the third holiest site in Islam and the location where the Prophet Muhammad is believed to have ascended into heaven, now stands where the Jewish temple once stood.

The Christian belief that the boundless nature of its compassion is what has protected and spread its influence throughout the world is historically inaccurate. The truth is that Christianity, with its hero narrative of Jesus' life to inspire its believers, was spread by early Christian martyrs and in the wake of courageous explorers, a conquering warrior class, brave merchants, and resilient settlers who were prepared to protect and bow to its moral certainty. What should be clear from this history is that without the belief of its followers and a successful warrior class prepared to protect and promote it, the moral certainty of any religion is ephemeral. If its followers are no longer prepared to sustain its existence, it will go the way of all other religious beliefs throughout history: into insignificance and possibly into myth.

Many free citizens in Australia today have replaced religious belief with ideology. Sexism, racism, gender ideology, and catastrophic climate change emergency are four ideologies that fanatical ideologues champion.

From the 1970s on, the UN has promoted a fear campaign against the citizens of the world concerning an environmental holocaust that will destroy the earth and us along with it. This environmental holocaust is said to be a product of human activity, changing humanity's relationship with nature from one of stewardship to one of destroyer. For example, pollution, water shortages, famine, ozone depletion, acid rain, biological diversity destruction, global warming leading to a catastrophic climate change emergency have all been blamed on human activity and promoted by the UN as leading to a catastrophic end of the world. In the words of Pogo, a cartoon character created by cartoonist Walt Kelly to celebrate the first Earth Day,

We have met the enemy and he is us.

For evidence of the beginning of this fear campaign refer to the 1972 United Nations Conference on Human Environment held in Stockholm which helped form the United Nations Environmental Programme (UNEP), and The Club of Rome, co-founded by Alexander King and Aurelio Peccei in 1968. Its first report was titled *The First Global Revolution* (1991). Since then, there have been many UN scare campaigns. For example, the Earth Summit held in Rio de Janeiro in 1992, The Kyoto Protocol in 1997, and the 2015 Paris Agreement, a legally binding international treaty on climate change designed to limit global warming to well below 2 degrees Celsius by implementing Nationally Determined Contributions (NDC) to limit carbon dioxide emissions.

This provides those Australian free citizens, lacking in religious belief, with a perfect moral certainty. It fills the emptiness in their lives created by a lack of spiritual purpose. Moral certainty as it relates to ideology results in ideological fanaticism, displaying similar effects on ideology as it has on intolerant religious behaviour. Their ideology replaces any necessity for reasonable analysis of facts or data. Those who question the established ideology are severely persecuted and cancelled by the morally certain ideologues. When confronted with objective truth that questions or disproves the moral certainty of their established ideological fanaticism, they are not prepared to tolerate any cross-examination of it, and merely double down on their fanatical belief with actions designed to reinforce the falsehood of their ideology and silence their critics with legal persecutions that financially destroys their opponents, since the fanatical idealogues' legal cost are paid for by the tax payers while their opponents' must be privately funded. For these reasons, moral certainty, when expressed by political ideologues, is more an exercise in vanity than morality; their moral vanity providing them with an unprovable superiority over their fellow citizens. The torture of the inquisition may have been replaced with persecution (both social and economic), but the result is the same: the silencing of opposing views.

The Racial Discrimination Act (RDA) was legislated into Australian law in 1975 and section 18c was introduced in 1995 to prohibit conduct that offends, insults, humiliates, or intimidates a person or group because of their race, colour, or national or ethnic origin. Section 18c has been controversial, notably in the Andrew Bolt case, which brought into focus its limiting effect on freedom of speech. In 2015 the eSafety Commission was established which has led critics to argue that its powers, particularly the Online Safety Act (OSA), threatens free speech in Australia by allowing censorship of certain content and promoting 'viewpoint discrimination'. Finally, the proposed legislation to provide the Australian Communications and Media Authority (ACMA) with powers to oversee mis/disinformation *could* be used to intimidate and persecute those with opinions that differ from the established narrative, particularly on the catastrophic climate-change emergency narrative.

Feminists, when countering what they believe to be sexist discrimination, use sexist discrimination to right the wrongs of the past and condemn those who question their methods by dismissing them as sexists; anti-racists use racial bigotry to counter what they see as racial privilege while condemning those who question their methods as racists; those who push gender spectrum ideology use charges of transphobia to counter doubters of their creed; those who question the mass immigration of people with values that differ from traditional Australian values are condemned as being racist etc. All these Australian citizens who voice opinions that differ from the established narrative could be charged under section 18c with offence. Those who champion catastrophic climate change emergency currently use persecution and individual cancellation to control those who are sceptical of their climate emergency ideology while condemning them as being climate deniers. These 'climate deniers' could be charged with spreading mis/disinformation under the proposed new legislation. To a rational thinking person all this name-calling seems childish, but the legislation is intimidating. I am reminded of an adage my mother used to combat this very nonsense in my childhood –

> *Sticks and stones may break my bones,*
> *but names will never hurt me.*

Of course, institutional sexism, racism, and gender bigotry already have been addressed by their liberal democratic societies in the past, so the morally certain, to maintain their moral superiority, are forced to go to absurd lengths to fight a continuing battle that has already been won. The charges of racism, sexism, and transphobia are becoming less effective as a consequence of its overuse on people believed by the Australian community at large to be innocent of this name-calling. Also, more and more people recognise the destructive cultural outcomes of radicals who use them. Climate emergency and renewable energy is being questioned today by an increasing number of scientists and social commentators on the grounds of validity, reliability and expense. In the past, those who questioned the established ideology were dismissed as climate change deniers and driven from the discussion, but this is becoming less effective as none of the predictions of the catastrophic climate change emergency prophets has materialised, and the cost of energy keeps rising. These are just a few examples of the illogical fanaticism displayed by the morally certain ideologues of present-day society.

The self-righteous fanaticism of the morally certain ideologues is also hypocritical. For example, these fanatics are strenuous in their condemnation of the actions of soldiers fighting for liberal democracy, like Israel, America, and Australia and are only tepid in their condemnation of terrorist or communist soldiers. They also claim that only white citizens are capable of racism. Non-white citizens are wrongly perceived to be in a position of constant powerlessness, thereby giving them a saintly appeal. Consequently, any racial attacks against white citizens are perceived as morally justified. Therefore, any condemnation is not equitability applied, making their moral certainty an exercise in political opportunism, not morality. Good intentions are no excuse for evil outcomes.

As you can see, moral certainty, although comforting for those who support it, can and does have a deleterious effect on those who question its validity, not to mention the corrosive effect it has on the integrity of the morally certain. Those espousing moral certainty always take the moral high ground in any argument, belittling others with their moral vanity. The biggest problem with moral certainty is that of extreme action taken in the name of purification and how that affects the kinds of interpersonal relationships within a society.

Moral certainty combined with absolute authority or totalitarian dictatorship terrifies me.

Can you identify any other uncivilised practices conducted by morally certain citizens either in the past or currently?

There is a significant argument that if moral standards are not set by religious belief with the authority to enforce it, one ends up with *moral chaos* leading to the decline and fall of the civilisation previously supported by the moral certainty of its chosen religion. The opposite argument states that there is a *natural order* of liberty that all people desire. These arguments centre around the twin concepts of the Divine Right of Kings and the existence of a natural social contract.

If you want a full understanding of these concepts please read Thomas Hobbes' book, *Leviathan* (1651), where he explores the necessity for an established authority to enforce any social contract, and that the state of nature is a state of war. The other is John Locke's book, *Two Treatises of Government* (1690) in which he advances his belief in natural law, social contract, religious toleration, and the right to revolution. From this you can see why the British chose a Parliamentary System with a Constitutional Monarch as its head, while the Americans chose their Constitution to uphold their belief in a separation of powers.

I can see how many today would be willing to accept Hobbes' argument concerning the necessity of authority to control the natural state of affairs after witnessing the decline of religious belief and the social/political chaos brought on by the post-modernists in Western countries in recent times. Additionally, there is the prevalence of wars in the world today. Shakespeare expresses his belief in the necessity of benign authority in his tragedies when he uses authority to intervene and restore order after social chaos has emerged. The sad truth is, however, that not all authority is benign, and once established, how does one rid their society of malevolent authority?

I will now present a modern example of partisan logic and how it divides those espousing moral certainty. Recently, Pope Francis (1936-2025) died. Journalists were gathered in St. Peter's Square interviewing the faithful about what sort of Pope they hoped would replace him. The word I heard most constantly used to describe their favoured replacement was *progressive* and they expressed a desire for the Catholic Church to adopt *modern values*, describing *traditional values* as out of date and likely to lead to a demise of the Catholic Church in the future.

Let's take their first recommendation, that of desiring a *progressive* pope. As I have already stated, 'progressive' is a vague, indeterminate term and should be avoided as a definition. Those claiming to be progressive actually seek radical change rather than reform. When progressives are finished with their 'progressive changes' they have actually changed the structural integrity of the thing they are setting out to change. This is true in religion, politics, bureaucracies, private organisations etc.

Their second recommendation is that of adopting modern values. Since "modern values' differ widely from "traditional values" this would actually change the moral certainty of the Catholic Church. Jesus Christ's resurrection (proving his divinity) and his teachings are the foundational moral values of the Catholic Church. When asked whether he wanted to change the established laws of the *Torah* (the *Pentateuch*), Jesus explained that he came not to *change* but to *fulfil* (Matthew 5:17-20).

This begs the question for those who seek 'progressive change' to the moral certainty of the Catholic Church. How do you change something that already has been *fulfilled* by its divine founder? Is it likely that progressives actually want a moral code different from that of the Catholic Church's traditional interpretation of Jesus' teachings? That is, does progressive moral certainty not differ significantly from that of the traditional moral certainty of the Catholic Church?

This has seen a division in the Catholic Church between those who follow *liberation theology* (another progressive term with positive connotations. Why not call it 'radical theology'?) and those following *traditional doctrine*. Those interested in this topic should consult Gustavo Gutiérrez's, *A Theology of Liberation* (1971) and classictheology.org, *Voices of the Past for Christians of Today,* June 2025. In future, will this lead to another Great Schism within the Catholic Church? In all likelihood this will occur if the progressives and traditionalists both maintain a position of moral certainty for their causes. If this happens, I wonder who will end up with Vatican City, the progressives or the traditionists.

Let's look at the moral certainty of ideology and its acceptance of actions taken by those fighting for the cause of climate emergency as being morally justified, even if they cause disruption to the commercial activities of society or the lives of other citizens, or even the destruction of private or public property, or a whole nation's economy through the economic destruction of its energy system. The majority of those who protest catastrophic climate-change emergency do not pay a price for their moral certainty. They continue to live and work in air-conditioned environments, drive air-conditioned cars, use mobile phones, use plastic products created from fossil fuels, and live in areas that are not affected by the loss of thousands of acres of fertile farming land, valuable grazing lands, the 'sterilisation' of valuable mineral resources in the ground, or the destruction of pristine rain and old growth forests, and endangered koala habitats.

One wonders how anyone can retain a position of moral superiority following the bulldozing of rain and old-growth forests and koala habitats (saveeunggella.com.au, 2025) and the clubbing to death of 'sick' or 'unviable' (due to injury) koalas and their cubs to make way for wind generators (abc.net.au, *Why claims about euthanising koalas to make way for Queensland wind farm are missing context*, Nov 2023). What is missing from the context? The 2022 biodiversity plan states,

Euthanasia will be conducted using blunt force trauma

and

This is a hard, sharp blow to the base of the back of the skull with a blunt metal or heavy wooden bar.

Sick and unviable koalas are being clubbed to death by construction workers clearing the site for wind generators.

The visual and noise pollution created by giant solar and wind generating energy factories is enough to ensure they never come to the districts of the morally certain. Imagine if the electorates of those espousing catastrophic climate change emergency and renewable energy were suddenly subjected to eminent domain legislation that compulsorily acquired the airspace above their properties and giant solar factories were installed there, or the same was applied to their parks and seascapes to install giant wind generators. Actually, there is a good economical reason for locating wind generators off the cost of major cities, because they would be close to consumers, negating the necessity for thousands of kilometres of transmission lines. If this were to happen, however, would the voters in those same electorates be so willing to embrace their moral certainty pertaining to climate change emergency and renewable energy?

There is a line from a Shakespearean play which highlights what might be the insincerity of those who shout the loudest for their cause –

> *The lady doth protest too much, methinks.*
> (*Hamlet*, Act 3, Scene 2)

This line suggests that when someone is overstating their insistence on something, they might actually be hiding the truth.

This reminds me of a joke I once heard that deals with over-complaining. A devout Catholic joined a monastery that upheld a vow of silence. The monks were forbidden from talking, except for once a year when a monk was allowed to say two words to the abbot. After the first year our devout Catholic addressed the abbot and said, 'more food'. The abbot nodded his head and released the monk. After the second year the monk said, 'more blankets'. Again the abbot nodded his head and released the monk. When the third year came around the monk said, 'I quit'. This time the abbot replied, 'That's good. You complain too much.'

Moral Equivalence

> *I believe in everything; nothing is sacred.*
> *I believe in nothing; everything is sacred.*
> (Tom Robins, *Even Cowgirls Get the Blues*, 1976)

This sentiment precisely describes the belief of those holding a morally equivalent approach to morality. The problem with this approach is that it paralyses all moral judgement, thereby rendering civilised society impossible. Because moral equivalence holds that all moral judgements are equal, its advocates cannot distinguish right from wrong, good from evil or justice from injustice. Rightness, goodness, and justice simply become a sliding continuum of differing morality, all of which are equivalent. Such is the ultimate outcome of sophist logic on morality. All cultures, societal values and political governance are equal and must never be brought into moral questioning.

The steps taken by feminists, anti-racists, gender identity activists, and anti-fascists, for example, are morally justified even if they expose some members of society to the same intolerance that those who take these steps are trying to eradicate. Moral equivalency when coupled with presentism becomes malevolent. In the minds of the morally equivalent, the measures taken by anti-colonialists are likewise morally justified if they destroy present-day culture and the institutions of those countries whose ancestors benefitted from colonialism. Needless to say, this course of action gives no credence to the fact that today's liberal democratic societies are in a constant state of social flux, with individuals rising and falling within the social hierarchy regardless of sex, race, gender, political affiliation or ancestral past. In this way, moral equivalence hinders appropriate responses to harmful action and encourages wrongful behaviour. For example, failure to administer equal justice on the grounds that someone's ancestors suffered historical injustice simply encourages wrongful behaviour to continue and creates yet another historical injustice.

Also, providing equal justice to both bullies and victims on the grounds that it takes two to start a fight, negates the right of the victim to self-defence. Taking this one step further, a failure to recognise the difference between a terrorist attack and a state-sponsored response fails to recognise the moral differences between these two actions. In this case moral equivalence is used to manipulate public opinion into accepting that both sides to the conflict are equally responsible.

I recently heard someone say that we have laws that govern wars today. Really? For laws to be effective they must be equally enforced. Applying rules of engagement to only one side in a conflict is not equally enforcing laws. A more just approach would be to allow for both sides to adhere to the same rules of engagement. If both sides adhere to the rules, fine. If one side doesn't, the opposing side should be given the option to respond with equal rules. This does not mean that they must use the same rules of engagement as their opponent but rather that they should have the option to, and not be condemned if they find it necessary to adopt some of the rules of their opponent. If one is going to protest the inhumanity of war, one must apply the condemnation equally to both sides of a conflict. My observation is that radical protests are directed against the side that is not supported by the radical protestors, regardless of what rules of engagement that side adopts.

When it comes to war, I have also heard the phrase 'proportional response', meaning one side can only respond to a violent attack in proportion to the damage levelled against it. I guess this would have given the Allies in WWII the right only to respond 'proportionally' to the attacks levelled against them. This would mean America had the right to sink only the same number of ships, and kill only the same number of Japanese as Americans killed in the attack on Pearl Harbour and then cease hostilities against Japan. The same logic would apply to Nazi Germany. With this logic, WWII would never have ended; we would still be fighting it today, or maybe the Japanese and the Nazis would have won by now because they had no commitment to 'proportional response', just like the terrorists or communists fighting today. Remember Hamas' promise to repeat October 7 over and over again, until they establish a Palestinian State 'from the river to the sea' thereby eliminating the state of Israel, and the war crimes committed by Russia against the innocent civilians of Ukraine in order to dominate them. Recently, Donald Trump cancelled a meeting with Vladimir Purin because Trump could see nothing productive coming from it. Putin retaliated by sending a swarm of killer drones which targeted a Ukrainian kindergarten, killing many innocent children and one six-month-old baby. Thankfully, Ukraine did not undertake a 'proportionate response'.

Moral equivalency can also undermine human rights by providing compassion for the criminal while ignoring the rights of the victim for justice. Recently, Magistrate Gail Hubble struck out almost 400 charges against a 14-year-old boy on a refugee visa, because,

> *He's been unable to comply with bail or satisfactorily complete a community order ... I don't think he can do a community order at this point. She went on to confess; I've lost count of how many times I've given him bail.*
>
> (tanea.com.au, July 2025)

In Victoria, separate Koori Courts already exist for the trial of Aboriginal and Torres Strait juveniles, and there have been proposals to investigate establishing a similar system for African Australians. This violates a fundamental principle of democracy: equal justice for all citizens.

This is an example of how boundless compassion, and morally equivalent laws and judgements undermine the citizenship rights of law-abiding citizens.

Finally, moral equivalence distorts reality in the minds of innocent civilians by ignoring important differences in intent, methods, and consequences. It creates dangerous logical fallacies that prevent a clear understanding of moral issues.

The biggest problem with moral equivalency, then, is its inability to identify malevolent activity. Moral equivalency has no moral standard because it has no values. Those who espouse moral equivalency would have us believe that 1 and 2 are equal because they are both numbers, without recognizing that 1 and 2 have different values.

What conclusions have you reached about moral equivalency? Do you accept that moral equivalency leads to injustice? Does moral equivalency impede our movement toward goodness by violating the fundamental principles of democracy?

Moral Clarity

Consider these definitions of moral clarity –

> *Moral relates to what is right or wrong.*
> *Clarity is the ability to think clearly.*
> (Collins English Dictionary)

So moral clarity seems to involve the application of critical thinking guided by logic, reason, wisdom, common sense, and empathy in establishing a code of moral behaviour that makes firm and unflinching decisions about what is right and wrong, and, once established, to live our lives accordingly.

Moral Clarity differs from Moral Certainty in that we must discover for ourselves what is morally right and wrong and not accept it from some source of authority or group identity, free from things like religious intolerance or ideological fanaticism. It also differs from Moral Equivalency inasmuch as it does produce a code of moral behaviour that its adherents recognise as right and wrong behaviour which immunises them against paralysing indecision. It is inspired organically by a study of transcendental truth; it is constantly examining itself at the transcendental and existential levels of truth to either confirm its morality, discover new moral truths, or make changes to existing morals that are proven wrong; and it recognises the potentially corrupting influence of the elements of archetypical truth. Moral clarity should not be confused with liberation theology because moral clarity is based on foundational tenets of truth and not a fusion of Christianity and Marxism. The essential difference being that moral clarity is more rational than utopian.

To combat the emergence of social chaos in a liberal democracy, moral clarity, as opposed to moral certainty, can be enforced by things like a social contract (i.e., the acceptance of constitutional law), citizenship rights, and a justice system that is applied equally to all citizens. For example, a country's belief in the primacy of liberty and democracy would involve the censoring of any religious belief or ideological conviction that violated these values. If any charismatic religious or secular leader were to try and replace liberty or democracy with any other form of religious or political system that robbed citizens of their constitutional rights, he/she could be charged with treason, and if found to be traitorous after a legitimate trial, have his/her citizenship revoked, be jailed, and where applicable deported. What is needed for this to work is a relentless pursuit of truth and clear definitions for liberty, democracy, and constitutional (as opposed to human) rights.

Just as moral certainty needs a strong warrior class to protect its believers, so moral clarity needs the same. Without a strong military, police force, and a court system based on equal justice, not social justice, to protect it, moral clarity will go the way of all other forms of moral codes that its believers failed to protect. America has developed an interesting combination of secular and religious beliefs that the might of its nation currently protects. If the American warrior and justice echelons are eclipsed, so too will the morals of its culture. This is a clear lesson that history has taught us. Lately, however, Europe and America are witnessing an interesting revival and commitment to Christianity and their warrior classes. Where this will lead to in the future is debatable.

Before we embark on discovering a moral code of behaviour based on moral clarity, we should first establish what its highest good should be, because our highest good is what will guide and direct the establishment of our moral clarity and through that our integrity and self-fulfilment. Should our highest good be based on power, money, fame, sexual gratification? Or some other good.

Let's consider power first. If our highest good is power, then our moral code would direct us to discover ways in which we can gain power over others and once having gained that power our moral code would be justified. Here is a quote from Machiavelli who promoted power as a means of influencing people and gaining dominance over them —

> *If an injury has to be done to a man it should be so severe that his vengeance need not be feared.*
> (Niccolo Machiavelli, *The Prince*, 1532)

Many people adopt this approach and gain their power through the use of violence. Power, when pursued in this way, only respects power. Such moral codes have plagued humanity throughout millennia, leading to much suffering, death and destruction. Hardly a desirable outcome. Clearly, our moral clarity should rule out power as our highest good, because it produces malevolent outcomes for humanity. However, we must accept that power will be needed to maintain our moral clarity, so it will be necessary to create and maintain a powerful force that will protect our moral clarity. Remember what Vegetius said —

> *If you want peace, prepare for war.*
> (Publius Flavius Vegetius Renatus, *Epitoma Rei Militaris*, late 4th or early 5th century AD)

Any civilisation upholding moral clarity must be able to defend itself, and this requires a morally sound warrior class capable of defending it. Here is a general observation of human nature and social dynamics that cannot be attributed to any single author —

> *In life, there are those who protect and those who need protecting.*

Another quote dealing with human nature and social dynamics comes from Danny Thomas, American comedian and actor –

> *There are two kinds of people in this world: the givers and the takers. The takers sometimes eat better, but the givers always sleep better.*
>
> (Stjude.org, 2025)

Both these quotes should be taken to heart by a warrior class upholding moral clarity. Although power should not be our moral clarity's highest good, it must be recognised that *righteous power* is needed to protect it. Just as the warrior class were and are prepared to bow their knees to the moral certainty of religions so too does moral clarity need a warrior class that believes its morals are worth defending.

A sad fact about power is that it has been, and will continue to be, used to promote and protect both liberty and tyranny. This is something that our moral clarity and righteous power must constantly contend with. Wendell Phillips, an abolitionist, when speaking to the Massachusetts Anti-Slavery Society in 1852 said,

> *Eternal vigilance is the price of liberty; power is ever stealing from the many to the few.*
>
> (thelatinlibrary.com, 2025)

Such is the reality when living in an imperfect world populated with flawed human beings.

Another highest good could be money accumulation. The greater our wealth becomes the more our moral code of money accumulation is justified. We have already spoken of the dangers associated with making money your highest good in the 'warning' section of Chapter Five, so I will not repeat those warnings here. Again, our moral clarity should rule out money accumulation as its highest good, because of its danger to our integrity. At the same time, we must accept the necessity of creating financial security for both ourselves and our civilisation, if we are going to maintain our moral clarity.

What about fame? Do you want to be known by as many people as possible? Do you want people to talk about you, to desire in their hearts to be you? When you travel would you want celebrity status? To achieve stardom, distinction, notoriety? Do you yearn for greatness, glory, even immortality? To become famous will require you to experience all these things. What effect do you think these things could have on your perception of yourself? Do you think you could become arrogant, opinionated, egotistical, perhaps even narcissistic? Would you be in danger of becoming a "cloud chaser" (a person intent on achieving instant fame)? Might you be tempted to use others as 'stepping stones' for you to use as you move from one source of fame to another? Is it possible to be famous and hold to your moral clarity? Maybe it is possible, but few achieve it. Most compromise their integrity for the sake of their fame, and if they lose their fame what are they left with? The once famous eventually will become yesterday's 'Ho hum'. Such a sad circumstance to find oneself in, especially after having lost one's integrity.

If our highest good is directed towards sexual gratification we are led into a moral code that can compromise important character traits like trust, loyalty, and commitment. Am I advocating a moral code based on chastity? Not necessarily. If you aspire to maintaining your chastity, there is nothing wrong with that if it suits your lifestyle. My generation believed that what two consenting adults do in the privacy of their bedroom is their business and not that of the government or others.

Do you think that statement is based on moral equivalence? What moral compromises do you think such a sentiment would entail? What if their sexual activity involved violence or undue coercion? Do you think there needs to be some laws that prohibit some sexual practices? Explain.

If you decide on a less demanding level of sexual restriction, that too is fine if it suits your lifestyle and does not compromise your integrity. I will not enter into the dangers of a plurality of sexual partners, like sexually transmitted disease (STD), human immunodeficiency (HIV) or acquired immunodeficiency syndrome (AIDS), because I'm sure you are well aware that they are a real danger to your health. What I am suggesting, however, is that

if you do not control your level of sexual gratification
it will control you

and potentially could lead you from desire to lust to perversion, as it has done to many in the past and present, especially if it is coupled with a pornographic obsession. All of which are less than desirable outcomes if you are to retain your integrity and realise your potential.

Attitudes towards sexual activity have changed, particularly with the younger generation. It saddens me to witness attractive young people proudly boasting about their 'body count' without realising how sexual gratification has consumed their *raison d'être* (reason for being), or even their inevitable inability to sustain such a moral code throughout their lives. As they grow older the opportunity for finding sexual partners with a similar outlook will decline. Some of the sexual practices I have heard about being played out on 'only fans' leaves me heartbroken about the unlit road some our youth have chosen to travel along.

Likewise, our moral clarity should rule out sexual gratification as its highest good, because of its potential to corrupt our integrity, exert control over our lives, and inhibit us from fulfilling our potential. At the same time we must recognise that our desire for sexual contentment must be satisfied both in a personal and family-orientated way. This is necessary for our own fulfilment and the continuance of our civilisation.

The truth is that those who are powerful, rich, famous, or hyper-sexually orientated, are less likely to maintain their integrity than those who put their moral clarity above all other values. This is the central issue to our current discussion on our highest good; that our moral clarity should be our highest good.

Our highest good, then, could be goodness itself as opposed to evil. Of course, this leads us into discussions about what constitutes good and evil and that is precisely the issue that must be decided upon when discovering our moral clarity. Once established, our moral clarity becomes our highest good. Remember, it is establishing a lifestyle that achieves our highest good that becomes our top priority in life. If we fall short of sustaining our moral code in our lives, it will involve us in a loss of integrity. Nevertheless, it is comforting to realise that no one is perfect, so redemption is a possibility with the correct course of action. Redemption is not an excuse for bad or evil behaviour. Rather, it involves taking responsibility, being remorseful, and demonstrating a genuine commitment to positive change. It is not used to justify past wrongs; it is used to transform past wrongs.

Once established by individual citizens, this moral code of behaviour becomes their moral compass to guide them through their lives' adventures. What we demand of ourselves we should also expect from others. For example, if we choose to treat others with dignity and respect we should also expect the same behaviour towards ourselves. Failure to meet this mutually agreed behaviour needs censure, and if it persists a dissolution of the association or friendship is not only justified but required. Does this mean I am advocating for cancel culture? Not really because I do not want to cancel others but rather their rude behaviour and avoid it on my own personal level. If our disrespectful friends become contrite and seek forgiveness, our commitment to dignity and respect towards others should guide us into accepting their apology. Unless, of course, the apology is not given in good faith.

Here is a quote from *Desiderata* –

Avoid loud or aggressive persons; they are vexations to the spirit.
(Max Ehrmann, *The Desiderata of Happiness*, 1948)

Having given due consideration to treating ourselves and others with dignity and respect, do you think this would be a good starting point to build our moral clarity upon?

Ernest Hemingway once said,

> *What is moral is what you feel good after,*
> *and what is immoral is what you feel bad after.*
> (Ernest Hemingway, *Death in the Afternoon*, 1932)

This emphasises the feeling of satisfaction that can follow decisions based on moral clarity. Obviously, what this moral code of behaviour depends on is a trustworthy, virtuous moral clarity that tells the individual what is right and wrong. Since most Australians have drifted from a more morally orientated life to a more secular life, this quote may have its limitations. However, if you possess moral clarity, this definition would be helpful in making life's choices.

I am further reminded of an interview Dr. Phil had with a Pro-Palestine activist who wanted Dr. Phil to understand the historical background to the atrocities committed by Hamas on 7th October 2024. Dr. Phil replied,

> *...No you don't. No you don't. That's either right or it's wrong and it was wrong, and I don't need a hundred years of conflict to know it was wrong. When somebody comes over a fence and goes into someone's house and burns their infant in its crib, I don't give a damn why they did it. It's wrong.*

This is moral clarity. One will not be swayed by sophist logic when one knows what is morally right and what is morally wrong.

There is also the interview that Elon Musk gave when advertisers had withdrawn their advertising from his newly acquired Twitter (now X) social platform. Elon Musk had bought Twitter because he believed in free speech as a cornerstone of democracy and was against the censorship being carried out on Twitter at that time. This had become an issue of moral clarity for Musk and the advertisers tried to dissuade him of his stance on free speech by imposing a monetary penalty on him. The interviewer questioned Musk about why he was willing to take a financial loss over his moral stance. In answering this question, Musk invoked the dialogue from the movie, *Princess Bride* (1987), where Inigo Montoya, when duelling with Westley (the man in black) who had killed his father, says,

> *Offer me money ... promise me power ... all that I ask for.*
> *Westley replies, All that I have and more.*

Montoya kills Westley and says, *I want my father back, you SOB.* Couple this with what Elon Musk said at CPAC in 2025 and we see his priority for purchasing Twitter for $44 billion dollars. He said,

> *Freedom is priceless.*

Again, this is an example of the uncompromising position of moral clarity once established. In Musk's case it is his unwillingness to compromise his moral clarity regarding free speech for the sake of money.

From these two examples, then, we can conclude that,

> *Moral clarity arises when we know that something is true. We know it is true; we do not have to be told that it is true, and we know it is true because of our enlightened understanding of transcendental truth.*

Do I intend to supply you with a moral code of behaviour that will enable you to operate on a level of Moral Clarity? Absolutely not. That would defeat the whole purpose of Moral Clarity. However, if you have paid attention to the topics under discussion throughout this book you will be well on your way to developing your own code of moral behaviour which will grant you a self-fulfilling life and enable you to reach your full potential.

When considering issues of morality, do your research first. Examine critically what other great thinkers have said about the moral issue you are contemplating. Be guided by the principle of always moving towards the good and away from evil, beneficence over malevolence. Once a decision has been reached, you should commit yourself to abiding by and upholding it in your life. If you do this, you will achieve moral clarity and integrity in your life. If you choose power, money, fame or hypersexual activity as your highest good, what compromises, what trade-offs, with your moral clarity might you have to make to achieve your goal? Do you think you will retain your integrity by making these compromises and trade-offs?

Having said that, I do not intend to supply you with a moral code of behaviour; may I instead supply you with an assessment of some moral issues for your consideration, which might help you in making your own assessment of moral issues of interest to you. I do this by way of example for you to follow when deciding your position on any moral issue. Why not start with what your code of moral clarity expects of yourself before considering what it expects from others. What have other great thinkers concluded when considering this moral principle? You will find there are many and varied ideas and opinions about this, so I will give you a starting point for your search for truth concerning this code of personal behaviour.

Let's start with the first of the ten commandments in the *Old Testament*.

Thou shalt have no other Gods before me.

This concept may be important to you because it places a limit on your pride. If you place God before yourself you cannot consider yourself a God, no matter how much power, money, fame or number of sexual conquests you accumulate in your lifetime.

Remember, in ancient times pharaohs and emperors considered themselves as actual living gods and their subjects worshiped them as such. On the other hand, conquering Roman generals returning to Rome often had a slave with them who whispered to them, *Memento Homo* (remember you are only a man). This was intended to remind the generals that their power and glory were not eternal. Think about today. Do you think there are some people who consider themselves to be all powerful? In fact, do we not say that the President of America is the most powerful person in the world? What effect might this have on the perception a President could have of himself/herself. Is this even true? Doesn't the American Constitution limit the power of the American President? Do you think it would be a good idea to limit your behaviour by your code of moral clarity, in the same way that the American Constitution limits the power of the American President?

If you are convinced that your moral code of behaviour trumps all other expectations you place on yourself, let us examine a few personal behaviour traits other great thinkers of the past have considered valuable.

Let us start with the expanded concept of justice that the Stoics followed. Have you already researched this concept like I recommended earlier? If not, why not do it now. Did you find it covers how we deal with others, even those of more humble circumstances than ourselves? That it strongly opposes the vice of injustice. That you treat others with kindness, fairness, and a spirit of public-spiritedness. What lies at the heart of stoic justice is our own integrity. It is something we impose upon ourselves first, before seeking it from others. That we do no harm to another, that we respect public property as belonging to all, and that private property belongs to its owners. That we deliver to others what they are owed, and to ourselves only what we are owed, nothing more.

Do you think that the expanded concept of stoic justice is a principle of moral clarity that could have relevance for you as you venture through life? Why do you think that?

What about the Confucian concept concerning filial piety found in Confucius' *Four Books*? Confucius believed that filial piety was crucial in maintaining harmony in our family and social relationships. It stresses the importance of showing love, respect and deference to one's parents and elders. Filial piety should also be guided by righteousness or doing what is right. That is, filial piety should not be used against you in such a way as to compromise your integrity.

Or the fifth commandment from the *Holy Bible* –

Honour thy father and thy mother: that thy days may be long upon the land which the Lord thy God giveth thee.

How can we do this? What if our parents are dishonourable? Do we still honour them?

If your parents treat you badly, should you treat them badly in return? Remember here the *Tu quoque* (you also) logical fallacy, which stops us from being misled into believing that just because someone else does something it gives us the right to do the same. Why not try to understand your parents. Be concerned for them. Try to forgive them. Treat them with love and respect, while at the same time explaining your position with courage, without anger in your heart or voice. Do you think this might have a better chance of changing their behaviour towards you? When your parents become old and frail, do you think you have a responsibility of care for them? Should you consider this responsibility a burden or a blessing, given how much they did for you in your lifetime?

Is filial piety a moral principle you might consider valuable in your lifetime? Explain your position in detail.

What about the 10th Commandment –

Thou shalt not covet...

It means that we should not desire anything that is not ours. Does this have any applicability for you?

Let me relate a shameful story from my childhood. When I was nine years old and attending a small country school, my cousin and I decided to play truant. We wandered around the neighbourhood and found a home that was unoccupied. On entering the yard we discovered a go-kart. It was a nice box go-kart that the father and son had built together. My cousin and I smashed it. Since truancy was a crime it was reported to the police who soon found out where we had been, and what we had done. The police came to my home and lectured me about breaking the law and how that could lead to me being removed from my family but said they would not charge me for the offence of destroying private property because the father, who owned the go-kart, did not lay a charge against me. My mother was in her bedroom crying. I was sufficiently chastised to arouse shame about my behaviour. The police then referred the incident to my father and charged him with the responsibility of disciplining me. My father explained to me what 'juvenile delinquency' was and told me that what I had committed was an illegal act which required him to discipline me. I had to drop my pants and bend over while he strapped me. The strapping I received did not hurt me as much as the shame I felt over the dishonour I had brought to my family. From that day on I knew with clarity that what was not mine was off limits for me, unless invited by its owner to enjoy his/her property. The same was understood by me about what was mine. Nobody had the right to use or damage my property unless invited by me to do so.

In my teenage years I reflected on my action of that day and realised that what I had done was out of envy. I had envied that boy and his go-kart. After coming to this realisation, I vowed never to envy anything others possessed and never did. Now that I am much older I can confess to you that that incident saved me from a lot of misery in my life. If I had not got control over my envy, it could easily have destroyed my life by leading me into recurrent acts of envy, jealousy, and resentment.

Does my experience help you to understand the importance of controlling your envy; to avoid coveting anything owned by someone else? I hope it does. Do you think it is important enough to add it to your moral clarity code of behaviour?

We could go on and examine other moral principles like moderation, charity, kindness, honesty, equality, fairness, duty, honour, trust, and loyalty, to name just a few, but it is best that you discover and articulate these for yourself. Now that you have developed a discovery process for arriving at moral clarity, you can appreciate that there are many things to consider when establishing a code of behaviour in your life that will provide you with a solid foundational stone for your character and your integrity. Now that you have made a start, don't forget to carry your moral compass with you as you journey through your life and always search for and adopt the good over the evil.

What an exciting adventure you now have before you. Enjoy it.

Consider this, can moral clarity play a role in our secular existence? Would laws, passed by our legislators, have more potential to be good laws if they were based on moral clarity rather than moral certainty or moral equivalence? Explain.

Do you think that our leaders only need to protect our security and provide a reliable food source for us so we do not go hungry? Should our leaders also provide for our moral character by living a life that provides us with examples of moral clarity? Our leaders may not be able to make us moral citizens but should they lead by moral example?

Well, you may ask, if you feel this way about morality, why don't you just choose a religion that best suits you and follow that moral code? I have partly answered that question in the section on moral certainty above, but there is more to it than that. The fact is that all religions have a bureaucracy that administer to their faithful, and like all bureaucracies they are vulnerable to corruption. The problem with religious bureaucracy is that it is absolute, and therefore beyond the reach of the faithful's censure. I have a deep and abiding distrust of absolute power of any kind and this forms my unwillingness to surrender my liberty to any religion. My free choice is also a part of my moral clarity code of behaviour, a part of my integrity.

If you find a religion that suits you and with which you are comfortable, far be it from me to advise you otherwise. There appears to be a revival in Catholicism currently happening which could be a good thing since it is the moral anchor of Western Civilisation, so long as the Catholic Church continues to emphasise salvation through the Grace of God and not descend into the power of papal infallibility. Let me go further. Religious freedom is a principal part of my moral clarity, so I would support your right to freely worship the religion of your choice, provided it does not violate my own moral clarity, then I would have to speak out against the moral certainty of your chosen religion.

Should a clash occur between the moral certainty of your religious authority and your own moral clarity, however, I would urge you not to surrender your integrity to any authority venerable to human corruption. I hasten to add that there are many examples of religious leaders who were, and are today, benevolent in their administration to their faithful, but so too are there examples of many who were, and are, malevolent in their treatment of heretics and infidels, and even abusive in their administration to their faithful.

Although I do not hold to any religious belief, I do believe in God, but now we have strayed into the area of personal truth. Remember the limitations that *personal truth* encounters when trying to reveal *general, objective, or universal truth*. Belief in God requires of us an exercise of faith, not just logic or reason. Our moral clarity is a product of our conscious perception of transcendental truth, which leads us to God, the creator of all things, including our consciousness. I believe in God because I have felt His presence in my life for a long time. I choose to believe in God and the moral clarity He has revealed to me.

My childhood was not influenced by religion, but my teenage

years were. During my Vietnam War experience, I lost my faith. When I was married and started to raise a family I became religious again, but later lapsed into scepticism. In my early 40s I suffered a personal crisis which drove me to pray to God for guidance. The only thought that came to me was to remain a teacher, a facilitator of learning for those who sought truth. After that, I remained in the teaching profession and, since retirement, have written three books. *The Lighted Road* is my fourth book.

This makes me a Deist, someone who believes in God but not religion. For me, the best thing that can be said about some religions is that they help people to treat each other better. Although this 'better treatment' can be selective at times, treating those with the same faith as oneself as deserving of better treatment.

I have reached a point in my search for truth where my highest good is goodness itself, the endeavour to live a life based on moral clarity which can only be perceived while searching for truth on the transcendental level. I must live in the existential level with all its confusion and contend with the archetypal level and all its hidden desires. I must control the confusion, and hidden desires, if I am to live a life based on moral clarity. I constantly find myself being tempted by and making foolish decisions based on existential and archetypal truth. When this happens I must recognise that the fault is mine, that I am the one to blame for my own bad choices and shortcomings and not try to rationalise my lack of moral clarity by convincing myself that someone else is to blame, that I would not have made the choice I did if it were not for the circumstances that someone else had forced me into. Only by accepting blame can I venture forth on a path to redeem my virtue.

On a more logical level, I cannot fault the arguments put for intelligent design in the creation of the universe and life itself. When I look at the universe I see benevolence in its existence. Mainly because I have a place in it, humble though that might be; I exist because the universe exists. I see it obeying the laws of mathematics, the most logical of all the sciences, which reveals the truth of its intelligent design. If the universe obeys laws, someone or something must have legislated those laws. I choose to call that someone God.

Just as death is personified by Donne, so God is the personification of my highest good. For me, God is the transcendental embodiment of His revealed moral clarity. My reason for wanting to live a good rather than an evil life. He encourages me to seek the good. Have I always achieved that? No. No I have not, and regrettably, in my frustration, anger, and shame I have even tried to blame God for my own shortcomings. At one time, I even screamed,

Can't You give me a break!

Of course it was not God who needed to give me a break but myself who needed to reevaluate my own choices.

I hope you do not conclude that I am sanctimonious or self-righteous. I do not claim to speak for God only that He has led me to my understanding of His will through the development of my moral clarity. I do not intend to impose my moral clarity on you, nor do I place my moral clarity above that of God. It is God who has led me to, revealed, and is the personification of my moral clarity. He encourages me to be faithful to the moral clarity He has provided for me through my consciousness. It is through adherence to this moral clarity that my integrity is sustained. It is God's will, not mine, that creates the moral clarity I adhere to. This is why my personal truth leads me to believe in moral clarity over moral certainty or moral equivalence.

There are good and bad people in those who follow the moral certainty found in religion and political ideology. They are the moderates and the radicals. The moderates are those who are benevolent, peace abiding, and just. They would not engage in disloyalty, dishonesty or malevolent activities. Ask yourself, are the moderates this way because they follow the moral certainty of their chosen creed, or because they choose to ignore the more extreme elements of it? If they do ignore the extreme elements, does this not suggest that they are actually following the moral clarity of their own transcendental truth and not that of the moral certainty of their chosen creed?

I will not impose my moral clarity on you, provided you do not try to impose your moral certainty or your moral equivalence on me. I do, however, reserve the right to question or criticise your actions, based on your moral certainty or moral equivalence, if it violates my moral clarity. Just like Dr. Phil did in the example previously mentioned.

One of the major benefits of choosing moral clarity as a guiding principle in your life is the happiness you will derive from it. Or as Marcus Aurelius puts it,

> *The happiness of your life depends upon the quality of your thoughts: therefore, guard accordingly, and take care that you entertain no notions unsuitable to virtue and reasonable nature.*
> (Marcus Aurelius, *Meditations*)

He also advises us that,

> *The best revenge is not to be like your enemy.*
> (Marcus Aurelius, Meditations)

Do you think you will find happiness if your thoughts are dominated by money, power, fame, or hypersexual gratification and not the moral clarity created by your conscious interpretation of transcendental truth?

The biggest problem associated with our adoption of moral clarity is in choosing it as our highest good while living in a society that is becoming ever more secular. By choosing the good while avoiding the evil we follow the lighted road instead of forcing our way through the darkness. That is, we become civilised and shun hedonism.

My life has been one spent giving aid, assistance, advice, and being a facilitator for learning. I have not been a leader. I don't believe I'd make a good leader in today's environment. I have served good leaders in the past. Those were the ones who showed integrity, empathy and powerful communication, as well as the ability to inspire and motivate others. Such leaders are rarely seen today. Perhaps the era of inspiring leaders, of great statesmanship, has passed, but then again, perhaps that is just me indulging my nostalgic memories. One thing for sure, however, is that people like me will become less and less valuable to the leaders of tomorrow as they turn more and more to available technology with the capacity to take what was once my position alongside them.

Many people today worry about the power of AI and humanoid robotics for humankind's future. Although this may be way off, and I'm pretty sure I will not be around when the full impact of this technology becomes available, it is still worthy of our consideration today. If AI is left to operate on the existential and/or archetypical levels of truth, and is allowed to be programmed by whomever, this could become a problem, because it would be searching for mere scientific or desire-driven solutions to our problems. In short, we could remain in the mess we are currently in. A mess created by an ever-expanding scientific discovery of amazing things coupled with an insatiable desire for gratification, but with no guiding principle upon which to control those discoveries or desires. Alternatively, if AI was programmed to look for solutions from the transcendental level of truth, our desire to use scientific discoveries purely for gratification may be eased. By giving the transcendental level of truth primacy in its decision making, AI would seek solutions based on truth, justice, goodness, and beauty; while rejecting lies, injustice, evil, and ugliness.

What sort of decision making would AI make if its decision-making capacity was determined by capitalists, communists, globalists, religious leaders, or criminal interests. Give a detailed explanation for your decision.

Imagine this scenario. A future AI has determined that the optimal human population for earth would be one with fewer people than currently exist. Would the solution to this problem be different for AIs programmed to make decisions based on transcendental, existential or archetypical levels of truth? In what ways could they differ from each other? Give a detailed account to explain your decision.

Whatever your future holds for you, always accept responsibility for your own actions. Don't try to pass the blame off onto others for the choices you make in your lifetime. Accepting blame enables us to grow our character and fulfil our potential. Additionally, always try to maintain your integrity while recognising perfection is not achievable in this world, but we have the ability to conceive of it and the struggle to realise it gives purpose to our lives.

Let me end this section on moral integrity with a sagacious joke told by Dushka Zapata, author of the book, *How to Build a Pillow Fort*, who said her mother had originally told it to her. It's a long joke but worth your while to wait for the ending,

An old man living alone hears on the radio that he has to evacuate his house due to an impending flood.

He switches the radio off.

His son calls. *Dad you have to leave the house. It will flood and it's too dangerous to stay.*

Son, his father replies, *I am a man of God. I have prayed fervently all my life. No harm will come to me.* The old man goes to bed and wakes up the next morning. He notices the rain is coming down hard.

Someone is banging on his door. *Dad, I'm here to pick you up! The car is right outside! Please get in. You can come home with me.*

His Dad refuses. The next day the man can only be on the second story of his house due to the rising water level. He hears a noise outside and his son yells through the window,

> *Dad! I rented a boat! Please, get in! It's so dangerous, I'm begging you!*

He refuses. The next day the man is sitting on his roof. His house is under water. He hears a noise above his head. His son is yelling from a helicopter,

> *Dad, please! I'm going to throw down a ladder! Get on! You are going to drown! Please, Dad!*

The man refuses. He drowns.
As he walks into heaven, he demands to speak with God.

> *I was good all my life! I prayed! I worshipped You! How could You do this to me?*
> *Look, my son, God replies, I sent you early warning. I sent you a car. I sent you a boat. I sent you a helicopter.*
> *And I sent you a loyal, devoted son.*

Political Integrity

Political integrity refers to the keeping of ethical principles like honesty and transparency. Politicians who hold their integrity do not mislead or lie to their constituents; their decisions are free from corruption, promote fair treatment and impartial governance while giving free access to their activities and financial dealings. They follow a strong code of conduct which includes things like disclosure of donations and lobbying influences as well as holding themselves and their colleagues to account for any breach of trust. When analysing this subject, I will first establish some definition for the *political terms* in use, then examine *political concepts* used to analyse political systems. Next I will survey the main *political organisation* and end with a *defence of democracy*.

Political Terms

> *But if thought corrupts language, language can also corrupt thought.*
> (George Orwell, *1984*)

The difficulty with discussing political terms is that the words used to describe them have been changed, some would argue deliberately corrupted and debased, so often that there is much confusion in the minds of the general public about what defines the actual terms themselves. For example, in 2023, Javier Milei became the new President of Argentina. He was described as a 'far-right libertarian'. Regardless of what people think of his presidency, this description is simply incorrect, some would say deliberately dishonest. A libertarian believes in liberty (freedom) which is far removed from far-right politics, which is dominated by authoritarianism. In simpler terms this is an oxymoron, but it has the effect of moving liberty from the centre of politics to the far right. No doubt this is the intention of those who create and use terms like these. So the use of this term is incorrect to say the least, and at worse a deliberate corruption of our thoughts for a political end. Perhaps in this case to give a negative connotation to liberty, making it easier for unscrupulous political operatives to remove liberty from the lives of their citizens, who would come to believe that liberty is a far-right plot to control their lives. Recently, I even saw a sign at a radical protest rally that read, 'Liberty is a right-wing conspiracy'.

'Social democracy' is another term that has been with us so long now that we no longer question its validity. Democratic socialism is actually a movement advocating for structural change to democracy, not reform within the democratic system. A correct perception would recognise that socialism, as a political ideology, is based on state control through the abolition of private property and free speech; while democracy would be seen as promoting individual sovereignty through the ownership of private property and open debate. By definition, then, the two words mean directly opposite things.

Again, the motives of those who use this term should be brought into question, because it has successfully (but wrongly) moved socialism from a left of centre position on the political spectrum into the centre left, which is rightly occupied by the reform movement.

Now that you know how some use language to corrupt our thoughts about politics, let us examine some political terms and come to some agreement about their meaning. In this way we can see clearly how the different thoughts concerning politics have arisen and what language was used to describe those thoughts. Hopefully, these definitions will help describe different thoughts about politics in clear-cut terms to help you construct an uncorrupted framework of definitions.

Let's now turn our attention to the words used to describe political ideas and corrupt political influences as opposed to political organisations.

Agent provocateur

A person who induces others to be violent or commit an illegal act in order to incriminate them or discredit them.
(Definition from Oxford Languages, 2025)

The activities of an agent provocateur (French for 'inciting agent') may include things like encouraging others to yell at opponents, display flags, banners or portraits of radical, extremist movements, all the way up to committing acts of violence like punching counter-demonstrators, breaking windows, burning cars, rioting or street fighting with police in order to discredit an otherwise peaceful demonstration and bring public condemnation upon the movement. This can even include undercover government officers and agents infiltrating social and political movements.

When co-ordinated with the media, an agent provocateur will create images for the media which they will run with to either discredit the issue that a peaceful demonstration is trying to highlight or promote it. In short, the media can either highlight the radical behaviour or violence of the protesters incited by the agent provocateur rather than their message or the actions of the police to restore order. If the violence of the protesters is highlighted, the message becomes a far-right issue rather than a conservative one. Alternatively, the media may highlight the violence used by police to restore social order after a peaceful demonstration turns violent. The lead-up to the police action is edited out while the police violence is emphasised. This encourages us to sympathise with the 'peaceful' protesters' message over the police violence, making the protesters' cause seem a reasonable, politically central issue.

Apolitical

Refers to those who are uninterested or uninvolved in politics. They are said to be unbiased in matters of politics, but at the same time they can be naïve or even ignorant of hidden agendas affecting their lives. They do not follow any ideology or political party and usually side with whatever political party they think would be the most beneficial for themselves. This can make them vulnerable to propaganda or vote buying. These voters are called the *swing*, or *independent* voters.

Authoritarianism

Is a belief that freedom leads to moral decay and social disobedience and, therefore, supports the strict enforcement of rules by authorities at the expense of personal freedom. Authoritarians show little or no respect for the opinions of others by enforcing laws designed to override freedom of speech and censoring what people can view, read, and hear. These laws are often described as being *draconian* (laws and their enforcement seen as excessively harsh and severe) by more liberal-minded citizens.

Bribery

Bribery is

> *the offering, promising, giving, accepting or soliciting of an advantage as an inducement for an action which is illegal, unethical, or a breach of trust. Inducements can take the form of money, gifts, loans, fees, rewards or other advantages (taxes, services, donations, favours etc).*
>
> (antibriberyguidance.org, 2025)

Corporate Welfare

Corporate welfare involves the government giving assistance to corporations, especially large corporations. This assistance may be in the form of *subsidies or grants* designed for specific purposes; *tax breaks* in the form of tax reductions, like deductions, credits, or exemptions; *bailouts* to stop companies from collapsing during an economic crisis; *favourable treatment* in the form of regulatory treatment, low-interest loans, or government contracts; and *public-private partnerships* in cooperative ventures.

Those who criticise corporate welfare argue that it benefits large corporations over small businesses and leads to market manipulation that distorts the free market. That is, that the private sector knows best what is most efficient for the market and not government. Those who favour corporate welfare claim that it is a necessary tool for economic growth, start-up companies that can't get finance from established sources of finance, and protecting defence and large industries from financial collapse and the loss of skilled labour. When implemented prudently it can create a more competitive business climate; when used wrongly it lacks transparency and accountability.

Corruption

Corruption is the abuse of entrusted power for private gain. It involves unethical and illegal actions like bribery, fraud, extortion, and misuse of public funds or resources. Corruption creates public mistrust and a drain on the economy making it less efficient. Excessive corruption of a system (political, social or corporate) can lead to a lack of trust in the public, who see the system as being incapable of solving their problems.

Cronyism or Favouritism
Refers to the granting of favours or positions of power based on friendship rather than merit. Sometimes cronyism centres on partisanship. Sometimes DEI can be used in this way. That is, individuals within a partisan group are given favoured treatment over others with more merit.

Dogma
A doctrine of belief in a religious or political system that should be accepted without proof. For example, Christians believe that there is one true God and that Jesus Christ is his son who rose from the dead; Muslims believe that Allah's will directs all human outcomes (known as Qadr or divine outcome); and communists believe that capitalism consists solely of workers who are exploited and capitalists who exploit them. In the minds of believers these tenets are beyond question.

Elitism
Elitism involves people who take pride in being a member of an elite group. This group could consist of those who see themselves as a member of an educated or academic group, a wealthy group, a powerful group, a stylish group, a physically attractive group or a group who sees themselves as having suffered a historical injustice, to mention just a few such elite groups. Selectivity into such groups makes one arrogant or snobbish in his/her attitude towards others. Not all people who are qualified to join these elite groups want to

become members, however, preferring instead to maintain their individual integrity rather than lose it to group identity. People who see themselves as elites believe they either are gifted or chosen to rule over others, or have the right to certain privileges denied to others in the community.

Extremism

Means political decision-making far outside the mainstream attitudes of society. The use of revolution or legislation to overthrow the existing socio/political structure of a society, or the use of terrorism or threat of nuclear war to achieve desired ends would be examples of extremism, although many people today wrongly use this term loosely to describe those who have differing opinions from themselves.

Extortion

When someone gains something (money, signing over property etc.) through the use of force or threats. An example of extortion is the demand for money from a business by gangsters for protection. If the business does not pay, the gangsters threaten or carry out violence on the business. Extortion can also be applied politically. For example, a politician can demand a percentage of a project's budget in exchange for granting the necessary permits, or high-ranking politicians can leverage their position by intimidating their subordinates, or a political party can use its influence to extract 'donations' from businesses or unions in exchange for favourable treatment or protection.

False Flag

> *A false flag operation is an act committed with the intent of disguising the actual source of responsibility and pinning blame on another party.*
> (Wikipedia.org, 2025)

The essential difference between the acts of an agent provocateur and a false flag operation is one of intent. The agent provocateur incites, while the false flag blames the opponent for actions they have already taken. The false flag operation is an act of deception where the true source of the operation is deliberately hidden. This can occur at a local level (i.e., a riot) all the way up to a nation that stages a fake attack on its own military and then blames the attack on another country.

Fanaticism

The word fanatic comes from the Latin word *fanaticus* meaning 'mad'. It describes someone who is insane with enthusiasm or behaviour involving uncritical zeal. A fanatic is someone who is incapable of critical analysis in a religious or political sense.

Fraud

Fraud occurs when someone dishonestly obtains a benefit, or causes a loss by the use of deception etc. An example of fraud is the use of deception to gain access to a victim's asserts without the victim's knowledge or consent. A *scam*, on the other hand, involves the victim voluntarily giving money etc. through deception. In a political sense fraud can occur when it is used to manipulate an election, or rig votes. Such actions are known as election or voter fraud. A scam may be used by politicians who use deception to garnish support for a project they want to introduce.

Graft

Graft involves the dishonest way in which compensation is given where no compensation is due. In politics, for example, it involves a politician intentionally misdirecting funds intended for public projects into the hands of private interests.

Liberty

The word 'Liberty' comes from the name of the Latin goddess *Libertas*, the personification of liberty or freedom, and she was the inspiration for the Statue of Liberty located on Liberty Island in New York Harbour in New York City. The torch that the Statue of Liberty holds aloft is a symbol of the Age of Enlightenment, lighting for us the road to liberty or freedom.

In its most basic form, liberty is the right to live as you choose and go where you want. It involves the right to free speech without the interference of arbitrary restraints like political censorship or social convention. It also includes the right to ownership of private property. Of course, citizens of a Nation State must live together in harmony and peace, so restrictions are placed on a citizen's liberty to achieve unity within the community of a Nation State. The laws of a Nation State define the social contract that individuals must accept to live in a given Nation State, and these laws, by necessity, restrict an individual citizen's liberty. Consequently, we have National and State laws and council by-laws that restrict our liberty. If citizens break these laws, they may receive a fine or have their liberty taken away and be required to serve a term of imprisonment. In this way Nation States encourage citizens to adopt a responsible use of their liberty.

Today, many Australians argue that there are too many laws and by-laws that restrict their freedom. What do you think?

Consider this. One question I was frequently asked by students is "Why does Australia's Constitution not have a Bill of Rights like the American Constitution?" As best as I can ascertain there are many answers. One is that our Founding Fathers believed that by defining our rights they would have been limiting them. A second was that they preferred parliamentary sovereignty (determined by a democratic process) to define them for us. That is, that there may arise future situations that would require new additions to our rights. Why they did not consider the use of a referendum for this purpose still puzzles me. Another is that existing common law (based on precedence) would sufficiently protect citizens' rights.

Many Australian citizens today are disappointed in their founding fathers for not having defined their citizens' civil rights, because of the changes that have been visited upon them in recent years. Firstly, as a result of the lack of definition regarding our rights, our politicians have signed on to the United Nations Human Rights Commission (UNHRC), which is an unelected body that stands outside our parliamentary sovereignty, and therefore our democratic process, and allows it to define (by recommendation) our human rights. Consequently, our founding fathers' preference for Australia's parliamentary sovereignty has been circumvented. Instead of having constitutional rights, Australians now have 'human rights' defined by the UN.

Similarly, Australia's Federal Governments have signed resolution agreements with specialised agencies of the UN. Australia's Federal Government just signed up to membership with the World Health Organisation (WHO), which gives WHO the right to *recommend* what our response to an international pandemic should be. Since the members of WHO are not elected by Australian citizens, do you think this agreement infringes upon your liberty to determine your own health decisions, either in partnership with your doctor or elected representative? Remember, when our politicians sign such agreements they often proclaim that the UN can only recommend, not enforce, their recommendations, but when these specialised agencies hand down their resolution agreements and Australia's representatives sign up to them, those same politicians argue that we must keep our word because we are signatories and then enforce the UN special agencies' resolutions on Australian citizens.

The United Nations Relief and Works Agency (UNRWA) sends funds and distributes aid to Gaza. In 2009, UNRWA suspended their aid operation after a second Hamas-linked theft of hundreds of tons of UNRWA food supplies (news.un.org, February 2009). UNRWA also sacked nine members of their staff because they had been involved in the 7 October 2023 Hamas-led attacks on Israel (news.un.org. August

2024). Australia donates funds to UNRWA which has, in the past, ended up funding Hamas, a terrorist organisation.

Moreover, the UN Intergovernmental Panel on Climate Change (IPCC) provides the scientific basis for net zero by 2050, affirming the need for net zero emissions around mid-century to limit global warming by 1.5 degrees Celsius. Despite this scientific evidence, the Paris Climate Accords, a formal international treaty adopted in 2015 under the United Nations Framework Convention on Climate Change (UNFCCC), allows China to reach net zero by 2060 and India by 2070.

Furthermore, the International Criminal Court (ICC), a specialised agency of the UN, can, and does, hand down verdicts on international criminals. Those countries who are signatories to the ICC are expected to enforce the ICC verdicts. These are all UN special agencies that Australia is a signatory to and provides funding for. They are also all unelected international agencies that make recommendations affecting the lives of Australian citizens, thereby nullifying their sovereignty.

Secondly, our High Court does not always follow tradition or precedent when formulating its decisions. They can, for example, follow the need for legal reform owing to what they perceive is an *evolving social context* and this has allowed an opportunity for making changes to the interpretation of our constitution that the majority of Australians (conservatives and reformists) sometimes find radical. Therefore, common law no longer offers Australian citizens the protection for their rights that our founding fathers thought it would.

Some changes that have taken place since our constitution was signed into law are –

Firstly, our right to own a gun. Australians at the time of Federation took this for granted, but the forced confiscation of our guns following the Port Arthur massacre in April 1996 didn't end there. Under the Queensland Weapons Act 1990, pepper spray is classified as a prohibited weapon and cannot be possessed or carried even for self-defence without a valid restricted weapons licence (bouchiekhan.

com.au, 2025). Those who support this legislation claim that without it protestors would use it against police, but this argument fails to address the underlying cause of the problem: the use of violence by protestors at what should be a peaceful demonstration. Why should Australian citizens have the right to defend themselves stripped because of the actions of a few violent protestors? Why should the law not address this issue by cracking down hard on violent demonstrators, and leave law-abiding citizens with the right and means to defend themselves?

Secondly, Australia's right to free speech is now determined by section 18c of the Racial Discrimination Act, or an eSafety Commissioner operating within the Online Safety Act 2021, who the Institute of Public Affairs (IPA) argues cannot be trusted to stick to online child protection (ipa.org.au, John Storey, *eSafety Commissioner Cannot Be Trusted On Online harm*, 5 July 2024, and Bella d'Abrera, *eSafety Commissioner No Longer Pretending To Hide Political Bias*, 26 July 2024). Recently, The Administrative Review Board found that the eSafety Commissioner made the wrong decision in the 'Billboard Chris' case (adfinternational.org, *Free Speech Victory in Australia for Billboard Chris as 'X' Post Censorship Overturned*, July 1, 2025). It appears limits to free speech no longer stop at defamation, incitement to violence or treason, but now include things like offence and online safety which increases the possibility for monitoring and attempting to censor certain political opinions.

Thirdly, our anti-discrimination laws keep expanding beyond just race and sex. They now include things like breastfeeding, sex work activity, family responsibility, association with others, and saying things where other people can hear what is said (qhrc.qld.gov.au, 2025). Is there anything we will be able to decide for ourselves in future? I remember being told that if you want to know how well a school is being run, look at the rules governing behaviour on the school noticeboard. If there is a long list of don'ts, it means that the students are incapable of exercising self-discipline. Examining the legislated rules governing the behaviour of Australians today, it is difficult not to conclude that Australians are no longer capable of self-discipline or courteous behaviour.

Finally, our right to equal justice has been compromised by a two-tiered justice system –

> *In Australia, while the law aims for equal treatment under the law, evidence suggest that societal biases and systemic factors can influence how judgements for violent crime are applied differently across various groups.*
>
> (AI Overview, 2025)

My father passed away in 2016, but he was a keen libertarian. Let me relate an anecdote to you that illustrates his strong sense of independence. When the Queensland Government first introduced seatbelt laws into our State, I remember him arguing strenuously that the Government has the right to force him to put a seatbelt into his car, but not the right to force him to wear it. That, he said, was something he would choose to do for himself.

Why did my father object to the state law that legally forced him to wear a seatbelt? Do you think he has a point?

This is an example of an Australian Government that passed a law *for our own good* that erodes the liberty of citizens. At the time I couldn't understand what had upset my father so much, but I do now. How many other laws can you identify that our local, state and national governments have introduced *for our own good*?

In my father's and my time, the only restriction on freedom of speech in Australia was *incitement* to violence, *defamation*, and *treason*. Today there are laws that restrict freedom of speech for *offence* (section 18c of Australia's Racial Discrimination Act), *controlled use* of our internet (eSafety Commission), and the possible introduction of *mis/disinformation* laws.

Do you think any of these laws infringe on your liberty? Do you consider the Online Safety Amendment (Social Media Minimum Age) Act which will prevent those Australians under 16 years of age from creating accounts on some social media platforms as an infringement on their rights or a protection of their innocence? How do you think the eSafety Commission will know the age of people wanting to use the internet?

In a Liberal Representative Democracy a plurality of candidates stand for elections at regular intervals, which allows citizens to decide if their members of Parliament and Council Chambers have exceeded their authority by creating laws that place unacceptable restrictions upon their citizens' liberty.

Some (J.S. Mill in particular, who wrote a treatise on liberty in the 19th century) argue that the only restriction that should be placed on a citizen's liberty is when it involves physical harm to another citizen, either through direct action or incitement to violence.

Do you think protestors who block the free passage of citizens or damage public or private property are infringing on the libertarian rights of citizens in a Nation State? Are property damage and the blocking of free passage acts of violence against fellow citizens? Is it logical, rational and wise to protect the rights of the protestors or the citizens? In the case of property damage or restriction of free passage, whose rights are more justified, the rights of the protestors or the citizens?

Libertarians also argue that because a citizen's freedom to choose has no restraints other than physical harm, individual citizens should be held personally responsible for the consequences of their own choices. In other words, the state has no responsibility to alleviate the consequences (suffering) of bad choices made by its citizens. Today, such an attitude is considered too harsh by our compassionate society and that the Nation State does have responsibility to offer relief for the needs of individual citizens.

What do you think? Do you think citizens need to admit that their bad choice is responsible for their suffering and commit to changing their behaviour before the Nation State offers relief?

Here is some research for you that will help you appreciate the struggle that your ancestors had to endure to achieve liberty for themselves and you. Read the following documents and look up the historical circumstances that gave rise to them. *Magna Carta* (1215), The Elizabethan Royal Compromise (1559), The Elizabethan Poor Relief Act (1601), *Habeas Corpus Act* (1679), *American Declaration of Independence* (1776), *The American Bill of Rights* (1791), the *Gettysburg Address* (1863) and *The Atlantic Charter* (1941). One idea you might like to research is *The Social Contract*. You will find information on this concept in the following books: Thomas Hobbes, *Leviathan* (1651), John Locke, *Essay Concerning Human Understanding* (1689) and John Stuart Mill, *On Liberty* (1859). Again, discover for yourself the historic circumstances that gave rise to this concept.

If you apply yourself to this research with structure and disciple your reward will be great. I can assure you of that. Do you now value your liberty? Why?

Nepotism

Is the granting of favours or positions of power based on family relationships rather than merit. The political dimension to nepotism occurs when political leaders promote members of their own families into positions of power.

Populism

This term emerged in the late 19th century and is most often used as a pejorative term. Someone who leads a popular movement is referred to as a populist, and is often accused of having hidden, ulterior motives from those he/she espouses to get elected. Put simply, populism involves a criticism of the elite who are portrayed as corrupt and self-serving, while holding up 'the people' as a morally good force. As a political force, populism most often arises in a democracy during periods of economic hardship (particularly high inflation and/or unemployment) and can be used by socialists and demagogues (someone who uses the desires and prejudices of ordinary people rather than rational argument to get himself/herself elected) alike to politically organise 'the people' against an existing political, economic, cultural system that the majority of the population see as not acting in their best interests. Those who favour populism claim that it is democracy in action, which, by definition, it is. However, when used to hide ulterior motives it can lead to undesirable outcomes, including the end of democracy itself.

Prejudice or Bias

Are irritational attitudes and sometimes hostile actions directed towards other individuals or groups. People who exhibit prejudice pre-judge others, usually on nothing more than their appearance or opinions. Political bias is detected in story selection, framing, tone, and the frequency of criticism or support of specific parties or people over others.

Realpolitik

Refers to diplomatic or political decision-making based on immediate circumstances rather than ideology. Realism and pragmatism are positive words often associated with realpolitik. Negative words used to describe realpolitik are opportunism, Machiavellianism (manipulativeness, deceitfulness) and expediency. Deng Xiaoping (1904-1997), Chinese leader, 1978-89, who oversaw the modernisation of China's economy, once said,

> *It doesn't matter whether a cat is black or white, as long as it catches mice.*
> (chinadaily.com.cn, 2025)

This is a clear expression of realpolitik, and was made by Deng in the 1960s as a way to promote his economic reform policies following the Great Leap Forward. The Chinese refer to this as the 'Black Cat, White Cat Theory', which emphasises that practical results are more important than ideological purity.

Rort

Rorting is taking unfair advantage of a public or private system. For example, when someone claims both a student allowance and an unemployment benefit at the same time. Or when someone makes the same insurance claim on two separate insurance companies.

Social Welfare

This involves government programs and services aimed at improving the economic and social wellbeing of citizens. This can involve providing income support, health services and educational assistance for the needy, but also involves assistance for groups rather than needy individuals. When social welfare goes beyond needy individuals it is sometimes referred to as middle-class welfare. Unemployment benefits, family support payments, pensions for the elderly and those with disabilities, and housing and employment assistance are examples of social welfare.

Terrorism

The Oxford definition of terrorism is

> *the unlawful use of violence and intimidation, especially against civilians, in the pursuit of political aims.*

Terrorists may commit criminal or violent acts to terrorise peaceful citizens, or they may threaten acts of violence to intimidate the innocent citizens of any given Nation State. They may also organise themselves into large paramilitary forces and go to war against smaller countries in order to conquer them and maintain their rule through a reign of terror.

Terrorist acts include assassinations and kidnappings. These acts are usually performed against the leaders of their perceived enemies, but they may include any targets of opportunity. Sometimes they will take a large number of hostages. For example, through carrying out raids or hijacking planes, ships, buses etc. This puts the countries of the hostages in a position of weakness and enables the terrorists to make demands against those countries that oppose the terrorists' agenda. They can carry out bomb scares and even do actual bombings, sometimes using suicide bombers who are difficult to detect. They carry out computer-based cyberattacks against the computers or data storage systems of countries and companies and demand huge payments in return for releasing their hold on the computers or their data. To date we have not experienced biological, chemical or nuclear attacks from terrorists against those countries that the terrorists deem as their enemies, but the possibility of such threats would take the death toll due to terrorist attacks to new heights and weighs heavily on the minds of innocent civilians and their leaders throughout the world.

Two of the more infamous terrorist attacks are the suicide 9/11 attacks carried out by Al-Qaeda against the United States in 2001 and the 7 October 2023 Hamas attack against Israel. The 9/11 attack killed 2,996 people and the 7 October attack killed around 1,200 Israelis and foreigners, while 252 were taken hostage.

Each nation state creates a designated terrorist list which includes those organisations deemed as terrorist organisations. Currently, the Australian National Security website lists 29 organisations which have been listed as terrorist organisations under Australia's criminal code. Obviously, Al-Qaeda, Isis and Hamas are listed as designated terrorist organisations along with some totalitarian organisations like the National Socialist Order and Sonnenkrieg Division.

Because of the suffering of innocent civilians and children from the October 7 Hamas attack on Israel and Israel's declared war against Hamas, which has resulted in urban warfare in Gaza, protests have erupted against Israel throughout the West. These protests have seen a rise of antisemitism in Australia. Slogans like *from the river to the sea*, which calls for the elimination of the Jewish state, *Where are the Jews?* and even *intifada* and *kill the Jews* have been shouted at rallies and painted on walls and fences in Australia. As well, synagogues and businesses have been attacked with graffiti and/or firebombed. The Australian Security Intelligence Organisation (ASIO) have even determined that Iran's Islamic Revolutionary Guard Corps (IRGC) gave the orders to firebomb the Adass Israel Synagogue in Melbourne that set Australia's social cohesion ablaze (afr.com, *The VW, the Tobacco Kingpin, and Iran's Revolutionary Guard,* Aug 26, 2025).

Furthermore, Australia has had its national flag burned in public while the flag of terrorist organisations has been proudly flown at pro-Palestinian rallies. This development is unconscionable. Jews living in Australia are not responsible for what happens in Gaza, and many people, who are not Jews, support what Israel is doing in trying to eliminate Hamas. Hamas recently referred to the success of their propaganda war against Israeli as

> *Palestinian State is one of the fruits of October 7.*
> (fdd.org, Ghazi Hamad, August 3, 2025)

This statement was made following France, the United Kingdom, Canada, Australia, and Malta announcing that they would officially recognise Palestinian statehood during the September meeting of the UN General Assembly, which they have subsequently done. This recognition is futile because Hamas has never accepted a two-state solution to their conflict. Instead they demand the elimination of the state of Israel. It has, however, encouraged Hamas and led to a continuation of the war. America, Australia's foremost military ally, has officially stated that recognising Palestinian statehood is rewarding terrorism.

On October 8, 2025, Israel and Hamas agreed to the first phase of President Trump's 20-point peace plan for ending the war in Gaza. President Trump has stated that recognising Palestinian statehood should come after the war has been peacefully resolved, not before.

Should Australian politicians allow any immigrants (not just

Palestinians) to bring their hatred and conflict into Australia? Should such immigrants pay a price for their refusal to leave their hatred behind when they migrate into Australia? What should that price be?

Since Australia is experiencing difficulty with Islamist terrorists, we need to clarify a few things about the Islamic religion. Islam is the religion of Muslims who are the devotees of Islam. There are approximately 1.6 billion Muslims around the world. Muslims are divided into two tribes, the Sunni (85%) and the Shia (15%) (history.com, 2025). The Shias believe that Mohammad and his descendants are divine and therefore Muslim leadership should be in the hands of Mohammad's family. Sunnis are opposed to this hereditary means of passing on Muslim leadership and prefer Muslim leadership to be decided by consensus. Iran is predominately a Shia Muslim country, approximately 90-95% of Iran's population adhere to the Islamic religion (AI overview, 2025).

Muslims are also divided into two groups according to their interpretation of the *Quran*, their holy text. One group sees Islam as a peaceful religion, the other as a political ideology that they can use to achieve their political goals. This more aggressive group of Muslims is called *Islamists*. Their aim is to achieve worldwide socio/political change including

> *the implementation of sharia law, pan-Islamic political unity, the creation of unified pan-Islamic political states, and the rejection of all other non-Muslim influences.*
>
> (Wikipedia, 2025)

It is from this group of Muslims that the terrorist organisations emerge. Unfortunately, both groups can support their beliefs through their interpretation of different passages found in the *Quran*. You see, the *Quran* contains passages on war and peace. The *Hadith* passages were collected and compiled after the *Quran*, and contains many passages on jihad, self-defence, conflict, and war.

The leadership of Islam is divided between Mullahs, Ayatollahs, and Muftis.

Mullah

This is a term used to describe a Muslim cleric. They usually have some education in Islam, theology, and Sharia law. Some are peaceful, even calling for reform, while others are radical, preaching the more extreme elements of Sharia law, the death cult of martyrdom, and the establishment of a caliphate empire.

Ayatollah

These leaders are found in Shia Islam. They are high-ranking religious scholars. In Iran, the Shia majority population relies on Ayatollahs, especially Grand Ayatollahs, to interpret Islamic law and guide the community. Some Ayatollahs are also Muftis.

Mufti

A mufti is a special type of Islamic scholar who is qualified to issue *fatwas* on matters of Islamic law. Fatwas are non-binding legal opinions in response to a question. It is a form of religious guidance intended to help Muslims understand and apply Islamic teaching in their lives. The Mufti have played, and still do play, a significant role in Muslim life, informing populations, advising courts and even mobilising resistance against foreign powers. One famous example of a fatwa was issued by Iran's Ayatollah Khomeini against Salman Rushdie, an Indian-born, British-American novelist, after the publication of his book, *The Satanic Verses*, in 1988.

Two other concepts regarding Islamic doctrine need defining. The first is *Jihad* or 'Holy War'. This war relates to the struggle that Muslims must undertake to stay on the path of Allah. This struggle is seen by Muslims to be both internal and external, that is, the *personal struggle* that a Muslim must undergo in order to live according to Islamic principles and the *effort* he/she must undertake to build a good Muslim society. This effort can potentially involve him/her in armed conflict.

The second is the phrase *Allah Akbar*, meaning 'God is most great'. This phrase is used by Muslims in prayers and as a general declaration of faith or thanksgiving. Unfortunately, it is understood by the public at large to be used whenever an Islamist kills an *infidel*. An infidel is not just a Jew or a Christian but anyone who is not a Muslim.

We could go on, but I feel that understanding these clearly defined terms will go a long way in developing your political literacy. Now we can consider the actual political organisations themselves.

Political Organisations

> *Political organisations are groups involved in the political process to achieve specific goals, typically benefiting their members, and include political parties, advocacy groups, interest groups, and think tanks. While political parties primarily focus on winning elections and controlling government by supporting candidates, other political organisations focus on activities like lobbying, campaigning, and producing policy alternatives to influence political decisions and the public.*
>
> (AI Overview, 2025)

Aristocracy

The term *aristocracy* derives from the Greek word *aristokratia* and was used to describe the mostly young men of the ruling class who led armies in frontline battle. In most cases, aristocratic titles and land titles were, and still are, hereditary. The aristocracy is a privileged class of people (both men and women) who derive their privilege through connections with the military and wealthy classes. Today, some would say they sustain their privilege through a successful social network. They were, and in some cases still are, seen to be noble, virtuous and *the best* of society. The head of the aristocracy is the Monarch who originally ruled with absolute power (the Divine Right of Kings).

The aristocracy, however, were and are a mixed bunch. The best of them maintain their integrity and behave with dignity and respect for others while guarding and maintaining their country's culture. The worst of them take their privilege for granted and act out of a sense of arrogance and entitlement.

Of course, this distinction between different members of the aristocracy was not recognised by the Jacobins during the reign of terror in France. Both King Louis XVI (1754-1793) and Marie Antoinette (1755-1793) of France died by the guillotine at the hands of French Revolutionaries during the French Revolution (1789-1799). At first, the revolutionaries only wanted revenge on all members of the aristocracy, but later, once the bloodlust had taken hold in Paris, the revolutionaries turned on Parisian landlords who had made their living from the rents they collected in Paris. Owing to the widespread executions and political purges ordered by the Jacobins, the revolutionaries eventually turned on those Jacobins who had led the revolution, like Robespierre (along with 21 of his followers), Saint-Just, and Georges Danton. This gave rise to the saying,

Eventually the revolution will eat its own.

This highlights the destructive nature of most revolutions.

Following the end of WWI (1914-18), all the main Crown Heads of Europe fell. In Germany, Kaiser Wilhelm II abdicated in 1918 and fled to the Netherlands. He was replaced by the Weimar Republic with a president as its head of state. The Habsburg Dynasty ended following WWI, the 1918 crop failure, and general starvation and economic collapse. The Holy Roman Empire that had been ruled by the Habsburgs was broken up into separate countries. Chief among these were Austria, Hungary, Poland, and the Czech Republic which adopted liberal democratic rule. Finally, the Romanoff family dynasty ended in Russia after Tzar Nicholas II abdicated in 1917. It was replaced first by a Kerensky-led liberal democratic government and then a few months later by a communist dictatorship led by Vladimir Lenin following a military coup d'état. After months of plotting, Tsar Nicholas II and his entire Romanoff family were assassinated by their Bolshevik captors in 1918.

Most of the remaining Monarchs left in Europe today are Constitutional Monarchs, having devolved their political power to the parliamentary process. The Vatican City, for example, is an absolute monarchy with the pope as its absolute ruler. Over time, some aristocratic families became part of the wealthy elite (the Grand Duke Henri of Luxembourg, for example, is estimated to have a net worth of $4 billion) while others, who were financially embarrassed, married into rich, but untitled families. Some resisted change, by clinging to their titles and traditional way of life despite facing financial hardship.

Bureaucracy

The term 'bureaucracy' originated in France when a French philosopher, Vincent de Gournay, combined two French words *bureau* meaning 'writing desk' and *cratie* meaning 'government' into the word 'bureaucratie'. When Anglicised, 'bureaucratie' becomes 'bureaucracy', so the literal meaning of bureaucracy is government directed from the desk.

The Cambridge Dictionary defines a bureaucracy as

> *a system for controlling or managing a country, company, or organisation that is operated by a large number of officials employed to follow rules carefully.*

Those who work in the bureaucracies of governments are referred to as *public servants* because they are seen as serving the public. Those in companies and other organisations are usually referred to as *administrators, managers* or more recently *executives* because they administer, manage, or oversee those organisations.

It would be remiss of me if I did not point out that without bureaucracies, governments, companies, and organisations could not function, and therefore would be unable to provide the goods and services to the public that they do. Clearly then, bureaucracies are a necessary part of modern life which provide citizens with the standard of living they all enjoy.

Critics, however, declare that bureaucracies are a necessary evil by pointing out a number of problems that bureaucracies create for the societies they serve. Chief among these are things like –

1) Bureaucracies can become so large that they become unmanageable. Officials in bureaucracies tend to create their own power bases within a bureaucracy by ever expanding their own departments. Companies that become *top heavy* are often rationalised by corporate raiders. A good example of this was when Elon Musk took over ownership of Twitter. He slashed 6,000 employees or 80% of Twitter's staff which did not affect the running of the company. In fact, it has become more efficient and profitable today than when he took it over (forbes.com, *Here's What Happened After Elon Musk Cut 80% of X's Employees – As He Eyes Reshaping Federal Workforce,* Feb 05, 2025). It is more difficult to rationalise government bureaucracies because they are seen as having *job security*. As of June 2024, Australia employed 2,517,900 public sector employees comprising 365,400 public servants in the Commonwealth government, 1,939,100 in State governments, and 213,500 in Local governments (abs.gov.au). Figures for June 2025 were unavailable as of September 2025. Of course, the more services that citizens demand from government, the larger the bureaucracy will become. Remember all this must be

paid for by the taxpayers or rate payers of the various governments offering these services.

Do you think there are too many people working in the bureaucracy of Australian governments? Do you think Australian citizens expect too much from their various governments?

2) To reduce costs, some governments, corporations, and organisations reduce the size of their bureaucracies and *outsource* the work to consultants. Some say this is economically beneficial, others that it is a false economy. The rationale behind this action is a belief that employees migrate from bureaucracies to more efficient consultancy firms that operate in the private sector. A possible drawback to this practice would be if contracts and agreements were created for trivial issues, family members, or friends. In short, this practice has the potential to increase the possibility of waste, nepotism, cronyism, graft, and corruption.

Do you think that corrupt politicians could use the awarding of consultancy contracts as political favours to those who support them?

3) The unelected department secretaries (department managers) of the bureaucracy could gain power over the elected officials because they could be seen as *experts* with more experience and *know-how*. I would urge you to watch two outstanding television series – 'Yes, Minister' and 'Yes, Prime Minister' – which dramatise this specific problem. We all remember the conversations between Sir Humphrey Appleby (Prime Minister's Secretary) and Prime Minister Jim Hacker that went something like this –

Sir Humphrey: "That's a courageous decision, Prime Minister."

Prime Minister: "No. No. No. I don't want to be courageous, Humphrey. I want to be practical. I think I should change that instruction. Can you see to it, Humphrey?"

Sir Humphrey (smiling): "Yes, Prime Minister."

And so the bureaucracy once again gets the decisions from its elected ministers that it wants.

Also, it is worth considering here the possible emergence of a partisan leadership of the public service. The public service is intended to be non-partisan so it can serve the different priorities of different governments. For example, a government with socialist priorities as opposed to a government with a capitalist leaning. In the past, departmental managers were promoted strictly on the basis of merit (qualifications, experience and integrity). Today, promotion is gained through DEI requirements.

Do you think a government or a company could use DEI to promote unqualified partisans into the leadership of their bureaucracies? Do you think a public service with a partisan leadership could impede the priorities of a government with priorities which differ from the partisan priorities of the public service leadership? Explain your position.

4) Bureaucracies can produce rules that citizens find excessive, rigid, or redundant. This is referred to as *red tape, green tape*, or more recently as *black tape*. Many claim that red, green, and black tape prevent companies from investing, acting, and making decisions. Many individual citizens also claim that such rules excessively restrict what they can do with their own property. What do you think?

5) Citizens and customers experience frustration from bureaucracies because their power is centralised and their rules seem arbitrary and generalised. That it is unsuited for the particular needs of individual people. Another frustration often cited by citizens and customers is the time needed to talk to operators on the phone. Often getting an answering machine that is difficult to navigate rather than a real person.

If you want a laugh and don't mind vulgar language, listen to comedian Rodney Rude's conversation with operator 42 working for telecom. You'll get a full blast of a customer's frustration when dealing with a corporate bureaucracy. Remember this is a comedy sketch designed to make you laugh. It is not intended as an example for dealing with operators. In fact, if you treat operators with dignity and respect, you will get better co-operation from them, not to mention retaining the integrity of your own moral clarity.

There are many other problems that can arise with bureaucracies that I have not dealt with here, but you get the general picture. Remember bureaucracies are a necessary part of modern life, so learn to laugh at your frustration when dealing with them (they make great anecdotes at parties) but be aware of the genuine dangers they pose to our liberty and democratic rights.

A good book that highlights the dangers of bureaucracy is *The Utopia of Rules: On Technology, Stupidity, and the Secret Joys of Bureaucracy*, by David Graeber.

Communism
The word communism comes from the Latin *communis*, meaning *common* or *shared*. This reveals the underlying philosophy of communism, which is *equity* (where no one has more than anyone else).

This word has its roots in the revolutions of 1848 in France. For Marx and Engels it is associated with revolutionary communism which seeks to create a society without economic division. That is, no class structure, hierarchy, or private property but rather a socio/economic order built upon the common ownership of all property and production, including real estate, finance, energy, manufacturing, and agriculture.

Communists believe that capitalist societies are divided into two classes: capitalists/workers, oppressors/oppressed, aggressor/victim, exploiter/exploited, or more recently coloniser/native, which are constantly challenging each other. Communism, they argue, would end this division.

Communists believe in *violent revolution* as a means to achieve their goals, while socialists believe in *political evolution* through the legislative process to achieve the same goals as communists. That is, the overthrowing of any other form of government and replacing it with a communist system of governance. In the West the goal is to overthrow capitalist markets and the liberal democratic system of government and replace it with a centrally planned economy and a communist system of government.

The word socialist was first used by Robert Owen in Britain in an article published in 1827 and Pierre Leroux (a French follower of Saint-Simon) in 1832. Both Owen and Leroux were considered *utopian socialists* who sought to replace the individualism and competition of capitalism with community-based ideals.

Four books that will lead you to a good understanding of communism are *The Principles of Communism* (1847), by Friedrich Engels; *The Communist Manifesto* (1848), by Karl Marx; *The State and Revolution* (1917), by Vladimir Lenin, and *The Rise and Fall of Communism* (2009), by Archie Brown.

To better understand communism we must examine the history of revolutions in Western civilisation that gave rise to it.

We begin with the American Revolution (1775-1783). As a consequence of the Seven Years' War between France and Britain (1756-63) over the control of territory and resources in North America, the British had accumulated massive debts and ongoing costs associated with the need to station a large army in North American to guarantee the security of their colonies and their newly acquired territories. The British argued that the American colonies needed to pay a share of the cost of the war and their future security, so the British attempted to impose taxes on their American colonies to recover some of their costs.

First the British tried to impose a stamp tax (1765) on the American colonies, which met with violent protests by the colonies who argued that they had fought alongside the British in the war and therefore had already contributed to the cost of the war. They created the slogan,

No taxation without representation

which highlighted their claim that they did not have representation in the British Parliament. Under the British constitution the King could not impose a tax without the consent of parliament (this principle was first introduced by King John of England when he signed the Magna Carta in 1215). Since the colonies did not have representation in the British Parliament, they argued that they had no legal obligation to pay the stamp tax. The British Parliament ignored their protest and introduced the tax. At that time, the dominant political power in the British Parliament refused to give the colonists representation in the British Parliament because they feared it would strengthen the democratic (at that time seen as radical) movement in Britain and intensify social pressure for political change at home.

The colonialists boycotted British goods, engaged in smuggling, harassed British officials, and organised secret, partisan resistance groups. The resistance grew, particularly in Boston where an effigy of the government official responsible for introducing the stamp tax was paraded through the town and hanged from a *liberty tree*. They also tore down the stamp office building.

The Tea Act of 1773 was originally intended to help the British East India Company that was struggling financially, but it also maintained parliament's right to tax their colonies. The American colonists planned to boycott tea by drinking coffee. This is why coffee became so popular in America even to this day. What followed was the Boston Tea Party where some colonists, disguised as Indians, boarded cargo ships carrying chests of tea and dumped the tea into the Boston harbour. This act irrevocably split the colonists into two groups: the *Patriots* (partisans) who rebelled against the British monarchy (who at that time controlled foreign policy) in favour of a Republic, and the *Loyalists* who remained loyal to the monarchy. Later the Patriots were joined by French soldiers (including most notably the Marquis de Lafayette) who joined their Continental Army led by George Washington. The British, led by General Cornwallis, employed German mercenaries (called Hessians) to fight for them owing to the British lack of manpower.

The American revolution was a very bloody and hard-fought war that ended in 1781 when Lieutenant-General (also Lord) Cornwallis surrendered his army at Yorktown because he was surrounded and faced a siege by a superior force of combined American and French soldiers. After the War of Independence had ended, the Loyalists were persecuted by the Patriots, so most of them migrated to Canada to the north of the 13 colonies which was still in the hands of the British.

Many thought that the American colonies would never be able to govern themselves. However, the Founding Fathers (the most prominent of these were George Washington, Thomas Jefferson, Benjamin Franklin, James Madison and Alexander Hamilton) drew up the American Constitution (1789). They were inspired by the ideas first promoted by the Enlightenment philosophers, in particular John Locke, and created a Republic based on a balance of power between a Legislative branch, an Executive branch and a Judicial branch. The American Congress recognised that their original constitution did not guarantee any citizenship rights, so they ratified ten amendments to the constitution called the Bill of Rights in 1791, which outlines the fundamental rights and freedoms guaranteed to all American citizens. Today there are 27 amendments to the American constitution; the first ten are known as the Bill of Rights. America never became a monarchy, because Washington refused it and the Colonies had no other person with enough standing to be accepted by all 13 colonies.

In 1812, America became embroiled in another war against Britain. I will not go into the details of this war but you could do a research project into it for your own expanded knowledge of America's history, if you are so inclined. The 1812 war, which saw Washington DC (the Capital of The American Republic) sacked by the British, was one which involved a naval bombardment of Fort McHenry in Baltimore, Maryland, inspiring Francis Scott Key to write *The Star-Spangled Banner,* the national anthem of the United States.

The success of the American Revolution and America's success in establishing a lasting form of government other than a monarchy was an inspiration for future revolutions throughout the world. However, not all revolutions ended in the forming of a republic and liberty for the people who fought in the revolution. Some resulted in establishing communist or military dictatorships, or religious theocracies.

The next revolution was the French Revolution (1789-94) fought by the French Revolutionists against the French Monarchy, which again was a very bloody affair. The slogan for this revolution was

Liberty, Equality and Fraternity.

Again you should research this for yourself. The revolutionaries eventually turned on Robespierre and the Jacobins (their leaders) who had established a revolutionary dictatorship and maintained control through a *Reign of Terror,* which became famous for its use of the guillotine. Napoleon Bonaparte, a French general and later First Consul, declared himself *Empereur des Français* (Emperor of the French) in 1804 following a coup de d'état. Later Pope Pius VII presided over the coronation of Napoleon. However, Napoleon took the crown from Pope Pius VII's hands and crowned himself Emperor of Europe following his success in wars against the other nations of Europe. Britain defeated Napoleon In the battle of Waterloo (1815) which ended the Napoleonic wars and exiled Napoleon to the island of Saint Helena until his death in 1821. During his exile, Napoleon is reported to have said to Charles Tristan,

Chapter 8: New World Issues

> *I have dethroned no one. I found the crown in the gutter. I picked it up and the people put it on my head.*

The Congress of Vienna (1814-15) sought to provide a long-term peace plan for Europe through a balance of power which tried to establish principles like state sovereignty and territorial integrity. These were principles that inspired later international organisations, like the League of Nations and the United Nations, which tried to maintain world peace. Despite the restoration of the monarchical system of government in Europe, these events gave encouragement to those who sought to overthrow the aristocratic rule in Europe and replace it with some form of government in which the people had a say in how they were governed.

Consider this nursery rhyme –

> *Humpty Dumpty sat on a wall*
> *Humpty Dumpty had a great fall*
> *All the King's horses and all the King's men*
> *Couldn't put Humpty together again.*

Do you detect any connection between this nursery rhyme and the events of the French Revolution and its aftermath?

Next came the revolutions of 1848, which were caused by the economic crisis of 1845-47, leading to the spread of ideas such as political liberalisation, nationalism, and socialism. For example, the French monarchy was once again overthrown and replaced by a republic; the leaders of Germany, Austria and Italy were forced to grant liberal constitutions in their countries. The separate states in Germany and Italy were forming into unified nations. These revolutions were led by the liberty-seeking middle classes and supported by the working classes in these countries.

This led Karl Marx to believe that the working class could govern themselves and establish a classless society, resulting in his writing of the *Communist Manifesto* (1848) and his cry for a worldwide communist revolution. Marx ends his manifesto with the slogan,

> *Working Men of All Countries, Unite!*

The 1848 revolutions, although fought to liberate Europe from autocratic rule, gave rise to the communist movement and their belief in a violent revolution of workers to overthrow the capitalist system and establish a classless society. It also created a political and economic struggle between those espousing individual liberty and those supporting dependence on the state, i.e., communism.

Another irony in this story is that Britain remained free from the 1848 revolutions that swept Europe, because of its industrial prosperity, political reforms (due to the success of the Chartists' movement, 1838-48), and the rising wages for workers. The irony is that Karl Marx sought, and was given refuge, in Britain where he conducted his research in the British Museum, London, which was the precursor to the British library. So the foundational works of communism were created in a country upholding individual liberty and the most successful capitalist economy in the world at that time.

In France, following France's defeat in the Franco-Prussian war in 1871, a short-lived commune was established in Paris. This was the first attempt at establishing a communist-inspired community.

This period of French history, the economic crisis of 1845-47, the revolution of 1848 and the establishment of the French commune in 1871, provides the historical backdrop for Victor Hugo's novel, *Les Misérables* and the musical of the same name. What is ironic about this narrative is that Jean Valjean, who loses his son in the revolution, recognises that God is love and calls on Him with the words,

> *God on high, hear my prayer. Take me now to thy care.*

Because the French commune is one of the inspirational

foundations of communism, it is ironic that communists are atheists who do not believe in an afterlife. Karl Marx even describes religion as,

> The opiate of the people.

The Fabian Society was founded in Britain in 1884 and is still active today, promoting socialist legislation through democratic parliaments. In the 20th century this legacy was further promoted by political parties with socialist policies like the Labour Party in the United Kingdom (founded in 1900) and the Labor Party in Australia (founded in 1901). The 21st century has seen an adoption of socialist-inspired legislation in most Western liberal democracies and the emergence of globalisation with global community aspirations that run counter to the principles of individual liberty and nationalism.

In 1917, the first communist state was created in Russia. A revolution in March (February under the Julian calendar) had led to the establishment of a Duma led by Alexander Kerensky and the abdication of Tzar Nicholas II. Kerensky's liberal government established things like freedom of speech, equality before the law, and the rights of unions to organise and strike. Unfortunately, Kerensky continued Russia's participation in WWI, which was highly unpopular and led to food shortages and more social unrest. In November (October under the Julian calendar) the Bolsheviks (communists), led by Vladimir Lenin carried out a military coup d'état and formed the world's first communist state, making Lenin the world's first communist dictator. What is noticeable about this event is that the first communist state did not come about by a bloody revolution conducted by the working class, as predicted by Marx, but by a military coup d'état.

Since then, a number of communist revolutions in other countries led to the establishment of other communist dictatorships. Most prominent among these were Mao Zedong in China, Fidel Castro in Cuba, Le Duan in Vietnam and Pol Pot in Cambodia. Again, all of these communist states were achieved through military conquest and not working-class revolution. In fact, Mao Zedong (1893-1976) is reported to have said during a meeting of the Chinese Communist Party (CCP) in 1927,

> *Political power grows out of the barrel of a gun.*

This saying was later popularised by its inclusion in *Quotations by Chairman Mao Zedong (*also known as *Little Red Book)* published in 1964.

All these communist dictators carried out mass killings and repression against what they called counter-revolutionary forces. They also oversaw the suffering and deaths of millions of their own people through the famines and starvation that their policies produced.

Communists refer to themselves as comrades. This term suggests a very close friendship shared by those who experience a common danger. It is used in both a political and military context. Communists use this term because they see themselves as being engaged in a war against capitalism and the counter-revolutionaries in their own countries. Their favourite colour is blood red, which symbolises the spilling of blood for the cause. Red is seen in all communist flags.

For an understanding of the malevolence of communist dictators, look up the history of Lenin's and Stalin's dictatorship of Russia, or Mao's dictatorship of China, or Pol Pot's dictatorship of Cambodia. To those who would say that true communism has never been tried, that it has always been hijacked by malevolent dictators, I would say that you seem to believe that you would have been able to introduce true communism to the world, when in reality you would have ended up like all your other comrades who thought that communist dictators were benevolent and offered 'dear leader' advice on how to improve the running of his country. At best, you would have wound up in a re-education camp (e.g., a Gulag in Siberia, Internment Camps in China, or Re-education Camps in Vietnam) or, at worst, been purged from the party as a counter-revolutionary, suffered the indignity of a show trial, and ended your life in a forest with a bullet hole behind your left ear. After the communist revolution in Russia, many Americans with communist yearnings went to the Soviet Union in the 1920s. Some joined various groups seeking to influence the new Soviet government, and faced the oppressive regime of Stalin. They finished up being purged, imprisoned, or executed.

Let us now consider how communism subverts the values of liberal democracies.

During the 20th century, citizens living in liberal democracies came to recognise the shortcomings in the communist paradigm and understood that they had liberty under a liberal democratic political system and were materially better off staying with the regulated Capitalist system they had. Disappointed that their revolution did not materialise in these countries, communists embarked on a subterfuge operation designed to create envy and hatred among the citizens and a lack of trust in the institutions of their liberal democratic nations.

The concept behind this innovation is *Critical Theory* or *Cultural Marxism*. Max Horkheimer (1895-1973) is a German philosopher and sociologist who made a significant contribution to developing critical theory, which provides the ideological framework for this new approach. Consequently, Marx's dialectic materialism, which did not produce the expected revolution to overthrown Capitalism, became Max Horkheimer's cultural dialectic which communists hoped would lead to the social and economic collapse of Capitalism and provide the fertile ground for a Marxist revolution. Critical Race Theory (CRT) developed in the 1970 by Harvard Law School Professor, Derrick Bell is based on the principles of Critical Theory.

Two books that will provide you with a better understanding of this process are Dr. Niranjan B. Poojar's book, *Cultural Marxism: The War On Consciousness* (2025), and *American Marxism* (2021) by Mark Levin.

Communists rightly recognised that the cultural and institutional systems of Capitalism were the structural framework holding up and unifying Capitalism and the liberal democratic nations that supported it. I would urge you to research the 1923 Frankfurt School of Critical Theory, the New Left political movement that arose in Western Europe and America in the 1950-70s, and the Postmodernist movement (a complex set of artistic, cultural, and philosophical ideals) first appearing in France during the 1970s and continuing until today. All of these movements promote ways in which communists can attack, what they see as, the cultural and institutional pillars holding up the exploitative capitalist system and its politically repressive system of government. It will give you a better understanding of how the aims of modern-day communists evolved and provide insights into the cultural and institutional changes taking place in liberal democratic nations today.

Once communists turn to destroying the cultural and institutional foundations of Capitalism they try to seduce the citizens of capitalist countries with a lie. Despite the historical evidence proving that communism leads to poverty, destruction, and malevolence, citizens in capitalist nations continue to succumb to the communist vision because of the seductive lie found in its ideology

that the government can take care of them from cradle to grave.

That all their problems can be resolved by government decree. The truth is that governments do not create wealth, they only redistribute it and this redistribution involves trade-offs not equity; it is the citizens who create a nation's wealth, and capitalism encourages citizens to create more wealth while communism discourages them. This communist vision, as it relates to the poor and those in need, is noble and valuable, but their vision of equity is unachievable and the historical evidence proves that its economic model is simply incapable of achieving this vision. Communism does not recognise the difference between *needs* and *wants*. Those in need rightly require our assistance. There is nothing wrong with people wanting a better life for themselves; what is wrong is expecting someone else to provide it for them.

Scholars have identified the cycles that Chinese Dynasties experience that led to their collapse. I will cover this in more detail later when we look at Empires. I have my own view of what I call the socialist cycle. Socialism is founded on the principle of unfunded welfare, both corporate and social –

1) At first, citizens in a liberal democracy enjoy the benefits of the *ever-expanding welfare state*.
2) Eventually however, this leads to the next stage of the socialist cycle: an increase in the national debt, higher taxes, and a decline in productivity.
3) If left unchecked the next stage of the cycle emerges: a *debt spiral* which produces a lower and lower credit rating and a correspondingly higher and higher interest rate on the money borrowed by the socialist government.
4) The next stage of the cycle sees the socialist country *struggle to pay off its debts* and might even lead to it defaulting on its payments or printing money which has no productivity backing it. This makes it even harder for a socialist country to raise loans and leads to a *hyperinflation* of the currency and the savings of its citizens are wiped out.
5) The socialist country's economy is now in a *state of collapse*, leading to social unrest, unlawful behaviour and ultimately *revolution*. Of course, the Socialists blame the economic failure on capitalism rather than their socialist agenda.
6) The revolution leads to a coup d'état and the establishment of either a *military or communist dictatorship* taking control of the country, thus removing its citizens' liberty and the source of its wealth creation.
7) Dictatorships are sustained by a *ruling elite* founded on *nepotism and cronyism* that eventually leads to a *two-tiered*

economic and justice system of government. Those inside the ruling elite do very well for themselves while those outside it are supressed and marginalised.

Such are the hardships, suffering and misery of all citizens and their descendants who allow themselves to be seduced by the great socialist lie. Unless this socialist cycle is short-circuited at some stage of the cycle by a return to liberal democratic values founded on prudently regulated capitalism, a dictatorship is the ultimate end for any country that embraces Socialism. This has been the fate of all those countries that embraced Socialism. Some notable examples include the Soviet Union, East Germany, some countries in Eastern Europe, China before it embraced capitalist reforms, Cuba, Venezuela, and Argentina before Miele introduced capitalist reform.

Also, socialists/communists are expert in conducting *hybrid warfare* (Frank G. Hoffman, *Conflict in the 21st Century: The Rise of Hybrid Wars,* Arlington, VA: Potomac Institute of Public Studies, 2007). Examples of some hybrid warfare tactics include –

1) *Blurred lines between open war and heightened tension.* The *wolf diplomacy* of the CCP is a good example of this. When a Chinese flotilla circumnavigated Australia and carried out a live firing exercise without informing the Australian Government of their intention, it left the Australian Government confused about what would be an appropriate response. Other incidents include a sonar attack against Australia's navy divers, directing laser lights into the cabins of Australia's surveillance planes and firing chaff into the flight path of Australia's airforce reconnaissance planes. Such activity is designed to heighten tensions between Australia's and China's armed forces without actually engaging in open warfare. The Australian Government responded to these attacks by declaring them *unsafe and*

unprofessional (abc.net.au, 2024). The Philippine Defence Chief responded to similar wolf diplomacy attacks against the Philippines as being *unwanted and malicious* (Security Talks with US, Manilla, 2025). I note that in an interview that Prime Minister Anthony Albanese gave after the 47th ASEAN summit (Oct 2025) he referred to the various diplomatic clashes that Australia has experienced with China as 'friendly disagreements'.

2) *Information warfare is conducted against the target country.* Things like disinformation campaigns, propaganda (lies) crusades, and cyberattacks are designed to manipulate public opinion, undermine trust in a target country's institutions, and sow confusion in the minds of its citizens. Often when the communist disinformation and propaganda is uncovered the communists will gaslight the target country's citizens by accusing them of spreading mis/disinformation.

3) *Non-state actors are also employed to create havoc in target countries.* This involves activating groups like protest rally organisers, terrorist organisations, radical groups, and hackers who hack into private and public data bases in order to hold governments and the public to ransom. The activity of these organisations, groups, and individuals usually operate with autonomy and anonymity, which leaves the target country unable to lay charges against the actual source of the attacks. As mentioned earlier, pro-Palestine protests have broken out in all Western liberal democratic countries. One wonders why the protestors do not show the same enthusiasm for protesting in support of Ukraine when the Russia military is deliberately killing Ukrainian civilians while the IDF is taking action to avoid civilian casualties.

These are just three examples of hybrid warfare which operates in a *grey zone* between peaceful co-operation and open warfare. This leaves target countries in a state of confusion, unable to respond effectively. When confronted with evidence of these activities, both the non-state actors and the totalitarian and autocratic countries funding and supporting them, simply deny, obfuscate, present strawman arguments, gaslight their accusers, and engage in character assassination.

Today, socialist political parties in many liberal democracies have been successful in legislating communist policies. Socialists and communists have continued to promote social unrest throughout the world, particularly in capitalist countries, by advancing a victim/oppressor model of society. For example, they aggressively advocate for communist-inspired movements like Social Justice Warrior, Antifa, Black Lives Matter, Critical Race Theory (CRT), Political Correctness, Cancel Culture, DEI, ESG and Anti-colonialism, which promote division between what they call the oppressors and the oppressed. This can lead to violence against property or, in some cases, even physical violence against other citizens deemed as being the oppressors. The hidden agenda of all these socialist movements is to create social division within liberal democracies and overthrow capitalism by creating distrust in its institutions. Some critics refer to these movements as *woke culture*.

These are destructive activities that start with altering the educational system (some even beginning in pre-school) through the teaching of ideology rather than creative and independent thinking. So racism, sexism, gender identity, colonialism, CRT, DEI, and presentism become accepted dogma indoctrinated into minors long after the *institutional discrimination* from these social evils has become illegal. The graduates of this indoctrination carry it over into the institutions of liberal democratic societies, for example, into their political, legal, and media institutions.

Let's take racism as an example. There are racists in Australian society today; white nationalists do exist. However, they are a small minority and do not constitute *institutional* racism but merely *isolated incidents* of racism. Nevertheless, communists point to these isolated incidents of racism to promote *white guilt* and prolong the flow of money for projects designed to counter institutional racism. People engaged in this activity are called *race hustlers*, because they gain monetary reward from their activities.

What is institutional or structural racism? This term was first used by Stokely Carmichael and Charles V. Hamilton in *Black Power: The Politics of Liberation* (1967) and means a form of institutional discrimination in society based on race, which provides an unfair advantage for people of one race over another. Ostensively, it can manifest itself in things like criminal justice, employment, housing, health care, education or political representation.

Today, institutional racism no longer exists, because laws were created to prohibit it, yet the fight to eliminate 'institutional racism' is still being fought by those who want to preserve the racial division in liberal democratic countries. In fact, the discrimination found in DEI, for example, does favour one racial group over another. For this reason, the definition has shifted its meaning into a perceived power relationship where one race is charged with having power over another even if no such power is discernible. One of the problems with this is that institutional racism has become an amorphous concept, which means it is not clear how we correct something when its meaning is ambiguous in the first place. Wealth, for example, is now distributed among all races. Members of all races are found in the wealthy sections of Australian society while all races are represented in the impoverished section of it. Surely, this suggests that assistance should be distributed according to individual need, not race.

During the civil rights movement of the 1960s, Martin Luther King delivered his famous *I have a dream* speech at the Lincoln Memorial in Washington DC on August 28, 1963, in which he said,

I have a dream that my four little children will one day live in a

> *nation where they will not be judged by the colour of their skin but by the content of their character.*
>
> (Martin Luther King, 1963)

For decades after this, all educational institutions in liberal democracies worldwide used this quote to fight racism in their societies. To judge people by their character and not their race, they believed, would overcome racism in their societies, and it was successful in eliminating institutional racism.

In learning institutions guided by Critical Race Theory (CRT) today, this quote is considered racist when white people use it to explain that they do not recognise racial differences, because CRT asserts that white people *must* recognise race in order to accept their historical guilt and unconscious prejudice regarding the treatment of black people. We even have the practice of racially segregated dormitories and graduation ceremonies being established and conducted in some American universities. Students in these institutions learn about the *micro aggression* and *unconscious racism* of white people and desire the creation of *safe spaces* to protect themselves from this unconscious white hostility. Obviously, this approach promotes *white guilt* in white people, but also a *victim mentality* in black people, both of which are harmful to white and black people alike. In short, CRT believes that we can use racism to fight racism. The logic of this argument disturbs me. To overcome racism, according to CRT, it seems one must first become a racist.

Perhaps the answer is more simplistic –

> *If you want to overcome racism, stop talking about it.*
>
> (Morgan Freeman, 2014)

> *If you want to overcome racial discrimination, stop discriminating on the basis of race.*

Chapter 8: New World Issues

(Vivek Ramaswamy, 2024, election town hall meeting in which he highlighted the danger of DEI)

A libertarian would argue for looking for common values between the different races; highlighting these; and through the use of logic, reason, wisdom, common sense, and empathy encourage members of different races to accept that all adult human beings are entitled to liberty and equal treatment.

When you were taught about racism at school, were these two differing approaches explained to you? Which approach do you think would be more effective in fighting racism? Do you think CRT is an example of teaching critical thinking or indoctrinating ideology? Can you identify any other social issues that were presented to you without adequately considering different perspectives?

This ideology then becomes pervasive in liberal democratic societies and moves into the legal, media, and political institutions of society. Selective enforcement of laws rather than their equal application becomes prevalent, even to the extent of selected persecution of those seen as opposing the CRT agenda while refusing to lay charges against those who support it. The police motto to *serve and protect* becomes one of *selective service and protection*.

Furthermore, punishment becomes unequally applied. In those cases where an individual is identified by the CRT agenda as being an oppressor it becomes harsh, while in those cases who fit their ideology of the oppressed it becomes lenient. This is known as a *two-tiered* legal system. All this is done in the belief that such actions will overcome discrimination and exploitation, without admitting that it is itself discriminatory and exploitative. In short,

> *our legal and judicial systems become instruments for imposing social justice rather than dispensing equal justice.*

Do you think that the CRT agenda undermines the trust

citizens living in liberal democracies would normally have for their institutions of law enforcement and justice?

The current symbol for justice, established over thousands of years by different people seeking a more just society and based on Themis the Greek Goddess of Justice, is a blindfolded woman with a scale in one hand and a double-edged sword in the other. This symbolises justice because she cannot see who is front of her so the law is applied equally, regardless of what section of society the guilty comes from. Also, the scales tell us that justice is achieved by weighing up the evidence before reaching a verdict, and a double-edged sword reveals that punishment is applied fairly and equally because the sword cuts both ways, regardless of class, race, sex etc.

Do you think a two-tiered legal system, implemented by CRT, alters this symbol? For example, does justice now wear her blindfold as a scarf? Can she now see who is front of her? Does she hold a book of ideology rather than a scale to weigh the evidence? And has she exchanged her double-edged sword for a single-edged sword? Does her sword of punishment now cut only one way? Can you think of any examples of a two-tiered legal system in operation today? Does it exist in Australia? Give a detailed explanation of your answer.

In parliament, politicians inspired by communist propaganda pass laws that fit their ideology with not enough thought being given to how they discriminate against certain sections of society. For example, policies like social welfare based on group identity rather than individual need are promoted, whether or not the taxpayers can afford them. Those opposed to group identity are shamed with cries of racist. Legalised mass immigration, leading to housing shortages, homelessness, congested traffic, overcrowded classrooms, ambulance ramping and long waiting lists for medical treatment, is adopted. Those opposed to mass immigration likewise are shamed with cries of racist. A constant stream of deficit budgeting, which spawns unsustainable levels of accumulated debt, becomes standard practice. This reliance on deficit budgeting achieves only one goal: it maintains a standard of living that the productivity of the nation cannot sustain and will lead, if not checked, to a collapse of the country's economy.

Can you see how this mentality is linked to the historical failure of all communist economies? Do you find any fault in my opinions and observations? Do my opinions reveal a bias on my part? Please explain your conclusion.

Let me go further. As stated before, communism promotes harmful ideology which plays upon the envy, jealousy, and hatred of liberal democratic citizens and inspires violent divisions within their societies. The cry,

> *Make the rich pay their fair share*

or more recently,

> *We need to address the intergenerational wealth gap*

are examples of communist-inspired sloganeering that divides us. The rich against the poor, the young against the old.

Whilst the rich do use accountants to minimise their taxes, their accountants only apply the taxation laws on our statute. Have you ever wondered why these laws never seem to change? Could there be a good economic reason to keep them? Could those who shout the loudest about the rich also be benefiting from the tax code that they condemn? Is strawman logic being used here? Instead of rationally discussing this issue, are you being led to envy the rich rather than address the root cause of the perceived problem: our taxation laws. What's more, there is a difference between tax avoidance and tax evasion. With tax avoidance citizens simply use existing tax laws to minimise their tax (a *legal* activity), while tax evasion is breaking the law to avoid paying tax, which is already *illegal*. Worse still, the cry to make the rich pay more tax or 'let's redistribute the elderly's wealth' sounds like this would solve the economic problem created by the excessive spending habits of the communist-inspired politicians, which it clearly does not because it will not raise enough revenue to achieve that. It does, however, divert your attention away from the government's excessive spending, our declining productivity, and any real inequality contained in our tax code.

What the intergenerational wealth gap fails to recognise is that today's old were once yesterday's young and started out with little or nothing, just like the young of today. It was the choices made by today's elderly as they aged that allowed them to buy their own homes. If young people today are unable to buy a home, that is the fault of current government policy, not the elderly. If today's elderly were able to purchase their own homes with the policies implemented by their generation's government, so too could the younger generation today if their government had similar policies.

One final piece of advice I will make about communism. Don't listen to what communists say, look at what they do, because it has been my experience that communist rhetoric does not match communist outcomes.

In closing this section on communism, I want to lighten our mood by leaving you with a joke that President Reagan told to a gathering of Republicans after becoming President of the USA –

Apparently, a couple had twins; one was an optimist while the other was a pessimist. In an attempt to cure their children and have them arrive at a more realistic view of the world; they filled one room with bright, shiny new toys and another room with horse manure. They put the pessimist in the room full of toys and the optimist in the room full of horse manure. Two hours later they came back to see what impact the rooms had had on their twins. First, they opened the door with the pessimist inside. He sat on the floor crying.

What's wrong? the astonished parents asked.

The pessimist pointed to his new toys one at a time,

That toy will soon break, that one will run out of battery power, that one will be stolen.

He then went through all the toys in the room finding fault with each one.

Shaking their heads, the parents left the pessimist's room and went to the room with the optimist inside. He was throwing the horse mature in the air while shouting,

Yippee!

Why are you so happy? the puzzled parents asked.

The optimist replied,

Well, with all this horse mature, there must be a pony in here somewhere.

If you are thinking the optimist will soon discover there is no pony, you are a glass half-empty kind of person. Which child would you prefer to be like? A bit of both? When you feel downhearted, believing that the world is incurable of its injustice and suffering, its cynicism and hypocrisy, remember this joke and start looking for the pony even if it is elusive. Stand up for your country, square your shoulders, and proclaim to the world how proud you are of Australia, its ancestors (both white and non-white), and its liberal democratic principles. Argue for optimism, mutual respect and co-operation rather than pessimism, division and conflict. Proclaim a belief in equality of opportunity over equity. Do you think this might help? In what ways?

Constitutional Monarchy

A Constitutional Monarchy is a system of government whereby a monarch shares power with a constitutionally organised government. The monarch's power is limited by the country's constitution, and their share of power may be in the form of a de facto head of state or merely a ceremonial head.

While a Constitutional Monarch is a unifying non-partisan head of state, only the elected parliament has the power to create legislation and enforce it through a government-led bureaucracy. Another important factor of a Constitutional Monarchy is that it provides continuity, stability and authority for liberal democratic governments. Australia has a Constitutional Monarch whose representative is our

Governor-General. Our monarch needs a representative because he/she does not reside in Australia. Our Governor-General is chosen by our prime minister and appointed by our monarch. Constitutional Monarchies have a much better record for longevity than Republics, whose Presidents seem to lead their countries into dictatorships during a political or economic crisis. The exception, of course, is America whose division of power arrangement contained in their Constitution and citizen guarantees found in their Bill of Rights helps to mitigate against the accumulation of power into one person's hands and stops any government's attack on its people's liberty.

One other point worthy of mention here is the emergency powers of a Constitutional Monarch or his/her Representative. Emergency powers are used to address urgent situations like natural disasters, civil unrest or external threats. Typically this calls for a suspension of some constitutional rights in order to address an urgent situation. At this time, a monarch's power can be limited to a check on the exercising of these powers by a government or even the dissolution of Parliament itself. If Parliament is dissolved a temporary period of martial law or the calling of an election can be used by the monarch to address the urgency of the situation.

Some examples of the exercising of a monarch's reserved powers in Australia have been the following. I was in Mount Isa during the 1974 floods when our city was cut off from the rest of Australia. A national emergency was declared by the Government of Australia and Mount Isa was put, temporarily, under martial law. When the army arrived we were subjected to rationing to get ourselves through this emergency and the army and police force maintained civil order. I was grateful for the army's support at this time because civilised behaviour was beginning to collapse. This took the form of rough and unruly behaviour in acquiring limited food in supermarkets and even the theft of things like petrol. I worked underground in the mines at the time and had to limit the amount of petrol I put into the tank of my motorcycle because thieves were syphoning petrol out of petrol tanks. Something similar happened in Darwin after Cyclone Tracy (December 1974) arrived and destroyed approximately 70% of Darwin. On 11 November 1975, the 'Whitlam Dismissal' occurred whereby Prime Minister Goff Whitlam was dismissed by the then Governor-General Sir John Kerr, who called a general election for December 13, 1975, to solve a supply crisis. Sir John also appointed Malcolm Fraser to head a caretaker government until the election was held. An Australian Parliament has never been dismissed by a Governor-General who then appointed military rule over all of Australia, but this has happened many times by the president of various republics who hold the same emergency powers as a monarch.

One point that Australians may not be aware of is that our monarch is the Commander in Chief of our armed forces. When members of our armed forces swear allegiance, for example, they swear it to the reigning monarch not our prime minister. Their oath also includes a commitment to uphold the laws of Australia and defend the nation.

Democracy

Democracy first emerged in the fifth century BC in Athens, a city republic of ancient Greece. The word itself is a combination of two Greek words, *demos* meaning 'people' and *kratos* meaning 'to rule'. So democracy, by definition, means the rule of the people. However, the definition of what *people* means has changed over the centuries. In Ancient Greece it meant only free men, so slaves, women and minors were excluded from voting; later it meant limiting the vote to men of property, then to all men and eventually to all adult citizens (men and women). *Adult citizen* has also changed its definition from those over 21 years of age to those over 18 years of age.

Consider this. 21 years of age was the 'coming of age' for my generation. That was the age at which we were given the right to vote, and we used to celebrate the occasion with a special 21st birthday party, which was our 'coming of age' party when we officially became adult citizens of Australia. When Australia was involved in the Vietnam War

(1962-1975), Selective Service (by ballot) was introduced during the Vietnam War for those who turned 20 years of age in the year of the draw. A tour of service in Vietnam for conscripted servicemen did not occur until after they had completed their training and this usually lasted for one year, so most National servicemen were 21 years of age when they toured Vietnam for one year. However, the median age for those who were sent to fight in the Vietnam War was 19 years of age. All 19-year-olds were regular soldiers who had volunteered for service. I was one of them. Reformists and those on the radical left argued that young people like me could fight in a war and drive a car but were not permitted to drink alcohol (legally that is) or vote in an election. I did not vote until I was 21 years of age.

Reformists and radicals argued that if politicians could send a 19-year-old to war, then a 19-year-old should be allowed to vote for those who would, or would not, send them. Since I was being used as an example to lower the age of voting, allow me to relate my personal experience. At 19 years of age I was immature. I had no responsibilities other than unto myself and was making a lot of irrational decisions which, at times, caused me considerable embarrassment. I was self-centred and, in many ways, selfish and egotistical. At 21 years of age I had matured somewhat. I was married, had a child on the way, was saving for our first home and, as you can see, had taken on responsibility for others and making rational decisions. In short, I had matured considerably during the three years between being 18 years of age and 21 years of age. You be the judge. When would have been the best age for me to have the right to vote in an election, at 18 or 21, regardless of what age I was expected to defend my country?

The Green Party in Australia today is now calling for those over 16 years of age to be given the vote. Some political parties lead the push to keep lowering the age for voting, because they see a political advantage in it for their party. A country's youth has always been more rebellious, more self-centred and more open to radical thought than older more mature adults who have seen the effects of radical legislation on their own and other countries over time. Consequently, radical political parties favour younger voting qualification, while more conservative political parties favour mature age voting qualification.

Do you think the policies of today's Green Party are more likely to be supported by radical, reformist or conservative voters?

Citizens in a democracy exercise their vote to determine who will represent them in Parliament. Parliament comes from the French word *parler*, which means 'to talk'. So our Parliaments, both Federal and State are where our Representatives go to talk (debate) with one another. Members of Parliament are decided by elections. Australia has a compulsory system of voting whereby all citizens must vote in our Federal elections or incur a fine.

The purpose of elections is to allow citizens to elect their representative voice to Parliament. In this way, democracies are said to reflect the *will of the people* through *Representative Government*. Over time our representative voices in Parliament joined together into political parties. Largely because political parties can provide the financial and membership support to conduct elections and give candidates a better chance of being elected.

Australia has a Bicameral Parliament. That is, a Parliament consisting of two Chambers. One Chamber is the House of Representatives containing 150 Representatives (popularly called the people's house because it is elected democratically). The Australian Constitution stipulates that on average the House of Representatives has 'as nearly as practicable' twice the number of members as in the Senate. Currently, Federal Electorates for the House of Representatives have about 120,000 electors, except for Tasmania which is guaranteed a minimum of five Federal Electorates regardless of the number of electors in each electorate. Australia uses a preferential system of voting for the House of Representatives, whereby voters must number all the candidates on a ballot paper in order of their preference. This is our chosen way of voting because then a candidate can only become a member of our House of Representatives if he/she is the preferred candidate (i.e., he/she must receive over 50% of the preferred vote to be elected) of his/her electorate. Many Australian citizens object to the preferential system of voting because it forces them to vote for a candidate that they may not want to cast a vote for.

The other Chamber is the Senate, which is referred to as the States' House, because each State has the same number of Senators elected to the Senate via proportional representation regardless of the number of citizens living in it. A quota is used to determine who is elected to the Senate. Any candidate must reach this quota, either by direct vote or by direct plus preference votes before being elected to the Senate. The Senate consists of 76 members; 12 Senators represent each State with 2 members from each of the two territories, the Australian Capital Territory (ACT) and the Northern Territory (NT). At each election only half of the Members of the Senate stand for election, so Senators are elected for 6 years and not 3 years as they are in the House of Representatives.

Our founding fathers designed the operation of our Parliament in this way because they wanted Australian citizens to be given a chance to reconsider their decision if a radical government was elected. You see, the Legislation Bills must pass through the Senate before they become law and a newly elected government is unlikely to have control of the Senate in its own right. The Senate can then block the Legislation Bill if it is highly unpopular with the citizens. If the Senate becomes obstructionist over popular legislation the Australian Constitution allows for the government of the day to call for a Double Disillusion of both Chambers of Parliament, whereby all members of both the House of Representatives and the Senate must stand for re-election. If the government of the day is popularly re-elected they will be able to pass their Legislation Bill through the newly re-constituted Chambers of Parliament.

The leader of the political party with the majority support in the House of Representatives becomes the Prime Minister. This majority party support may be in the form of a political party with an absolute majority or in coalition with another party or a group of independents or both. Such an arrangement is called minority government which is usually highly unstable and prone to make compromises on Legislation Bills that few citizens are happy with. Since the formation of the Fisher Ministry in 1908, the Australian Labor Party caucus has elected its ministers and the prime minister has allocated portfolios. The caucus is comprised of all the Labor Members of the Senate and House of Representatives. The Parliamentary Members of the Liberal Party elect their leader and he/she chooses his/her ministers and allocates their portfolios.

The Prime Minister is the Head of Government, but the Governor-General is the Head of State.

Pre-selection is the process by which registered political parties choose who will be their endorsed candidates in any given federal, state, or local election. A pre-selection ballot is where members of a political party vote in a poll for preselecting a candidate for endorsement. Two ways of unduly influencing pre-selection are branch stacking and parachuting candidates. Branch stacking involves the act of recruiting or signing up members for a local branch of a political party for the principal purpose of influencing the outcome of the pre-selection vote. A parachute candidate is a pejorative term for someone who does not live in the area they are running to represent. A parachute candidate is usually someone who is favoured by the party leadership.

Do you think citizens in Australia vote for a party or an individual candidate? Do you think party representatives in Parliament would reflect the will of their constituents or their party's policy? Why do you think that? If they reflect the will of their party and not that of their constituents, would this practice erode the democratic rights of citizens? Who do you think voters would vote for if their member consistently voted along his/her party line but against the wishes of the majority of his/her electorate? Sometimes voters prefer none of the candidates standing for election and are forced to vote for the least bad candidate. Colloquially, this is known as 'holding your nose' as you vote.

Do you think voters should be put in this position? What might be some reasons why voters feel it necessary to 'hold their noses' when they vote?

Sometimes political parties allow their members a conscience vote whereby the representatives can decide for themselves which way they will vote on a given piece of legislation, but this is rare. On most occasions representatives are expected to vote according to the party's position on any given piece of legislation. Colloquially, this is known as *toeing the party's line*. Each party has a party 'whip' who is expected to deliver the party member's vote for the legislation announced by the government or against it by the opposition parties. Sometimes party 'whips' are referred to as 'toe cutters'.

What do you think the term 'toe cutter' says about the duties of a 'whip'? Why would a 'whip' be referred to in such negative terms? Since a party whip cannot literally cut off his party members' toes, what forms of coercion do you think he could use in its place?

Sometimes representatives lose their party endorsement if they vote against the party line, and sometimes they resign from their party on principle and become independent members of the Parliament.

Do you think the two-party system limits choice for the voters in a democracy or do you think the party system helps to stabilise discussions in Parliament and the running of our government?

Those who support the party system of government argue that without it nothing would ever be decided by Parliament because there would never be a majority consensus on any piece of legislation since there would be so many differing opinions. Sometimes the two major parties adopt a bipartisan approach on issues that the majority of voters oppose. In such a situation, how can the majority of voters influence change?

We have already examined the issue of mass-immigration, which was upheld in a bipartisan approach, but is now being questioned by both major parties. Another issue is net zero by 2050 which has always been opposed by one minor party and is now opposed by another minor party and questioned by one major party but still enjoys a bipartisan approach by both major parties. What do you think is the majority view of Australian citizens today about net zero by 2050? Are the majority of citizens happy with what is happening to their energy supply and cost of living as a result of this policy?

As you can see, democracy has its faults. However, it is still the most equitable and fairest system of governance yet devised, or as Winston Churchill (UK Prime Minister, 1940-45, 1951-55) cynically put it,

> *Democracy is the worst form of government – except for all the others that have been tried.*

The five pillars of democracy have been identified as,

1) *The Constitution.*
2) *Strong Institutions (a justice system, a defence force, a foreign affairs department etc.).*
3) *Federal, State and Local Governments.*
4) *Citizen responsibilities.*
5) *Political parties and a free press.*

(inspire.education.gov.ng)

I would add to this list one pillar of my own: *Citizen Rights*. One of which is *Individual Sovereignty*, the right of a citizen in a democracy to cast a single, individual vote in elections and not have their vote or the election interfered with in any way. Another is *Free Speech*, the right of citizens to hold opinions (excluding incitement to violence, defamation, or treason) and express them publicly without interference from authority, public, or government. Yet another is the right to *private property* which fosters individual freedom and responsibility; economic stability through its citizens' aspiration, innovation, and efficiency in the use of resources; and protection from arbitrary government power. One more is the right to *freedom of religious worship* which is essential to a citizen's identity and conscience. Yet another is the principle of equal justice in its justice system. John Locke would add the *right to revolution* which provides citizens with the justification to 'alter or abolish' a government acting in an unrighteous way against the citizens' interests or safety (John Locke, *Two Treatises of Government*, 1689).

What is your opinion about the validity of these pillars of democracy? Can you think of any other pillars that you think should be included? Do you think politicians should be *limited* to a set time to hold elected office? Some think this would help overcome corruption within our political system. Also, some see danger in what they call *career politicians* who are more interested in their careers than in serving their constituents. Some also believe in limiting the time citizens can be employed in the public service, for the same reasons. What do you think about the American system whereby the president can *appoint* the ministers heading separate departments from the private sector rather than his own government? Do you think public service heads of department should be appointed on merit alone or through DEI? Should a public service head of department be appointed for a set period of time or should the elected prime minister make appointments that he/she is more capable of working with?

To research democracy, I would recommend Plato's book, *The Republic*, and Aristotle's treatise, *Politics*. Both Plato and Aristotle criticised Democracy, believing it was flawed because of the inherit danger of majority, popular demands being prioritised over justice and the common good. What is your opinion? Can you think of a way to counter this danger? How far do the pillars of democracy go in combating the *tyranny of the majority*? A more modern book on democracy is *Modern Democracies, vol.2.* (1921) by Viscount James

Bryce, who examines democracy in the US, Australia, and New Zealand.

President Lincoln (1809-65, 16th President of the USA) in his 1863 Gettysburg Address described democracy as,

> *Government of the people, by the people, for the people.*

Do you agree with President Lincoln's description? Explain your opinion. Do you think his definition of democracy has aged well? Why do you think that?

When it comes to democratic elections President Harry S. Truman (1884-1972, 33rd President of the USA) is believed to have made the following observation,

> *You can please some of the people all of the time and you can please all of the people some of the time, but you can't please all of the people all of the time.*

Here President Truman suggests that governing a country involves a trade-off between competing interests. Do you agree?

Cynics substitute *fool* for *please* in the above quote. This suggests that electors in a democratic election do not always get things right, but that eventually they do. That is, that an unscrupulous prime minister or president, who gains votes by utilising things like lies and bribes and a childish petulance that refuses to take responsibility for any consequences arising from his/her actions by blaming everybody and everything other than himself/herself, will eventually be unmasked by the electors.

Do you think it is possible for a prime minister or president to be elected by using these tactics? Do you think that such a politician will eventually be unmasked by the electors? How might this happen? Can you think of any examples that highlight this?

Dictatorship

The term 'dictatorship' first emerged during the period of the Roman Republic. It described a period when a 'dictator' was given temporary power to handle an emergency.

Unfortunately, dictatorships became prevalent at different periods in European history. Some famous dictators in Europe were Oliver Cromwell (1599-1658) who was Lord Chancellor for 5 years in England and Napoleon Bonaparte (1769-1821) who was a dictator of France for 11 years. Since Napoleon crowned himself monarch, his rule was not considered legitimate by other nations, so he is remembered as a dictator rather than a monarch. During the interwar period of European history (1918-39) Fascist, Nazi and Communist dictatorships became popular. WWII defeated the Fascist and Nazi dictators but the Communist dictatorship survived and has emerged in those countries that embraced communism/socialism. After WWII many Republics were created, especially in Africa and Asia, as European Nations surrendered their empires to the local citizenry. A large number of these newly formed Republics descended into dictatorships following social or economic emergencies in their countries.

A dictator is someone who has total control over a country. He/she usually maintains this control through force (militarily, police, secret service, propaganda, and a politically corrupt judicial system are some of the ways this force is maintained). Elections, where the people could remove the dictator, are either never held or rigged in such a way that the dictator always wins.

People living in dictatorships have every part of their lives controlled by the dictator, who has absolute power over them. Justice is also controlled by the dictator in such a way that legal appeals either do not exist or are always decided in the dictator's favour. When the dictator levels a charge against a citizen, the case is heard in a *show trial* where the defendant is always found guilty and the dictator wins a propaganda victory.

Dictators also try to control what the citizens in their country think, through censorship and propaganda. The people living in dictatorships usually grow tired of the excessive control over their lives and, when their country faces an economic crisis, they revolt. This is put down in a brutal suppression by the police and military. Sometimes, however, a people's revolt can overthrow a dictator. Dictatorships always produce economic crises because of the cost associated with maintaining their power. Military, police, and surveillance costs mean a country's wealth is diverted away from wealth creating enterprises.

Dictators usually create a war economy and when faced with an economic crisis may go to war. They do this in the hope that their conquest will fund their war economy and give rise to patriotic zeal among their citizens.

Some people support dictatorships, believing that the dictator can solve their problems. Consequently, many dictatorships begin from a people's revolt against a political system they believe is letting them down. Dictators always come to power promising to overthrow a corrupt government. Those who are against dictatorships believe that the loss of liberty is too high a price to pay and that their country's problems can be solved in other ways.

Many democracies have been overthrown by dictators in modern times, because of corruption, economic mismanagement, political instability, and social unrest/revolt/civil war or revolution. What steps do you think a democracy can implement to ensure these disrupting elements are controlled?

Empire
Empire is a system of government which rules over many different peoples outside its original borders (sometimes referred to as a parent country, *motherland* or *fatherland*) and can be ruled by a supreme ruler (Emperor), an oligarchy or the parliamentary body of a Republic or Democracy. An Imperial Dynasty exists when an empire bases its leadership succession on heredity. The most famous Chinese

Dynasties were the Quin, Han, Ming, and Tang Dynasties. Scholars have identified a political theory to describe a Dynastic Cycle that Chinese Dynasties went through –

1) The first phase is the *rise of the dynasty* where the dynasty gains power.
2) The second phase is where the *dynasty flourishes*.
3) The third phase is where it *declines* owing to corruption.
4) the final phase is where the Emperor loses the *Mandate of Heaven* and his dynasty *falls*.

In the past, Empires have brought benefits and disadvantages to the people who fall under their rule. Examples of benefits include civilizational things like protection for the people now included in the Empire. In Rome's case it was called *Pax Romana* or Roman Peace; in Britain's case it was *Pax Britannia*. Many countries today rely on *Pax Americana* to keep the peace, although America has not established an Empire in the classical sense, preferring instead to protect the rights of independent Nation States and keep the sea lanes free and open. Other benefits include things like increased trade in luxury items leading to an expansion of the merchant and manufacturing sectors of the colonies' economies, the building of ports, roads, bridges and public buildings, the introduction of stable governance, law and order, educational institutions, medical treatment and hospitals, water management with the building of dams and canals for irrigation, the building of railways for not just military and commercial purposes but also for the transportation of people and food, to name only a few of the benefits. Disadvantages include things like the loss of language and cultural identity of the people outside the parent country. In the more severe cases of Empire, it can include exploitation of colonial resources and suppression of the conquered people. For example, all ancient imperial powers forced conquered countries to pay tribute or taxes or deliver valuable items to them, which included things like gold, grain, livestock and even slaves.

One example of the mistreatment dispensed by an Imperial power relates to the people of the Congo who originally followed Kongo mythology which was animistic and pantheistic. However, in 1885 King Leopold II of Belgium established the Congo Free State and ran a private enterprise for his own personal gain, which brutally mistreated the Congolese people. This was not an example of European Imperial power but rather the personal greed of a European monarch and it led to international pressure being forced on him to hand over the Congo Free State to the country of Belgium in 1908.

After the arrival of the Europeans, the majority of the Congolese people converted to Christianity leaving their Kongo mythology behind. The Islamic religion spread to the northern areas of the Congo from North Africa in the mid 19th century. Under the governance of Leopold II's Congo Free State (not a Belgium colony at this time) the people of the Congo were forced to labour for valued resources, including rubber and ivory, and deliver cash crops to personally enrich Leopold II. During times of hardship when the cash crops were not delivered, their private enterprise overseers cut off the right hands of those who failed to deliver, which was the Islamic punishment for stealing under Sharia law. Such punishments were not a part of Christian theology, which the Congo Free State had brought to the Congo. Although these actions were undertaken by a private enterprise and not an imperial power, it is a good example of the extreme measures King Leopold II was willing to enforce in order to enrich himself and how a people's culture was lost owing to the outside governance of the Congo Free State and later the colonisation by Belgium. To be sure, this is an example of the mistreatment of people from an outside power, but it is by no means unique to European private enterprise or European Empires.

The Ottoman Empire, for example, castrated their African and European slaves so they could not procreate. It is not possible to know definitively how many died from this practice because records were not kept, but some sources suggest that as many as two out of three boys died from castration (wikipedia.org, 2025 and academic.oup.com, 2025). Many people from Eastern Europe and Africa were taken into slavery by military raids with the purpose of supplying the slave markets of the Ottoman Empire. Young, white, female children and adolescents were highly prized and extremely badly treated by their masters, often ending up in harems and sex slave markets. Young white male children were trained to become members of the Sultan's army after castration. This practice continued until 1924 when the Turkish Republic finally dissolved the Imperial Harem and freed its slaves.

All empires have a cycle of existence which eventually comes to an end. This can be because the people within the empire see themselves as being 'in' the Empire but not 'of' the Empire and rise up and overthrow what they perceive as their oppressors. Alternatively, the parent country may see *the writing on the wall* (Book of Daniel Ch.5) and peacefully withdraw. Such was the case with the British Empire, who perhaps left their Empire with more pride in their accomplishments than those before them.

Following the American War of Independence, Britain was reluctant to force its will on its colonies. Britain provided security from outside threats, protected the minorities within and upheld the rule of law, but declined to force their will on them, preferring instead to move them towards self-government. Within Australia there was not a single War of Independence but rather many acts of resistance leading to the granting of self-governance, first to the separate Colonies and finally to the Australian Nation State. Some acts of resistance include *the Battle of Parramatta* in 1792 where approximately 100 local Aboriginals led by Pemulwuy tried to attack the colonial settlement at Parramatta and were met by British Imperial forces; the *Castle Hill Rebellion* of 1804 where approximately 233 Irish convicts led by Philip Cunningham rebelled against British authority and were put down by a British force, and the *Eureka Stockade* in 1854 when approximately 150 gold prospectors led by Peter Lalor were overrun by British government forces at Ballarat. Following the Eureka Stockade and *The Age* newspaper's highly critical appraisal of the Victorian colonial administration's handling of the Eureka Stockade incident, Britain embarked on a slow process of granting self-government to its former colonies in Australia. Worldwide, many of Britain's former colonies had already achieved Dominion status, involving self-governance within the British Empire for former colonies, by 1910, even before President Woodrow Wilson announced America's preference for national self-determination at the Paris Peace Conference in 1919.

For Australia, what is clear is that the struggle for independence and national self-governance was conducted by Aboriginal and non-Aboriginal Australians alike. That the British Empire and its Australian colonies came to an end when Australia became a Nation State in 1901. The era of Colonialism ended and all Australians embraced their independence and were willing to fight alongside each other in two world wars and many smaller wars to maintain their liberty, independence, and democratic rights.

Why not set up a research project of your own and discover the details of the three acts of resistance against British Imperialism listed above. What do these acts of resistance tell you about the desire of Aboriginal and non-Aboriginal Australians for independence from the British Empire?

After WWII the Imperial powers of Europe became economically exhausted; the cost of running their Empires had become an enormous burden on their tax-paying people already exhausted by the expense of the war. European countries also changed their priorities. Of primary importance now was the welfare of their own people, which saw their governments taking an ever-increasing role in their well-being. They also suffered from a lack of political will which was driven by a humanitarian 'backlash' over the exploitation of colonial natives. This exhaustion is what the French refer to as *ennui*.

Recently, Imperialism (or as the radicals like to call it, Colonialism) has been portrayed as a foundational sin of Western civilisation. By using presentism the radical left uses the sins of things like slavery and racism (both present in all Empires since the beginning of recorded history) to castigate Western civilisation (Bruce Gilley, *The Case for Colonialism*, 2018). Such things rightly are considered wrong by today's standards and have been addressed by our present-day emphasis on human rights. However, there is nothing unique or different about Western civilisation adopting Imperialism once it was in a position to do so. One wonders, then, why Western civilisation has been singled out for condemnation while all other civilisations that adopted Imperialism have been given a pass.

Some examples of Ancient Empires (up to 50 AD) include, Egyptian Empire (3100-30 BC), Indus Valley Empire (2550-1550 BC), Babylonian Empire (1792-1595 BC), Shang Empire (1751-1111 BC), Bantu (African) Empire (dates are speculative but believed to have started about 2000 years ago and is still culturally active today), and the Roman Empire (264-476 BC).

Some Pre-Modern examples of Empire (50-1500 AD) include, Ethiopian Empire (50-1974 AD) spanning both pre and post-modern periods, Byzantine Empire (330-1453 AD), Sung Empire (906-1278 AD), Burmese Empire (1057-1287 AD), Mongol Empire (1206-1405 AD), Aztec Empire (1345-1521 AD), and Holy Roman Empire (1254-1835 AD), which again spans both the pre-modern and modern periods of Empire.

Some Empires of the modern period (post 1500 AD) include Ottoman Empire (1453-1923 AD), Spanish Empire (1492-1898 AD), Mughal Empire (1526-1805 AD) including South Asia and most of India, British Empire (1607-1980 AD), French Empire (1611-1980 AD), Ch'ing Dynasty (1644-1911 AD), Comanche (American plains Indians) Empire (18th-19th century AD), and the Japanese Empire (1889-1945 AD).

These are just a few of the literally hundreds of Empires that have existed over the millennia of human history. All of world history, therefore, is a history of Imperialism or Colonialism. There is no present-day country, including European countries, that at one time was not a colony of another country. Furthermore, all Empires have provided advantages for and inflicted misdeeds on their colonised peoples. To single out the brief period of the 18th-19th century and zero in on European Imperialism (Colonialism) is a fundamental misunderstanding of the history of Imperialism.

Europeans did have racist views towards the people they colonised. However, they were no more racist than any other Imperial power that had colonised other groups of people. In fact, owing to the Christian foundation of their civilisation, it has been argued (Bruce Gilley, 2018 and Nigel Biggar, 2021) that they were less racist because they looked on the peoples in their colonies as being morally equivalent to themselves and therefore capable of becoming civilised. Over time, for example, they abolished the practices of human sacrifice, slavery, infanticide, cannibalism, Hindu sati, female circumcision, and child brides in their colonies. Something that no other Imperial power before them had even contemplated let alone enforced.

With all this happening, one wonders what the motive behind singling out Western, and in particular British, Civilisation and condemning it for its past Imperial (Colonialist) practices is. Do you detect a hidden agenda here? Can you identify a new power base and a new flow of money emerging from this condemnation? Who are the beneficiaries and who are the losers? Explain what the goal would be for those who benefit.

Kingdoms

Kingdoms have a history stretching back into the ancient world. The Jewish kingdom, for example, was divided into two kingdoms (north and south). The northern kingdom was called the Kingdom of Israel and existed until 722 BC when it was absorbed into the Neo-Assyrian

Empire. The southern kingdom was called the Kingdom of Judah and was eventually absorbed by the Neo-Babylonian Empire in 587 BC.

Kingdoms derive their name from the fact that they are ruled by Kings. The King is the head of state and rules, via heredity, for life or until he abdicates. Sometimes the succession of kings will form a dynasty, a long period of direct family succession. The line of succession is usually determined by the Crown, the symbol of the King's authority, passing to the eldest son (known as the Crown Prince). However, if there is no son to inherit the Throne, a seat reserved solely for the King, the eldest female may become Queen, the name given to the female ruler of a Kingdom. Once a Queen has children the eldest son will eventually inherit the Throne. A Queen Mother is the mother of a ruling king's children. A Queen Consort (e.g., Camilla) is the wife of a reigning monarch, but not the mother of his children. When one continuous period is reigned over by the one family, this is referred to as a 'House'. For example, in England's case, the House of Lancaster, the House of Tudor or currently the House of Windsor. Sometimes historical periods can take on the name of the ruling Kings. For example, The Plantagenets, The Saxons, The Hanoverians, or today the Windsors. Also, an era (period of time) can be named after one individual monarch. For example, the Elizabethan era (1588-1603), the Victorian era (1837-1901), the Edwardian era (1901-10).

In earlier times, Kings were rulers whose power was autocratic and absolute. Kings ruled via a Royal Court, the place where the King and his trusted nobles would meet to discuss current events affecting the Kingdom and the King. A benevolent King might produce a period of peace and prosperity for a Kingdom. However, in times of conquest (either by the King himself directed against neighbouring Kingdoms or challengers to his own lands or Crown) a period of instability may arise. For this reason, Kingdoms generally needed the rule of a strong King to unite the people of the Kingdom and to be victorious in battle. Strong Kings are also needed if the Kingdom itself is divided and the King faces challengers from among his nobles. When such a scenario occurs, the Kingdom becomes weakened by divisions within, making it a target for ambitious neighbouring Kings. Such a time existed in English history during the period known as *The War of the Roses* (1455-87 AD). Perhaps you would like to research this period of English history and discover what the *roses* were all about.

The rise of Kings and Kingdoms in Europe and England occurred after the Romans withdrew from their lands. In England's case this led to a period of instability when the former Roman province of Britannia was no longer under Roman protection (*Pax Romana*). Violent, warlike tribes from the north conquered and settled in their lands. These tribes were the Anglo, Saxon, and Jutes tribes from land which today we call Denmark and Germany, who settled in parts of the area that is known today as England. Later Nordic tribes, commonly referred to as Vikings, carried out raids throughout Europe and northern England. Some of these also settled in England. These conquerors called themselves Kings and established Kingdoms, but they were little more than violent warlords who were constantly at war with one another. This was a very violent time for the Britons, those left behind when the Romans withdrew. Eventually, some warlords were absorbed by the more powerful warlords, which eventually led to the rise of England, a Kingdom ruled by one King. Since the newly emerging King needed warriors, the strongest and more successful warriors in battle became the Kings' nobility and were given lands (fiefdoms) to administer in the name of the King. Athelstan (924-939 AD), called The Glorious, was the first King of England. So, following the Roman withdrawal from England (around 410 AD) it took 514 years for a Kingdom to be established which united all of England. Those 514 years were bloody, terrifying years filled with much death and destruction by feuding warlords and their armies not only involving themselves but also the common people.

Incidentally, the word 'England' has its roots in Old English, specifically the term 'Engla land' which translates to 'land of the Angels'. 'Great Britain' is the term used to describe the uniting of England, Scotland and Wales, while the United Kingdom includes

Great Britain and Northern Ireland. Originally, Britain was a term used to describe the uniting of England and Scotland, but when Wales joined Britain it was superseded by Great Britain. Today Britain has become a more general term used to describe either the island itself or the political entity of the United Kingdom.

The most successful of Europe's Kings was Charlemagne, the King of the Franks, who inherited his throne after his father's death. In 732 AD the Moors (Muslims from North Africa) crossed the Pyrenees where they were met by Charlemagne's grandfather, Charles Martel, at Moussais-la-Bataille and were defeated in the battle of Tours, thus ending the Muslim conquest of Western Europe. After Charlemagne inherited his throne he went on to conquer most of Western Europe and Northern Italy. For his effort in uniting Europe, Pope Leo III crowned Charlemagne Emperor of Europe. His empire was broken up by his children after his death.

Kleptocracy
This is the rule of an elite that exploits and steals public wealth for their own gain. This can be achieved in the form of embezzling or misappropriating government funds or passing legislation that steals land (without compensation) or wealth from one group of individuals and gives it to another favoured group. Some legislation can also be passed that involves a financial burden on one group while exempting another favoured group.

Examples of kleptocracy are found in the taxes levelled on non-Muslims living in Muslim countries, who are subjected to Jizya, a type of taxation levelled on non-Muslim subjects of a state governed by Islamic Law. Zimbabwe under the leadership of Robert Mugabe and South Africa under the leadership of Cyril Ramaphosa are both examples of Kleptocracies, because both leaders confiscated farms from white farmers, without compensation, and gave the farms to their black citizens. These are examples of socialist leaders of liberal democracies who devolved their countries into Kleptocracies. Muslim kleptocracies have more success than socialist liberal kleptocracies, which historically degenerate into revolution and dictatorships, because the existence of Jizya in Muslim states brings many converts to Islam, making their states majority Muslim.

Nation States

The concept of a Nation State is a relatively modern idea. As the feudal system broke down, populations in Europe began to recognise that they had some things in common with each other. National identities began to emerge as groups of people organised themselves around a common or shared identity. This identity was (and is today) based on things like a common language, religion, culture, politics, or geography. If you wanted to destroy a Nation State without starting a revolution or going to war with it, you would attack and undermine its shared identity, which is the aim of cultural Marxism. Nation States eventually emerged containing a centralised political organisation that ruled over a population within a territory that identified itself as a Nation.

Some benefits of Nation States are the creation and maintenance of a uniform national culture through state policy. It also guarantees the liberty of its citizens, the right to vote, to hold public office, to own private property, access to public education and health services, and the rights and protection of citizenship, to name just a few.

There is much dissention over the drawbacks of Nation States. Some claim that it can lead to an unhealthy level of nationalism that was responsible for much of the conflict in the 20th century. Others claim that this only occurs in extreme cases, and that the benefits far outweigh the drawbacks. Some argue that Nation States impede the progress of globalisation, which they see as a greater benefit to world development than Nation States. They argue for a one world order with open borders and rule through globalist organisations like the United Nations (UN), the World Bank Group, and the World Economic Forum (WEF). Others shudder at this prospect, claiming that these organisations are not democratically elected and represent the interests of a ruling elite (an oligarchy).

Many Nation States are comprised of a collection of states which form a federation or a union. 'Country' is a term often used interchangeably with 'nation state'. A country is a clearly defined geographic Nation State with one unifying government.

Australia is a Nation State with a Liberal Democratic Government and a Constitutional Monarch as Head of State. Australia's economy is organised around a regulated, capitalist market. This arrangement, guaranteed by our constitution, has served Australia well in the past. We have endured periods of social unrest, political and economic crises, but, until recently, have remained united and strong.

Many in Australia today claim that this arrangement is currently under threat from those espousing Communism, Republicanism, Globalism, Theocracy, Open Borders, Mass Immigration, Multi-culturalism, among many other assaults on our Nation State. All of which attack what were the unifying values and identity of the Australian people. What do you think?

Ochlocracy
The word 'Ochlocracy' is derived from the Greek language by combining two Greek words, *Ochks* meaning 'mob' or 'mass', and *Kratos* meaning 'to rule'. Ochlocracy, then, means government by the populous or mob rule. *Mobocracy* is another word for mob rule which usually contains violence and intimidation by those in authority. Individuals in a mob usually adopt the behaviours and attitudes of the mob that differs significantly from their own personal beliefs, morals, and ethics.

Oligarchy
Aristotle was the first to coin the term 'Oligarchy' by combining the Greek words 'oligos' meaning few or scanty, and 'kratos' meaning to rule. So, an Oligarchy denotes a form of government run by a

few individuals who usually gain power through their economic status, religion, kinship, prestige, or even language. Whatever their background, oligarchs usually exert power in terms of their own interests or the interest of their own class or group.

It is very difficult to arrest the emergence of oligarchs as they have been identified in ruling monarchies, dictatorships, democracies and even organisations like Trade Unions and large multi-national companies. The Mafia Godfathers in America, Italy and Sicily can also been seen as oligarchs of the criminal underworld class of those countries.

There seems to be a pattern in all forms of governments and organisations for an elite to emerge that are accepted because they *get things done* and are more efficient than the endless meetings of bureaucracies that produce a preponderance of impractical conclusions. A drawback of oligarchies, however, is that they do produce a rigorous order and ideology that lacks human dimensions. In short, oligarchies produce material gain but have little empathy or compassion for others.

I worked in Singapore for eight years, and at one time visited an ear, nose and throat specialist. Discovering that I was an Australian, he asked, 'What do you think of Singapore?' Not wanting to offend, I offered an uncritical comment that highlighted its financial success. His reply was telling –

No, it's not. Singapore is successful but has no heart.

That is a common sentiment expressed by those living under an oligarchy.

Plutocracy
Plutocracy is a term first used in England in 1631 (Merriam Webster) and was invented by combining two Ancient Greek words, *ploutos*, meaning 'wealth' and *kratos* meaning 'to rule'. Therefore, this term

links money with power and control. The idea of a plutocracy is not rooted in any political philosophy but signifies the control of people by means of great wealth.

It is a derogatory term used to alert people to the danger from people who use their wealth to dominate their societies. Plutocrats are criticised for abrogating their social responsibility; of using their wealth to further enrich themselves while making others in their society impoverished and undernourished.

Countries where plutocrats are prominent become politically and socially unstable with the alienated members of society calling for revolution. Fascist Italy and Nazi Germany arose primarily because the revolutionaries in those countries convinced the people that their democracy and capitalism had been compromised by plutocrats. Many citizens in Western countries today are coming to the same conclusion with the same social and political unrest resurfacing. In Russia, Communism took root in a similar way.

Plutocrats are not interested in political power for themselves but rather in the power of money, believing everything (including people) has its price. The plutocrat's creed can be found in the quote by Sir Robert Walpole (Prime Minister of Great Britain, 1721-1742) taken from a speech he gave in 1734 –

All those men have their price.

Which gave rise to the popular saying,

Everything has a price.

For the plutocrat, that price always can be measured in money; for others the price of things can be measured in other entities like the sacrifice of time, family, integrity etc. needed to realise great personal achievement.

Republicanism

Republicanism first emerged in ancient Rome. At this time it meant a group of men forming a Senate and deciding political issues which would rule the citizens of their state. The word 'Republic' comes from the Latin phrase, *res publica* meaning 'public affair'. When the legions of Rome went into battle they carried a banner displaying the letters SPQR, an abbreviation for *Senatus Populusque Romanus* meaning

The Senate and People of Rome.

The two major social groups of ancient Rome were the patricians and the plebeians. These two groups (the wealthy, powerful group and the free Roman citizens group) struggled for political power. Slaves and women also made up a large social group in ancient Rome, but they had no political power. During the time of the Roman Republic, Senators were not elected but appointed by consuls and later the censors. The Senate initially only came from the patrician group, but later some members of the plebeian group were appointed as Senators. Regardless of which group the Senators came from, the majority of Senators came from the richest social group whose wealth was derived primarily from large agricultural estates.

When ancient Rome became an Empire, it was ruled by an Emperor who appointed all Senators. During the time of Empire, the Senate lost much of its power to the Emperor, and when the Empire fell in 476 AD the Senate disappeared until its revival in the American Constitution where its members are determined not in a democratic fashion and not by appointment, but rather by the electors of each State of the Union in the United States electing the same number of Senators for each State, regardless of the State's population. The President is also elected via an electoral college system which is undemocratic while the House of Representatives is a democratically elected body of representatives. So America is a combination of the two systems, or a Democratic Republic. The United States of America is the only country in history to survive more than 200 years with a democratic republican form of government.

Some people argue that the American Republic is under threat from the forces of globalism, communism, and Islamic theocracy. If this is true, one would expect a hero to emerge and fulfil the criterion of a heroic narrative. Can you think of an American politician who believes he is on a quest to save his country from destruction? Someone who endured extreme establishment persecution, perhaps even to the extent of attempted assassination, only to return and continue his fight against the establishment, gain popular support, and enjoy seeing other political leaders emulate his example.

Here is a joke that highlights the way Americans feel about their Democratic Republic which protects their liberty. In the 1980s, President Reagan told those gathered at a conference that he was collecting jokes circulating in Russia that had been created by the Russian people. He also said that he had told it to Mikhail Gorbachev (General Secretary of the Communist Party of Russia and leader of the Soviet Union, 1985-1991) and that Gorbachev had laughed.

Apparently, an American citizen was talking to a Russian comrade. The American said,

I can go into the White House, pound on the President's table and tell him that I don't like the way he is running the country.

The Russian replied,

I can do that.

The astonished American responded,

You can?

Sure, the comrade answered, I can go into the Kremlin, pound

> on the president's table, and tell him I don't like the way the
> **American** President is running his country.

Totalitarianism

Totalitarianism is a belief that insists that government must be centralised while requiring complete subservience of citizens to the state. It supresses all opposition, exercises strong centralised control over the economy, media, and social institutions. It holds that a single political party must have unlimited control over every part of its citizens' lives. Under a totalitarian system of government citizens have no rights, only duties to perform for the state. In essence, a totalitarian state has absolute authority over every aspect of its citizens' lives.

Tyranny

The word tyrant is derived from the Latin word, *Tyrannus,* meaning 'illegitimate ruler'.

Tyranny is a system of government in which all political power is in the hands of a single person. The rule of a tyrant is characterised by cruelty and harshness. The people suffer from domination and coercion without any appeal to justice or redress. Ancient Greek Democracy fell in 404 BC following Athens' surrender to Sparta after Athens' loss of the Peloponnesian War. Political power in ancient Athens passed from the Assembly (Ecclesia) into the hands of Thirty Tyrants. Thereafter, democracy disappeared from the world until it was revived by the American Constitution in 1789 for the election of their House of Representatives. The revolutionaries during the American War of Independence believed that King George III of Great Britain was a tyrant.

> *Resistance to tyrants is obedience to God.*

This was a saying adopted by Thomas Jefferson (Founding Father and contributing author of The American Constitution) as a personal motto (AI Overview, 2025).

Political Concepts

Let us now turn our attention to some political concepts that underpin our understanding of politics and political systems.

The Political Spectrum

After deposing French King Louis XVI (1754-1793), the political leaders of France met in a tennis court they named the National Assembly. What occurred was that those leaders who favoured equality sat to the left of the gathering while those favouring various forms of hierarchy sat to the right. Ever since, those favouring the *reform* of political policies are referred to as being on the left of politics, while those favouring the *conservation* of political policies are referred to as the political right. Hence the terms reformist and conservative and the emergence of a political spectrum involving the left and the right. We have also seen the terms 'far left' and 'far right' being used to describe political parties with extreme views. Some people may refer to political parties displaying a radical proclivity as 'extreme left' or 'extreme right'.

Given the definitions of the various political organisations highlighted above, place those organisations on a political spectrum of your own. Where would you place terrorism on your spectrum? If you have difficulty assigning terrorism to your spectrum, you acknowledge that both extreme left and extreme right factions utilise terrorism as a tactic to gain and hold power. As the saying goes,

> One man's terrorist is another man's (or should it be radical's) freedom fighter.

A saying that lacks any sense of moral clarity. The truly sad reality of people who believe this is that they fail to recognise that this statement belongs on both fanatical edges of the political spectrum.

My own political spectrum differs from the established norm. At the centre of my political spectrum sits *liberal democracy* which rests on the principle of *the consent of the governed* by upholding *individual sovereignty* and *liberty*. It contains both *reformist* (not to be confused with socialist) and *conservative* (not to be confused with the religious right) political movements.

Since I have claimed a difference between reformists and socialists, and conservatives and the religious right, I feel the need to clarify my position. Reformists are those who stand in a centre left position within liberal democracy. Reformists, for example, will unite with conservatives over the issue of free speech, which they see as a central tenant of liberty, while at the same time conservatives will stand with reformists in condemning the evils of bigotry, both religious and ideological. On the other hand, socialists are those who stand left of centre. They are *in* a liberal democracy but not *of* it. That is, while still maintaining a position within the liberal democratic process, they stand outside liberal democracy itself with the intention of using totalitarian ideology and the erosion of free speech to tear down the liberal democratic process which they view as structurally unjust. Many religious believers are socialists. These are the religious group that espouse the principles of liberation theology and fundamentalist (united order) theology.

The difference between conservatives and the religious right is that conservatives hold a centre right position within the liberal democratic process, while the religious right stand in a right of centre position. That is, the religious right, while maintaining a position within the liberal democratic process, stand outside it and seek to destroy it, which they view as morally decadent and inherently evil owing to its belief in, what they see as, excessive freedom. The religious right, for example, use authoritarian ideology which views conservatives as supporting a system of government that is unrestrained and ungodly while they would prefer to return to a system where a religious leader or a monarch would rule through the word of God and not the inherent weakness of human beings.

I hasten to add at this point that I am highlighting the religious right and not all religious people. Many religious people are conservatives who stand to uphold the liberal democratic system of government largely because they recognise that human beings have the God-given right to exercise their own 'free will', and that liberty, found only in liberal democracy, facilitates that religious principle. They also recognise that liberal democracies uphold the principle of religious freedom.

Today both reformists and conservatives unite to condemn things like group identity over individual sovereignty, discrimination over individual merit, and intolerance (be that religious or ideological) over reason, to name just a few common grounds shared by those championing the liberal democratic cause. The underlying philosophy of my political spectrum can be found in Aristotle's golden mean which holds that virtue lies in the middle ground between two extremes of deficiency and excess, and the Stoic belief in treating others with dignity and respect. Its moral correctness can be found in Jesus' golden rule found in the gospel of Mathew, which states,

In everything, do unto others as you would have them do unto you.
(Mathew 7:12)

Two other groups, oligarchs and plutocrats, can be found on both the far left and far right of politics. However, these groups are more interested in the power of money than the power of politics, although both groups are willing to use politics to accumulate more wealth for themselves.

Now that these distinctions have been clarified let's move on to how socialism and the religious right lure citizens away from their liberal democratic rights.

On the far left is socialism which is the bridge over which dictators (Communist, Fascist and Nazi) march to establish their far-left *totalitarian* states. You see, all these political movements start as socialist movements promising economic, social, and political change to alleviate the suffering of the poor and needy, especially during times of economic downturn and the destruction of the working and lower middle classes, but end in dictatorships, giving the dictator and his inner-circle elites total and unchallengeable power over their society. Consequently, all totalitarian dictatorships rightly belong at the far left of the political spectrum. My view here differs from the consensus view that Fascism and Nazism belong on the far right. The difference in our views rests on the principles of totalitarianism and authoritarianism.

Some argue that socialists see society divided into two groups, workers/capitalists, while Nazism and Fascism divide society into races. That is, only Fascists and Nazis believe in selective breeding to produce a master race. That racism is a social infliction of only the far-right wing of the political spectrum. It is more accurate, however, to point out that the left has always been racist. For example, eugenics, a belief that society can be improved by things like selective breeding, contraception, abortion, sterilisation etc., has always been a belief and practice of the left. Even Karl Marx and Friedrich Engels, the founders of communism, were racists (tandfonline.com, *Marx and Engels Theory of History: Making Sense of the Race Factor*, 2019). Later, major believers in British socialism (Sidney and Beatrice Webb, George Bernard Shaw, Harold Laski, John Maynard Keynes and Marie Stopes) promoted eugenics. Margaret Singer, an American socialist, argued that birth control would reduce the number of 'unfit people' and improve the overall health of the human race (pubmed.ncbi.nim.gov, *Was Margaret Singer A Racist?* 1985). As late as 1976 the Swedish (socialist) government was carrying out forced sterilisations (theguardian.com, *Eugenics and the master race of the left*, 1997, by Jonathan Freedland). Today, the antisemitism plaguing the West is supported by far-left politics (theconversation.com, 2023; adl.org, 2023). So those pursuing this narrative are, to put it mildly, historically inaccurate.

Another argument designed to put Fascism and Nazism on the far right of the political spectrum is the claim that these political movements do not nationalise private industry. Something that communist dictators do. However, Fascists and Nazis are also socialists in that they nationalise individuals and establish dictatorships with a centrally controlled economy. An SS report in 1944 puts it this way –

> ...*National Socialism (Nazism) takes the position: the state directs the economy, the state is not there for business, business is there for the state.*
> (mises.org, *Hitler's Views on Private Property an*d *Nationalisation*, 2022)

You see, the Nazis did not have to nationalise private industry; they had total control over it and all aspects of the socio/economic structure of Germany. They determined what would be produced, in what quantities it would be produced, and what it would sell for. Nazis sat at the table of the (so-called) private industry Boards and woe betide any Chairman or Board Member who differed from the Nazi orders. In this way, Fascists and Nazis belong to the socialist left and not the right of politics. Put it this way, Nazis and Fascists did not have to nationalise industry or business, they nationalised people. I refer here to communist leaders like Joseph Stalin, Mao Zedong and Pol Pot. Did they not run their countries in the same fashion as Mussolini and Hitler.

I see the fundamental ideology of Fascism and Nazism to be totalitarianism while others see it as authoritarianism. I find their view confusing. Which is what I suspect is their main purpose since they do not want to associate Socialism or Communism with Fascism or Nazism. To claim that Hitler persecuted the communists is, in my mind, only to state the obvious; he saw communism as his socialist competitor and therefore wanted to eliminate it.

Right of centre is the religious right which follows a well-worn pilgrim's path leading directly to religious intolerance and the *absolute authority* of its religious leaders, regardless of which religion is involved. The leaders of Christianity are the heads of the churches, who gain their absolute authority from God, and their political leaders are

Monarchs, who gain their absolute authority from the 'divine right of Kings' bestowed upon them by their country's official religion; both are authoritarian in nature, relying on the authority of God. Islam, on the other hand, combines its religious and political leaders into one. In Iran, for example, the Supreme Leader is the head of state and holds ultimate authority over the country's political and religious affairs, including the military, judiciary, and state media. The overriding problem with authoritarianism is that those who hold God's authority are answerable only to God. A pretty cool idea for the holders of God's authority, but not for the rest of their believers, because history has shown that such absolute authority always leads to corruption and abuse of power by those in authority, and misery and repression for the faithful.

One of the biggest problems with the religious right is their failure to recognise the importance of the separation of church and state; a political principle that took many centuries to develop in Western Civilisation. When Jesus said,

Render unto Caesar the things that are Caesar's and unto God the things that are God's

(Matthew 22:21),

He was making this distinction between church and state. In short, the things of government (like the supply and distribution of money) are the jurisdiction of secular politics, while the things of salvation (like the spiritual awakening of the faithful) are the providence of God. In their ignorance, the religious right try to integrate politics (the secular) with religion (the spiritual). Religion is at its best when operating on the transcendental level of truth through the promotion of *salvation through grace or moral jurisprudence*. It is at its worst when dispensing secular, *existential justice* on heretics or infidels.

Another way of looking at the difference is that Totalitarianism achieves its right to govern through military power while Authoritarianism achieves it through the divine authority of God.

To those socialists who say that they are progressives, I say, leave your radical socialist group identity and move to the political centre where you will find the reformist movement. When you do, be aware of the *unintended consequences* that may arise from the reforms you promote and the *hidden agenda* of the radical socialists. Be prudent, look ahead. To those religious followers who long for a return to the absolute authority of the church, I say, leave your radical religious group identity and move to the political centre where you will find the conservative movement. When you do, *be mindful of the prudent reforms* suggested by the reformists. When you cannot reach an agreement, end your discussion with a continued respect for each other's position, rather than resorting to violence to settle your differences. In short, move to the centre and drop all radical aspirations.

To sum up, my spectrum places *liberty* in the centre, *totalitarianism* on the far left, and *authoritarianism* on the far right –

Totalitarianism----Liberty----Authoritarianism.

With liberty, citizens have rights that their Nation State protects, while totalitarian comrades have duties to perform for their state, and authoritarian devotees have service and sacrifice performed for their chosen faiths.

People living in totalitarian or authoritarian states have no choice in deciding whether they accept or reject the totalitarian dictates of their dictators or the authoritarian edicts of their autocrats. Authority as it exists in a liberal democracy (the centre) is consensual, being decided by the consent of the governed through elections. In other words, people who hold authority over citizens in liberal democracies can be accepted or rejected by electors, whilst those with central control on the far left or far right are absolute rulers who are unable to be rejected by the governed.

It is much easier for individuals to live in a totalitarian or authoritarian state, where 'dear leader' or 'holy father' make all the decisions for them than a liberal democracy where they have to think and choose for themselves who is best to have authority over them. After all, it is more convenient to blame someone else when things go wrong –

> *I was following orders, or I was told that was God's will,*

and easy to become elated by claiming that

> *I contributed to the success of my state or religion,*

when things go right.

When things go wrong and people begin to question the wisdom of their leaders, both the far left and far right employ repression through terror and military power. The Supreme Leaders use Islamists terror organisations and their military to control and supress their believers. In the past, Christians used the Inquisition to keep their believers in line and Monarchs used their military power to supress their subjects when they became unruly. Dictators use their secret police and military power to terrorise and enforce their totalitarian state dictates on their people. They also create a surveillance state in which their people are constantly spied upon, even in some cases by their own family members. This places people living in a dictatorship in a constant state of fear, anxiety and, in some cases, even paranoia.

Conversely, liberal democracies and their political leaders (reformists and conservatives) use their military power to protect the liberty of their citizens and their police to uphold the legal rights of their citizens from those who would challenge them or try to remove them. Through legislation, reformists try to improve the lives of their citizens by introducing new laws or amending or repealing old laws. Conservatives try to conserve those laws that they believe have a proven efficacy for protecting their citizens' liberty and legal rights and a history of providing them with a prosperous life. Things like free choice, free speech, private property rights, and equal justice are just four things that conservatives guard against change.

Both reformists and conservatives try to make liberal democracy work better for their citizens; they do not want to replace it with a different political system. They also are dedicated to the holding of free and fair elections at regular intervals (usually every three to six years) where any citizen has the right to stand for election. In short, citizens in a liberal democracy have their liberty and rights protected by their politicians, while the far left and far right want to replace the liberty and rights of their citizens with blind obedience to the state or a religious order.

The danger to a liberal democracy, however, does not exist only from outside the democratic process; it also is vulnerable from within. Unfortunately, corruption from within is ever present, where money and power is pursued relentlessly by those holding political power (oligarchs and plutocrats), even to the extent where the powerful create a socio/political/economic elite within a liberal democracy and are willing to compromise the integrity of their elections in order to hold on to their power. The stifling of free speech through hate speech or mis/disinformation laws, the spreading of propaganda lies through the use of *ad hominem* arguments that include things like gossip, inuendo and false charges coupled with trial by media, unjustified character assassination of political opponents, and buying votes by making promises that are broken after elections are just some of the ways that the integrity of elections can be compromised. As well as this, there is the deliberate corruption of the voting system itself achieved by the manipulation of electoral boundaries and how votes are cast and counted. This can occur when electoral rolls are not kept updated or new rules are introduced to make some votes invalid.

Furthermore, we have seen the revelation by the Department of Government Efficiency (DOGE) in American that millions of citizens in America are over 120 years of age and collecting social security. The oldest living person in the world in 2025 is Inah Canabarro Lucas from Brazil. She is 116 years of age. The oldest living person in history was Jeanne Louise Calment. She was 122 years of age when she died in 1997 and is the only verified person to have lived beyond 120 years of age (sciencefocus.com, 2024). Have you ever wondered how many dead people are still on the electoral roles of some liberal democratic nations?

Vote early and vote often.
(brainyquote.com, Al Capone, Chicago gangster, 1915)

Many other politicians have made this same remark in jest about the voting process in their countries. However, the phrase can raise doubts in the minds of citizens about the integrity of their electoral system.

From this observation, can we conclude that liberal democracy works best when citizens use their logic, reasoning, wisdom, common sense, and empathy to evaluate the policies of different political parties at election time and avoid following the narrative promoted by the socio/political/economic elite, being swayed by the *compassionate society* argument so often pushed by socialists to disguise their hidden agenda, or giving into the temptation of 'free stuff' offered by socialists and communists?

The liberty and individual sovereignty that exists within a liberal democracy is an anathema to the fanatics on both the far left and far right, and the corrupt elite. The far left view liberal democracy as upholding inequality, while the far right view it as promoting moral decadence. Both are willing to end democracy in pursuit of justice for *the people*. The corrupt elite within liberal democracy see free and fair elections as an impediment to their power over what they perceive as the 'ignorant masses'.

What annoys me most about radicals and elitists is their tiresome insistence on ideas that lack historical accuracy, rational consistency, or even common sense. When challenged by reformists or conservatives they do not consider the accuracy of the challenge, they simply double down on their intolerant ideology. Unlike discussions with reformists or conservatives with whom one can engage in logical conversation and end with,

> *Well, we'll just have to agree to disagree.*

Try that ending with a radical or an elitist.
George Orwell puts it best –

> *One has to belong to the intelligentsia to believe things like that. No ordinary man could be such a fool.*
> (George Orwell, *Notes on Nationalism*, 1945)

One tactic I have adopted when dealing with radicals and elitists is to engage the Socratic tradition of asking questions that test the logic of their position. Of course, what usually follows is descent into sophist argument, usually containing obfuscation and strawman argument. Hopefully, they will eventually come to see the error in their logic by, at least, admitting it to themselves. This is a hollow victory, however, because remember the end for a radical or an elitist always justifies the means, even if it entails lying to others or themselves.

Milton Friedman also warns us about the concentration of power threating our liberty –

> *Our minds tell us, and history confirms, that the great threat to freedom is the concentration of power.*
> (Milton Friedman, *Capitalism and Freedom*, 1982)

And may I add that the moment those who step to the far left or far right of the political centre or attempt to corrupt the democratic process from within, even if their intention is to rid democracy of injustice, moral decadence, or ignorance, are on a road that leads directly to the concentration of power, the death of free and fair elections, and the end of democracy. It is a sad fact of history that citizens living in a liberal democracy can vote in dictatorships or a powerful elite but have to fight their way out of it. Therefore, the citizens of liberal democratic nations must be forever vigilant in guarding their liberty and democratic rights from those who would steal it from them or have them trade it for totalitarianism, authoritarianism or elitism. I find my political spectrum helps me rationalise an otherwise overcomplicated system of categorisation.

What do you think about my political spectrum? Is it helpful? Can you suggest some changes that would make it more accessible?

The Overton Window
Overton was an executive of the Mackinac Centre for Public Policy in the 1990s who created what has become known as the Overton Window.

The Overton Window tells us what policy ideas politicians can support to gain widespread popular support. What is interesting about this model is that the political ideas and concepts a society holds change over time and can influence what policies politicians will run with at election time. Simply put, politicians generally, but not always, will run with policies that are widely accepted by society as legitimate policy options while rejecting policy options that are generally less popular.

The concept of a political pendulum has been around for a long time and is similar to Overton's Window. However, Overton chose the image of a window over that of a pendulum because it presents us with an image of a window of opportunity.

In times past, most political policies were formulated by the centre left or centre right of this spectrum, because that was where the overwhelming popular support resided and where the Overton Window was located. However, much political change has occurred in the 21st century, and the Overton Window has shifted. First further to the left, but lately it is gravitating back to the right. The problem is that the Overton Window has a tendency, once it starts to move, to go further and further one way or the other until it creates economic and social crises which brings it back towards the opposite direction.

What causes the Overton Window to reposition itself? It could be the charisma of a popular leader. This leader can be from the left or the right who courageously endorses policies outside the Overton Window, but whose charm and persuasive ability carries the day, or it simply could be when economic reality catches up with ideological intolerance. Alternatively, it could be the result of a deliberate commitment by some determined individuals to move the window in a desired way through social and cultural engineering over a long period of time. Those most favourably positioned to affect this change are those who can influence change. This power is concentrated in the hands of the socioeconomic and political elite. In the past, it was those who controlled the mainstream media and our public education who, to a large extent, controlled the positioning of the Overton Window. More recently, digital media has become an influential form of information distribution and therefore a more prominent player in the positioning of the Overton Window. It is not by accident that the established political elite now seek to censure digital media. For our own good, of course.

A good example of how the Overton Window works in practice can be found in Milton Friedman's introduction to his book, *Capitalism and Freedom*, xxviii, 1982 –

> *That, I believe, is our basic function: to develop alternatives to existing policies, to keep them alive and available until the politically impossible becomes the politically inevitable.*

This Overton Window seems to vindicate the veracity of Breitbart's Doctrine that

politics is downstream from culture
(Wikipedia.org, 2025)

and is the driving force behind postmodernist cultural theory which sees communists focusing on influencing cultural institutions like media, entertainment, academia, education, and the judiciary rather than directly on political campaigns and politicians which were left largely to the socialists.

How do you think the mainstream media or educators could affect change in the position of the Overton Window? Do you think the manipulation of greed, envy and/or fear in the general population would have an effect on the position of the Overton Window? What affect do you think the digital media is having on the position of the Overton Window today? Do you think economic reality has a part to play in the positioning of the Overton Window? How so?

In Defence of Liberal Democracy
May I take some time to offer you my views and opinions concerning the history of liberal democracies. I urge you to question and evaluate them for yourself before deciding if they might be valuable to your understanding of the importance of liberal democracy as it pertains to world peace and prosperity.

At first it was the writings and ideas introduced by The Enlightenment in Europe that gave rise to liberal democracies. Some of the great philosophers and thinkers of the Age of Enlightenment were people like Descartes (1596-1650), a French philosopher, scientist, and mathematician, who championed reason and mathematical analysis over superstitious, oppressive theology; John Locke (1632-1704), a British empiricist who championed individual freedom, natural rights, and limited government; Sir Isaac Newton (1643-1727), who formulated the three laws of motion which revolutionised our understanding of the physical world; David Hume (1711-76), who advanced the theory that all knowledge originates from sensory experience (empiricism), and that morality is rooted in feelings (sentimentality) not reason; and later John Stuart Mill (1806-73), who informed us that actions are right in proportion to the happiness derived from them. He was also a champion of liberty. That is, freedom, especially freedom of speech and choice. I hasten to add before moving on that many of the enlightened philosophers were Christians who believed in God. Not all were atheists, although many French philosophers were.

Obviously, I have not done these Enlightenment figures justice in my all too brief summary. However, it is not my intention to explain the intricacies of their contribution to the Enlightenment, but rather to provide a simple understanding of how Enlightenment thought facilitated the emergence of Liberal Democracy.

Enlightenment thought, then, celebrates *knowledge, freedom* and *happiness* achieved through the *power of reason*. Central to Enlightenment thought were things like *natural law* which Enlightenment thinkers saw as *the expression of God's will,* as opposed to the expression of *legal positivism,* which does not require ethical or moral justification. The enlightened view believes in the expression of logic and reason to *the rule of law; individual liberty* as opposed to subjugation and bondage; *religious freedom* as opposed to *religious persecution; constitutional* and *representative government* as opposed to *absolute authority or totalitarian power; equality* before the law as opposed to *selective or arbitrary* legal enforcement; *free speech* as opposed to *censorship*; and the *separation of church and state* rather than the imposition of religious morality applied to the legislative and executive arms of government.

Bolstering their contribution was the influence of Christian charity that encouraged much of the empathetic change in those liberal democracies, like the abolition of slavery, child labour and the alleviation of poverty. Like all political and religious thought, however, both Enlightenment thought and Christian worship can be taken to extremes. Christianity's compassion and the Enlightenment's emphasis on reason and freedom can lead to extreme action that attacks the social fabric of any society. The compassionate society does have its limitations. The fact is that all societies must work within limitations, and that fact engages us in trade-offs and compromises, not absolutes. We have learnt how to tame our environment to better suit our requirements and how to provide better for our needs, but we are not living in a perfect world. What is needed, then, is a prudent balance between our reason, happiness, and compassion; not a triumph of any one over the others.

The Enlightenment and Christianity led to the creation of liberal democratic nation states and a belief in, among other things, individual sovereignty, the acquisition and free exchange of private property, freedom of speech, and individual choice. This accelerated the emergence of the agrarian and industrial revolutions which brought great wealth and technological change to liberal democracies worldwide. All these developments encouraged Europeans to believe that Western Civilisation, with its morality grounded in Christian values and its political organisation shaped by liberal democracy, was on an upward path towards perfection and a betterment for all people around the world.

However, the 20th century witnessed Western Civilisation become involved in WWI and WWII, thus spawning a moral crisis for their vision of a perfecting society. What nauseated people in Europe about both WWI and WWII the most was that it, once again, involved Christians killing Christians. Europeans believed they had left all that behind with the ending of the religious wars (1517-1648) between Catholics and Protestants, the Napoleonic wars (1800-1815) and the wars of unification (mid-to-late 19th century). The European belief that they had created a civilisation, based on Christianity and liberal democracy that would bring peace and prosperity to the world, was laid waste by the World Wars because of the slaughter and vicious brutality on an industrial scale that it had produced. A scale of cruelty and human suffering that had never before confronted any other civilisation. Europeans asked themselves, how could Western

Civilisation be on a path towards perfection when it had produced such a horrendous outcome for humanity?

Historians lay the blame for the outbreak of hostilities in 1914 on a number of things. Chief among them were national and Imperial rivalry and treaty alliances.

I would like to revisit these points and see if we can recover some balance in the argument which favours liberal democracy. First is the point involving national rivalry. WWI did not break out between nations governed by liberal democracies. It broke out between nations supporting liberal democracy and nations governed by autocracy. This is a vital distinction because using my political spectrum we find that autocracy lies at the far right of the political spectrum. So the conflict actually involved liberal democratic nations occupying the centre of the political spectrum being attacked by autocratic nations at the extreme right. Unfortunately, Christianity was unable to provide a check on the aggressive ambitions of the autocrats in those countries. We can conclude that it is not nationalism per se that was the cause of WWI, but rather the authoritarianism of the far right that is responsible for the outbreak of WWI. That is, radical, authoritarian nationalism. Liberal democratic nations were only defending themselves against aggressive, autocratic extremism. The same can be said about WWII, only this time the centrist liberal democracies had to defend themselves against the aggressive, far-left dictatorships of Germany, Italy, and Japan. This time, it was the far-left totalitarians, who again pursued radical nationalism, that was the underlying cause, not nationalism itself. The fact is that liberal democratic nations have never gone to war against each other; they have only done so in defence of themselves against radical aggression. In short, liberal democratic nations view war as a failure of their diplomacy, while authoritarian or totalitarian nations see it as an extension (a part) of their diplomacy. Liberal democracies create moderate nationalism which provides unity for their people. Authoritarian and totalitarian states create radical nationalism which take their people to war against the moderate nationalism of liberal democracies.

Since WWI and WWII saw the end of radical nationalism expressed in authoritarianism and totalitarianism in Europe in the 20th century, one would have imagined that Europe would have recognised the triumph of liberal democracy, especially after it brought relative peace and unparalleled prosperity to Western Civilisation in the latter half of the 20th century. This was not to be however, because autocrats and dictators still existed in other parts of the world.

Communist and later military dictatorships dominated Russia; communist dictatorships controlled China, North Korea, North Vietnam and later all of Vietnam, and other less powerful nations like Cuba and Venezuela; while religious autocracy took hold in Iran. Since then, communist and Islamist propaganda has taken hold in liberal democracies and filled their citizens with a *guilt complex*. This is promoted through a perceived oppressor/oppressed model of capitalism underpinning democratic economies. Because current liberal democracies lack moral clarity (owing to the demise of Christianity in the West, the acceptance of moral equivalency, and the adoption of a 'guilt complex' related to colonialism) in their thinking, democratic citizens too easily accept this radical narrative. The shaming from this narrative enabled extremists to develop an educational system promoting this 'guilt complex' and their political ideology and religious beliefs.

Racism, sexism, homophobia, Islamophobia, climate change denial, cancel culture, multi-culturalism, mass immigration, and mis/disinformation are some of the ideas created by radicals to promote guilt and anxiety while shutting down free speech in liberal democracies. While it is true that racism, sexism and homophobia were a blight on civilised Western society, liberal democracies have legislated against any institutional discrimination pertaining to these forms of prejudice in their societies and done so much more in correcting this error than has either the totalitarians or the authoritarians. Catastrophic climate change emergency, cancel culture, multi-culturalism, mass immigration, and mis/disinformation have done so much to divide, confuse and create anxiety in the minds of liberal democratic citizens than has any other challenge of the past. The saddest fact of all is that these challenges are self-inflicted and have created one group of citizens with a *guilt complex* and another with a *victim mentality* in liberal democracies not present in either the authoritarian right or the totalitarian left. This 'guilt complex' in liberal democracies has made acceptable things like borrowing excessively to placate citizens' guilt, allowing their institutions to be overwhelmed by administrators who believe the only way forward is to destroy liberty (particularly free speech) along with its market-driven capitalistic economic system, pursuing catastrophic climate change emergency policies that destroy the economic viability of liberal democracies, and implementing a mass-immigration system based on multi-culturalism that threatens to destroy the social/cultural fabric of liberal democracies by allowing people with radical views to become citizens. What the two world wars had rid liberal democracies of is now being restored by the far left and far right from within.

Second is the issue of Imperial rivalry. It is true that Europe's expanding Imperial interests led to increased Imperial rivalry between the different European nations. Unfortunately this occurred at a time when the opportunity to acquire new colonies had already declined. For example, Kaiser Wilhelm II sought Germany's *place in the sun*. He coveted the empires of France and Britain in African and Asia and wanted the same for Germany, but the colonies had already been established, leaving little for Germany to acquire. Did this make conflict between Imperial powers inevitable?

Third, treaty alliances materialised as a consequence of Imperial rivalry. In WWI, the Triple Alliance involved Germany, Austria-Hungary and Italy. Italy withdrew from the Tripple Alliance in 1915 and declared war on Austria-Hungary. The Triple Entente included England, France, and Russia. Lenin withdrew Russia from the war after he come into power in 1917. In the same year, the Americans joined the Allied cause because of Germany's resumption of unlimited submarine warfare on merchant and passenger ships in 1917.

In WWII, it initially involved the Allies of England and France. Russia signed a non-aggression pact with Germany and participated in attacking and carving up Poland. France fell to Germany following the Battle of France in 1940. After Germany launched Operation Barbarossa in June 1941 against Russia, Russia joined the Western Alliance. Later that same year, America also joined the Allied cause following the Japanese attack on Pearl Harbour in December 1941. Opposing the Allies were the Axis powers of Germany, Italy and Japan. What these Alliances (involved in both WWI and WWII) meant was that, once hostilities broke out between any two countries from different Alliances, it meant all countries in the alliance would become involved. A *one in all in* approach to the resolution of national conflict generated from Imperial rivalry had led to two world wars. After WWII, liberal democratic nations in Europe relinquished their colonies by helping their colonies become self-governing.

What appeared after the collapse of European Imperialism was the emergence of free trade between nations, made possible by America's military commitment to keeping the trading routes open. For global trade to exist the supply lines between trading nations must be kept open. Eventually, globalism came to dominate liberal democratic thinking but is now being questioned by some as being at the radical end of free trade. Today, many see globalism as producing a transfer of wealth and technology from liberal democracies into the hands of countries supporting radical political positions. This is now at a point where it is, once again, threatening the security of liberal democracies and an outbreak of worldwide hostilities.

Following the withdrawal of Western Imperialism, unregulated private enterprise returned to dominate world trade, and with it a return to child labour (lithium mines in Africa), slavery (Ghana and Nigeria), and forced-labour camps (Chinese repression of Uyghurs). Remember what Leopold II and his Congo Free State enterprise did to the Congo in the 19th century. As a consequence of these developments in world trade, the citizens of liberal democracies are beginning to support a concept of *fair trade* rather than *free trade*, which would consider the costs of production relating to labour and energy. President Trump has now introduced a new concept for trade, *reciprocal tariffs*. In short, liberal democracies would like to see the living standards of developing nations rise, but not at the expense of their own citizens' living standards. Globalist free trade has already led to worker exploitation worldwide and the deindustrialisation of liberal democracies, thereby making liberal democracies dependent on overseas manufacturing and technology. These developments have created a major threat to liberal democracies (now dependent on fragile supply lines) and the disappearing dream of a prosperous, peaceful world achieved through citizenship rights and liberty. Ask yourself, is this wise?

As world tensions rise, nations are, once again, turning to alliances to protect themselves against the outbreak of hostilities. China, Russia, North Korea, and Iran are reaching international agreements and aligning themselves militarily. China and Russia now conduct joint military exercises, and North Korea has sent troops to help Russia in its war with Ukraine. The appearance of BRICK+ nations and their desire to trade in their own currencies rather than the American dollar is another example of global fragmentation. Remember these are all nations that sit at the far left and far right of our political spectrum, dedicated to the destruction of market capitalism and the elimination of liberty in liberal democracies. America, NATO countries, England, India, Australia, New Zealand, Canada, The Philippines, South Korea, and Japan have either formally signed treaties or entered into understandings designed to guarantee their protection against foreign aggression.

The UN was created specifically to stop this from happening but seems powerless to placate current conflicts and rising tensions. Remember Russia (led by a military dictator) invaded Ukraine (a liberal democratic nation state), and the terrorist organisations Hamas and Hezbollah, proxies established by the Iranian Ayatollah, have attacked Israel (a liberal democratic nation state). Meanwhile China (led by a communist dictator) threatens to invade and capture Taiwan (a liberal democratic nation state). All nations involved in these conflicts were or are now member nations of the UN, an organisation designed to protect the territorial integrity of their member nations. Taiwan was a charter member nation of the UN until 1971 when its membership was withdrawn. Since then, Taiwan has reapplied to become a member nation of the UN but China keeps blocking Taiwan's re-entry.

To become a member of the UN every member nation must sign an oath to uphold the territorial integrity of all other member nations. Where then does the UN stand on these acts of aggression? These invasions of liberal democracies worldwide are justified by the aggressor nations through the same propaganda that the Nazis used in the 1930s, namely *historical injustice*. In Germany's case it was the historical injustice wrought against their people by the liberal democratic nations of Europe in forcing the Treaty of Versailles on the German nation and the loss of German territory to existing and newly formed liberal democracies in Europe. Today, the historical injustice may have changed (now it's colonialism) but the propaganda techniques remain the same. Are we witnessing the same pattern emerge that led to WWI and WWII? It is not liberal democracies that have started these conflicts; it is dictators (from the far left) and autocrats (from the far right) who have initiated these conflicts, and the UN seems powerless to even mitigate this new emergence of international tension.

What all these developments will produce from now on is anyone's guess, but one thing is certain, if the world were governed solely by liberal democracies free from radical politics, these tensions would disappear. It is the exclusive belligerence of the far right and far left that keeps worldwide conflict and tensions rising. Given the impotence of the UN and the fact that it took the revolting slaughter and destruction of WWI and WWII to end extremism in Europe, one shudders at what horrors it would take to remove it from the world. Make no mistake, liberal democracies worldwide are currently in an existential conflict with the far left and far right. The resolution of that conflict will determine whether we will be governed by Consent, Totalitarian dictate or Authoritarian edict.

What liberal democracies now need is a heroic narrative to unify their people. It can be found in the sacrifice endured by their ancestors to create and maintain their liberty, which is so beautifully articulated in their constitutions. Those reformists and conservatives who have lost their way and joined the radicals on the political far left and far right must now surrender their rhetorical weapons, rejoin the liberal democratic centre, and take up the challenge to defend the liberty that their ancestors fought so bravely to bequeath them.

Today there is much radical criticism of regulated capitalism and liberal democracies on the grounds that they create an unequal society in terms of their distribution of material wealth, or that it leads people into moral decadence. Actually, this is the tedious Marxist idea of material determinism and the religious nonsense that seeks to strip individuals of their free choice. In any event, one must ask the obvious question –

What do you propose to replace it with?

What always follows is a referral to some utopian ideal that has never existed. The simple truth is that liberal democracy and regulated capitalism, although not perfect, has produced more freedom and a higher standard of living for their citizens than any other political system. The obvious truth that history tells us is that liberal democracies can only be replaced by a totalitarian dictatorship or an authoritarian autocracy. Both of which will lead to a lower standard of living and much suffering on the part of the very people that the radicals claim compassion for.

The new utopian ideal of the radicals is a multi-polar world where separate nation states (be they liberal democracies, totalitarian states or theocracies) compete equally in the international arena. In reality, what history has shown us is that this would create another warlord era, only on a grander scale, where separate states would be in constant battle with one another for supremacy. I guess the old adage applies here –

Be careful what you wish for, you just might get it.

Have I engaged in ideology myself by presenting my views and opinions about 20th century history? I think not, because they are just my views and opinions and I prefaced my presentation with that overriding principle; they were not presented to you as absolute truth. It is up you whether you find merit or fault in them, and I encourage you to question and evaluate anything I have offered you in my nonconformist presentation.

Economic Integrity

Economic integrity is built upon honesty, transparency, consistency, and fairness. Two important moral principles that establish economic integrity are *good faith* in agreements and *honest conduct*. This is important because it establishes public trust and combats corruption, misinformation and biased decision making. Economic integrity results in increased investment, innovation, efficient allocation of resources, increased productivity, and best of all economic prosperity. All economic systems are subject to human fallibility. These range from our tendency to make mistakes, to make decisions without sufficient knowledge, to engage in partisan reasoning, and to surrender to our emotional flaws (i.e., excessive anger, persistent irritability, and inability to control one's moods). Any attempt at creating economic integrity must consider these potentially destructive human fallibilities.

There are three major economic systems I will analyse here: *capitalism, communism,* and *globalism*. In the modern world, these three economic systems arose in this order. I hope you will find my examination helpful in determining your own evaluation of their effectiveness in providing

> *the greatest good for the greatest number.*
> (Jeremy Bentham, *A Fragment on Government*, 1776)

Capitalism

Capitalism is an economic system which allows for the means of production and property to be controlled and owned by private individuals operating in a free market which determines the production and price of goods. Modern capitalist theory was first defined by Adam Smith (1723-90), a Scottish economist of the 18th century, who promoted the theory that prices in the market were determined by *supply* and *demand*. Supply being the number of goods in the market and demand being the amount of money chasing those goods.

When capitalism first emerged there were no restrictions placed on it. This *laissez faire* (a French term meaning 'allow to do') approach to capitalism led to many social problems, like the failure of unchecked growth leading to economic depressions, environmental pollution, child labour, and the inhumane treatment of workers. This caused governments in capitalistic countries to regulate their capitalist economies. However, the excessive use of regulation on an economy can lead to economic stagnation. We now have red, green, and black regulation controlling our economy, as well as cultural policy (DEI, ESG, etc.) that regulates and protects cultural ideology. All this regulation has an effect on investment decisions shaping Australia's economy. For this reason, economic regulation needs to be prudently applied to allow for economic expansion, not to irresponsibly supress it with ideologically driven legislation. Like all things in life, the regulation of Australia's economy involves a trade-off not the ideological triumph of regulation over economic development.

Consequently, much disagreement has arisen over what constitutes an appropriate level of regulation. For example, the *Keynesian* and *Monetary* approaches concentrate on the demand side of the capitalist economy, thereby prioritising greater governmental regulation and wealth distribution; while the *Neoliberal* approach concentrates more on the supply side of a capitalist economy, thereby emphasising economic growth (productivity) with minimal government intervention. These two different approaches are known as *demand* side economics and *supply* side economics.

Following the Great Depression (1929-39), which was a severe global economic downturn characterised by unacceptable high rates of unemployment and poverty, John Maynard Keynes (1883-1946) detailed his macroeconomic theory about the economic policy of government. Basically, his economic theory promotes the idea that a capitalist economy is incapable of avoiding severe economic downturns without the government putting purchasing power into the hands of the working (consumers) population through government spending, hence creating more *demand* for goods and services. He believed that if governments accumulate surpluses during times of economic growth and spend the accumulated surplus during times of economic downturn, it will maintain an economy that will reduce the extremes of economic growth and depression. That is, a capitalist economy using these government practices will experience mild growth of 2%-4% while maintaining an inflation rate of 2%-3%, and a rate of unemployment around 3.5%-5%. This is known as demand side economics which tries to achieve periods of mild economic growth combined with economic recessions while avoiding the larger swings of economic booms and busts.

Unfortunately, once governments became involved in trying to control the economy, their electorates in liberal democracies began to demand more and more services from government. Thus, increasing government spending and taxation to ever greater heights and a corresponding return to extremes of increasing demand which was not supported with increasing productivity. Thus, creating inflation that had to be dampened down before the economy entered another economic depression. Today, the established way to dampen down inflation is with the Reserve Bank of Australia (RBA) increasing interest rates and the Australian Government cutting its spending. However, if the government refuses to cut its spending to meet ever-growing citizen expectations there follows an accompanying rise in inflation and interest rates. Here we see the impact of human fallibility on economic integrity.

To counter this development, Milton Friedman (1912-2006) created the theory of supply side economics. That is, Friedman suggested that demand, and by extension inflation, in an economy could be controlled by government spending. His neoclassical macroeconomics school of thought promoted the concept of *rational expectations*. In other words, the electorate in capitalist countries had to limit their expectation about what services government could supply them with according to what the economy could afford. Therefore, government spending had to be limited to raising levels of productivity (supply) rather than expectations (demand).

> *Additionally, he theorised that there existed a natural rate of unemployment and argued that unemployment below this level would cause inflation to accelerate.*
>
> (wikipedia.org, 2025)

Current economic theory holds that as the unemployment rate gets below 5% the economy is very close to or at full capacity (dspace.mit.edu, 2025).

Furthermore, he revived a novel approach to minimum wage setting, first suggested by Dame Juliet Rhys-Williams (1898-1964), a British writer and politician, by suggesting a system that reverses the flow of money to taxation. That is, wages set by the market below a certain level should receive money from the tax office to make up the minimum level, while money above the minimum would pay tax in the normal way. This would reduce the minimum labour costs of small businesses by linking it to market prices. Since small businesses are the largest employers of labour, this also would help in controlling unemployment. The cost of this system would be lower than that of paying unemployment benefits, and the unemployment level would not rise above 5%.

As another counter to socialist theory, he argued that capitalism leads more people out of poverty created by discrimination than any other economic system –

> *The right to private property under the capitalist system is the most effective means that leads to the liberation of groups suffering from discrimination.*
> (Milton Friedman, *Capitalism and Freedom*, 1962)

In Friedman's mind, then, there is no need for DEI or ESG, because the principle of open access to private property under a capitalist economy will take care of any forms of discrimination.

Another possibility (my own) along Friedman's lines but not argued by him, would be to set government spending relative to the GDP of a nation's economy. In this way, the total amount of government spending would be fixed as a percentage of the GDP to allow the private sector some guarantee of its share of the GDP. This would be one way to enforce Friedman's rational expectations. Clearly, this would allow only for increased government spending on voter expectations in accordance with a growth in the country's productivity, thereby avoiding excessive inflation. With these amounts fixed by the economy's ability to pay, it would prevent any temptation for political parties to bribe voters. Australia's government spending (Federal, State and Local) relative to GDP in the FY2023-24 was 28%, up from 21% 10 years prior. This has led the Institute of Public Affairs (IPA) to conclude that,

> *It is critical that Federal and State Governments cut spending and red tape, as well as put policies in place to deliver sustainable economic growth based on increased productivity.*
> (ipa.org.au, 2024)

This suggests that the percentage of GDP allocated to government spending should not rise above 20%.

Obviously, in times of national or economic crisis, borrowing would be necessary, but once the crisis is over a set percentage of GDP would be allocated to pay back the debt, and this would reduce the amount of GDP available for government spending on voter expectations and money available for private enterprise. That is, everyone would have a stake in paying back the national debt. The crisis would be declared for a fixed term. For example, for the duration of a drought, flood, fire, economic downturn or war. Any political party unable to get control of a crisis over a fixed period of time would be prohibited from running for government in the following election.

Do you think my suggestions would help solve the problems with democracy first articulated by Plato and Aristotle that we covered earlier? Do you remember what they said about the demands of the majority? If you think my proposal is too inflexible, can you suggest any modifications that would make it more flexible without rejecting it outright?

One thing that has puzzled me about the extraordinary productive capacity available to humankind through AI and humanoid robotics is what would happen to the consumer base of today's capitalist economies. In capitalist economies today, increases in productivity and consumption is achieved through the aspiration of the working and middle classes. In future, with AI and humanoid robots this aspiration will no longer be needed to increase productivity, but the demands of a consumer base will.

Consider this. The living standards of both the advanced and emerging nations could be overcome with humanoid robotics. Elon Musk, Tesla's CEO, described his Optimus humanoid robot as a robotic assistant. He told the 8th Future Investment Initiative at Riyadh, Saudi Arabia, in 2025 that he expects at least 10 billion humanoid robots priced between $20,000 and $25,000 to be sold by 2040. Optimus will perform tasks in health and manufacturing and carry out unsafe, repetitive and boring tasks currently performed by human beings. If this is our future, it will have benefits for our future society. Problems related to our declining population, lack of housing, mass migration etc. will cease to exist as our productivity growth will increasingly be achieved by humanoid robots while our population continues to decline. Obviously, at some time in the future we will have to maintain an optimal population or breed ourselves into extinction. The downside would involve people finding some other form of fulfilment outside of their work. Perhaps greater involvement in family, the educational pursuit of integrity as opposed to ideology, and increased participation in recreation pursuits would achieve this need for fulfilment.

As fanciful as this might sound today, do you think it has enough merit for consideration? Explain your conclusion by way of a detailed analysis of the history behind and the development and ownership of AI and robotics. Can you suggest any other forms of fulfilment outside of work that people could pursue? What are they, and would people accept them given the human fallibility factor?

To conclude, capitalism provides its people with a higher standard of living than other economic systems, but there is a limit to how much it can provide. Governments, therefore, must engage in trade-offs when considering what services they can provide to their citizens and not pander to their unlimited expectations. Those citizens in true need are the old, those in crisis, and the physically and mentally challenged. The rest are all citizen wants and need to be determined after all other budget considerations are met.

Communism

A recurring theme in the history of communism is its failure to achieve an economic model that can sustain its long-term equity goals. You see, the communist economic model, based on equity, always collapses a nation's economy through uncontrolled inflation. This happens owing to huge government spending programmes, designed to create equity and state surveillance without a complementary growth in productivity. Under communism, such government programmes are funded by debt or the printing of money rather than productivity increase.

Clearly, the assumption underpinning communist philosophy is that when someone becomes rich someone else becomes poor. Is this assumption true or fallacious? Historically speaking, working people living in capitalist countries have raised their standard of living, while working people living in communist countries have lowered theirs. It is an economic fact that the middle and working classes are the aspirational source of a capitalist economy which raises their standard of living through increased productivity. Also, in liberal democracies with capitalistic economies social mobility exists within the society, while in a communist country the society suffers under social stagnation. Capitalist economies incentivise the aspiration of their middle and working classes, but communist economies first diminish and eventually eliminate theirs.

Thus, the shortcoming of communism is that it robs aspiring individuals of any incentive to create personal wealth and, consequently, a more prosperous Nation State. Rather, it produces a citizenry lacking initiative and resourcefulness, because there is no individual incentive to produce more than anyone else since everyone gets the same. Entrepreneurism, creative genius and individual achievement is discouraged since it leads to the individual rising above the community. This is why communist countries either buy or steal the superior technology of capitalist societies like the US, Britain, and Germany.

Do you find any truth in my analysis of communism so far? Do you have an alternative view? Explain.

For a good appraisal of the difference between capitalist and socialist/communist economies, discover the principles and ideas of three eminent economists. The first is Richard D. Wolff, a prominent contemporary socialist economist and founder of Democracy at Work. He is renowned for his work in making accessible explanations of socialism and his critique of capitalism as well as his focus on class analysis. His explanation is that capitalists become rich by *stealing* a large portion of the wealth created by those who work and produce things. His suggestion promotes the idea of worker ownership of the means of production. Of course, this overlooks the existence of co-operatives which already exist in the capitalist system and allows for worker ownership of the means of production (fed.coop, *Part One: Understanding Co-operatives*, 2025). Richard Wolff's latest book is *Understanding Capitalism*, 2025.

The second is John Kenneth Galbraith, a Canadian-American economist, diplomat, public official, and intellectual who argues that the obsession with production and consumer goods, driven largely by advertising, has led to a disconnect between actual consumer needs and market outputs. His most famous book is *The Affluent Society* (1958).

The third economist is Milton Friedman, an American, neo-liberal economist who received the 1976 Nobel Memorial Prize in Economic Science. He proved that inflation is caused by excessive, unsubstantiated government spending and not rises in prices or wages. He discovered that government spending is the *cause* of inflation while rises in prices and wages are merely the *effects* of inflation. This tendency towards excessive spending is exacerbated by socialist policies. Milton Friedman's last book was *Milton Friedman: Why Government Is The Problem*, 1993.

The fourth economist is Thomas Sowell, the Rose and Milton Freeman Senior Fellow on Public Policy at the Hoover Institution, a brilliant American economist and statistician, who believed in *analysing economic data* as opposed to following ideology to establish socio/economic policy. Both Friedman and Sowell proved that communism does not produce an economic system that can sustain itself; it always ends in runaway inflation which collapses the socialist/communist economy, owing to uncontrolled government spending with a lack of increased productivity to fund it. Thomas Sowell's latest book is *Social Justice Fallacies*, 2023. His latest audio book is *Basic Economics, Fifth Edition: A Common Sense Guide To The Economy*, 2024.

To meet this criticism, socialists have created a new economic model that they call *Modern Monetary Theory* (MMT).

> *Put simply, MMT decrees that such governments (sovereign countries with a fiat currency) do not (have) to rely on taxes or borrowing for spending since they can print as much money as they need and are the monopoly issuers of the currency.*
> (Deborah D'Souza, *MMT: Definition, and Principles*, 2024)

Milton Friedman and Thomas Sowell would point out that MMT fails to recognise that the more money in an economy chasing a limited number of goods in the market leads to inflation. Government spending must be matched by a growth in the economy's productivity (more goods and services) or it will lead to inflation. If the value of new money is not supported by an increase in productivity it will lead to inflation, simply because there will be more money chasing the same number of goods and services.

What are your ideas about MMT? Do you think a government can print as much money as it likes to fulfil its country's wants or vision for a better life without leading to inflation?

Argentina's President, Javier Milei, published a new book on May 1, 2025, titled *Capitalism, Socialism and the Neo-classical Trap*. His book makes a strong defence of free market policies and rejects any form of market intervention from either socialist or neo-classical ideology. On Wednesday, 29 May 2025, he delivered a speech to the Hoover Institution in which he said,

> *Stop viewing every inconvenience discovered in the economy as a market failure needing government intervention.*
> (President Javier Milei, *The Market Is Ourselves*, 2025)

What has been the socialist history of Argentina before the market orientated reforms introduced by President Milei? Look up the current state of Argentina's economy, then give a detailed explanation for your conclusion. You will find there are both positive and negative trends.

During WWII (1939-45) the Australian Government spent a large amount of money to wage the war. It was funded through the sale of war bonds which had to be paid off. My father's generation and my generation were tasked with the burden of paying off this debt. My generation was happy to accept this responsibility since we recognised that without that spending to wage war we would have lost our Nation State. Also, the Australian economy experienced exceptional growth at this time owing to an increase in productivity created by an expansion in our farming, manufacturing, and mineral and energy sectors. As well as this, we expanded our population through a sustainable, controlled, and harmonious immigration policy based on cultural assimilation not multi-culturalism.

Today, Australia's socialists are trying to increase national GDP with mass immigration. Whilst this does increase national GDP, it may decrease the individual citizen's share of the increased national GDP, particularly if the mass immigration is based on unskilled labour and their dependents who may end up on long-term welfare dependency –

> *An extensive body of research has consistently found that immigration is a huge cost to the UK Treasury...*
> (migrationwatchuk.org, June 2025)

Another program that socialist governments in Australia have embarked on is renewable energy targets, to counter what they believe is a catastrophic climate change emergency, which is destroying the standard of living of their citizens. Climate change projects replace cheap, reliable fossil fuels with expensive, unreliable renewable energy which not only increases the energy costs of citizens, manufacturing, and heavy industry but also makes our exports uncompetitive and drives Australia's factories and industry offshore. The cost of all government-owned enterprises, like Competency based Economies through Formation of Enterprise (CEFE) and National Reconstruction Fund Corporation (NRFC), are currently recorded as off-budget costs, so they do not contribute to Australia's budget deficit, which will reach $1 trillion AUD this financial year.

On 30 September 2025, Peta Credlin reported that environmentalist, Steven Nowakowski and his colleagues at Rainforest Reserve Australia, had done a costing of the government's renewable energy project. The total land space required for the project comes in at 433,572 hectares or 4,500 square kilometres, not including the land needed for transmission lines, at a cost of $1.3 trillion AUD.

Future Australian generations might not hold the same attitude, as the generation that paid off Australia's war debt, towards the current generation who spend money they do not have to fund an economy based on their vison for a *better world* rather than their ability to pay for it. Future generations might conclude that they were left with a debt they cannot repay, an energy system that is expensive and unreliable, a welfare system (both corporate and social) that is unsustainable, a property market they cannot access, and a multicultural and mass-immigration policy that has led to the emergence of cultural enclaves causing national division and social disharmony.

What is your assessment of this observation? Do you think it is immoral for one generation to steal the wealth of their descendants to fund their dreams of a better life?

Lately, some socialist-inspired governments are trying to control inflation by giving government-funded grants of money to relieve cost of living pressure. For example, the Australian Government is paying part of their citizens' energy bills to lower the inflation rate. Furthermore, the Australian Government has soaked up rising unemployment by expanding the public sector. Clearly, this will only postpone higher inflation rates and unemployment, because the government must either raise taxes or go into more debt to pay for the extra spending. If they raise taxes it will remove more money from the private sector, thereby reducing productivity. If they go into more debt they will enter a debt spiral which will initiate an unstoppable increase in interest rates on the debt they are carrying, making it increasingly harder to pay down the accumulating debt. If the government prints more money in an attempt to cover their debts and maintain their citizens' standard of living, it will lead to hyperinflation, wipe out the savings of their citizens, and inflict immeasurable suffering on the poorest Australians. In short, these steps are a giant Ponzi scheme which will ultimately collapse at some future time, as it historically has done to all socialist governments in the past.

Socialists spend money their economies cannot afford and make up the shortfall with an ever-increasing taxation burden on their citizens and by borrowing more and more money. They also over-regulate their economies by enforcing centrally planned, uneconomical projects and rules and regulations that smother private investment initiative. The inevitable economic collapse is blamed on capitalism (they claim capital went on strike when it left their country rather than admitting that investors went looking for better investment opportunities) and not their socialist governance and overspending policies. Thus, creating the fertile ground for a revolution.

In August 2025, the Australian Government held an economic roundtable on how to improve the Australian economy. The Government concluded that what is needed is to increase taxes to pay down the debt and accommodate government spending, and not so much on increasing productivity or cutting government spending. Apparently, The Australian Government wants to be the first government in history to spend and tax its way to wealth creation.

I encourage you to study the history of communism for yourself before making any conclusions about communism as an economic philosophy worthy of adoption. Suffice to say that those countries that either fell under or adopted communism voluntarily never progressed beyond dictatorships and caused the death of millions of their comrades in trying to achieve their goals. The communist motto was and still is,

The end justifies the means,

which corrupts their integrity, moral clarity, and human decency.

Why then do socialists and communists persist in promoting an economic model that has been proven incapable of achieving the desired ends promised?

> *George Orwell's book, The Road To Wigan Pier (1936), explores the educated class's complicated relationship with the working class, revealing a mixture of genuine sympathy, condescension, and even unconscious distain ... he also observed how some socialists, despite their stated ideals, retained a subconscious prejudice against them.*
>
> (AI Overview, 2025)

Could it be that socialist are not really interested in meeting the needs of the poor and needy or their vision of equity, but rather in the power they gain from overthrowing Capitalism. This would explain why they continue to promote envy and division within the societies of capitalist countries, while, at the same time, accumulating greater personal wealth than the average citizen.

Can you identify any political parties in Australia today who pursue socialist policies? What about communist policies?

Finally, Karl Marx, in his book *The Communist Manifesto*, describes how and why he wants to abolish private property and allow for the distribution of a nation's wealth through what he called

the dictatorship of the proletariat.

His guiding economic principle being

from each according to his ability to each according to his need.

Of course, these are political slogans which require economic policies to achieve them. Something that communists have never achieved in any sustainable way.

President Ronald Reagan explains how to tell a communist from an anti-communist –

How do you tell a communist? Well, it's someone who reads Marx and Lenin. And how do you tell an anti-communist? It's someone who understands Marx and Lenin.

(goodreads.com, 2025)

Globalism
Essentially, globalism is an ideology that promotes the concept that economies and foreign policy should be planned on a global scale rather than separate Nation States. So Nation States would be

reduced to administration centres that would take their orders from globalist organisations (the multi-polar world mentioned above). For example, the UN and its subsidiary organs like the ICC, UNHCR, WHO, UNESCO, IMO to name just a few subsidiary organs within the UN that would override the sovereignty of Nation States with regard to justice, human rights, health, education, science, culture and immigration. The World Bank would control global finance, the World Trade Organisation would control international trade, and the World Economic Forum (WEF) would control the world's economy.

I must stress that today these organisations do not control any decisions made by Nation States. However, membership of these organisations allows national governments to argue that they are signed-up members of these organisations and as such should abide by their suggestions and recommendations, even if those suggestions and recommendations are unpopular at home. Such is the case of those Nation States that have signed up to Net Zero by 2050 but whose people are now questioning their countries' economic capacity to deliver if they use renewable energy as their main source of energy. Also, Australia recently signed up to allow the WHO to determine the global response to any future pandemic. Given their track record on COVID-19, one wonders at the wisdom of this, since the WHO followed whatever the CCP decided was the best approach. First, the CCP denied COVID-19 existed, then it was merely a slight influenza, then it required international, national, interstate, and community quarantine including city lockdowns. The CCP still insists that COVID-19 came from a wet market in Wuhan, while the rest of the world argues that it most likely came from a Biolab in Wuhan. The WHO acknowledges the need for more research into COVID-19 origins and has not definitively pinpointed a single origin. The WHO has suggested sharing early genetic sequences, detailed market information, and data on lab biosafety conditions in Wuhan. However, the CCP has yet to share this requested information with the WHO. This is one of the problems with signing up to these globalist organisations; some nations abide by their suggestions and recommendations while other do not. Clearly, this places those nations who do abide by the suggestions of globalist organisations at a distinct disadvantage to those who do not.

Different people have different ideas about globalism. Some see it in a positive light while others see it in a negative light. Those advocating for globalism argue that it reduces world poverty; gives access to new cultures, resources and markets; lowers the cost of production; helps spread new technology and human talent; and provides a higher standard of living worldwide.

On the other hand, those who reject globalism argue that it increases global inequality through worker exploitation, not only in poorer countries compared to richer countries but also income disparity and inequality between the more educated and less educated members of all societies, even in countries with developed economies. They further argue that it leads to a loss of jobs and hollowing out of the working and middle classes in developed economies while creating environmental degradation worldwide; increasing corruption among the elite members of all Nation States; and generating a rise in technology which facilitates the monitoring, control, and power over peoples of the world by governing elites.

In economic terms, then, the main criticism of globalism is that it raises the standard of living in poorer countries by lowering it (managed decline) in richer countries, while widening the wealth gap globally. Critics of globalism suggest that a better system would be to raise the standard of living in poorer countries without lowering it in richer countries by implementing liberal democracy and prudently regulated capitalism worldwide.

The biggest problem that globalism has yet to address is maintaining the rights and protection of individual citizens in Nation States. It has been argued that globalists believe in open society; that is, open borders, mass immigration, and multi-culturalism, which erodes the national identity of the citizenry by the establishment of cultural enclaves within Nation States. The unprecedented mass exodus of refugees and migrants from Middle Eastern and African countries into Western countries, for example, is creating enormous pressure on the economies and populations of these destination countries. Some look on this development favourably, but increasingly others are alarmed at the use of violence and intimidation by these refugees to advance their agender for cultural change, and the establishment's use of force to assist cultural change. The political effect of this dissatisfaction with multi-culturalism is beginning to take root in those countries most affected by it.

Do you think globalism attacks the democratic principles of Nation States, or do you think this observation is merely a conspiracy theory?

Furthermore, some see globalism as attacking their liberty. For example, more and more young people are being driven out of the property market because of foreign investment and the effect of mass immigration, which drives up the cost of owning one's own home to such an extent that it becomes out of reach for the younger citizens who are now limited to renting. This restricts their right to the ownership of private property, a cornerstone of liberty in a capitalistic society.

Also, the push for catastrophic climate change emergency legislation, which forces people (through the increased cost of energy and tax on petrol- or diesel-powered cars etc.) to reduce their disposal income, has taken the right of choice from individual citizens. Moreover, the drive for renewable energy is forcing farmers and graziers to surrender their property to wind and solar factories and transmission lines. Couple this with the enforcement of laws limiting the use of fertilisers for their crops and diesel for their tractors has seen farmers witness a steep decline in farm production and therefore farm income. Attempts by some countries to limit the number of livestock of graziers has heightened sociopolitical tension in those countries. On top of this, governments worldwide, with globalist sympathies, have run up huge debts trying to maintain a living standard for their citizens that their economy cannot afford, and are now introducing new taxes on farmers, graziers and property owners generally that have sent family-owned farms and grazing stations into receivership or forced sale, and robbed those, especially the elderly, of their accumulated wealth. This has resulted in the rise of political activism from a section of society that is usually politically stable.

New taxes already imposed on property owners has seen further stress paced on rental accommodation, and the proposed tax on unrealised capital gains will place further pressure on rental accommodation. A new taxation development is the proposal to introduce a tax on the family home which until recently has never been contemplated. All these new taxes are necessary because of the inflicted managed decline on developed economies by globalism, and the government's attempt to maintain a standard of living for their citizens that is fast disappearing.

Scientists began to identify human activity's effect on changing the world's climate in the 1970s. Catastrophic Climate Change Emergency (the calling for net zero targets by 2050) became more prominent after Al Gore first published his book, *An Inconvenient Truth* in 2006. Globalism emerged at different times and different stages. However, it has accelerated during the period from the 1980s to the present. Both of these trends called for the advanced economies of the world to limit their use of fossil fuel while, at the same time, allowing the emerging economies unlimited use of them.

When fossil fuel energy systems are replaced with renewable energy systems, it puts even further pressure on the standard of living for citizens of countries with advanced economies. This places the emerging economies at a huge trading advantage over the advanced economies since they enjoyed not only cheaper labour costs but also cheaper energy cost than their competitors. However, this arrangement enables globalists to cash in by producing or buying their goods from countries with emerging economies while selling their goods to consumers in countries with advanced economies.

All nation states with developed economies have three sectors, the primary sector (agriculture, grazing and mining), the secondary sector (industry and manufacturing), and tertiary (service) sector. The primary and secondary sectors constitutes the productivity of a nation state while the tertiary sector forms its purchasing, or consumer base. What globalisation does is hollow out the secondary sector of a developed economy by moving it offshore to a developing economy; thus, making the developed economy reliant on the developing economy for its manufactured goods and the supply lines between the two economies. It also depletes the wealth (created from its secondary sector) of the developed economy by transferring it to the developing economy.

The wealth of Australia's richest 200 people nearly tripled over the last two decades.
(australianinstitute.org.au, David Richardson and Frank Stilwell, *Wealth and Inequality in Australia*, 2024)

(While) the lowest 60% of Australians has seen a 55% increase in their household wealth.
(AI Overview, 2025)

I mention this wealth gap, not to encourage envy or jealousy but rather to highlight the fact that in countries with advanced economies the wealth gap becomes more pronounced under globalism than it does in countries governed by a liberal democracy with a prudently regulated capitalist market system containing all three economic sectors.

Do you think globalism has led to a free global market economy, or a controlled global market economy?

Globalism has allowed the CCP to re-establish a mercantilist economy in China, not seen since the days of Empires and Colonies.

The CCP accumulated huge wealth which it used to build a massive armed force enabling it to threaten its trading partners. For example, Australia has experienced military threats, cyberattacks and a trade embargo from the CCP; the Philippines has experienced CCP harassment over disputed islands in their internationally recognised territories; and Tiawan is under constant threat of invasion from mainland China. Any criticism of the CCP for these actions is simply ignored. Similarly, the CCP ignores any criticism regarding their claim to the South China Sea and their unfair trade practices like

> *intellectual property theft, state subsidies, forced technology transfers, and market access restrictions.*
>
> (wikipedia.org, 2025)

Thanks to globalism we have seen the emergence of a Chinese dictator who dreams of a world replete with communist-dominated vassal states, a Russian dictator who dreams of re-establishing a Russian empire based on the old borders of the USSR, an Iranian Ayatollah who dreams of a worldwide Islamic califate, and a WEF (an oligarchy of plutocrats) that dreams of a *Great Reset* (Davos, 2020) that will allow its members control over the world's economy and the establishment of a *New World Order* where,

> *You will own nothing but you will be happy.*
>
> (Davos, 2022)

Also, the WEF has called for 15-minute cities (Davos, 2023); and regaining lost trust by the implementation of censorship (Davos, 2024). None of these dictators, autocrats, oligarchs, or plutocrats believe in globalism, yet all of them have profited from favourable, globalist-inspired trade with the developed economies of liberal democratic countries.

The term *New World Order* has a long history dating as far back as the end of WWI when Woodrow Wilson (1919) outlined his vision of achieving world peace through the League of Nations. More recently Mikhail Gorbachev (1988) used the term when he urged (among other things) the UN to oversee an end to the economic blocks and the emergence of one world economy, and Tony Blair (UK Prime Minister) who used the term in 2000 when he stated,

There is a new world order like it or not.

Many other politicians have used this term ('new world order'), so we have a long history of the political use of it. However, when people today use the term to describe what they fear is a newly emerging totalitarian world government, they are accused of spreading a conspiracy theory.

In conclusion, globalism delivers a top-down organisational structure to society, while liberal democratic national states deliver a bottom-up approach. Without democracy, individuals are robbed of their sovereignty and liberty, especially their freedom of speech and choice. With globalism individuals get what the globalist elite allow them to have, not what they earn for themselves.

I am reminded of a quote by J Edgar Hoover (Director of FBI 1924-72) about the communist conspiracy of the 1950s-60s in America –

The individual is handicapped by coming face to face with a conspiracy so monstrous they cannot believe it exists.

(imdb.com)

Having read what I have written about globalism, what are your conclusions? Explain. Do you object to my opinions? Why? Do you believe that globalism poses a danger to Nation States and their citizens' sovereignty and liberty, or do you conclude that these dangers are just an unfounded conspiracy theory blocking the emergence of a better tomorrow for all? The answer to these questions is the challenge for your future. Which control do you prefer, top-down or bottom-up?

A General Observation

Currently, the world is in a time of crisis and turmoil. Where we will end up is difficult to say, but it will require clear thinking on the part of concerned citizens if we are to come through to a resolution that does as little damage to our liberty and democratic rights as possible. The political and economic terms we have discussed in this section will help you with your task of clear thinking, if you keep the terminology outlined here firmly fixed in your mind and don't allow others to redefine them and shift them on the political spectrum you have arrived at. Political and economic terminology are like mathematical definitions; without them it is impossible to reach a correct solution.

Before leaving this section I want to explain the people's participation in a liberal democracy. We obviously start with the people's vote which gives individual citizens sovereignty over their government. But what redress do citizens have when they feel that their votes do not bring about the changes they desire? You will be pleased to know that our liberal democratic process does have a way to address this possibility. The process involves the freedom of speech, and peaceful protest. The High Court of Australia has ruled that although the Australian Constitution does not explicitly protect freedom of expression, it does imply a freedom of political expression free from government restraint (Australian Capital Television Pty Ltd Vs the Commonwealth, 1992).

Free speech and peaceful protest have been won for us by our ancestors and have existed as part of our cultural inheritance for hundreds of years. Since the mid 1800s a speaker's corner has existed in Hyde Park in London, England, where citizens are invited to voice their beliefs and objections. There are similar parks in Australia, for example Sydney's beautiful Domain Park. As well as this, peaceful protests involving assembly is permitted. Different State Governments have different laws governing these activities. In Queensland these laws are contained in the Peaceful Assembly Act (1992) and Human Rights Act (2019). However, if a peaceful assembly or demonstration gets out of hand it may be declared an unlawful assembly, thereby giving police the power to arrest and charge individuals. Let's look at how these assemblies or demonstrations can *get out of hand*.

First, is the blocking of other citizens from going about their daily lives or conducting legitimate commerce. Another is using force against the police. Such activities can and do involve an infringement of our peaceful assembly laws, thereby eliciting an appropriate response from the police. Also, individuals involved in a peaceful assembly do not have the right to incite violence against others or cause damage to private or public property. These actions are deemed unlawful since they can lead to worse behaviour on the part of protestors. Unfortunately, radicals deliberately provoke police in order to get a physical response from them, then claim that the police used excessive force to restore order. Sadly, past experience proves that the mainstream media, when radical protest aligns with their own political narrative, are willing to portray the police use of force on radical protestors without showing the lead-up to the violent confrontation. Thereby, creating a biased portrayal of events.

Riots are one form of worse behaviour from protestors, where damage is done to private and public property and lives are endangered. Clearly, such behaviour tears at the very fabric of a liberal democratic society and must be stopped, otherwise it can lead to even worse behaviour in the form of a revolt, civil war or revolution. All of which seek to overthrow the very process of our democracy.

Revolts and revolutions can be peaceful or violent. Revolts seek to overthrow an existing government and replace it with new leaders. A good example of a revolt was the Peasants' Revolt (England, 1381). Revolts do not seek to change the actual form of governance. For example, a revolt may seek to replace a king with another king or a political party with another political party in a democracy. Revolutions, on the other hand, seek to replace the ruling form of government with a different form of government. The American Revolution (1775-83) is a good example of a revolution because its success led to a new form of government being created in the former colonies of America. The American revolutionaries replaced an autocratic form of government with that of a democratic republican form of government. Those involved in revolts are called rebels and revolts can lead to Civil War. Those involved in revolutions are called revolutionaries and can lead to revolutionary war.

Revolts, civil wars and revolutions are usually very bloody affairs which create much physical pain and suffering for the people of those countries involved, and can become long lasting. A report by *The Economist*, April 2023, suggested that the average length of Civil Wars worldwide had increased to nearly 20 years. Factors contributing to longer durations include multiple warring factions, a lack of military victory, and increasing complexity.

Another way that governments are overthrown is through a military coup d'état. Many democracies have ended in this way in the past. Such actions usher in military dictators who can only be overthrown by a popular uprising, another coup d'état or having their power taken from them by a Foreign Power.

As I stated earlier, these are politically unstable and violent times, riots, wars, and rumours of wars are present which can escalate at any time. The changing cultural and economic circumstances inflicted on people throughout the world has led to much anger, hatred and violence. Such times call for courage on the part of citizens and a commitment to equal justice on the part of those who govern us. Nothing can trigger a revolt or revolution quicker than citizens believing that injustice is being forced upon them.

David Betz (1987-), professor of *war in the modern world* at the Department of War Studies, King's College, London and a senior fellow of the Foreign Policy Research Centre has claimed that Civil

War will engulf Europe and Britain within the next five years unless something is done to course correct. He believes this because the cultural narrative pertaining to the precursors of Civil War have all been met. For example, the continued support for multi-culturalism and mass illegal immigration, in particular, as well as things like the undeserved public shaming of people with cries of racism, sexism, gender identity, and Islamophobia, who do nothing more than question the wisdom of multi-culturalism, mass immigration, gender identity, and illegal immigrant attacks on underage girls, is leading people into distrusting their authorities and institutions. This distrust is confirmed in the minds of the majority of native Europeans by things like the selective enforcement of the law against them and in favour of those who they see as trying to destroy their culture, and a two-tiered legal system, which again, they see as favouring those whose ambition is to destroy their culture. They believe their cries of,

> *I want my country back.*
> (newstatesman.com, June 2016)

are being ignored by those in authority. In David Betz's own words,

> *...the reasons that this situation has arisen (are): a combination of culturally fractured societies, economic stagnation, elite overreach and a collapse of public confidence in the ability of normal politics to solve problems...*
> (David Betz, Civil War Comes to the West, Part II: Strategic Realities, Military Strategy Magazine, Volume 10, Issue 2, Spring 2025)

All this creates in the mind of the majority of native Europeans and British people a lack of loyalty towards their institutions and a firm conviction that the established political system is incapable of solving their problems. This situation, they believe, is intolerable and urgent and can only be solved with insurgency.

David has outlined what he believes is a likely scenario for the coming Civil War. It will first break out in one European country and then spread to others. The cities, which house the majority of illegal immigrants, will have their vital infrastructure attacked. Things like energy, transportation, water supply, and communications will be attacked from the country, their most vulnerable point which is extremely difficulty to secure. David points out that this has already happened in France when its rail network was attacked before the Opening Ceremony of the Paris Olympic Games, which was criticised on the grounds that it displayed scenes that derided and mocked Christianity.

David further reminds us that during Civil Wars the civilian population suffers enormously from deprivation, starvation, and bloodshed. He implores European and British Governments to take his warning seriously and take immediate action to make a course correction in their policies.

There are two sources for this information. The first is David Betz, *Civil War Comes to the West. Part II: Strategic Realities,* Military Strategy Magazine, 2025. The second is *Are We Headed for Civil War – David Betz,* in which David Betz is interviewed by hosts Konstantin Kisin and Francis Foster on their podcast Triggernometry, July 2025.

On September 10, 2025, Charlie Kirk was assassinated while addressing a large audience on the campus of Utah Valley University (UVU). Charlie Kirk had been a popular mentor of the youth of America, and around the world. My own grandchildren had often consulted his blogs on YouTube. They were deeply moved by his death and heartbroken that his family attended his open debate and witnessed his assassination; especially on hearing his little 3-year-old daughter rushed to her father after hearing the shot from the assassin's rifle. This is a truly disturbing development since it contributes to the dwindling confidence in open debate as a force for change in a liberal democracy. The response on social media to Charlie Kirk's assassination is also deeply unsettling, with some celebrating his death while others are losing faith in open debate as a form of protest.

On 13 Sept 2025, a *Unite The Kingdom Rally* (a mass-immigration protest rally) led by Tommy Robinson, attracted what the mainstream media reported as over 110,000 protesters (reuters.com). YouTube bloggers, *Geoff Buys Cars,* reported attendees at least three times the number published in the mainstream media, while *The Podcast of the Lotus Eaters* reported the number of attendees at somewhere between 500,000 and 1,000,000. Such speculation about the number of attendees at the rally underscores the distrust that British citizens have for the established media. I must say that I viewed the footage of the huge crowds lining the streets and concluded that the official numbers were underestimated.

On 21 Sept 2025, a Memorial Service for Charlie Kirk was held at the State Farm Stadium in Arizona. The Trump Administration, past and present, attended the service along with over 90,000 people. Overflow attendees were sent to Desert Diamond Arena holding 20,000. These numbers are indisputable. However, the number of viewers who watched the service on cable news draws attention to the huge social divide in America. The *New York Post* reported CNN had 372,000 viewers (nypost.com, 2025), *The Hill* reported MSNBC had fewer than 300,000 viewers (thehill.com, 2025), while Fox News claims to have drawn nearly 5 million viewers (press.foxnews.com, 2025). Overall viewership (cable and online) claimed by *The New York Post* was at least 20,000,000 (nypost.com, 2025).

On 23 Sept 2025, US President Donald Trump addressed the UN General Assembly where he delivered a scalding attack on the globalist agenda of the UN. Among other criticisms, he warned Western nations about the UN's continued support for its open border policies and how uncontrolled immigration threatens the social fabric of Western societies by

> *overwhelming (them) with different customs, religions, with different everything...*

> *They (the immigrants) repaid kindness with crime. It's time to end the failed experiment on open borders. You have to end it now.*

> *Your countries are going to hell.*

> *The UN is supposed to stop invasions, not create them and not finance them.*

Trump went on to describe the UN's climate change policies as,

> *The greatest con job ever perpetrated on the world.*

and issued a warning to Western countries about how destructive the UN's climate change policies would be to their economies,

> *If you don't get away from this green scam your country is going to fail.*

On 24 September 2025, Anthony Albanese, Australia's current prime minister, delivered a speech to the UN Trusteeship Council that refuted President Donald Trump's warnings –

> *This is the decisive decade for acting on the environmental challenge of climate change – and seizing the economic opportunities of clean energy.*

> *Australia's 2035 target is to reduce emissions by 62 to 70 percent on 2005 levels. This target is ambitious – importantly, it is achievable.*

> *Just as our traditional resources have helped power the extraordinary economic transformation in our region, our*

renewables can underpin new prosperity for the growing economies of the Indo-Pacific.

Australia has had a long-standing Alliance with America but now it has broken ranks with America on not just climate change but also America's stand on the recognition of a Palestinian state. If an ally like Australia is prepared to so publicly denounce America's position on these important global issues, one wonders about the unity of the whole Western Alliance.

These are serious developments that can no longer be ignored and will require all the persuasion and political skill of our leaders if we are to avoid the future predicted by David Betz.

Let me offer one piece of advice. As you become more aware of the political movements trying to gain power over our liberal democracy and regulated capitalist economic system, do not let anger or revenge cloud your judgement. Remember democracies support individual opinion, open debate, and peaceful protest assemblies and parades. Democratic countries do not support any form of violence as a weapon of protest.

Try to control your emotions by recognising that life involves us all in a venture, the venture of our personal lives, our families, our local community, our national identity, and our global vision. There are no absolutes, no Utopia in our ventures, only trade-offs, because Utopia can never become a reality in the world we currently inhabit. Those trade-offs are determined by a reality involving cost/benefit, and risk/reward results. Every venture we embark on comes with a cost that someone must pay and a benefit that someone will receive, a risk that someone must take and a loss that someone must take or a reward that someone will reap. Keep in mind that all ventures are subject to human nature. Greed, envy, fear, anger, and revenge, for example, will be corrosive elements to any human venture, while generosity, co-operation, friendship, and courage will strengthen it. Again, all these ventures operate on a scale from the personal to the global.

Over time we have learnt to divide these ventures into political, economic and social realms.

The political realm requires trade-off decisions involving *power*. Political power is usually arranged via totalitarianism, authoritarianism or consensus arrangements. Arguably, the best power trade-off we have managed to create so far is documented for us in the American Constitution and involves a *balance of power* arrangement, and a government determined by the *consent of the people* that upholds their rights contained in the American Constitution's Bill of Rights.

Regardless of which power arrangement governs us, to remain in existence it requires a vigilant commitment on the part of the participants or it will inevitably collapse. That commitment can be total in the case of totalitarianism, submissive when administered by authoritarianism or resolute when determined by consent. Once that commitment wanes, however, the power arrangement is in danger of being replaced with a different power arrangement. A power arrangement, however, will always exist because our political ventures are timeless. It's just that over time one power arrangement is replaced with another, even if the power arrangement grows from the tribal to the global or is reduced from the global to the tribal some form of power arrangement will remain.

The economic realm requires trade-offs involving *money*. In money ventures, money is distributed via markets, and markets are governed by supply and demand and designed around free, regulated, or controlled systems. Much disagreement exists regarding which system is the best. The capitalists and globalists claim to believe in a free market system (even though this has never existed) where unimpeded *supply and demand* controls the distribution of money. Communists and autocrats believe in a *centrally controlled system*. Theoretically, Communists seek to control supply and demand through the redistribution of money according to the equity principal. That is, everybody gets the same amount of money regardless of effort or competence. What communism has delivered, however, is a system based on a political ruling elite which enjoys a much higher standard of living than their comrades. Autocrats *control* their economies according to their need to maintain order and control over their subjects/believers and protect their crown or faith. Plutocrats control their economies by their individual wealth. Centrists (reformists and conservatives) prefer to *regulate supply and demand* in an attempt to deliver a fairer distribution of money based on personal effort and need, not unfunded compassion for separate groups.

One of Jeremy Bentham's theories was *the greatest happiness principle*, which gave rise to the utilitarian principle of *the greatest good for the greatest number* since he conceived *final utility* (actions based upon their consequences) as *human happiness*. In his book *Hard Times*, Charles Dickens satirises Bentham's greatest happiness principle. Cicilia 'Sissy' Jupe, one of Dickens' leading characters, for example, epitomises the importance of individual experience and emotional connection over efficiency and rational principles.

Here is a puzzle for you. How did Jeremy Bentham attend a meeting after his death? Have I aroused your curiosity in Utilitarianism? I hope so because the more philosophy you understand the better your understanding of our human condition will become, regardless of which ethics you find useful or doubtful.

All money distribution systems are a trade-off producing less than perfect results. Some systems generate more wealth than others, while all systems have their flaws. The capitalist system produces more wealth than the other systems but is prone to worker exploitation and booms and busts, which produce a huge gap between the rich and the poor during boom times and crushing misery for the poor during times of bust. Regulation produces considerable wealth but leads to either inflation or stagflation requiring economic pain to correct, while communist control produces an ever-dwindling supply of wealth which ultimately ends in economic collapse.

Whatever money distribution system is followed, from a personal all the way up to a global scale, it will involve a trade-off, so the best that can be hoped for is a finely tuned balance between supply and demand, giving rise to a just distribution of wealth. Regardless of our personal commitment to one system of wealth distribution or another, one thing seems certain: ever since money was invented it has remained a constant in our lives and we have never stopped squabbling and fighting over its distribution.

The social realm requires trade-off decisions involving a *social hierarchy*. Social hierarchies are usually determined by the power distribution established by the society. In times past, social hierarchies were determined by autocrats (powerful warriors) because societies were mainly concerned with security. Religion can also be a determining factor of a social hierarchy if a society fears an all-powerful God with even the mightiest of warriors kneeling in its presence. Of course, this arrangement can be benevolent or malevolent depending on the disposition of God's highest spokesperson.

Money, technology or competence can also be determining factors in the arrangement of social hierarchies. The social hierarchies organised around money possession are dominated by plutocrats or oligarchs, while social hierarchies dependent on technology are controlled by technocrats, and social hierarchies rewarding competence are organised around a meritocracy.

All social hierarchies produce benefits and costs for their members. However, the most stable social hierarchies are ones that involve equal justice for all, free speech, and the possibility for social mobility. Two-tier justice, discrimination, censorship, and a rigid stratification in social hierarchies breed corruption, division, vilification, and violence.

One last point. Autocrats try to control their subjects or their faithful through fear; Dictators try to control their comrades through suppression; and Plutocrats try to control consumers through money. All three are power blocks that can sometimes co-operate with one another to achieve a common goal. All three believe that they can control the other through fear, suppression or greed. History contains a litany of the struggle between these three power blocks exercising their power over others or over each other.

Have you found my observation helpful? I hope you have. Do you find fault with it? In what way? Have I overlooked something you believe would improve it? Why not discuss your ideas with others.

Cultural Integrity

A society that upholds its cultural integrity is a society that values the gathering of data and facts followed by the application of logic, reason, wisdom, common sense, and empathy over blind adherence to a partisan ideology. Cultural integrity is achieved through the preservation of a society's history, knowledge systems, language, traditions, customs, institutions, and values and ensures that these elements remain intact and valued by others in the society. One way that Australia upholds its cultural integrity lies in the defence of its liberal democracy. Specifically, the right of citizens to liberty (i.e., freedom of speech and choice), national and individual sovereignty (the right for only their elected government representatives to make decisions and take responsibility for all laws affecting the social contract of its citizens and for individual citizens to vote in free and fair elections), equal opportunity (all citizens being equal and entitled to equal treatment), and equal justice as opposed to social justice under the law (i.e., all citizens expected to uphold its laws and justice being applied equally, regardless of group identity). In analysing Australia's cultural integrity I will focus on only three major issues: *human sex and preferred sexual behaviour, Identity Politics,* and *Native Title and Land Rights*. I am sure you will be able to identify other cultural issues that you consider important to address. When you do, you might like to follow the approach I take here.

Human Sex and Preferred Sexual Behaviour

I recognise that this topic is highly controversial and can lead to the harassment of those who do not *toe the ideological line*. Despite this, I have decided to venture into this dangerous area and try to maintain what I consider an objective, neutral approach. I hope my observations do not cause too much controversy or distress among my readers. However, this topic is clearly a prominent new world issue that I feel compelled to cover.

A starting point for our analysis would be to consider the two opposing definitions for sex –

1) Biological scientists tell us that sex is *established* at conception and *recognised* at birth if not before.
2) Those who believe in gender fluidity tell us that sex is *assigned* at birth.

Clearly, these definitions of sex cannot both be correct. One establishes that sex is a *biological reality*, while the other concludes that it is a result of *individual preference*. I hope that the following discussion will help you determine which of these judgements best aligns with what you believe to be the truth about sex.

First, what does biological science tell us about human sex? Human beings are primarily divided into two sexes: male and female. A minority of human beings are born hermaphrodite. It has been estimated (not factually determined) that up to 1.7% of the population may have been born with this intersex trait (Anne Fausto-Sterling, *Sexing the Body*, 2000). On the other hand, Leonard Sax estimates that approximately 0.018 of the world's population is born hermaphrodite (Leonard Sax, *How common is Intersex? a Response to Anne Fausto-Sterling*, National Library of Medicine, 2002). Whatever number is more accurate, there are no recorded cases of human hermaphrodites giving birth through self-fertilisation because their gonads (sex organs) do not mature. For this reason, hermaphrodites are not considered a separate sex by biologists. Self-fertilisation does occur in the animal kingdom (given the right conditions, for example, some frogs can self-conceive) but not so in human beings. This makes intersex a biological exception to the rule in human sex but not the rule itself. Of course, intersex people are real and need to be accepted by all, and proper understanding, treatment, and care afforded them. They should not be summarily dismissed.

According to biological science, male and female sexuality is determined through their sex-linked genes; males have XY sex-linked genes and females have XX sex-linked genes (hermaphrodites usually have a combination of XX and XY sex-linked genes). These sex-linked genes produce the gonads of males and females at birth. Gonads must mature before they can function to produce offspring. Immature males are called boys, while immature females are called girls. Mature males are called men and mature females are called women. So, biologists define a man as an adult human male and a woman as an adult human female.

XY and XX sex-linked genes also produce different hormones in the different sexes as their gonads mature. As a girl matures into a woman, she produces oestrogen which affects her reproductive tract, urinary tract, heart and blood vessels, bone and muscle density, breasts, skin, hair, mucous membranes, pelvic muscles, pelvic bones, and brain. As a boy matures into a man, he produces testosterone which affects his bone density, fat distribution, muscle mass and strength, penis size, production of red blood cells and sperm, and brain. It is also thought to regulate his sex drive (libido). These sex-linked genes are immutable, so they remain with you for the duration of your life.

What does science tell us about the decision-making effects of oestrogen and testosterone on the human brain?

Taking oestrogen first. It appears that estrogen affects different women differently –

> *Estrogen effects differ between women because (of) factors like genetics, body composition, overall health, and lifestyle influence estrogen levels and receptor sensitivity.*
>
> (AI Overview, 2025)

Chapter 8: New World Issues

With this provisor in place, what general conclusions can be drawn from the emotional effects of oestrogen on the female brain –

Estrogen is a major player in regulating moods. Estrogen effects everywhere in the body, including the parts of the brain that control emotion.
(webmd.com, *The Effects of Estrogen on Women's Emotions and Mood*, 2024)

Some research suggests a connection between estrogen levels and emotional perspective-taking, a key component of empathy.
(AI Overview, 2025)

Estrogen levels rise during the mid-follicular phase and then drop precipitously after ovulation.
(ncbi.nim.nih.gov, *The Normal Menstrual Cycle and the Control of Ovulation*, 2018)

What we can conclude from this scientific evidence is that oestrogen affects different women differently, but that it is at its highest concentration during the mid-follicular phrase of a female's menstrual cycle. That is, it can and does affect emotional changes in the female brain. That it may increase a woman's ability for empathy. What affect does testosterone have on the male body?

Testosterone levels vary significantly between men due to factors like age, time of day, genetics, overall health, and even environmental factors.
(AI Overview, 2025)

Studies have shown that higher testosterone levels can be associated with increased risk taking ... especially in situations

> *involving competition and status, reduced empathy ... (being) less able to understand or share the emotions of others, and more utilitarian moral judgements ... where the best outcome for the majority is prioritised.*
>
> (AI Overview, 2025)

Again, it is difficult to draw generalised conclusions because the level of testosterone varies with individual males. However, we can conclude that the decision-making processes in males may be different from that of females, owing to the effect of oestrogen and testosterone in their bodies and brains. The higher the oestrogen the more empathetical a female becomes, while the higher the testosterone the more decisive a male becomes.

Second, psychology and psychiatry are concerned with the preferred sexual behaviour of human beings. They are not concerned with the study of biological human sex. Biologically speaking, there are only two mature sexes in human beings, but there are many preferred sexual behaviours in human beings. In order to categorise and describe these preferred sexual behaviours in human beings, psychologists and psychiatrists adopted the linguistic term 'gender' to describe these behaviours (John Money, 1955, https://www.ubcpress.ca). Originally, gender was a linguist term used to describe the pronoun reference in language and not preferred sexual behaviour. So, following this categorisation sex is a biological term describing a biological reality, while gender is a psychological term describing preferred sexual behaviour.

Initially, the preferred sexual behaviours in human beings were identified and defined as heterosexual, nymphomania and hypersexual activity, bisexual, homosexual, transvestite, and transsexual. There are some other preferred sexual behaviours that I will not examine here because they are illegal. As these words suggest, heterosexuals prefer sexual behaviour with the opposite sex; nymphomania is the uncontrollable or excessive sexual desire in women; while hypersexual activity is the same condition in males, homosexuals prefer sexual behaviour with the same sex; bisexuals prefer sexual behaviour with both sexes, while transvestites and transsexuals also prefer sexual behaviour with the same sex. Transvestites and transsexuals differ from homosexuals in that transvestites like to *dress and act* in a style opposite to the sex they were born with, while transsexuals *identify* with the opposite sex they were born with.

Heterosexual, nymphomania, and hypersexual activity are practices that do not involve gender confusion and since we are examining sexual behaviour which can lead to gender confusion, I will concentrate on those which exhibit this behaviour, namely bisexual, homosexuals, transvestites, and transsexuals.

Gender dysphoria in minors contain many groups with differing identity confusion. Tomboys, for example, are girls who grow up preferring the company of boys and like playing and competing with them. As tomboys mature their hormones bring the changes to their bodies described above, which results in them no longer looking like or able to compete with boys, resulting in some disliking their bodies. Mature tomboys, however, eventually come to accept their bodies, are comfortable with their sex, and prefer sexual behaviour with men. Most marry and want to have children. Some prefer working in traditional male occupations. Boys with a more effeminate nature prefer the company of girls in their childhood and tend to avoid the roughhouse play and competition with boys. When they mature, however, they accept they are men, want to get married and have children, and get satisfaction from providing for their families (the traditional role of males). Some prefer working in traditional female occupations.

Bisexuals are a group who are confused about their sexual identity in childhood, but who also come to accept their preferred sexual behaviour in adulthood. Most bisexuals end up in long-term relationships. Some commit to open marriages and must contend with issues arising from open marriages which include things like trust, commitment, and loyalty. Research shows that most adult bisexuals end up in opposite-sex relationships. 84% commit to heterosexual relationships while only 9% to homosexual relationships (Pew Research LGBT Survey, 2013).

Another group suffering from gender dysphoria in minors is homosexuals, who, at first, do not understanding why they are attracted to the same sex. However, as this group matures they come to accept their preferred sexual behaviour, 'come out', and live rewarding and fulfilling lives. Now that Western societies have accepted homosexuals for who they are, they do not suffer from the undesirable effects of gender dysphoria as much as they did in the past. Some homosexuals transition to heterosexual behaviour later in life and some heterosexuals transition to homosexual behaviour. Those who do this freely, of their own free will, have more success than those who are forced or coerced into the transition.

Transvestites are yet another group who suffer gender dysphoria as they mature, but they generally have been comfortable with their preferred sexual behaviour throughout their childhood (in Asia they are referred to as 'ladyboys' by both others and themselves). It is only when transvestites feel that their lifestyle is unfulfilling or in some way wrong that they suffer greater distress from gender dysphoria. It doesn't help if they also feel that other adults do not accept them for who they are.

Parents of transvestites report that their transvestite children were born different from their other children in that from birth they wanted to dress and act in a way different from the sex they were born with. The citizens of some Asian countries have been better at accepting transvestites for who they are than some Western countries have been in the past. One thing I have noticed about most, not all but most, transvestites is that they do not have the appearance of most women. Their hair, makeup, dress, voice, and mannerisms seem like a parody of women. This makes their identity unique to them, and not one they share in common with most women. For centuries,

Western citizens have enjoyed live stage entertainment by men and women dressed opposite to their biological sex on stage but feel uncomfortable when it is displayed in public. This is not the case in some Asian countries.

I remember an incident that occurred when I entered a male toilet in a major shopping centre in Bangkok, Thailand and saw a transvestite standing at a urinal. At first I thought I had entered the female toilet, but then realised that the transvestite was using a urinal. We both checked each other out as we used the urinal.

One problem that has arisen between conservatives and radicals concerning transvestites is the emergence of transvestites performing drag shows for children at parties or in public, especially if the performance enters into explicit sexual suggestiveness intended to provoke sexual arousal.

Do you think this is a radical belief because it seeks to change the underlying structure of Australia's culture by not only seeking an acceptance of transvestite activity, but also promoting it with children, or do you think this is a reformist belief giving rise to a better acceptance of transvestites in society?

Some argue that drag shows for children are designed only to entertain and educate children into accepting the existence of transvestites. Another involves Drag Time Storytime conducted by transvestites in primary school libraries. One side believes it is healthy for children to accept transvestites at an early age, while the other side claims it is confusing to young minds that have not worked out their own sexuality. Conservatives also claim that sexualising children is actually grooming them for later exploitation, that children should be allowed to find their own sexuality naturally.

Do you have any comments regarding transvestites? Perhaps you would like to share them with your parents.

Transsexuals are yet another group who suffer from gender dysphoria. Studies on transsexuals, however, have reported a high frequency of childhood emotional, sexual and physical abuse, perpetrated by their parents and caregivers, that transsexuals had to endure during their childhood (Pauly, 1974; Devon, 1994; Cussino et el., 2017; and many others). At least one study (Littman, 2018) has suggested that the rapid onset of gender dysphoria (rather than from birth) could be a social coping mechanism for other disorders, such as anxiety (fear about the future) and depression (fear about the past) caused by trauma. Transsexuals suffer extreme discomfort and distress from identifying with the sex they were born with, creating within themselves a belief that they were born into the wrong body; that they are actually a woman or a man in the wrong body, and this feeling does not ease with the passage of time.

> *About 0.9% of Australia's population is trans and gender diverse. Studies suggest that around 1% of the adult population worldwide identifies as transgender.*
>
> (AI Overview, 2025)

Do some research on Stockholm Syndrome. Do you detect any similarity between those with transsexual identity and those with Stockholm Syndrome?

This belief about being born in the wrong body among transsexuals has caused a great deal of confusion in modern Western societies, giving rise to an acceptance that individuals are actually the *sex* they *identify* with. This has inspired a concept that human sex is actually a spectrum, or non-binary. Clearly, this is an attempt to change Australia's culture, which, in the past, marked a clear distinction between sex and preferred sexual activity. Essentially, then, gender has become an imaginary spectrum with males at one end of the spectrum and females at the other end, with an abundance of sex categories between them.

This has blurred the distinction between human sex and preferred human sexual behaviour (between sex and gender) and has created a spectrum with an infinite number of gender categories as more and more genders are identified. At this point in our discussion, I must confess that I find the distinction between sex and gender has been made confusing. I hope not deliberately. Mainly because I don't see any consistency in its logic. On the one hand, sex is defined as male and female, while gender is defined as preferred sexual behaviour. On the other hand, sex and gender become interchangeable, your preferred sexual behaviour becoming your sex. I think that this is what is at the heart of the confusion and conflict regarding gender in some Western countries today.

Some psychiatrists, being concerned about the higher than average suicide rate among transsexuals, advanced a new type of treatment for transsexuals called affirmative care. This treatment affirms the gender identity of the transsexual and provides the medication and surgery necessary to make physical changes to transsexual bodies, rather than psychoanalysing transsexuals and providing psychiatric treatment via helping them understand why they identify with the sex opposite to the one they were born with. Transsexuals usually identify with the sex of their childhood abusers. That is, the dominate parent or caregiver. Those who criticise affirmative care are charged with being transphobic.

Because the affirmative treatment for transsexuals achieves best results before children's immature bodies undergo the changes resulting from their biological hormone production, affirmative treatment recommends giving hormone suppressants (to supress their patient's biological hormone growth) and chemical hormones, opposite to the ones produced by their biological sex. This is done in an attempt to produce the physical changes to a minor's body opposite to the ones produced by their biological sex. However, the sex linked genes (XX, XY) are fixed at conception and do not change throughout the lifespan of individual human beings, so this treatment only affects the level of hormones in the body (testosterone and oestrogen); it does not change the sex-linked genes which continue to produce the hormones of the sex one was born with. Therefore, this affirmative treatment of transsexuals comes with a high degree of post treatment complications, like high blood sugar and blood pressure, altered physical growth, probable infertility, lowered sex drive, and weight gain, to name a few. This usually results in a lifetime of drug dependency to supress their biological hormone growth and control these complications.

Some surgeons also carry out sex-altering surgery on minors. Full mastectomies and removal of sex organs are sometimes performed on minors. The removal of both testicles and both ovaries significantly reduces or stops the primary hormone production of testosterone and oestrogen. This obviously ends fertility in both sexes. For females the removal of both ovaries does not only ensure hormone reduction, but it also causes permanent menopause, including potential symptoms like hot flashes, vaginal dryness, mood changes, decreased sex drive, and loss of bone density. For males the potential side effects are decreased sex drive, hot flashes, loss of muscle mass, fatigue, and emotional changes like depression and low self-esteem. Special clinics were opened to perform these treatments. The most famous of these being the Tavistock paediatric clinic in England. Naturally, some parents and psychiatrists objected to this treatment being performed on minors. Some governments passed laws requiring psychiatrists to affirm transsexual identity, and some schools assisted minors to undergo sex change treatment without informing parents. This led to an obvious confrontation between some psychiatrists and parents on one side, and other parents and authorities (governments and schools) on the other.

When addressing this issue, Michael Shellenberger points out that

> doctors, surgeons, therapists and others who are engaged in this (affirmative treatment) admit that the parents and kids do not understand that they are facing lifelong sterility as well as potentially a significant loss of sexual function. They don't understand these treatments and that is called informed

> *consent and that is right up there with 'do no harm' and I think this a violation of medical ethics.*
>
> (Rising Hill interview, *Leaked Files*, 2024)

Keeping in mind our earlier discussion regarding which minors suffer from gender dysphoria, it should be obvious that many minors who have had sex change treatment performed on them are not actually transsexuals. Later, as these minors mature, they became distressed about the decision they had made and horrified that in many cases the treatment is irreversible. Many began class actions against the governments that had passed legislation that had facilitated their treatment. The claimants believed that they should have been challenged more before the irreversible treatments were undertaken. This led to Tavistock, the world's largest paediatric clinic conducting such treatments, being shut down by the British Government, owing to a lack of evidence showing the benefits of affirmative treatment, risk of harm, and operational failures.

Add to this a new study that found –

> *There is an elevated co-occurrence of autism in trans individuals, which recent meta-analysis suggesting that 11% of trans individuals are autistic.*
>
> (Lancet Reg Health West Pac, 2024)

One advocacy group in favour of affirmative care is the World Professional Association for Transgender Health (WPATH) who argue that affirmative care reduces the suicide rate of transsexuals. However, long-term studies have yet to be conducted to confirm or disprove these claims, so much dispute remains about the long-term effects on suicide rates.

When considerations concerning suicide are made, one should keep in mind that suicide thoughts generally are treated as a mental disorder for all other members of society and psychiatric treatment for the disorder is recommended. People who are suicidal, for example, are incapable of making rational, logical decisions. They feel isolated, fearful, anxious, and depressed; all mental disorders requiring psychiatric treatment. Why, then, should it be different for transexuals with suicidal thoughts?

This raises an inescapable question –

> *What is the central motivation for the argument against transgender affirmative care: transphobia or child protection?*

If you are troubled by this, may I suggest you discuss it with your parents.

In a unanimous decision, the UK Supreme Court decided,

> *The terms 'woman' and 'sex' in the Equality Act 2010 refer to a biological woman and biological sex.*

It also decided that a person with a Gender Recognition Certificate in the female gender,

> *Does not come within the definition of a 'woman' under the Equality Act.*
> (commonslibrary.parliament.uk, 2025)

Before closing this section, I want to mention the rise of transspecies (otherkin) in Western societies. Transspecies are human beings (minors and adults) who suffer from species dysphoria, which is a mental state giving rise to a feeling of distress from being an animal in a human body. Most common animals *identified* with are cats, werewolves, and vampires, although some children *identify* with unicorns. Newspaper articles report a rise in such cases in classrooms, particularly primary school classrooms (theguardian.com, 2023).

Transspecies believe that

their present state is a result of ancestry (werewolves, vampires), reincarnation, or a non-human soul dwelling in a human body.
(Tristan Briggs, *Otherkin – A Balanced View*, 2023)

Some transspecies undergo things like tattoos, whisker and canine tooth implants to gain the appearance of the animal they identify with. They also behave in ways that imitate their chosen animal, crawling around on all fours, licking their hands, purring, meowing and hissing, rubbing themselves up against others, and in the case of werewolves, howling to a full moon while squatting on a hilltop, while vampires avoid sunlight, preferring to focus on nighttime activities, for example.

Clearly, this poses a major problem for those advocating for the *identity principle* as the determining factor for sex categorisation. If your sex can be determined by whatever sex you identify with, why can't it also determine that you are a cat (an animal) or a werewolf or a vampire (both fictional characters) or a unicorn (a mythological creature) because you identify as such. Should a new form of affirmative treatment be implemented for those claiming transspecies identity or should they be given psychiatric care? And if psychiatric care is preferred, why would it not be preferred for transsexual identity?

Which of these approaches (affirmative or psychiatric care) for transsexuals and transspecies do you consider the more humane?

Before closing this section I want to point out that gender dysphoria in transsexuals and non-human identity in trans-species are genuine problems afflicting human beings. The deep depression and anxiety suffered by those who experience it is acute and deserving of our understanding and treatment. The issue, therefore, is not whether or not it exists, but rather what the most appropriate treatment for it is. Facing a problem with a truthful appreciation of the facts is, in my opinion, the most appropriate approach, and more likely to lead to a better resolution. Falling back on ideology as a cure, on the other hand, seems to be a recipe for disaster as the Tavistock enquiry has proven.

Identity Politics

Consider these two quotes –

> *Those who control the present, control the past and those who control the past control the future.*
> (George Orwell, *1984*)

> *It is a simple but sometimes forgotten truth that the greatest enemy to present joy and high hopes is the cultivation of retrospective bitterness.*
> Robert Menzies: Australian Prime Minister (1939-41; 1949-66)

They both address the underlying problems with identity politics. The first is that it is a deliberate invention; and like all deliberate inventions, it must have been invented for a purpose. Those who support identity politics say they want to correct historical injustice, but as we already have seen their historical injustice is selective, which suggests a hidden agenda. The second is that identity politics creates bitterness. Again, we need to ask why those who support it want to divide Australian society along the lines of bitterness.

The observations I make here are my own and will be controversial. Again, I ask you to question all my assumptions and conclusions before arriving at your own evaluation and conclusions.

Identity Politics centres around Group Identity. That is, certain groups in society demand political rights and privileges based on their identity within a group, such as sex, race, gender, etc. and not by any achievement or merit they have individually attained. Some individuals also claim intersectionality. That is, they say that they intersect with different groups, thus creating unique experiences of discrimination and disadvantage known only to themselves as individuals. For example, an Aboriginal lesbian could claim that she is a member of the Aboriginal racial group, the women's group, and the gender group, thus providing her with a higher priority for affirmative action. Identity politics is linked to a historical grievance or perceived injustice that the group suffered from, and the group's protest focuses on its fight for special political and privileged rights pertaining to these grievances. These political and privileged rights usually take the form of special political and economic benefits or compensation which are unique to the group and stand apart from the rights and benefits pertaining to all other individual Australian citizens. From a cost perspective, the claims for special privileges and benefits demanded by a rapidly expanding number of groups within our society will make it difficult for any future government to meet their demands and may have reached crisis point already.

As highlighted before, liberty is based on individual rights and individual choice, not group rights. For a libertarian, individuals within a society may be part of a group, but they still only retain their individual rights within their society. What group rights activists demand are special rights and privileges that are added on top of their individual rights, they do not replace them.

For a libertarian, benefits and compensation should be based on individual need or injustice committed against an individual during his/her lifetime. Not someone who does not need an extra benefit or never had injustice committed against them personally. The notion of reparations for a crime committed against a particular group in past generations is not something that a libertarian would hold present-day individuals accountable for since they are in no way responsible for those crimes (the child does not inherit the crimes of his/her parents) and holding them accountable for those crimes is seen as an infringement against their individual rights. Since identity politics is an attack on the liberty rights of Australian citizens, it is a radical movement, not a movement for reform.

Do you concede the difference between identity politics and individual rights as outlined here? Does Group Identity challenge the principle of individual rights in a liberal democracy? Which of these two political movements, identity politics or individual rights do you consider the more just?

There is a further argument that Australia is a Nation State which protects its citizens' individual rights, one of which is equality of opportunity, not equality of outcome, or equity. Communist countries, on the other hand, want to achieve equity. In your opinion, should Australia try to achieve equal opportunity for its individual citizens or equity for groups of citizens? If you decide on group equity, who should pay for the cost of the privileges and benefits incurred to achieve group equity? If you believe that the government should pay, you are actually advocating for all taxpayers to pay, some of whom had nothing to do with the selective historical injustice you are attempting to correct.

Is this fair, since many taxpayers' ancestors never took part in the selective historical injustice under question? What do you think would happen to the aspirations (self-reliance) of those who want to achieve things based on their own merit, if they were forced to pay benefits to a group of individuals whose selective historical injustice they do not consider they are responsible for? Do you think this might have an impact on Australia's economy? How does the principle of group equity play out in practical, everyday terms? Do you think that group equity would provide benefits and compensation to individuals who do not need them? Should benefits and compensation be distributed on the basis of group identity or individual need in a Liberal Democratic Nation State?

The simple truth is that everyone on earth has ancestors who suffered historical injustice. This includes both sexes, all genders, and all races. Why then do radical Australians concentrate only on those who suffered under European colonialism? Why do they only want to attack European culture for the same crimes committed by all cultures of the world over time immemorial? Why not Turkish, Chinese, Native American, African cultures among many others, for example. What about Aboriginal Australians who engaged in tribal warfare against each other which led to much death, destruction and female enslavement, or who still engage in blood feuds today, even when they no longer know the reason why the blood feud started?

My personal truth is that over 60% of my DNA is Celtic. Celtic history is replete with historical injustice: Roman conquest, Viking raids and settlement, Anglo Saxon settlement, Norman conquest, Barbary Coast slave raids, British Imperialism, to name just a few of the historical injustices suffered by my ancestors, but I am not bitter about it, nor do I obsess over it, because I am an Australian. I celebrate my Celtic ancestors and their struggles with injustice and their triumph over adversity, but I am now a 5th generation Australian with a rich Australian ancestry that is my primary identity. My observation here in no way lessens the Australian identity of new migrants to Australia who have taken out Australian citizenship. My wife, for example, has been living in Australia for over 20 years and has taken out Australian citizenship. She likes to refer to herself as an 'Aussie chick' and I love her all the more for it. I do not belittle her as a latecomer.

The question to address, therefore, is do we compensate everyone for the historical injustice suffered by their ancestors, or do we recognise that historical injustice existed in the past, empathise with those who suffered, and simply put it behind us and move on while guaranteeing everyone equal individual citizenship rights today? In actual fact, the injustice of the past cannot be changed, and attempting to change it only creates new, present-day injustice. Let's acknowledge it and commit ourselves to not repeating it in the future. Let the past stay in the past and move on to a better future for all.

Do you agree? Which of these two approaches does Robert Menzies advance in his quote displayed the beginning of this section? Why does he believe this?

In a liberal democracy it is the individual that is sovereign, not a group. Identity politics, therefore, attacks the fundamental philosophical principles of liberty and democracy. Let's turn our attention to how Group Identity attacks liberty and democracy, and in particular how Group Identity uses Multi-Culturalism and a newly emerged movement called diversity, equity, and inclusion (DEI) to attack the individual rights of citizens living in liberal democracies.

We need to establish the difference between a multi-racial and a multi-cultural society before we proceed, because those who criticise multi-culturalism are often wrongly, and I suspect deliberately, condemned as being racists. A multi-racial society is one where different races peacefully co-exist because they share common values, and in the case of liberal democratic societies these values have already been clearly defined when we considered national identity. In other words, multi-racial societies that peacefully co-exist are those societies that have achieved racial assimilation, while those that do not peacefully co-exist are those with no shared, common values and no racial assimilation.

Multi-cultural societies, on the other hand, are societies with not just different races but also different cultures. A multi-cultural society does not share things like beliefs, values, social norms, traditions, and a common language. That is, a multi-cultural society is one where different groups of people have different beliefs, values etc., yet live in the same society. Is this a good idea? How does an assimilated society differ from a multi-cultural society?

It takes a limit on the number of immigrants and a significant time lapse before different cultures can be assimilated into sharing common values. It cannot be achieved through mass immigration, and it cannot be achieved if ethnocentric enclaves are established in a liberal democratic society and allowed to thrive, because some ethnocentric enclaves speak different languages, continue to identify with the values of the countries they have emigrated from, and continue to hate those from opposing cultures. The burning of the Australian flag at a radical rally, for example, is a rejection of Australian cultural values.

The term 'Multi-Culturalism' is defined as

> *the state of a society or world in which there exists numerous distinct ethnic and cultural groups seen to be politically relevant, and a program or policy promoting such a society.*
> (sciencedirect.com 2024)

Those espousing multi-culturalism believe that there is strength in diversity. That is, in separate ethnic and cultural groups being allowed to live their lives according to their culture and acquire separate socio/political and economic rights in the same society. However, history teaches us the opposite. All civilisations collapse because of the confluence of many challenges, but one challenge always present in the collapse is tribalism. Multi-culturalism promotes tribalism or ethnocentric enclaves, so rather than a strength it is a weakness, dividing a society and creating disharmony rather than uniting it.

Do you think *unity in diversity* as a concept is a reality or a utopian ideal? What would happen if a cultural group of people immigrating into a country espousing multi-culturalism did not believe in multi-culturalism themselves, particularly if they were striving to become the majority group in a democracy? What does the history of liberal democratic nations that adopted multi-culturalism tell us about the problems they face today? Do you think liberal democratic nations that embraced a process of mass immigration and the establishment of multi-cultural societies containing ethnocentric enclaves face unique problems that other nations, who did not embrace it, do not? Do you think these unique problems can be solved? In what way?

Another problem faced by societies embracing multi-culturalism is that of moral equivalency. It denies citizens their right to make value judgements about their country's values and principles and those of other cultures, since *different from* must never equate to *better than*. Thereby negating the right of citizens to exercise their moral clarity, a moral clarity based on their shared values.

How does this play out in practical terms? Do we accept the practice of misogyny, female circumcision, arranged marriages, child brides, child abuse, child labour, slavery, terrorism etc. on the grounds that such things are found in some cultures both inside and outside of Australia, or do we set aside multi-culturalism and adopt the more civilised approach of Cultural Assimilation based on the moral clarity of Australia's shared liberal democratic values?

Over many years now Australia has witnessed religious and politically motivated violence which has escalated recently. For a timeline of terrorist incidents in Victoria since 2005 go to www.police.vic.gov.au. Why not discover for yourself the size of terrorist escalation in Australia. The current national terrorism threat level is PROBABLE. That means there is a greater than 50% chance of an onshore attack or attack planning in the next twelve months (nationalsecurity.gov.au). Are you surprised by what you have discovered about terrorist activity in Australia? Some Australian politicians have responded to this development by arguing that such actions (antisemitism in particular) are 'un-Australian'. My question to them is: does the Australia you refer to still exist, or has that Australia been partly destroyed in the name of multi-culturalism over the past 50 years? A multi-culturalism that Australia's politicians deliberately created and fostered on their citizens. I am reminded what my father once told me –

What you tolerate, you accept.

I am paraphrasing Andrew Bolt here who once put it this way:

Australia was once a family home in which all Australians lived as one big, happy family. Now it is more like a hotel where new arrivals take up residence in separate rooms and immediately call for room service.

(Andrew Bolt, *The Bolt Report*, 2025)

Mike Burgess AM, current Director General of Security in charge of the Australian Security Intelligence Organisation (ASIO), has warned Australians of assassination threats by at least three foreign powers. He also warns of a fraying of Australia's social fabric –

> *Community cohesion (social harmony) remains a great blessing seven years later (after Frank Lowy 2018 lecture) but it is under siege, under threat, and under attack. Our social fabric is fraying, fraying in ways we have never experienced before and this is not an accident.*
>
> (2025 Lowy Lecture)

My plea to Australian politicians, then, is to abandon multiculturalism as an immigration policy and adopt cultural assimilation based on moral clarity where immigrants can still celebrate their parent culture but they cannot practise it in Australia. In Australia they must adopt and practise Australian liberal democratic values and principles as a condition of their citizenship. These values and principles must also be taught in our educational institutions and not watered down by moral equivalence.

What is cultural assimilation?

> *Cultural assimilation is the process in which a minority group or culture comes to resemble a society's major group or assimilates the values, culture, behaviours, and beliefs of another group whether fully or partially.*
>
> (Wikipedia, 2024)

Clearly, the strength of cultural assimilation is that of social harmony, unity, and accord regarding cultural values and principles. A weakness is that it can lead to cultural stagnation. This can be overcome, however, by allowing all cultures to celebrate their ancestral cultures, during a Cultural Day of Celebration which can be established in our country's calendar. In this way the more valuable elements of minority cultures can be observed by the majority group and value judgements based on moral clarity made about the appropriateness of adopting them.

Some politicians may claim that immigrants are expected to swear the Australian citizenship oath (that mentions God) or pledge (that does not mention God) before being granted Australian citizenship. The oath reads as follows –

> *From this time forward, under God, I pledge my loyalty to Australia and its people, whose democratic beliefs I share, whose rights and liberties I respect, and whose laws I will uphold and obey.*
>
> (immi.homeaffairs.gov.au)

For the pledge, one just drops the (under God) of the oath.

Does this oath or pledge sound like a commitment to multi-culturalism or cultural assimilation? Consider the terms 'loyalty to Australia and its people', 'democratic beliefs', 'rights and liberties I respect'. Do these terms sound like a commitment to multi-culturalism? Do all cultures contain these principles? There seems to be a lack of clarity about what precisely our immigration policy is. It appears we espouse multi-culturalism but make immigrants swear an oath or pledge their allegiance to cultural assimilation before becoming Australian citizens. Do you think this could cause confusion in the minds of some immigrants about how they should adjust to life in Australia? Is Australia taking a schizophrenic approach to its immigration policy? Why not dispense with the confusion and doubt and be honest. Abandon multi-culturalism and call our immigration policy what we really expect our immigrants to accept: Cultural Assimilation.

Can you see from this how multi-culturalism attacks the democratic rights of Australia's citizens?

DEI does the same –

DEI are organisational frameworks which seek to promote the fair treatment and full participation of all people.
(Wikipedia, 2025)

While this sounds reasonable it disguises a hidden agenda. What this seeks to achieve is *equity,* over *equality.* Equity is a principle which has nothing to do with individual merit and achievement which are the cornerstones of liberal democracy. Also, who exactly decides what is *fair* and *full*? DEI is a direct attack on the individual rights of liberal democratic citizens because it promotes the rights of groups (sex, race, gender etc.) over that of the individual citizen. Unscrupulous operators, in both the private and public sectors of the economy, also could use DEI to promote citizens with partisan leanings into positions of authority.

Multi-Culturalism and DEI are the Hydra heads of Identity Politics, ready to regenerate (ESG, Cancel Culture, Mis/Disinformation etc.) the moment they are attacked by individual liberty. It is where Australian liberty goes to die. The correct order of identification for all Australians living in a liberal democracy is Australian citizenship first and foremost then a group identity, not the other way around. When we put Australian citizenship first, groups within Australian society are sub-groups not the primary group, and as such not entitled to any special entitlement or consideration outside their individual rights as Australian citizens. Cultural sub-groups can be celebrated as such but not held up as a primary source of identity.

Here is another debating topic for you to consider –

That identity politics radically changes Australia's cultural integrity.

Do a little research on the Greek myth involving the monster Hydra. Do you think this myth helps us understand how regenerative ideology is so difficult to conquer? In this Greek myth, how did Hydra die and bring an end to its endless regeneration?

Another problem with Identity Politics is that it cultivates a victim mentality within the groups living in a society that promotes it; thus depriving individual citizens of the opportunity to grow through the acceptance of personal responsibility. It negates the responsibility attached to the freedom of personal choice, because someone or something else is to blame for the circumstances a group finds itself in. In reality, a free lifestyle is a coin with two sides. The freedom of individual choice within a free society comes with the individual responsibility arising from those choices. Without the responsibility side of freedom's coin, bad choices will be enabled by the society that takes on that responsibility on behalf of the individuals within favoured groups, thereby depriving them of the personal growth required to take them from dependency into independence. Freedom comes with responsibility; a free life is not a double-sided (two-headed) coin.

Let me round out my observations about the divisive nature of identity politics by using two quotes. The first quote comes from the *New Testament*. Jesus is reported to have said,

> *Every kingdom divided against itself is laid waste, and no city or house divided against itself will stand.*
>
> (Matthew 12:25)

The second comes from Abraham Lincoln (1809-65), the 16th President of the USA (1861-1865), during the American Civil War who alludes to Jesus' words –

> *A house divided against itself cannot stand. I believe this government cannot endure, permanently half slave half free. I do not expect the Union to be dissolved – I do not expect the*

house to fall – but I do expect it will cease to be divided. It will become all one thing, or all the other.
(Abraham Lincoln, *Illinois Republican Convention in Springfield*, June 16, 1858)

Our ancestors, who were willing to die for their and your liberty, would be shocked by the voluntary surrender of our liberty to identity politics. They would also be disappointed in our reluctance to take responsibility for our own actions and choices.

What are your conclusions about identity politics and group identity? Do you believe group identity erodes the individual rights of Australian citizens? Do you think it divides Australia's national unity? Do you think identity politics has a hidden agenda to change Australia's libertarian culture? Explain.

Native Title and Land Rights

One of the outcomes of Native Title and Land Rights is that it has locked away access to private property ownership and land held in common in the form of national, state and council parks and reserves from all the citizens of a liberal democracy and given it to a select few on the basis of tribal hereditary. The following quotes outline the arguments, both in favour of and in opposition to this outcome.

Land back means a reckoning with 'so called' Australian history and the unjust ways land was stolen.
(Gemma Pol, 2022, commonground.org.au)

We need to get to a point where real reconciliation is accepted by all of us as one with the Australian flag, with all of us underneath it, and the way I was bought up in traditional terms is that when you are conceived on this country your baby spirit leapt from the ground into your mother's belly giving you your personal

> *dreaming and it didn't matter what your racial heritage was, you belong and have a spiritual connection to this country.*
> (Australian Senator, Jacinta Nampijinpa Price, 'It's time to reform Native Title'. Centre for Independent Studies, 2024)

This appears to be the central contention pertaining to Native Title and Land Rights that continues to divide Australian society along the lines of Aboriginal and non-Aboriginal group identity in Australia today. On the one hand is the view that the history of Australia since 1788 is wrong and that Aboriginal tribes had their land stolen. This view seeks to structurally change our Australian citizenship rights to land ownership and our Australian history which is an important element of our shared cultural and national identity. On the other is the view that we are all now Australian citizens who live in a Liberal Democratic Nation State and as such entitled to equal access to our land.

Before starting our discussion I would like to get the meanings of some words defined. This is important because words have distinct meanings that carry clear thoughts. As explained above, if our thoughts are controlled by the words we use, then it surely follows that those who control our language control our thoughts. If the words we are allowed to use are controlled by those who conflate words with violence and wish to control what we are allowed to say by charges of their being offended, are we not allowing our free speech to be censored and our thoughts to be corrupted, in particular if that 'offence' is subject to privilege? This is a radical attack on our standard English language. For example, if privileged groups in our society are allowed to set the offensive agenda at the expense of others whose offence is cancelled.

The reality of free speech is that there will always be some who will find offence at what is said; that is a part of the 'free speech' code established by the Enlightened philosophers. I have already pointed out the difference between offence and vilification, so I will not go into that again.

However, there is another distinction that needs to be made before we continue, and that is the genuine difference between a slang word and a standard English word. Depending on its usage, a slang word can be intended to deliberately offend or vilify while the other is merely trying to establish a clear definition for our thoughts. Then there is the difference between slang words which are used by specific social groups and colloquialisms which are used by a wider population in everyday conversation. I am, therefore, only interested in slang words that are intended to offend or vilify and standard English which is not. With this in mind, let me define the words used in this discussion.

Aborigine (noun), aboriginal (adjective).

> *A member of the original people to inhabit an area as contrasted with an invading or colonizing people.*
> (Merriam-Webster).

For example, we would say, 'he is an Aborigine' or 'he is an Aboriginal person'. When referring to a person belonging to a specific Aboriginal tribe, we use the name of the tribe. For example, 'he is a member of the Butchulla tribe (or people)'. Aborigines is the plural.

I note that some people today claim that the term 'Aborigine' is offensive. Let me relate a true story to you. When I was a History/English Master at Brisbane Grammar School (BGS), the school invited an Aboriginal spokesperson to address our 6th Form (Year 12) students. At that time a slang term for Aborigines was in fairly common use. It was a contraction of the word Aborigine and some did use it to vilify Aborigines. He went to great lengths describing how that slang word was offensive, and it could be taken as such, and explaining that we should all use the standard English word 'Aborigine' and not the slang word. Notice that this Aboriginal spokesperson was advocating substituting a slang word with a standard English word. From that day on I pointed out the offence Aborigines took from the slang word and encouraged my students to substitute it with the standard English word when discussing Aboriginal culture and tribal life. Imagine my surprise when I was told that what the Aboriginal spokesperson had recommended and what I had been teaching all my life is considered offensive by some people today.

As far as I can ascertain the offence rests on two claims. The first is that it has racist connotations with Australia's colonial past. However, the word 'aborigine' is derived from the Latin phrase, 'ab' meaning *from* and 'origine' meaning *origin* or *beginning*. Combined 'aborigine' means *from the beginning*. If words with Latin or Greek derivates are to be deemed offensive because they have a 'colonial connection' should we be expected to delete them from our English language? Given the number of words in the English language with Latin derivatives, that would do serious damage to our ability to communicate with one another in standard English. The second claim is that it lumps people (different Aboriginal tribes) with diverse backgrounds into one group. Do not the words 'Australian', 'European' or 'Asian' also do this? There are many words in the English language that lump people of diverse backgrounds into the one group. Again, if we were to do this, we would do serious damage to the effectiveness of standard English as a means of communication. As stated before, there was a slang word that was used to describe Aborigines that could be taken as offensive. That word is rightly condemned by most Australians today as being offensive and has fallen out of popular use. What I am suggesting is that there is a difference between offensive slang and standard English. The first category rightly should be avoided while the second should not be interfered with in any way.

Having stated my objection concerning the censoring of the word 'Aborigine', I cannot in all good conscience now bow my head to someone else's privileged offence because it trumps my offence at the attack on standard English. Please understand I am not being insensitive by refusing to accept this offence but rather faithful to my resolve to reject the forced censoring standard English.

Non-Aborigine (noun), non-Aboriginal (adjective). A citizen of a county other than an Aborigine, i.e., native-born or naturalised citizen of Australia.

Native (noun or adjective).

> *Belonging to a particular place by birth*
> (Mirriam-Webster).

For example, 'he is a native of Sydney, or he is a native of Australia. Obviously, 'native' includes both Aboriginal and non-Aboriginal (native-born) people.

Indigenous (adjective).

> *produced, growing, living or occurring natively or naturally in a particular region or environment.*
> (Merriam-Webster)

For example, 'the eucalyptus is an indigenous tree of Australia'. Koalas, kangaroos, emus, and platypuses are also indigenous to Australia. Applying indigenous to Aborigines is incorrect since it is a term that usually applies to the flora and fauna of a particular area, and if applied to Australian citizens it would also embrace non-Aboriginal, native-born Australians since both occur natively in Australia.

I recognise that at least one dictionary defines Australian Aborigines as indigenous to Australia, but I suspect this has more to do with ideology than concept clarification.

If our scientists are to be believed, Homo Sapiens originated in the northern plains of Africa then migrated out of Africa and settled throughout the world. This would make all Homo Sapiens indigenous to Africa. One can plant whole forests of Australian eucalyptus trees in California and Israel, as has been done, but this does not make the Australian eucalyptus indigenous to either of these two regions.

Naturalized (adjective).

> *(of a foreigner) admitted to the citizenship of a country.*
> (Oxford Languages, 2025)

For example, 'a naturalized Australian (who was) born in China.'

For the purpose of our discussion, I will use the word 'Aborigine' to mean someone who lived in what we now call Australia prior to 1788, the coming of the first fleet and British settlement, and his/her descendants. The word 'non-Aboriginal' will encompass the original British settlers and their descendants, native-born, and naturalised Australians.

Now that our definitions are clear, let us examine the issue of Native Title and Land Rights. From the start you can immediately detect a definitional error in the title 'Native' used in Native Title. Obviously, it should be 'Aboriginal Title'. Why do you think the High Court of Australia got their standard English wrong?

I recognise that my observations and questions about this topic are controversial, so I want to begin by making my views on the position of Australia's Aborigines in Australian society clear. Aboriginal tribes were the first to settle in what we now call Australia. No one disputes that. Additionally, many Aboriginal tribes suffered historical injustice at the hands of British colonisation, but that should not result in today's non-Aboriginal Australians developing a debilitating 'guilt complex' and engaging in trying to correct the wrongs of the past, because this only produces a paralysing 'victim mentality' in Aborigines. Furthermore, the correct priority for Aboriginal people is that of Australians first and Aborigines second, because they are citizens of the Nation State of Australia and derive the benefits of being such. Moreover, adult Aborigines are capable, resourceful, responsible citizens. They are not hapless as the history of Aboriginal tribal past testifies and, therefore, should not be treated as hapless victims. Such paternalistic attitudes have created much of the problems that Aborigines face in today's Australia. Given responsibility for their own actions would go a long way to solving those problems, as it does for most non-Aborigines living in Australian society today. What's more, the low expectations many non-Aboriginal Australians have placed on Aborigines has created a sub-group (remote communities) of Aborigines who have become marginalised and dependent. This is a genuine social phenomenon referred to in the social sciences as the *tyranny of low expectations*. This needs to change if Aborigines are going to fulfil their potential in a modern Nation State. I know that some will argue that my view does not address the issue of 'stealing' Aboriginal land. My views on this issue will become clear as my case proceeds. With my view having been clearly defined, I offer the following opinion about Native Title and Land rights.

To begin our discussion, we need to look at *origins and history*. Current scientific evidence suggests that hominid beings first emerged in North Africa over 2 million years ago. Our Homo sapiens ancestors first appeared in North Africa between 200,000 and 300,000 years ago. Homo sapiens began migrating out of Africa about 70,000 to 100,000 years ago and became so dominate that all other forms of hominid beings became extinct, including the Neanderthals of Europe. It seems like the first act of genocide was committed by our Homo sapiens ancestors. It also appears that we are all immigrants from North Africa, some of whom settled on other peoples' land.

Our Homo sapiens ancestors first went through three stone age periods — Palaeolithic, Mesolithic and Neolithic — before the emergence of the first civilisation. *Palaeolithic* means a period of history characterised by the sole use of rudimentary stone tools for hunting and gathering purposes. *Neolithic* refers to a period of time in the stone age characterised predominately by farming and herding prior to the emergence of a civilisation. *Mesolithic* is the period of transition between the Palaeolithic and Neolithic eras where both hunter/gathers and farmers/herders lived together. Obviously, the hunter/gatherers would raid the animals and farms of the farmers and herders. What followed the Neolithic era was the emergence of civilisations with labour division including a warrior class who protected the farmers and herders from marauding tribes of hunter/gathers and the other warriors of emerging civilisations.

The first civilisation, that we know of, emerged in the valley between the Tigris and Euphrates rivers around the 5th millennium BC. It is known as the Sumerian civilisation. This spot was favourable because it was a fertile valley suitable for the growing of crops and the domestication of animals. This was important because the population pressure on the land was such that the people living there required a reliable and abundant food source to sustain itself. The first leaders of these newly emerging centres of population were the religious leaders who heavily influenced governance through a theocratic system of religious beliefs. Later, as the centres of population developed into cities, they were joined by kings, who led in war and maintained order. The kings reinforced the priests and religious belief, which provided them with the legitimacy for their rule.

Because the Sumerians created this abundant food production, individuals living within their cities could develop specialised labour skills. The first division of labour to emerge were the priests, warriors, artisans, merchants, and managers. Later, conquering kings united the cities and formed the first civilisation. This is how the Sumerian civilisation, the world's first known civilisation, emerged from the Neolithic Stone Age. Following the invention of the plough, the increased food production, and the freeing up of labour enabled new specialised labour to emerge, like potters, smiths, and scribes. The Sumerians also created a textual code (cuneiform) for writing instead of having to rely on an oral tradition, thereby developing their own religious scripture, legal code and literature. We have discovered Steles (tall stone structures) in the locations of Sumerian cities that record Sumerian military victories. The Babylonian civilisation that followed the Sumerian civilisation under the rule of Hammurabi produced the first-known legal code, which was based largely on reciprocity (an eye for an eye) and was recorded on a Stele located in the centre all of his cities.

We can conclude that the foundation of all civilisations is the existence of a farming and herding economy that produces a surplus of food production, which enables the emergence of specialised labour and a civilisation to flourish.

Many other civilisations emerged around this territory after the Sumerian civilisation and absorbed Sumer into their Empires. For example, Akkadian Empire (2334-2154 BC), Babylonian Empire (1894-1595 BC), and Persian Empire (550-331 BC) all succeeded each other; all successively conquering the other and occupying their lands. As well as this, other civilisations began to emerge in other river valley systems, for example, the Indus Valley Civilisation in what is now Pakistan and northwest India, the Ancient Egyptian civilisation on the Nile delta, and the Chinese Civilisation along the Yellow River. The civilisations in these areas expanded their domains by conquering other civilised groups of people and creating Empires. Kingdoms and City States outside of these fertile river systems next emerged. All fought against each other conquering and taking land from previous owners, so a second condition of civilisation seems to be that you have to fight to keep your land and if you are not victorious in your defence it will be taken away from you, and the laws and culture of the conquering civilisation will alter yours.

In the 20th century, Australia was nearly invaded by the Japanese who were creating a Japanese empire in Asia by conquest. All Australians, both Aboriginal and non-Aboriginal alike, united in a spirit of mateship to defend their country and its liberal democratic way of life. Had the Japanese succeeded, Australians would have lost their country, their culture, and their lands to the Japanese. If, in the future, we are faced with a similar threat from a dominant power, we would have to defend our country or lose it. If we lost to a triumphant conqueror, our land would be lost and our culture would be altered to become more like theirs. That is why Australia has maintained a Defence Force since its foundation in 1901, and alliances and agreements with like-minded liberal democracies like Britain and America.

Presently, there is some dispute about the coming of Homo sapiens into Australia from Asia. Some argue that there was more than one wave of migration, others that there was only one. In 1974, Jim Bowler, a geological scientist, discovered human skeletal remains on the shores of the now dry Lake Mungo. These remains became known as 'Mungo Man'. Later tests discovered that Mungo Man's skeleton was around 42,000 years old, making it the oldest skeleton ever found in Australia.

Gregory Adcock, along with a team of other scientists, released an Australian National University (ANU) study of Mungo Man's DNA in 2001, which claimed Mungo Man's DNA showed that he was not ancestral to any other human population. This caused great controversy within academic circles, because it suggested that the current Aboriginal population is not descended from the original Australians. A new paper, released in 2016, claimed that the DNA used by Gregory Adcock had been contaminated and this raised concerns about the validity of his conclusions (theconversation.com, *New DNA study confirms ancient Aborigines were the First Australians, 2016*). The traditional owners of the Willandra Lakes Region, which includes Lake Mungo, demanded the return of Mungo Man's skeletal remains because they had not given permission for them to be removed. The government granted their demand and Mungo Man was buried in a secret location known only to the traditional owners.

Only a handful of DNA studies have been done on Aboriginal fossil remains and any future DNA study will need the permission of the traditional owners. Also, there is a growing movement to limit access to physical remains, data, visual depictions of certain people, artifacts and ceremonies, archaeological field notes, photographs, and interviews (Quillette, 2025). Clearly, this creates a serious impediment for the scientific research into Australia's Aboriginal past.

The emerging civilisations outside Australia did not affect the palaeolithic Aboriginal tribal culture in Australia, because they remained in splendid isolation, remote from the rest of the world until British settlement in 1788.

An important question arises from this historical fact. Why did Australian Aboriginal tribal culture never evolve into a civilisation? Think back to the reason why civilisations emerge in the first place. Remember it was the population pressure on the land which first inspired palaeolithic tribal people to farm and herd animals. Such population pressure never arose in Aboriginal tribal culture, so there was no need to increase food production. But why? Why didn't tribal Aborigines living in what we now call Australia ever develop a population pressure on the land? Didn't their women conceive the same way as all other homo sapien women? These are questions I will leave for you to ponder for yourself. However, there are a few issues you might like to consider.

First is the harsh topography of their tribal landscape. Was this a limiting factor to population growth? Actually, there were plenty of fertile lands (the Murray/Darling basin, for example) for farming and open grasslands for the grazing of domesticated animals. Our colonial ancestors exploited these assets, so Aborigines also could have exploited them by developing grains for farming and domesticating and breeding animals for grazing. Some rightly argue that the indigenous animals were not conducive to domestication and the grass seeds were not suitable for agriculture. This is true, but so too were the original animals and grasses of the other river valley civilisations and some Aboriginal tribes did domesticate dingoes. Consider also the didgeridoo, boomerang, and woomera which were in use in some Aboriginal tribes. A truly remarkable and extraordinary technological achievement. So Aborigines had the technical mindset to think creatively and develop ways of increasing their food supply. Instead of doing that, however, the Aborigines chose to limit their population and survive by exploiting the natural flora and fauna they found in their tribal lands. The very fact that they were able to survive in this manner for so long (around 40-50,000 years) is evidence of their resourcefulness and determination. The answer as to why tribal Aborigines never developed into a civilisation, then, does not seem to lie solely in the harshness of their tribal landscape nor in the lack of their technical ability. Could the answer lie in Aboriginal tribal culture?

You might consider the personal relationships between different members of an Aboriginal tribe. That is, how did men, women and children relate to each other? What roles did each play in their culture? What was the lifestyle of male and female children in Aboriginal culture like? What weapons did men develop to hunt for food, protect their tribes, raid other tribes, and go to war against other tribes? Was Aboriginal tribal culture dominated by elders (older male members of the tribe)? Did the initiation ceremony that the elders performed on the young boys entering manhood contribute to a difficulty for Aboriginal women to conceive? Modern Australian women maintain a birth rate below replacement level with the use of contraception and abortion. How, then, did Aboriginal tribal women maintain a birth rate of no more than 2.1 when, without contraception or abortion, they would have produced many more than this number?

What adaptive measures did tribal Aborigines have to adopt in order to survive in their hostile environment? How did Aborigines, for example, overcome the challenges of drought, floods and raging bush fires that would have torn through their limited tribal lands? Were some Aboriginal tribes wiped out by these natural disasters and the famine that would have followed? What was a major reason for Aboriginal tribes raiding each other or going to war against each other? When Aboriginal tribes went to war with one another, were some tribes wiped out? What is an Aboriginal blood feud and how did they come about? You may be surprised by what you discover. A good place to start your research is with *Triumph of the Nomads* (1975) by Geoffrey Blainey (AC). Then, there is William D. Rubinstein's article, *Life and Death in Pre-contact Aboriginal Australia,* published in the October 2020 edition of the *Quadrant. You* might also like to read an online *Quadrant* article entitled *Infanticide in Traditional Aboriginal Society* (2022). D*o* not give credence to *Dark Emu* by Bruce Pascoe. It has been debunked by many reputable professionals. The latest is a new book, *Farmers or Hunter-Gatherers? The Dark Emu Debate* (2021) by esteemed anthropologist Peter Sutton and archaeologist Keryn Walshe. Many ask, if Aborigines were farmers and graziers, why is it not represented in their oral history or their cave paintings, and why did it not lead to the development of a civilisation like it did elsewhere? Two other publications that look at traditional Aboriginal tribal culture are *The Politics of Suffering* (2011) by Peter Sutton, and *The Burden of Culture* (2022) by Gary Johns.

Do you think Aboriginal tribal culture was harsh and brutal? Would you like to live in a palaeolithic tribe? Do current Aborigines live according to their tribal culture today, or have they modified their lifestyle by incorporating the rewards and benefits provided to them by the Australian Nation State?

The population of Australia in 2024 passed 27 million people (abs. gov.au, 2024). As previously stated, Australia has established a Nation State with a regulated capitalistic economic system and a Liberal Democratic form of Government with a Monarch as its Head of State. What value do you think palaeolithic tribal culture has for present day Australians? Could palaeolithic tribal culture sustain 27 million people?

Could it be said that some Australian Aborigines today want the rewards and benefits of a modern nation state but want to live a life separate from it? If individuals want to accept the rewards and benefits of a modern Nation State should they have to contribute to it? Remember, Australian Aborigines who experience no 'gap' in their lives relative to non-Aborigines are those who have successfully assimilated into the Australian Nation State; something that the colonial founders originally had hoped for the Aboriginal people.

Explain your answers to these questions by way of detailed, factual reference. From your research, do you think it is possible to romanticise palaeolithic tribal culture? That is, by adopting what Rousseau romantically described as a 'noble savage' concept about tribal culture (Rousseau, *Discourse on Inequality*, 1754). It needs to be understood that Rousseau never experienced living in, or even seeing, a palaeolithic tribe. Rather, he devised his theory from the comfort of his home in Paris.

I understand that the above questions I have asked as well as what I am about to offer from this point on is, in many ways, at odds with present day concepts about the position and entitlement of Aborigines living in contemporary Australia. Most contend that Australian Aborigines are the deposed original owners of this land, which they are. This is historical fact. No one disputes that. However, does that entitle Australian Aborigines to special privileges alienated from non-Aboriginal Australians? That is the question we are now faced with. No doubt, compassionate Australians will answer 'yes', but increasingly empathetic Australians are beginning to have doubts about the wisdom of such an approach. For asking this question, some Australians will accuse me of lacking compassion. Uncharitable Australians might even accuse me of being a bigot or a racist. However, I do have concern for Australia's Aborigines, but my concern lies with those individual Aborigines who are in need, not with those who are not, and devising a scheme which would best tackle those needs. A cause, I believe, that would be supported by many Aborigines today, but I do not presume to speak for them. I am empathetic towards Australia's Aboriginal past, but believe that the current level of Australia's compassion is damaging to both Aborigines (victim mentality) and non-Aborigines (guilt complex).

During the Age of Discovery, European nations engaged in world exploration, largely because they had built large, square-rigged, ocean-going sailing ships, and developed navigation skills that enabled them to plot exactly where they were by the use of compass, sextant and marine chronometer. They had also developed steel swords, muskets and cannons as their weapons of choice which gave them a technological advantage over those they encountered outside Europe. When they left their home ports and set out to discover what lay outside the confines of their known world, they had no idea what they would encounter, what dangers they would face and have to overcome. They were courageous and enticed to venture out by a spirit of curiosity and adventure. In practical terms, they initially undertook this exploration to acquire new trading routes and knowledge (discovery of new lands, winds, and currents, for example) about the world.

However, this soon developed into the establishment of European Empires built on the principle of *Gold, God and Glory* (This period embraces some of the Old Imperial period, 15th to 18th centuries, and the age of New Imperialism, 1870-1917). That is, for the wealth it created for the parent country through trade, settlement, or conquest; the saving of souls for Jesus in competition with other religions; and the glory of the monarchs and the power, prestige, and national pride of the countries that sent forth the colonisers. It also afforded the explorers and adventurers a coveted place in history.

The early explorers sought to enrich themselves by discovering and taking gold and establishing new trade routes. Later their European monarchs encouraged others to trade, settle, or conquer these new lands to create wealth and prosperity not only for their own kingdoms but also for their colonies. The Monarchs used this new wealth to enhance their military which made them strong, powerful and prestigious, thereby securing the safety of their Empire. By bringing the Christian message of *peace on earth, goodwill toward all* into new lands and the changing of tribal laws, language, and culture the Imperial powers hoped to spread their civilisation throughout the world; to make the world more like themselves. During the Age of New Imperialism, there was also the motivation involving *the white man's burden* (Rudyard Kipling, 1899), which saw British Colonialism and American world influence as a mission of spreading Western Civilisation for the benefit of all by fostering the emergence of nation states and the maintenance of peace and prosperity worldwide. Although the period of New Imperialism saw many social reforms at home, like public education, and some progress in the colonies, like the abolition of slavery, it did inspire an intense, competitive nationalism and Imperial rivalry among the Imperial powers of Europe.

We may think that such values are deficient when compared to today's values, but should we judge those in the past by the values we espouse today? Some would argue that the Imperial powers never achieved any of these things; that what they did achieve was the exploitation of other people through Colonialism. That is, establishing control over other people for economic gain. This is true and no doubt you are familiar with these criticisms of European Imperialism since it dominates our education system today. However, doesn't this opinion fail to understand and empathise with the settlers who faced deprivation, hardships, and challenges we do not face today? Do you think that the modern appreciation of Australia's colonial past lacks empathy and gratitude for what those colonial explorers, pioneers and settlers endured? Do you think our descendants will find some of our present-day values primitive? Can you identify some present-day values future generation may find primitive?

The First Fleet set up a convict settlement at Sydney Cove which marked Great Britain's settlement and colonisation of what today we call Australia. On 26th January 1788 Captain Arthur Phillip raised the Union Jack (the British flag) and took possession of the land in the name of King George III. This is why untitled land is called Crown Land. What Phillip did was consistent with what had always existed, and with international law as it existed at that time. It is also the legal right underpinning all freehold land owned by Australians today under the Torrens Title system of land ownership. It confirms the ownership of all individual Australians holding freehold title to their property. Phillip's action also conferred British subjectship to all peoples living in Australia, including Aborigines. That is why this date is celebrated today as Australia Day by the majority of Australians as the foundation of modern Australia.

Who was Woollarawarre Bennelong? Why did Governor Phillip kidnap Bennelong? Did Bennelong assimilate into colonial life?

It is not possible to definitively know how many Aborigines were living in what we now call Australia at the time that the First Fleet arrived, simply because there had never been a census taken. Estimates range from 300,000 to 950,000. Estimates also tell us that there may have been approximately 260 distinct language groups and 500 dialects (www.workingwithindigenousaustralians.info). Clearly such a wide variance in opinion and approximations on this matter is not helpful. Again, it is impossible to determine exactly how many Aboriginal tribes were living here at that time but there may have been as many as 500. Today there are 983,700 Australians claiming Aboriginal descent. This includes those of mixed race. Also, there are 250 Aboriginal tribes (*mobs* is a colloquial term used by Aborigines, which embraces different family clans) living in Australia today.

In the early stages of settlement, it is true that many British people considered themselves superior to other races, that they had an arrogant attitude towards others, and that they were insensitive to the feelings of others. This attitude probably arose because of the more advanced technology that they possessed. However, in this they were no different from the millions of other peoples who had established Empires throughout history. They believed, as others before them had, that their dominance gave them the timeless and universal rights of the subduer over the land and peoples of their colonies.

I would like to relate a personal anecdote at this point. In the 1970s I worked for the General Electric Company (GEC) in its Perth sub-branch as an office manager. GEC (an English company) was given a multi-million-dollar contract to install a centralised traffic control system (CTC) on the railway linking Mount Newman (an iron ore mining operation) and the export port facility at Port Hedland. GEC was given the contract because they had successfully installed a CTC system between Edinburgh and London. Consequently, two English electrical engineers were sent to our office in Perth where I overheard them talking about our local paper, *The Perth Times*.

> *One said to the other,*
> *Do you find the local paper parochial?*
> *The other replied,*
> *Yes. But it's always been that way in the colonies.*

I guess for some, old habits die hard, but in today's world they are to be pitied more than persecuted, because they have failed to accept the passing of European Empires and the emergence of independent Nation States in the 20th century.

Although European Imperialism did involve attitudes of superiority on the part of European Imperialists, concentrating only on this facet fails to understand and empathise with the settlers who faced deprivation, hardships, and challenges we do not face today. Do you think that the modern appreciation of Australia's colonial past lacks empathy and gratitude for what those colonial explorers, pioneers, and settlers endured?

Do some research of your own and discover what deprivations, hardships, and challenges European explorers, pioneers, and settlers faced that we do not face today. In doing your research you might like to set up a family project by answering the following questions –

Who were the early explorers of the Australian continent? What did they hope to achieve? Were they encouraged to explore Australia by the British and Colonial Governments of the day? Why?

Look up the brief biographies of the following explorers: Captain James Cook (1728-1779), George Bass (1771-1803), Captain Matthew Flinders (1774-1814), Gregory Blaxland (1778-1853), Sir Thomas Mitchell (Major Mitchell) (1792-1855), Allan Cunningham (1791-1839), Ludwig

Chapter 8: New World Issues

Leichhardt (1813-1848), and the Burke and Wills expedition of 1860-61. These are just a few of the more prominent explorers of Australia.

What contribution did they make to the opening up of Australia to the farming and grazing industries? How old were they when they died? Do you expect to live longer than they did? Do you think they would have experienced hardships and deprivations during their explorations? Can you think of some? Do you have your favourite explorers? Why not look deeper into their stories.

Who was James Ruse and why was he so vital to the survival of the early convict colony of New South Wales? Do you detect a link between James Ruse and the necessary precursor of creating a food surplus for the emergence of a civilisation?

Who was John Macarthur (1767-1834) and his wife Elizabeth (1766-1850)? How did they come to Australia? How did John Macarthur make his initial fortune? What was his role in the Rum Rebellion (1808)? Why is Macarthur known as a pioneer of the Australian Merino wool industry? How did Macarthur acquire 5,000 acres of the Cowpastures near the Nepean River? Why was it called the Cowpastures? Why did he name his grazing farm 'Camden'? How did he acquire his Merino breeding stock? What role did Elizabeth play in breeding the superior Australian Merino? Why was wool production so important to the colony of New South Wales and England? What role did the Napoleonic Wars (1803-1815) play in all this? What did Macarthur suffer from before his death in 1834?

Who was Lachlan Macquarie (1762-1824)? Why did he bring his own Highland Regiment of soldiers when he took over the governorship of the Colony of New South Wales? What was the relationship between Macquarie and Macarthur? Why did Governor Macquarie introduce the first currency into the colony? What is the 'Holey Dollar'? What vision did Macquarie have for the colony of New South Wales? What were some of the buildings he commissioned to be built? Who was the convict Francis Greenway? What is his connection with Governor Macquarie? What was the controversy surrounding what is now the Sydney Conservatorium of Music's castle-like building located at the top of Bridge Street on Macquarie Street? Why did Macquarie emancipate convicts? What opposition did Macquarie face over his policy of emancipation? What impact did the Bigge enquiry have on Macquarie's governorship?

Consider the following –

> *The Native Institution was established at Parramatta by Governor Lauchlan Macquarie on 10 December 1814 as a school for the education of the native children.*
> (findandconnect.gov.au, *Native Institution*, 4 Aug 2025.)

'Native children' included both Aboriginal and non-Aboriginal native born British subjects of the colony of New South Wales.

Who was Mary Yallamundi? What achievement did she reach as a student of The Native Institution? How successful was she as a British subject of the colony of New South Wales? Do you consider Mary Yallamundi successfully assimilated into British culture?

To what extent can it be claimed that Macquarie's vision represents the beginning of a role for government in Australian society and Macarthur's that of the commercial vision for Australia? Look up the definitions for the words, *enlightened, pragmatic and egalitarian*. Which of these words do you think best describes Macquarie's governorship? Explain your choice in detail.

For further reading, read *Henry's Empire* by Bob Bennett (2022). What role did Ernest Henry play in the establishment of Queensland's cattle and mining industries? What hardships and challenges did he face? Do you admire his ambition and determination to overcome the setbacks he faced? Do all Queenslanders owe Ernest Henry a debt of gratitude?

Three colonial writers who captured the deprivations and poverty faced by the pioneers and settlers, as well as the courage and stoic humour needed to overcome the austerity they endured, were the poet Andrew Barton (Banjo) Paterson, CBE (1864-1941) made famous for his penning of the iconic Australia poems *Waltzing Matilda* (which tells the tale of an itinerant worker's struggle against authority) and *The Man from Snowy River* (a story illustrating the importance of horsemanship and courage during colonial times). Henry Lawson (1867-1922), renowned for his *bush* poems and short stories, was another poet and author who depicting the harshness of life and unforgiving landscape in outback Australia in the 19th century. His characters depict determination, resilience, independence, and mateship, as well as humour and loyalty coupled with loneliness and isolation. Finally, Steele Rudd (1868-1935) a distinguished novelist, playwright, and short story writer, was best known for his short story collection entitled *On Our Selection,* which portrays his many humorous colonial characters. Many of his stories were turned into movies in the 1920s and 30s.

Also active during the 1880s and 90s was the Heidelberg School of Australian impressionist painters known for their depictions of the Australian landscape and rural life. The best-known artists of this movement are Tom Roberts (1856-1931), Arthur Streeton (1867-1943) and Frederick McCubbin (1855-1917). Roberts is well renowned for his famous paintings depicting colonial workers and bushrangers, *Shearing the Lambs* (1890), *A Breakaway* (1891), *The Golden Fleece* (1894), and *Bailed up* (1895). Streeton painted many memorable landscapes. The best known of which are *Still glides the stream, and shall for ever glide* (1890), *Fire's on* (1891), *Sunlight (Cutting on a road)* (1895), *From my campsite (Sirius Cove)* (1896), and *The purple noon's transparent might* (1896). McCubbin was one of the key founders of the Heidelberg School who painted memorable outdoor scenes depicting pioneers. Among his most famous paintings are *The Letter* (1884), *Lost* (1886), *Down on His Luck* (1889), *A Bush Burial* (1890), *On the Wallaby Track* (1896), and *The Pioneer* (1904). These paintings are available for viewing in most Australian Art Galleries.

My favourite is *Lost*, which is available for viewing in the National

Gallery of Victoria. This painting depicts what must have been one of the most terrifying anxieties faced by Australia's pioneers. That of having a child wander into the Australian bush and become lost. The poor little girl in McCubbin's painting has her head bent in sorrow while the Australian bush seems so indifferent to the human tragedy playing out in front of it. The possibility of a child getting lost in the Australian bush was very real for Australia's colonial pioneers. That is why they taught their children to shout *cooee* in response to the searchers who would use the same long, loud call ending on a shrill rising inflection on the *ee*, when looking for lost souls in the Australian bush.

Would you like to face the privations suffered by our colonial explorers, pioneers, and settlers who laid the foundation of our great Australian Nation State? Are you grateful for the benefits that their sacrifice produced for you? You have your own challenges that you must face today. Can you draw inspiration from the courage of those colonial explorers, pioneers, and settlers to help you face your challenges today?

You might also like to look up the meaning of Mercantilism which was the underlying economic system driving Imperialism. Adam Smith offered a criticism of Mercantilism. What was his criticism based on? For even further research, seek an understanding of the Imperial rivalry between England, Spain, France, Russia, and Germany during the time of European New Imperialism. How might this have contributed to the enthusiasm European countries displayed for establishing their Empires?

Was Imperial rivalry unique to European Imperialism, or was it present throughout recorded history, in both the ancient and modern worlds? Can you identify some other sources of Imperial rivalry from history? Do modern nations today compete for world dominance and prestige? Identify those nations and determine what the underlying cause of their rivalry is. Do you think there is a hidden agenda for those who have singled out European Imperialism for harsh criticism, including substandard moral degeneracy? If you do identify a hidden agenda, what might be the motivation for such selective condemnation?

I will now return to outlining the emergence of Australia as a Nation State. Present during this period were two distinct groups of colonialists. The free British subjects of the King and the convicts. The free British subjects included soldiers who acted as guards and free settlers. They were predominately Protestants. The convicts were British and Irish (predominately Catholic) political prisoners and criminals sent to the colonies to serve out their time. Some convicts were transported for 'the term of their natural life'. Following the establishment of a convict colony at Sydney Cove, free British subjects harboured attitudes of superiority and racism towards others. The goldfield riots against the Chinese in Lambing Flat (1860-61 AD) led to a restriction of Chinese immigration into Australia. This carried over into the Immigration Restriction Act of 1901 infamously known as the *White Australia Policy* (1901-1958 AD). This is best understood in terms of a fear generated from the concept of a *Yellow Peril* (Jacques Novikov, a Russian socialist, first used the term in his essay *Le Peril Jaune*, 1897). Kaiser Wilhelm II also used the term extensively in an attempt to rally European nations against Japan, and in the USA following increased migration from Asia. So a fear of the peoples of the East and Southeast Asia was not unique to Australia; it was prevalent throughout Western countries. It was a fear that the West generally held over an existential Asian threat to Western Civilisation. When the Japanese bombed Darwin and Townsville, infiltrated Sydney harbour with miniature submarines, and tried to establish a military base in Port Moresby, New Guinea from which to launch an invasion of Australia, this fear became not just an intellectual theory but a stark reality for all Australians. As stated previously, Aborigines and non-Aborigines alike united in the defence of their nation. This indicates an Aboriginal preference for the Australian Nation State that existed at that time over that of Imperial Japan. Australians (both Aboriginal and non-Aboriginal) prevailed over their Japanese adversary and kept their country.

Racism has been found in all peoples throughout history and was not unique to colonial settlers. There is a heated argument today about whether racism is a foundational survival skill established in homo sapiens from their first emergence on the plains of Africa or whether it is acquired by cultural conditioning. I do not want to enter this debate here but merely observe that it could be a combination of the two and not singularly acquired. However it is acquired, it has been a blight on humanity for thousands of years and if it cannot be eliminated it must be controlled. Perhaps Australian soldiers have recognised this better than most. To win in war they must present a united front with a high *esprit de corps*. Soldiers, for example, fight as one, under one flag, for the protection of shared values, regardless of race, religion, ideology or culture.

Unfortunately, racism is still found in many countries around the world today. However, liberal democratic nation states like Australia have passed laws to eliminate institutional or structural racism and have gone a long way in controlling the excesses of isolated incidents of individual racism in their countries. Sadly, the emergence of anti-Semitism within Australian society today has seen racism become more prevalent than in the past. Let's hope the Australian Government can take steps to once again control the excesses of racism within Australia. Perhaps the example set by liberal democratic nation states will be adopted worldwide in future.

In establishing their settlement of Australia, The British observed international law, established by a legal precedent stretching back since the beginning of homo sapien migration from Africa and all of recorded history (more than two millennia) which legalised a dominant power to take territory by cession (treaty), settlement, or conquest. Therefore, the British took legal sovereignty of Australia and established a penal colony. At that time, settlements were established by all Empires where there was no other existing Kingdom or civilisation with a central government and common laws. Such was the case in Australia because what the British found here was many different tribes practising palaeolithic tribal culture, each with different laws, languages, and leaderships. There was no Kingdom or civilisation in Australia at the time of British possession. So ascribing the terms 'nation' or 'Australia' as in *first nation's people* or *first Australians* status to Aborigines today is historically inaccurate. Australia became a Nation State on 1st January 1901 and all people living in Australia at that time (Aboriginal and non-Aboriginal alike) were the 'first nation's people' and 'first Australians' because they had all participated in the creation of Australia as a nation state. Before that the people were British subjects, and before that, members of various tribes. Had the British found a Kingdom or civilisation here they would have had to have either conquered it or established a trading treaty. Given that initially they were trying to establish a penal colony, that would have been highly unlikely.

Later the penal colony developed into a free settlement colony with the settlers bringing with them their own culture and the general body of English law, including common and criminal law, which was grounded on the principle of precedence. In the 19th century both the Colonial Supreme Court of New South Wales and the British Privy Council (Cooper vs Stuart, 1889) found that Australia had been settled and not conquered. This is highly contested today, as some argue that Australia was invaded and not settled. That the lands of Australia were never ceded but stolen.

When pioneering squatters first moved outside the boundaries of settlement and squatted on land, they had to protect their sheep flocks, cattle herds, and families themselves. A timeless and universal act of protection not unique to British settlement. Consequently, violent acts were committed against those who would kill or steal their sheep or cattle or attack their families, because the Colonial Governments were incapable or unwilling to provide the necessary protection for these squatters, their families or their property. The Colonial Governments had encouraged the squatters to go beyond the boundaries of settlement and establish their sheep and cattle stations, as they depended on the revenue raised from the squatters to remain solvent but offered them no protection. What emerged from this development was a squattocracy, established by their immense wealth, social prestige, and political influence arising from their vast pastoral empires. The squatters were not all of this wealthy group, however, many struggled to survive, and few of the squatters had legal title to the land they developed.

Of course, the protection of their holdings or families does not justify or legalise any brutal acts of violence other than those of self-defence. In response, Colonial Governments hanged Colonists for murdering Aborigines and Aborigines for the same crimes committed against Colonists. Clearly, not enough was done to protect either the squatters or the Aborigines from the inevitable conflict which arose from the ensuing clash of cultures. That is, cultures based on individual private property vs communal tribal property. Essentially, this clash of cultures lies at the heart of the conflict between the Aboriginal tribes and British settlers. Today, Australia faces a similar class of cultures owing to its policies of mass-immigration and multiculturalism. This modern-day clash of cultures has not reached the level of violence experienced by the settlers and Aborigines during the period of colonialisation.

It is true that some convicts and ex-convicts led by the overseers of sheep and cattle stations, and in later years even free settlers, did conduct massacres of Aborigines, and that is a brutal historical fact that we must recognise, because it is a part of Australia's colonial history. It is also true that some Aboriginal men attacked isolated settlers, which led to reprisals obsessed with revenge, especially when the women and/or children of the settlers were involved in the Aboriginal attack (theconversation.com). A massacre is defined today as the intentional killing of six or more relatively undefended people in the one event (c21ch.newcastle.edu.au). All these actions were, of course, illegal. In some cases they were also racist.

The most commonly recognised massacre of about 28 Aborigines was the Myall Creek Massacre (1838) which occurred between Moree and Inverell in Northern New South Wales. At the time there were acts of violence being committed against Aborigines and non-Aborigines alike. Twelve Europeans were involved in the massacre. Following the arrest and trial of the perpetrators, seven were found guilty of murder and publicly hanged at the Sydney Goal in 1838 for their crime, four were acquitted, and their leader, John Henry Fleming, evaded arrest and was never tried (mhnsu.au, Dec 2022).

There are also records of Aborigines killing squatters or settlers. The largest and most publicised massacre of white settlers occurred in 1861 at Cullin-la-ringo in central Queensland when a group of at least 50 Aborigines, in a revenge attack for the murder of several of their men in a separate incident not related to these newly arriving settlers, attacked and killed 19 (including men, women, children and one infant baby) of the 25 white settlers who had set up a temporary camp. What followed was a frenzied revenge attack on the Aborigines when police and native police carried out a massacre of their own. From the official account, the number of Aboriginal casualties was *very high*, but there is no further detail. Another contemporary account said the police, 'overtook a tribe of natives, shot down *sixty or seventy*, and ceased firing when their ammunition was expended' (Wikipedia, 2025). Another contemporary account estimates the death count as 'probably not under 300, and of these 100 may be assumed as the number of fighting men' (SMH, *The Wills Tragedy*, 16 Nov 1861). Since no official number of Aboriginal casualties was recorded in official reports at the time, it has left the size of this massacre open to speculation.

What is most disturbing about this whole tragedy is the number of innocent Aboriginal and non-Aboriginal victims who were caught up in these massacres. Such is the sad, bitterly painful history of the colonial settlement of Australia.

What can be observed from both these incidents, the Myall Creek Massacre and the Cullin-la-ringo massacres, is that tension was high between the Aborigines and the settlers and that any incident could spark reprisal or revenge attacks against each other. However, these massacres were mainly isolated incidents. What was more common was Aborigines who raided and stole isolated settlers' property, and sometimes killed them, as well as pioneering squatters and settlers who killed Aborigines in defence of their property and families.

This violent activity was by no means universal. Some districts, for example, were peacefully settled while others ended in conflict, and acts such as massacres were never sanctioned by the Colonial Governments. In fact, the official policy directive of the Colonial Office in Britain charged the Governors with the responsibility of maintaining *friendly relations* with the Aborigines and *assimilating* them into the new settlement. It is true that the Queensland Mounted Native Police, which consisted of Aboriginal troopers and trackers led by white officers was given orders by the Colonial Government to disperse gatherings of Aborigines by firing at them. Each detachment of Native Police consisted of six or eight Aboriginal troopers led by one European officer. How many Aborigines were killed under this order is disputed, and it is difficult to determine or estimate how many fell victim to this order, owing to bureaucratic neglect, natural disasters (fires, floods etc.) destroying records, and intentional destruction of records.

Some historians today argue the case for the existence of a *frontier war*. The most prominent historian to argue the case for this is Henry Reynolds (1938-), Professor of History and 2015 Tasmanian Senior of the Year Award in his books, *The Other Side of the Frontier* (1981) and *Forgotten War* (2013). His main critic is Dr Keith Windschuttle (1942-2025), historian and author, whose book *The Fabrication of Aboriginal History* (2002) offers a counter argument. Reynolds argues that an estimate of violent Aboriginal deaths during the colonial period of settlement amounts to about 10,000+ and therefore constitutes a war against Aborigines. This figure is arrived at by mathematical formula. Since the number of settler deaths at the hands of Aborigines is known, it was assumed that the death rate would be 10 to 1 (AI Overview, 2025). Notice that even the 10 to 1 ratio does not account for the over 300 Aborigines claimed to have been killed by the SMH in the Cullin-la-ringo massacre, since the settler death toll was only 19. Windschuttle argues that the incidents of violence and massacres were isolated and sporadic and that Aboriginal and settler deaths owing to violence can be totalled in the 100s. How do these two eminent historians arrive at such differing totals for Aboriginal and non-Aboriginal deaths at the hands of each other?

I would urge you to read these two books before coming to any conclusions about a frontier war. There is also a fine debate on YouTube between these two historians debating this topic that you should view.

Having done your research, what is your opinion about the frontier war? Which argument do you consider the most probable?

Two other observations about this issue made by those who question the validity of a Frontier War relate to archaeological evidence and settler celebration. We know what the bones of people who died in their hundreds from sabre attack or musket fire look like. Archaeologists have unearthed the bones of those who died in the battle of Waterloo (a battle fought with similar weapons to that of the suggested frontier war) and were buried in mass graves. This tells the story. We also know what two battles fought in the frontier war in the USA look like. You can go to the battleground of Little Big Horn where the US 7thCalvary (260 troopers) was wiped out and the battleground at Wounded Knee where approximately 150-200 Lakota Indians were massacred. To date, no similar bones or battlegrounds that would suggest massacres of this scale have been found by Australian archaeologists searching the sites that have been identified as likely massacre sights by Aborigines, nor are there any official historical records of such events (dark-emu-exposed.org, 2025).

The second observation is that if the majority of settlers and the colonial governments conducted a frontier war or engaged in deliberate genocide, why then did the settlers and governments not celebrate the Aboriginal massacres? Which is also a universal and timeless practice of those at war at this time. Why is it that known incidents of massacres were investigated and the murderers brought to justice? Even if a claim for a guerilla war is made, the incidents of resistance must be on a scale much larger than we have evidence for, otherwise we simply have a history of isolated incidents which does not represent a war. Dr Keith Windschuttle argues that these incidents were mainly ones of violent robbery with no intention of armed resistance against colonial settlement. There is no solid evidence of armed resistance on a scale that would represent a guerilla war. Separate Aboriginal tribes did not unite and attack settlers, and neither did the Colonial Governments mobilise an army to deliberately track down and kill Aborigines. In fact, separate Aboriginal tribes continued to engage in 'blood feuds' against each other which still exist, even today. Those Aborigines who were tracked by Aboriginal trackers had been deemed criminals with a warrant put out for their arrest. Also, wars end in treaties, and there were no treaties signed by Aborigines and Colonial Governments.

Those who argue the frontier war theory claim that those who massacred Aborigines disposed of their bodies by cremation in order to hide their crime. Keith Windschuttle points out a problem that arises with this theory when the amount of fuel (timber) needed to dispose of massacred corpses in this way is considered. In some remote marginal areas there is simply not enough fuel, and larger cremation activities would leave archaeological evidence for us to discover today.

Some point to the extinction of Tasmanian Aborigines as an example of *deliberate Colonial genocide*. The only existing Tasmanian Aborigines today, for example, are of mixed race, so Tasmanian Aborigines did cohabit with settlers, some Aboriginal Tasmanian women marrying or living in de facto relationships with male settlers and establishing families. Statistics do not reveal as to how many colonial women entered into relationships with Tasmanian Aboriginal men and produced offspring (utas.edu.au, 2025).

What happened to the Tasmanian Aborigines? European settlement of Tasmania first travelled up the Huon Valley from Hobart (established in 1804) then on to Launceston (established in 1858), south to north. The seasonal migration of Aboriginal Tasmanians travelled from the east to west. This meant the paths of the settlers and the Aborigines brought them into constant contact.

Over time it became apparent that the Tasmanian Aborigines were in danger of becoming extinct (the impact of tribal warfare; diseases introduced by passing ships, mainly seal hunters, before colonial settlement; settler-introduced diseases and to a lesser extent settler conflict was taking a terrible toll on them). Diseases like smallpox, influenza, measles and tuberculosis could possibly account for somewhere between 70% and 90% of Tasmanian Aboriginal deaths (AI Overview, 2025). At the time of settlement, European settlers had little understanding of the causes and spreading of these diseases and died from these diseases themselves, although not in the same devastating numbers as that experienced by the Aborigines. In 1830, Governor Arthur recruited over 2,000 men to form a line and move all remaining Tasmanian Aborigines into the Tasman Peninsula for their own protection. This failed because the line lacked the required number of men to prevent the Aborigines from slipping through it at night. This became known infamously as *The Black Line*. The decline in Aboriginal numbers continued.

To deal with this issue, George Augustus Robinson, with the support of Tasmanian Aborigines like Truganini and Woureddy, were able to move the remaining Aborigines to Flinders Island in the Bass Straight where they established the settlement of Wybalenna which provided food, shelter, clothing, education, and spiritual guidance for the Aboriginal settlers. The intention was to bring Tasmanian Aborigines into the modern world by establishing a settlement of their own. This too failed. Nobody knows definitively why the numbers continued to decline, but they did. Some have speculated that the new settlers on Flinders Island failed to acclimatise, that the climate and terrain did not suit the new settlers and was unsuitable for establishing a modern settlement. Others have argued that they suffered from a spiritual sickness over a longing for their ancestral lands. Whatever the reason, as a race, they continued to die out. Much is made about the cemetery at Wybalenna. Some graves were reserved for particular Tasmanian Aboriginal settlers and some were buried in unmarked graves, but this is not unusual practice for cemeteries, even today.

In 1847, the few remaining Tasmanian Aborigines from Wybalenna were relocated to Oyster Bay, south of Hobart. Regrettably, this did not arrest the decline. The last of the Tasmanian Aborigines to die was Truganini, who died in 1876 in Hobart.

Looking back over what I have written about this sorrowful event leaves me with a sense of regret that my objectivity has failed to encapsulate the full tragedy of the extinction of a race of people. However, what this objectivity has revealed is that successive Tasmanian Colonial Governments were aware of the danger posed by the colonial settlement on Tasmanian Aborigines and that they took official action, however ineffective, to address that danger. This was a tragedy but does not suggest a *deliberate act of genocide* by either the colonial settlers (intermarriage) or the Colonial Governments. Nevertheless, it is an undeniable fact of history that the colonial settlement of Tasmania did lead to the extinction of Tasmanian Aborigines.

Clearly, both sides of the conflict arising between colonial settlers and Aborigines, in Tasmania and on the Mainland, suffered injustice and violence at the hands of each other. This was indeed a dark chapter in our history, but we need to understand and empathise with both sides of this conflict. The Aborigines because they saw their land being used for a purpose different from their hunter-gatherer culture and the Colonists because they were protecting their own families and property. What needs to be kept in mind about this conflict, however, is that if the graziers and farmers had not established a successful primary industry in Australia, we would not have the Nation State we have today. For a nation such as ours to exist today it had to be founded on a food surplus being produced, which is true with all other nations and civilisations throughout history.

If you condemn outright the graziers and famers of our colonial history today for what they did, are you failing to recognise your ancestral debt by continuing to enjoy the benefits of the nation that their sacrifice established for you?

Later when Colonial Governments sought the close settlement of land occupied by some of the squatters, they passed individual land acts that allowed for the free selection of Crown Land. Since most of the land occupied by the squatters had not been granted to them by the Colonial Governments, it was subject to the new land acts. Consequently, both the squatters and the selectors sought to maximise their advantages in the ensuing scramble for land. Many pioneers who had opened up the unsettled lands for the running of sheep and cattle stations lost their lands to the new selectors. The conflict between the existing squatters, the new landowners, and the Aborigines continued, but by this time the Colonial Governments had established a constabulary which included Aboriginal troopers and trackers, enabling them to enforce the laws of the colonies more efficiently.

According to Stuart Banner, the concept (but not the term *terra nullius*) was first used in a tax dispute case between Barron Field and the Governor of New South Wales Lauchlan Macquarie in 1819. It was not until 1835, however, that New South Wales colonial Governor Richard Bourke proclaimed the legal principle of *terra nullius*, some 47 years after Captain Arthur Phillip's proclamation (Stuart Banner, Professor of Law at UCLA, *Why Terra Nullius? Anthropology and Property Law in Early Australia,* published in *the Law and History Review,* 2005). Professor Banner argues that *terra nullius* was a deliberate fiction concocted by the British Government to justify their taking of aboriginal land and not an accurate reflection of the land's actual state. So the term *terra nullius* is a 19th century concept and not a concept used at the time of Australia's foundation in the 18th century when the land was taken by proclamation.

Since the term *terra nullius* is a Latin expression meaning 'nobody's land', does this suggest an apparent change of concept about the settlement of Australia? That is, the international right of an Imperial power to settle and establish colonial governments in lands occupied by separate paleolithic tribes with no legalised system of land ownership, as opposed to a dominate power invading and occupying unceded land. The truth is that there was no change. This is not difficult to understand, because those declaring *terra nullius* as the legal justification for settlement did recognise that there were people already living here. The British established a free settlement colony and created the agricultural and grazing industries necessary for a Nation State to develop precisely because they knew that they had a legal right to the land by way of the internationally recognised laws of settlement. They knew this, because they viewed the land as belonging to 'nobody' owing to it not being used for farming or grazing, not because it was unoccupied. The Australian Aborigines lost the land they occupied in the same way that the squatters lost theirs at a later date. They both lost it because they had no legal title to it. If this were not the case, why would the settlers have endured all the hardship and deprivation needed to achieve what they did?

So their interpretation of *nobody's land* meant that the land was not being used in a productive capacity, not because there were no people living here. The claim that present-day Aborigines make about their ancestors not ceding their tribal land to the settlers is legally invalid, because Britain had the legal right to settle those lands according to internationally recognised law as it existed at that time. The land was never ceded because it was not necessary for it to be ceded. There was also no treaty signed to end a war, nor any treaty to facilitate the establishment of a trading colony, because these too were not necessary. Also, Aborigines past and present accepted the rights and benefits afforded to them from British subjectship, wards of the State, and later Australian citizenship. Is this not also an acceptance of the colonial and later the national system of governance that provided those rights and benefits to them?

If Australian Aborigines past and present accepted and today accept the rights and benefits provided by the settlement and development of Australia, have they not also accepted the land ownership laws that in the past provided and today provides those rights and benefits?

The British colonial settlement of Australia, then, led to the creation of our independent Nation State. That is, that the British Empire faded into history and all Australians today have equal citizenship rights under our current liberal democratic form of governance which protects the liberty of all Australians. British colonialism in Australia ended following the passing of The Commonwealth of Australia Constitution Act 1900 by the British Parliament. On 17th September 1900 her majesty, Queen Victoria, proclaimed that the Commonwealth of Australia would come into existence on 1st January 1901 and on that date Lord Hopetown, our first Governor General, declared it so, and the Nation State of Australia was born. So you see the struggle for independence from the British Empire by Aborigines and non-Aborigines has already been fought and won. What some are suggesting now has nothing to do with British colonialism. Rather, it involves the breaking apart of the Australian Nation State, so may I respectfully ask, what precisely are you suggesting we exchange our Nation State and Australian citizenship rights for?

Australia became a nation state after six separate colonies became states of the Commonwealth of Australia. Crown Land then came under the control of Local Councils, and State and Federal governments. Also, there is confusion today over the ownership of Crown Land. Our current Constitutional Monarch, King Charles III, holds Crown Land *in trust* for the people of Australia. The people of Australia own their country, not the Crown. In this way the country of Australia is owned by the individual citizens of Australia. When Crown Land is released for development, for example, the Crown derives no benefit from it, only the different councils and governments releasing the land receive benefits in the name of the people of Australia. The councils and governments of Australia have full control over Crown Land, not the Monarch who symbolically endorses the actions of our councils and governments. They make the decisions regarding its release, how it will be used and derive the benefits for its release in the name of the citizens of Australia. Today, when Crown land is ceded to Native Title, it is not ceded by the Crown but granted by the citizens of Australia through their elected government representatives.

When Australia became a Nation State in 1901, the status of Australian Aborigines shifted from British subjects to wards of the state. This was a patronising attitude by the Founders of Australia, because it highlights a belief that Australian Aborigines were incapable of looking after themselves and needed the protection of the State to care for them.

On 27th May 1967, a Constitutional Amendment referendum recognised that Australian Aborigines and Torres Strait Islanders should have equal rights to other Australians. The referendum passed with an overwhelming majority (more than 90% of Australians voted 'Yes', *reconcilliation.org.au*, 2025) and any forms of discrimination against Aboriginal and Torres Strait Islander peoples was removed. If you consider the age limitation for voting at this time (21 years of age), you discover that the only 'baby boomer generation' (1946-64) citizens, the post WWII generation, who voted in this referendum were those born in 1946, others were simply too young to vote, so this referendum was carried overwhelmingly by the parents of the baby boomers, those who had fought alongside Aborigines to protect Australia from a Japanese invasion, and who believed that Australian Aborigines should have equal rights to all other Australians. Also, there is a common misconception that Australian Aborigines and Torres Straight Islanders were given the right to vote in this referendum. This is not true because both groups already had full voting rights before this referendum (museum.wa.gov.au, *Right Wrongs: 67 Referendum 50 years on*, 2017). Another misconception is that this referendum overturned a 'Flora and Fauna Act' that classified Aboriginal people alongside Australia's flora and fauna. No such act ever existed (abc.net.au/news/fact-check, 19 March 2018).

Chapter 8: New World Issues

In 1972, the baby boomer generation were finding their voting power and imbued with feelings of compassion over the impoverished images of Aborigines living in remote communities displayed regularly on their television screens. Consequently, the Australian Government established the Commonwealth Department of Aboriginal Affairs to assume responsibility for all issues related to Aboriginal and Torres Strait Islander peoples. Once again, for compassionate reasons, the Aboriginal and Torres Strait Islander people were placed back into a dependency role by a Federal Government who maintained a paternalistic attitude towards them. What emerged from this was a program to 'close the gap' between Aborigines living not only in remote communities but throughout Australia and other non-Aboriginal Australian citizens.

What this program fails to recognise is that those Aborigines living in remote communities are expected to maintain their tribal culture (guaranteed by Native Title) yet reach a standard of living equal to that of a fully industrialised and economically diverse culture. Since Aboriginal tribal culture cannot produce a standard of living equal to a modern developed economy without movement from the remote communities and significant change to the tribal culture itself, this placed those Aborigines in a constant state of dependency. Even non-Aboriginal citizens living in remote, isolated regions of Australia today are unable to maintain a standard of living equal to that of city dwelling citizens. The only Australian Aborigines who had liberated themselves from this state of dependency and 'closed the gap' were those Aborigines who had successfully assimilated into mainstream Australian culture, while still recognising and respecting the tribal culture of their ancestors, similar to what all other non-Aboriginal members of Australian culture are expected to do. What this created was a division within the Aboriginal community between those who had successfully assimilated into mainstream Australian culture and those who had not.

Terra nullius was overturned by the High Court of Australia's Mabo decision in 1992. This established Native Title based on traditional ownership of land and water and recognises a *pre-existing title*. That is, pre-existing to colonial settlement. Native title is inalienable and enduring. It cannot be sold or transferred freely like other freehold land; it can only be surrendered to the Crown or extinguished. Native Title grants land to different Aboriginal tribes and gives them the exclusive right to occupy an area at the exclusion of all other Australians, including Aborigines from other tribes.

Since the Mabo decision of the High Court of Australia created a structural change to Australia's land ownership based on prior ownership, it was not a reformist but a radical change. It was based on the socialist principle of selective historical injustice and overturned the democratic principle of equal access of all democratic citizens to the land of their country once it is released by the Crown.

Recently, the Federal Court recognised Native Title *non-exclusive* rights over 365,000 hectares of land and water located on the Sunshine Coast in Queensland. These waterways, freehold title, and Crown lands were already owned by the Queensland State Government, the local councils (parks, costal shoreline, and vacant crown land) and private citizens under the Torrens Land Title system of land ownership. Since then, an Indigenous Land Council has requested a surf lifesaving club on the Sunshine Coast pay $500 for a Welcome to Country Ceremony before they use the beach (couriermail.com.au, 2024). The Butchulla tribe have native title rights over the land at Hervey Bay and a strip of foreshore at Burrum Heads. There was a claim by some residents of Burrum Heads that they had been denied access to the beach (news.com.au, 19 June 2025). However,

> *the Butchulla Native Title Aboriginal Corporation has clarified that they do not seek to prevent public access to the beach or charge visitors for access.*
>
> (AI Overview, 2025)

How this will play out in future is yet to be determined, because in 2023 the Western Australian Government repealed similar Land Rights legislation for practical reasons.

Native Title land is not subject to the same rates and taxes imposed on land owned under Freehold Title. Royalties paid for mining on Native Title aboriginal land, for example, are not subject to taxation if the money is used for the tribal community. Senator Jacinta Nampijinpa Price has called for a forensic audit of the distribution of these royalties and government funding to remote communities flowing into these tribal communities since the improvements, in her opinion, do not match the royalties and government funds paid into them.

Land rights, on the other hand, are rights created by the Australian States, and Territory Governments. This usually establishes freehold or perpetual lease title to Aboriginal Australians only.

Whenever a group of Australian citizens, identifying as an Aboriginal tribe, files a Native Title or Land Rights claim, the Australian or State taxpayers pay all their legal costs. If individual Australian citizens want to challenge the claim, they must pay their own legal cost. If a Local Council challenges the claim, ratepayers must pay the legal costs. If a State Government or the Australian Government challenges the claim, their taxpayers must pay the legal costs. The legal costs of Native Title claims alone has already cost the Federal Government of Australia 100s of millions of dollars (cgc.gov.au). Native Title and Land Rights has created a bonanza for the legal profession.

The Mabo decision by five of six judges of the High Court of Australia, not democratically elected by the citizens of Australia but rather appointed by the Governor General on the formal advice of the Attorney General following the approval of the Prime Minister and Cabinet, I contend, was ill-considered on three counts: legality, democracy, and national division.

The legal decision was ill-considered because it overturned the legal precedent of settlement stretching back as far as our homo sapien ancestors' migration out of Africa and the recorded history of all civilisations since the emergence of the first civilisation in the fertile river valley of the Tigris and Euphrates rivers. It had been confirmed by the Supreme Court of New South Wales, the Privy Council of Britain, and the High Court of Australia up until 1992, so the legal precedent had clearly been established.

It was also ill-considered on the grounds of being an undemocratic decision made in a democratic nation. In a democratic nation all the citizens, both Aboriginal and non-Aboriginal, own the unreleased land of their country and have equal access to newly released land. This is covered in their unwritten but culturally accepted rights to private property ownership and is a cornerstone of their liberty.

Furthermore, it was also ill-considered on the grounds of national division because it created a second Australian nation, one based on tribal racial hereditary rather than democratic equality of access to land ownership. To be clear, it was an undemocratic decision made in a democratic nation which divided the Australian nation into two separate people based on race. One group of Australians based their land ownership on the Torrens Land Title of land ownership and the other on Native Title and Land Rights State legislation of land ownership. The decision, in the minds of some, transitioned an ever-growing proportion of land ownership, currently standing at 40% (AI Overview, 2025) with more to come (dailymail.com.uk, *Stunning map shows the extent of Native Title control in Australia, Sept 1, 2025*) in Australia from a democracy (upholding equal citizenship right to private ownership of land) to an autocracy (upholding a privileged class of land ownership based on heredity).

Here is another debating topic for you and your family and friends, and again, ask your teacher if he/she would set up a class debate on this topic –

> *That the High Court Mabo decision has established a landed aristocracy based on heredity in democratic Australia.*

The Australian people were promised that the granting of Native

Title and Land Rights would result in reconciliation and a 'closing of the gap' between Aboriginal and non-Aboriginal Australians. They received the opposite result. The division between Aboriginal and non-Aboriginal Australians widened and deepened, and the standard of living gap has never been overcome. Such was the result of the decision of five High Court judges, an undemocratic and divisive decision based not on legal precedent, democracy or national unity but the principle of selective historical injustice found in radical, socialist ideology.

Ask yourself, why are socialists selective in addressing only the historical injustice found in European Colonialism and not the historical injustice found anywhere else in history? This is not historical injustice but rather selective historical injustice that is being pursued. Do you detect a hidden agenda at work here? Does the cause of selective historical injustice create a new political power base and a new flow of money? If so, who are the beneficiaries of this new arrangement of power and money? Who are the ones who not only fail to benefit from this new arrangement, but are disadvantaged by it?

What is not clearly understood by non-Aboriginal Australians today is that the principle of *prior ownership* of Australia does undermine the legal standing of those who own freehold title under the Torrens System of Land Title. This principle underpins the cry of 'Stolen Land!' by those who claim Aboriginal tribal ownership of all the land of Australia. When Aboriginal and non-Aboriginal Australians alike say things like 'we are standing on (insert Aboriginal tribe's name) land' or 'this land always was, always will be Aboriginal land' they are referring to the principle of prior ownership established by the Mabo decision of the High Court of Australia. It is precisely because of the expectations raised by this undemocratic decision of the High Court of Australia that has led to these new claims.

At the Anzac Day ceremony conducted at the War Memorial in Canberra on 25th April 2025 some in the audience booed when the *Welcome to Country Ceremony* was being performed. Later, a veteran said that he was offended by the ceremony which suggested that Australia did not belong to him and those who had fought, bled and died for their country. This created a controversy that is still debated today.

Does the Welcome to Country Ceremony conducted by Aborigines at many events in Australia have a hidden agenda? Dr Stephen Chavura (Senior Lecturer in History at Campion College) has suggested that

> on the surface we are told that the ceremony is nothing more than a friendly, non-political ceremony. Much like one person welcoming someone else into their town. That it should not be seen as a divisive instrument. However, academics when talking to a left leaning audience deliver a very different story. For example, Associate Professor in Indigenous Studies at Melbourne University, Jessa Rogers wrote in the Sydney Morning Herald, after the Anzac Day Ceremony, that the Welcome to Country Ceremony is about reminding Australians that they are standing on sovereign indigenous land that has never been ceded.
>
> (Topher Project, 2025)

This suggests that, in the eyes of radical socialists and those who support them, the public explanation stating the purpose behind Welcome to Country is duplicitous.

Again, does this suggest a hidden agenda? If so, would this create a new flow of money and who would be the beneficiaries and who would be the losers? What new power structure would be created? This is an issue that greatly affects all Australians so why not discuss it with your family and friends.

Since prior ownership does now exist, how can the High Court of Australia justify carving out freehold title and prohibit Aborigines from claiming it? Surely, if prior ownership does give land ownership to individual Aboriginal tribes, then does it not logically follow that the Torrens System of Land ownership merely give its title holders possession of stolen property? Today the High Court says 'no', but didn't the Colonial Supreme Courts, the Privy Council and High Court of Australia once declare the right of land ownership exclusively to the Crown, British subjects, and Australian citizens who bought land once it was released by the governments of the day?

Once again, I am now moving into the area of personal truth, so make allowances for that fact when evaluating what I am about to say. When I explain that none of my ancestors killed any Aborigines, that they and I paid for all the land we owned in the past or own today, that Aboriginal Australians fought alongside my ancestors and me in defence of our nation state and the liberty of its citizens, that all Australians were willing to die for their liberal democracy and our Nation State and, therefore, must have seen something worth preserving in it, I am mockingly informed,

Oh. So that's how you justify stealing our land.

I tire of such condescension but must admit that the High Court of Australia's Mabo decision has created a logical and legal case for their argument. Most Australians would point out that these words are only spoken by a radical minority. However, radical minority dissention, usually violent and unlawful, has a nasty habit in Australia of creating expectations that grow into fully-fledged legal challenges to established socio/political norms. Especially if it is supported by radical socialist academics who are not subjected to outspoken resistance from conservatives wanting to protect those established norms, or if the laws protecting the majority are not enforced.

The legal principle of prior ownership makes second-class citizens of non-Aboriginal Australians. Love of country is something that non-Aboriginal Australians have fought for and expressed a love for in their literature and actions since Australia's foundation. Yet, those same Australians are now told that their love for and ownership of this land is subordinate to that of selected Aboriginal tribes. Should all Australian citizens have equal access to their local parks, their beaches, their rivers, the natural forests of their state and national parks as those of selective tribal Aboriginal descent? Remember some of these parks have now been granted to individual Aboriginal tribes, like Uluru (previously Ayres Rock National Park), Kati-Thanda (previously Lake Eyre National Park), Dyurrite (previously The Mount Arapiles-Tooan State Park), Wollumbin (previously Mount Warning National Park), and K'gari (previously Fraser Island National Park). Other Aboriginal tribes and non-Aboriginal Australians must now first seek permission from the traditional Aboriginal tribal owners before being able to enjoy what was once equally available to all Australians. Those in authority who have allowed this takeover of Australia's National and State Parks should be ashamed of their lack of political courage to stand for democracy over the radical socialist ideology that has robbed all Australian citizens of their free democratic right to enjoy the delights of what was once their own State and National Parks.

And so our discussion has come full circle. Now we must decide who are the enlightened heroes in this scenario? Are they the ones who cry for justice for a radically conceived, assertively pursued selective historic wrong, or the ones who insist on the established norms of liberty and liberal democracy? Australia now has reached a point where its citizens must choose between land ownership based on private property ownership or a return to a system of land ownership based on tribal hereditary. You may argue that we can have both, but that is not the position of radical socialist academics and radical dissidents, and even if it were it would not be the position of an enlightened liberal democratic society.

Let's move out of the personal and back into a more objective element of truth. How is the High Court's decision in the Mabo Case undemocratic and divisive?

> *Private property ownership is a fundamental element of free and democratic societies.*
>
> (Jacinta Nampijinpa Price,
> 'It's time to reform Native Title', CIS, 2024)

Chapter 8: New World Issues

What should be clear about Native Title and Land Rights is that it overturns the legal standing of land title established by the colonial period of Australia's history, and in doing so destroys a fundamental principle of our liberty, which holds that individual citizens living in a Nation State with a Liberal Democratic form of Government have an equal right to the property ownership of the land of their country either through the release of land to freehold title or the granting of leases, i.e., pastoral leases. That is, that the property of their country, once released by the Crown for private ownership, should be freehold or leased and available for purchase, lease or trade by all individual citizens. Alternatively, land reserved for National and State Parks should be open to all Australians and not taken from all Australians by Native Title or Land Rights legislation.

The existence of two separate land title systems is clearly undemocratic, owing to its attack on the democratic rights of Australian citizens to equality of land ownership. But can it be reversed? Land Rights legislation can be repealed, because it has been established by State legislation, so it can be repealed by State legislation. However, land ownership by citizens living in a liberal democracy cannot be taken away by government legislation without compensation, so Land Rights legislation can be repealed with adequate compensation being given to those already granted it. That is, Land Rights title can be replaced by freehold title under the Torrens Land title of ownership. Land Rights title given to individual Aboriginal tribes on State Parks would need compensation so that the parks would once again become freely available to all Australian citizens.

Native Title, however, has been granted by the High Court of Australia so can only be set aside by the High Court reversing its decision. That is, the High Court can overrule their previous decision regarding Native Title. This is highly unlikely given the current divisions within Australian society over this issue. Alternatively, a referendum can be held stating that only the Torrens Land Title system, and the principle of 'terra nullius' and no other land title system be constitutionally valid. If it carries, the High Court would be forced to reverse its decision, thereby ending the legal principle of 'prior ownership' and reinstating 'terra nullius'. Existing land title covered by Native Title would then be converted to the Torrens Land Title system, or adequate compensation being given in the case where National Parks are handed back to the citizens of Australia.

These actions would be beneficial for Aborigines currently holding Native Title since their land would then become valuable freehold land that they could sell or develop, within the rules governing all freehold land. In other words, they would gain the same ownership rights over their land as all other Australians. Alternatively, compensation for Native Title land on National Parks would need to be made so that all Australians could once again enjoy equal access to their National Parks. Consequently, all Australians would once again own their country and have their liberal democracy and equal citizenship rights restored.

Do you believe that all Australians should have equal rights to the ownership of their own country, or do you believe that some citizens should have rights to land ownership at the exclusion of all other citizens?

Seth Godin (American author and former dot com business executive) argues that,

> *Before we react, though, it might be worth asking 'and then what happens,' five times.*
> *Five steps from here to there...*
> *If any of the steps involve, 'and then a miracle happens,' or 'we'll deal with that later,' it might be worth taking a few more moments to reconsider the first step.*
> (https://seths.blog, 2022)

Is there a direct causal link between the High Court's Mabo decision and Senator Lidia Thorpe, after having burnt the Australian flag, standing with a large crowd of radical, dissident Australians on a street in Melbourne (2024), brandishing an Aboriginal war stick, and raising a hand coved in fake red blood while shouting, "This is war"? More recently, she shouted at King Charles III to 'give us our land back. Give us the land you stole from us. You are not my King.' (Royal couple's Parliamentary Reception, Parliament House, Oct 2024). Since then, she also has addressed a large crowd of pro-Palestinian protestors at a rally in Naarm where she claimed that those present were standing on stolen land. Recently, she stood outside Buckingham Palace in London and gave a rude gesture to those inside.

Do you think that the joining together of radical socialists and Islamists, claiming that the stolen lands of Palestine and Australia is the same struggle against colonial oppression, is a development destined to tear (potentially with violence) at the very fabric of Australian society? How could such a violent division in Australia's society have been allowed to fester and grow? If only the five Judges of the High Court of Australia had asked themselves, "and then what happens?" five times before handing down their decision, perhaps they would have foreseen the division their decision would bring to the streets of Australian cities, the halls of Australia's Parliament, and Australia's society over time.

It is an indisputable fact that Native Title and Land Rights have led to neither *reconciliation* nor a *closing of the gap*. I well remember being shocked and appalled by the squalor and poverty clearly evident in remote Aboriginal communities when their images first appeared on our television screens back in the late 1960s; images that have carried on ever since. This led to an outpouring of compassion and support for Aboriginal people. Australians always have been a fair-minded and generous people in their approach to these problems and have been disappointed with the results produced. Over the 50+ years of its implementation this approach has clearly failed, because reconciliation is nowhere in sight and the gap has not been closed. It is now time to question the efficacy of this approach by asking why it failed. Remember the popular definition of insanity –

> *The definition of insanity is doing the same thing over and over and expecting different results.*
>
> (quora.com, 2018)

One other development in Aboriginal rights worth mentioning here is the claim that Aborigines have a mystical, spiritual relationship with the land that non-Aborigines do not have. This results in non-Aborigines being told that they must respect the existence of Aboriginal, mythical, spiritual beings to the extent that billion dollar projects are cancelled because it might disturb these mythical creatures. One example of this is the cancellation of a billion dollar gold mining project in New South Wales because it would disturb the bees that floated down from the Southern Cross constellation and settled near a creek that a mining company wanted to use as a tailing dam, even after the local Aboriginal tribe had stated that they had never heard of that myth and had approved the project (theguardian.com, 2024). Other projects have been cancelled because of the existence of spiritual rainbow serpents in our waterways (www.smh.com.au, 2021), spiritual ocean serpents (www.afr.com.au, 2024) and spiritual whales that talk to Aborigines when they are over 100 kilometres from land (www.afr.com.au, 2024).

Also, there are a growing number of atheists and radicals, when told of Christian stories about Moses who parted the Red Sea or Jonah who lived inside the belly of a giant fish, who laugh and say those who believe in such nonsense are foolish. Clearly, Australians should respect the stories of transcendental truth arising from all religions and cultures, but not allow any of them to cancel vital national projects.

Another issue is the existence of Aboriginal sacred sites which trumps any form of development. What is now Suncorp Stadium was once Brisbane's first major cemetery. In the 1930s the last of the remaining memorials and headstones were removed from this site to make way for the improvement of drainage facilities at the then Lang Park sporting facilities. If the sacred Christian grave sites of non-Aboriginal citizens can be moved to make way for redevelopment, why can't Aboriginal sacred grave sites be subject to the same approach?

This is not to say that there are not some locations and buildings of significance that should be preserved. For example, the Customs House in Brisbane is listed with the National Trust on the grounds that it is culturally, architecturally and historically significant. Consequently, there are strict rules governing what can and can't be done to this building. On the other hand, Cloudland was demolished in 1982 to make way for an apartment complex. Although Cloudland was historically and culturally significant, it was deemed not to be architecturally significant. Similarly, Australian Aboriginal cave paintings and bora rings are rightly deemed culturally, historically, and artistically significant and in need of preservation, but are all rocks claimed as significant by Aborigines entitled to Aboriginal exclusivity? What about the climbing rights of Australian citizens to the mountains and cliff spaces found on national parks or the beauty of national parks themselves? Should these national treasures be the exclusive preserve of individual Aboriginal tribes?

What practical solutions can be suggested to 'close the gap'? If Aboriginal Australians are going to 'close the gap' and 'reconcile' with non-Aboriginal Australians, there must be a reconsideration of the non-Aboriginal, paternalistic approach to their needs.

This statement by Dr. Phil makes it abundantly clear –

> An enabler is a person who, acting out of a sincere sense of love, loyalty, and concern, steps in to protect, cover up for, make excuses for and become more responsible for the chemically dependent person. This can prevent the chemically dependent individual from confronting the crisis that might bring about change, and thereby prolong his/her illness.
>
> (Dr. Phil, *Are You an Enabler?* 2023)

Could it be that the approach adopted by non-Aborigines to solve the Aboriginal crisis is that of an enabler? Just like the enabler who prevents a chemically dependent person from confronting his/her addiction. In other words, is it the non-Aboriginal's paternalistic belief that is holding back Aborigines from confronting for themselves their own crisis? Could such an approach to this problem create a culture of low expectations? Put differently, does the paternalistic approach encourage those espousing it, including Aborigines, to believe that Aborigines are not capable of looking after themselves? What effect do you think this might have on the self-esteem of Aborigines? Surely, this is an example of the tyranny of low expectations.

Do you think it is better for individuals to believe that they can make a difference in their own lives through merit?

Warren Mundine, in his autobiography, *Black and White: Race, Politics and Changing Australia,* 2018, states that it is essential for welfare dependent people (both Aboriginal and non-Aboriginal) to participate in economic activity if they are to move out of poverty.

Good parents know that if they shower their children with money and privilege that their children have not earned for themselves, they will spoil their children; thus, making them unable to confront the hardships of modern life. Alternatively, if parents encourage their children to acquire the ability to become independent and self-reliant, they produce responsible adults. Might this self-reliant approach have relevance in bringing today's Australians together and help in closing the gap not only between Aborigines and non-Aborigines but also between all poverty-stricken Australians and others alike?

In conclusion, it is true that some Aboriginal Australians still suffer deprivation, but so too do an increasing number of non-Aboriginal Australians. Homelessness, poverty, and drug addiction have reached new heights among non-Aboriginal Australians since the 1960s. Some non-Aboriginal people now sleep on our city streets, in their cars, in our parks and in tents on the banks of our rivers. The majority of our elderly are undernourished or malnourished. Our aged pensioners make decisions about *eating or heating*. Of course, something must be done to alleviate the situation of those people who stand in need of help today, and that includes individuals from both Aboriginal and non-Aboriginal sections of the Australian community. What is questioned is not the need, but how Australians seek to resolve this issue.

Should help given to any individual (excluding those incapable of self-reliance, like those who are confronting a crisis, mentally or physically challenged, or elderly) be preceded by a commitment to change by those receiving the help, and should it be based on individual need and not group identity? In future, should society's help be matched by a commitment to self-help by capable citizens receiving assistance? In short, should we only help those who are prepared to help themselves? Do you think that those offered help without their commitment to self-help would remain dependent on their society and incapable of fulfilling their potential?

Given an honest, objective, and empathetic assessment of the above, while at the same time avoiding white guilt or impractical compassion, one can only conclude that the decision of five unelected High Court judges in their ill-considered Mabo determination was not based on legal precedence, was undemocratic, and was divisive.

Do you find my questions callous? Does my suggestion about granting benefits on the grounds of individual need and not group identity leave you cold? Or do you think that my suggestions regarding land ownership and individual need offer a way out of Australia's present-day crisis and avoid a potentially violent situation emerging in future?

How do we proceed from this point on? I suggest you ask yourself who you are as an Australian. What is your identity? Remember the importance of beneficence over malevolence, moral clarity over moral certainty or moral equivalence, unity over division, liberty over totalitarianism or authoritarianism. What are the principles you stand by? Proclaim those principles to other Australians and other nations throughout the world. Proclaim them, promote them, and stand by them. Do not surrender them to radical socialist ideology, radical elitism, or radical protest.

National Integrity

Here is one definition of national integrity –

> *National integrity refers to cohesion, unity, and harmony within a nation, where citizens respect each other's rights, uphold shared values, and work towards common goals, regardless of differences in ethnicity, religion, or socioeconomic status. It involves fostering a sense of belonging and loyalty to the nation, promoting social justice, and preserving the sovereignty and territorial integrity of the country.*
> (medium.com, Saku Khosa, *Definition of national integrity* Aug 29, 2024)

This definition of national integrity includes 'social justice'. Here I differ from Saku, because I believe in *equal justice* rather *social justice*. Social justice promotes disunity (divides a nation into groups) and equity (where big government takes a larger share of a nation's GDP through higher taxation), while equal justice achieves unity (through individual rights) and equality of opportunity (through lower taxation and equal access to private property). Under social justice individual members of a nation state are not equal because members of select groups are entitled to more government benefits than other individual members. Under equal justice government benefits are distributed according to individual need and not group identity.

One of the ways that a nation achieves integrity is through the telling of its heroic narrative. Mythologist Joseph Campbell first described the overarching Heroic Narrative in his book, *The Hero with a Thousand Faces*. In his book he points out the elements of a heroic narrative found in Classic Mythology and Modern Literature. From the Greeks we have figures like Heracles and his impossible

Twelve Labours, Achilles the greatest of warriors and his desire for a tragic fate, Jason leader of the Argonauts and his quest for the Golden Fleece, to mention just three. From the British we have King Arthur and his knights of the round table fighting for his people, and St. George who slayed the dragon that threatened an English village. Even very modern stories fulfil the heroic narrative. For example, the stories of Harry Potter who seeks to destroy Lord Voldemort and Luke Skywalker from Star Wars who struggles to find the hidden Sith world of Exegol. Without going into the elements of a heroic narrative, I will describe the hero narrative that, in the past, maintained Australia's national integrity.

It begins with the arrival of Australia's Aborigines at least 40-50,000 years ago. Australian Aborigines settled Australia and took up tribal lands. Within their tribal lands, they exploited the natural recourses they found in its flora and fauna, controlled their tribal population sizes, and developed the technology necessary for life in a palaeolithic tribe. Theirs was a heroic achievement based on courage, superb hunting and tracking skills, and tribal unity, as well as a dreamtime connection with their tribal lands. However, Australia's Aborigines had no concept of Australia, because their experience was limited to the borders of their tribal lands.

Next came the British who established convict and free settlements around all of Australia, Tasmania, and the Norfolk and Torres Strait Islands. It took courage to cross the oceans in sailing ships that were highly vulnerable to the weather. They were at risk of strong winds, rough seas, and capsizing. It required accurate weather forecasting, precise navigation, seamanship, and skilled boat maintenance to make each journey as safe as possible.

Later, the explorers needed all their bravery, optimism, and adaptability to complete their explorations, discover the continent of Australia, map it, and open it up to the graziers and farmers who followed them. They also needed the necessary material items to sustain them. If they were on foot, they needed backpacks, compasses, and essential supplies like food and water. Larger expeditions also needed horses, wagons, and camping gear, as well as essential supplies.

The colonial graziers and farmers required the courage and bravery of their predecessors as well as resilience, determination, resourcefulness and a capacity for hard work to establish their stations and farms. They also required livestock, which they had to know how to handle and bring with them, and materials to build simple structures like huts and homesteads, using local timber, bark, and mud. Finally, they needed access to capital, and vacant Crown land in order to turn unproductive land into the food surplus gained from their ambitious and enterprising ventures. Theirs was a different, but complimentary story to that of Australia's Aboriginal people, both being settlers who sustained their cultures.

Next our Aboriginal and non-Aboriginal ancestors had to struggle against the British Empire to establish our current nation state based on liberal democracy and regulated capitalism. Sometimes this struggle entailed the spilling of blood, but the venture eventually achieved its goal on 1st January 1901. Again, this took bravery and courage along with determination, and a fierce commitment to liberty.

In the wars that followed to protect our Nation State and its liberty, both Aborigines and non-Aborigines combined in a spirit of mateship that maintained Australia's national integrity. Additionally, the immigration of people from all the countries of the world has created Australia's magnificent cities, and its vibrant and versatile economy which includes our primary, secondary, and tertiary industries. All Australians contributed to this accomplishment so all Australians should take pride in their hard work, diligence and resourcefulness in creating the outstanding, modern, Nation State of Australia and its national integrity.

Australia's national flag is an appropriate symbol for Australia's heroic narrative. First is the sky-blue background of the flag. Those Australians who travel overseas, as well as visitors to Australia, always comment on the uniqueness of Australia's deep blue sky. This represents the beauty of our nation and its embrace of all Australians. It is a unifying symbol for all Australians. The Southern Cross signifies Australia's geographic location in the southern hemisphere with its ancient, timeless quality, and Australia's rich, Aboriginal history and their dreamtime connection to it. It also acts as a symbol of the navigation skills of its early voyagers and explorers together with its historical significance by having been used in earlier colonial flags and as a symbol of defiance during the Eureka stockade. The Union Jack represents the foundation of modern Australia and the British cultural traditions found in Australia's current culture, like liberty, democracy, regulated capitalism, equality, and fairness. Finally, the seven-pointed star represents the unity of all the people who inhabit the six states and territories of Australia.

What better symbol could Australia have to represent its national integrity and the unity of its people. An integrity that Australia's current generation must fight, with all the courage, bravery, and determinisation of their ancestors if they are to keep Australia's cohesion, unity, and harmony, currently under threat from globalist aspirations, communist subversion, and theocratic control.

Possible Solutions for Three Current Problems

Australians today face a number of problems other than integrity. I will address only three of the more prominent ones I consider need urgent attention. They are obesity, overweight and pride in Australia, the dignity of work, and housing affordability. Although these problems are not related to integrity, if addressed they will make the task of Australia regaining its integrity a little easier.

Obesity, Overweight and Pride in Australia

One serious problem Australians face today is an undesirable high level of obesity and excess of body weight. Another is holding pride in their country.

> *2 in 3 (66%) of adults were overweight or obese in 2022. 34% were overweight but not obese and 32% were obese. Australia had the 10th highest proportion of overweight or obese people aged 15+ among 21 OECD member countries in 2022.*
> (Australian Institute of Health and Welfare, 2024)

Another problem is the number of young people who are too ashamed to fight for Australia –

> *One in five young Aussies are not proud (of being Australian). Researchers say the figures are a result of the indoctrination of young people at school to feel embarrassed about their own country.*
> (Dailytelegraph.com.au, 2022)

> *Only 32% of those aged 18-24 said they would stay and fight (for their country) and 40% said they would leave the country (28% were unsure) ...*
> (The Institute of Public Affairs, 2022)

Another problem for Australia generally is the shortfall in ADF recruitment. In a Senate Estimates committee held in February 2024, the then Chief of Defence Force General Angus Campbell said,

> *'Recruiting and retention, Defence is addressing retention and recruitment as a priority. As of 1 January 2024, the ADF is 6.9%, or 4,308, below its authorised strength (of total 62,735)'.*
> (defenceconnect.com.au 2024)

These are disturbing statists about our younger generation and Australia's defence recruitment. Remember, if you are obese or overweight you *will* suffer health problems and if you are not prepared to defend your country you *will* lose it. Better to lose weight and keep your country.

Both these problems can be addressed by the same possible solution: the introduction of National Service.

Please hear me out before dismissing this possible solution. Our youth could participate in a one-year National Service programme for all 17-year-olds at the end of their High School years before becoming adults at 18 years of age. It should be considered as part of their education, not as expanding Australia's military capacity. It could also be mandatory for all immigrants (with an exception given for the elderly under our family reunion scheme) wishing to take out Australian citizenship.

National Service would be divided into two six-month sections: one section for *military training* and the other for what President John F Kennedy called the *Peace Corps*. Both the military training and the peace corps would require all members to participate in a physical fitness program at the start of every day and follow a healthy diet. An IQ test designed to tell them what their potential is and a personality test that would tell them what their preferred occupations are would be conducted. This would help individuals know what occupations they are best suited for and where they would most likely be competent and happiest. These tests would be conducted as part of their military training or peace corps experience. Those born between January 1 and June 30 could do six months military training first followed by six months participation in the Peace Corps. Those born between July 1 and December 31 could undertake a reverse timetable. This would put less strain on those conducting both courses.

What would be the benefits of National Service?
Military training would be designed to get our youth into physical shape while developing their potential and character. It would also contain basic or recruit training designed to develop self-discipline, task orientation, and group participation as well as acquiring basic military skills should the case ever arise where they would be needed to defend Australia. Following *recruit training*, they would be posted

into the corps most suited for them where they would undergo *corps training*. This will provide them with specialist skills needed to conduct their daily duties. Finally, they would be posted to an ADF unit and participate in an exercise where their newly acquired specialist skills would be put to use and appraised.

Participation in the Peace Corps would also be designed to get our youth into physical shape while developing their potential and character. Essentially, the Peace Corps would require those members of our National Service programme to engage in development projects conducted by the Australian Government as national emergency projects within Australia, foreign aid to our nearest neighbouring countries, and UN development projects that our Government deems in the national interest. They would be working, in their service uniforms alongside overseas local citizens, in services like education, health, agriculture, and community projects that address locally prioritised needs. The Australian Government would co-ordinate these projects with the various governments in our neighbourhood and Australian relief organisations. Financial support would be provided by the Australian Government for these projects, and this would be the only foreign aid payments given out by Australia. Direct cash payments to overseas governments would no longer be given.

At the conclusion of their National Service all participants would be required to complete an evaluation assessment on the strengths and weaknesses of their experience and how to improve the National Service experience of future participants. All data from the evaluation assessment would be collected, correlated and assessed by those leading the National Service programme. A written report would be submitted to the government at the end of each year which would contain a response to the evaluation assessment, suggestions on how to improve their programme, and an evaluation regarding the success or failures of the cohort's progress.

This would achieve four things. The first would be the necessary attitudinal and physical changes required in Australia's youth.

The second would be the gratitude and friendship that citizens in neighbouring countries would have for both Australia and its armed forces. The third would be the pride our youth would develop for their country and its Foreign Aid programme. Also, seeing how people in other countries live would give our youth a better appreciation of the culture and lifestyle of their own country. Then there is the fourth, and perhaps greatest benefit of all, that of realising the personal joy of doing something for someone other than yourself. That is, to participate in a truly altruistic act.

National Service of this sort should not be viewed as a cheap way of boosting our defence force personnel, but rather as a final stage in educating our youth before they become responsible citizens. The military portion of National Service should be seen as a preparation for a national emergency should it be required. All military deployment outside of a national emergency would be undertaken by the full-time professional members of the ADF or the Australian Reserves and not those who complete their National Service. Any major national emergency entailing a rapid expansion of our military would be met by conscripting 20-year-olds or older, not this younger cohort.

Following graduation those chosen by a military selection board would be encouraged, but not forced, to join either the ADF or Australian Reserves. However, those not voluntarily recruited for service in the ADF or Australian Reserves would be required to register for immediate call-up should our country be facing a national emergency, and they would be required to undergo refresher courses from time to time.

Also, all those who complete their national service would be required to take the Australian citizenship oath or pledge (previously mentioned) before being registered as an Australian citizen. They would then participate in a graduation ceremony and be discharged. Those who claim conscientious objection would be offered a non-combatant training schedule in their military training.

A new category of non-voting citizenship could be established for those born in Australia but who refuse to participate in National Service and take the oath or pledge of citizenship. Those who fall into this category would still become Australian citizens but remain ineligible to vote in elections. Their status would change should they have a change of heart at a later date, but they would still be required to complete their national service and take the Australian citizenship oath.

Those eligible immigrants wanting to become Australian citizens who refuse to undergo National Service and take the Australian citizenship oath or pledge would be offered permanent residency but would be ineligible for citizenship. National Service would not be required for permanent residents or those on working or tourist visas. Hopefully, Australians would no longer be overweight or obese, have developed lifelong skills applicable to civilian life, and be proud of their country and willing to defend it.

One further point that needs to be made before we leave this topic is the current state of global insecurity and Australia's spending on Defence. Australian Prime Minister Anthony Albanese (1963-, 31st Prime Minister of Australia) said this about global insecurity –

> *Today I want to take the opportunity to share my vision for an Australia that is stronger, safer and more resilient ... more prepared to meet the challenges and threats of a less certain world.*
> (lowyinstitute.org, *An Address by opposition leader Anthony Albanese, 2022*)

Since then, global insecurity has reached the highest level since the end of WWII –

> *Global insecurity is currently at its worst point since World War II, with a record number of countries engaged in conflict and a growing sense of fear and instability.*
> (AI Overview, 2025)

In response to this crisis, America has announced that it can no longer protect its Allies unless they increase their commitment to their own security.

> *US President Donald Trump called on NATO members to lift their defence spending from the current target of 2 percent of GDP to 5 percent.*
> *Australian defence spending was $53.3 billion in 2023-24, which was 2% of GDP. The Treasury expect it will reach 2.4 percent of GDP in 2027-28.*
> (aspistrategist.org.au, 2025)

Will this be enough? The US spent 3.45% of its GDP on defence in 2022 (AI Overview, 2025) and intends to increase defence spending in future.

> *President Donald Trump last week (April 2025) announced new plans for a $1 trillion defence budget in 2026.*
> (mises.org, *Federal Spending Is Only Going Up: Trump Pushes Trillion-Dollar Defence Budget*, 2025)

With this in mind let us consider what our attitude to defence spending has been in the past and what it needs to be in future.

> *Australia is a nation that has always prided itself on "punching above its weight" in its relationship with the United States... While the rhetoric and continued debate surrounding the nation's increased defence spending is welcomed, the time for debate is over, it's time for the rubber to hit the road and for real capability to be delivered in a timely manner.*
> (defenceconnect.com.au, *Step it up: Trump 2.0 will expect increased defence spending*, 2024)

US Defence Secretary, Pete Hegseth, in a meeting with Australia's Defence Minister, Richard Marles, in Singapore, asked Australia to raise its defence budget to 3.5% of GDP (defensenews.com, 2025). Given all this attention on new global insecurity, the US request and the current level of Australia's defence spending, what should Australia's response be?

The Australian Prime Minister stated that it is not a question of how much Australia spends on defence but the quality of the spending (defenceconnect.com.au, 2025). Why is this an either/or proposition, Prime Minister? Of course, the spending must have a quality priority but so too must the spending be adequate to meet the needs of our current situation.

Currently, Australia spends approximately 2% of GDP on defence, 9-10% on health, 8-10% on social security, and 5-6% on education.

(AI Overview, 2025)

Does this represent wise government spending at a time of heightened global insecurity? Why do we seldom hear Australian governments level the quality argument on these other departmental expenditures? For example, Australia's level of spending on education is slightly above the OECD's level, yet its global ranking has continued to decline (AI Overview, 2025). Why then is the quality argument not levelled against education? During every election campaign, both political parties in Australia enter into a bidding war over health, education, and social security, but seldom mention or even downplay the importance of defence spending.

The fact is that our defence forces have been seriously depleted because the government has diverted funds away from previous commitments. For example, the purchase of a fourth squadron of F35s was cancelled (australianaviation.com.au, 2024), and 22% of acquisition costs have been cancelled (David Uren, *National Defence Strategy: Cancellations cover 22% of acquisitions*, aspistrategist.org.

au, 2024) to meet the purchase of our future nuclear-powered submarines. The F35 was the weapon that the Israeli Airforce used to gain dominance over Iranian airspace in the recent 12-day war which erupted on 13thJune, 2025.

> *Great Britain just announced that it will purchase 12 F35A stealth fighter/bombers capable of carrying nuclear bombs from Lockheed Martin.*
>
> (reuters.com, 2025)

Does this cancellation sound like a quality decision regarding Australia's defence spending?

What seems clear is that Australia will have to increase its defence spending in the near future. At a time when cost of living is high with people increasingly turning towards the government for financial help and the majority of young people lacking pride in and becoming reluctant to defend their country, this will not be easy. Drastic times call for drastic measures. Perhaps it is time to get ahead of the curve and introduce National Service.

What is your opinion about the introduction of National Service and the current spending level on defence? Do you think National Service would help solve the fitness and loyalty problems of our younger generation and the recruitment problem currently being experienced by the ADF? Please discuss this with your family and friends. Would you be willing to participate in a National Service programme? Do you think it would be beneficial for you? In what ways? Be specific. Do you think it might even be an exciting challenge and help develop your character? Do you think anyone born in Australia should be entitled to Australian citizenship regardless of whether they are willing to participate in National Service and take the citizenship oath or pledge? Do you think Australia should increase its defence spending in line with our other Allies? Do you think Australia should spend 3.5% of GDP on defence at this time of heightened global insecurity? Would the introduction of National Service and our ADF receiving 3.5% of GDP increase your pride in Australia?

The Dignity of Work

> *By the sweat of thy brow thou shall eat bread until you return to the ground, since from it thou were taken.*
>
> (Holy Bible, *Genesis 3:19*)

I worked at Brisbane Grammar School (BGS) for 14 years as a History/English Master. BGS is a successful, independent, non-denominational secondary school that was established in 1868, so has a tradition that stretches back for many years. The original main building and school house are still in use today. The school's motto is *nil sine labore*, which is a Latin phrase that translates to *nothing without work*. This is a motto that the masters and students at BGS still adhere to today.

The dignity of work is a belief that all types of work are respected equally, be that professional, trade or unskilled work. Also work in small business or big business is admired equally, including work in all sections of the Australian economy, from the dirty, dangerous jobs to those receiving the highest rewards. There is no such thing as essential or non-essential employment, because all work provides goods and services to citizens that they want to consume. In times of emergency, however, it is necessary to curtail the consumption of what the government determines to be luxury goods and services to free up the economy to meet the challenge of the emergency.

The Institute of Public Affairs issued a report in 2019 which stated the following –

> *Too many young Australians are missing out on the dignity of work. Work is what provides meaning and enables the formation of self-sustaining families and communities ... Australia is facing*

> *a growing crisis in underemployment. 1.7 million Australians are either unemployed or unable to find their desired amount of work. The rates are worse for young people with nearly 30% of the youth labour force being underutilised.*
>
> (ipa.org.au, *244,000 Young Australians Missing the Dignity of Work to Inflexible Industrial Relations,* April 2019)

Although Australia's unemployment rate in June 2025 was 4.3% (abs.gov.au, 2025), it is estimated that the 'hidden unemployment' could be significantly higher for the following reasons –

1) The official rate only includes those who were actively seeking work in the last four weeks and able to start immediately. This is a very narrow definition of 'unemployed' and likely to miss many people who would like to find work.
2) The number of people in underemployment do not show up on the ABS figures. These are people who would like more work but are unable to find any.
3) Some workers may have become discouraged from looking for work and simply given up looking.
4) Then there are those who enrol in education courses, like those conducted by TAFE colleges, where they could receive better benefits than those on unemployment benefits, like Youth Allowance, Austudy, or ABstudy, depending on their individual circumstances. Courses conducted by TAFE are fee free.
5) The youth unemployment rate in Australia was officially 10.4% as at June 2025.

Additional to this is the percentage of youth in the 16-24-year-old bracket who were suffering from mental health disorders which rose from 26.4% in 2007 to 38.8% in 2020-2022 (ABS National Study of

Mental Health and Wellbeing, 2022).

When people are unemployed or underemployed they are forced to turn to social welfare for relief. This saps their dignity since they move from independence to dependence. Only work can restore their independence and dignity, so any form of work is dignified because it leads workers towards self-sufficiency and pride in their accomplishments. Participation in the workforce also engages workers in companionship and social involvement, thus overcoming the problems associated with isolation.

When young, inexperienced workers enter the workforce, they generally start at a less prestigious job but then rise through the ranks of workers. Therefore, should minimum wages be set at a rate so high that it forces small businesses to dismiss young workers? If minimum wages were set at a lower rate for young workers, would that be fair to workers in other businesses that can afford to pay their workers higher wages? Should young workers be allowed to work at rates lower than the minimum so they can find employment? Would this disadvantage older workers? Should the setting of minimum wages acknowledge what small businesses are capable of paying? Should the minimum wage be set at different rates depending on what businesses workers are employed in? Explain your reasons for the answers you provide.

I have already mentioned Juliet Rhys-Williams' and Milton Friedman's suggestion regarding negative taxation that addresses this issue. The minimum wage would still be set by the Fair Work Commission (FWC). The market would determine the actual wages of workers. Those workers who earn wages above the minimum wage would pay tax, while those workers who earn wages below the minimum wage would have a supplement paid by the taxation office to raise their wages to the minimum wage. This would not involve creating a new government department since the supplement would be paid by the taxation office, and it would cost the government less since unemployment payments for the out of work citizen would cost the government more than the negative taxation supplement.

Do you think some small businesses would take advantage of this scheme and offer wages below what they can afford to pay? Most conservatives are against government subsiding wages for this reason. Can you suggest a solution for this possibility? What about a cap being set on negative taxation? Has a cap on Medicare payments to GPs helped reduce consultation costs for patients or encouraged higher consultation costs?

Whatever your answers to the questions above, the youth of Australia must not lose sight of the dignity of work by looking down on some forms of labour. The work of unskilled labour is just as essential to a functioning society as the work of professionals. Both forms of work should be respected equally. No work is undignified. Only refusing to work because you consider the work beneath you is undignified. It is more dignified to work at any job than it is to rely on social welfare.

Would a belief in the dignity of work help some of today's youth restore their self-respect and provide a remedy for their lethargy, indifference, isolation, and depression? Give a detailed explanation for your answer.

As stated previously, AI and humanoid robotics will fundamentally alter the necessity for much skilled and unskilled labour in our marketplace, but the need for a large consumer base for Australia's economy will continue. If the solution to this problem is found in a government-directed redistribution of Australia's wealth, those who will remain permanently unemployed will have to find some other way than work to maintain their self-respect and purpose to life. Again, Australians could devote more of their time and effort towards raising a family, engaging in life-long education, or pursuing recreational activities.

Everybody needs a dream that they dedicate themselves to achieve. This gives them a purpose in life and the motivation to work hard. Currently, my dream is to collect my thoughts and ideas and publish them in a book that I can leave for my descendants. This is a labour of love that I am motivated to complete. What is your dream? Does it involve work, either paid or unpaid?

Housing Affordability

Young people often say they have given up trying to buy a home because they will never be able to afford one. It is true that house prices have risen steeply over the last 10 years –

> *The data shows that in Sydney, Melbourne, Brisbane and Adelaide, house prices have increased by an impressive 80-100%.*
> (propertyupdate.com.au, 6 June 2024)

The housing market, like any other market, depends on supply and demand to set house prices. The only way to reduce this rise in prices is for this ratio to change. Leith Van Onselen (Chief Economist at the MB Fund and MB Super) puts it this way –

> *To solve the structural housing shortage, Australia needs to run a migration system that is below the nation's capacity to build housing and infrastructure.*
> (IPA Free Views, *Australia's Out-of-control Migration System*, Leith Van Onselen, 2025)

To meet this requirement we need to determine what Australia's demand for housing would be without migration –

> *Without migration, Australia would need to build significantly fewer houses, likely closer to the rate it built in the 2010s (around 170,000 to 190,000 annually), to meet demand driven by natural population increase and household size changes, rather than the 240,000 dwellings targeted for the National Housing Accord.*
> (AI Overview, 2025)

So Australia must build 170,000 to 190,000 homes annually

before any consideration is given to Australia's immigration numbers. Australia's prime minister promised to build 1.2 million homes by 2030. To meet this target Australia would need to build 240,000 homes per year. The record number of homes built in Australia in one year is 220,000. Current data shows that the government is falling 15,000 homes short every quarter. This leaves the National Housing Accord on track to be at least 300,000 homes short (realestate.com.au, 2025). Given these numbers, it appears that Australia is currently capable of building somewhere between 200,000 and 220,000 homes annually.

In the year ending 30th June 2024, overseas immigration contributed a net gain of 446,000 people to Australia's population.

(abs.gov.au 15 Dec 2024)

For a country with a population of 27,204,809 people as of 30th June 2024 (abs.gov.au, 14 Dec 2024) and the housing requirements to meet the needs of Australia's natural population, this level of immigration is unreasonable and contributes to higher demand being placed on the real estate market for both housing and rental properties. The gap between housing construction capacity and demand necessitates a more balance approach to immigration. The current government policy for permanent migration into Australia is 185,000. This number is still unreasonable unless the ratio between supply and demand for housing changes.

This ration can only be achieved if demand is lowered, or met with increased housing construction, or both simultaneously. To achieve this, compromises and trade-offs must be met from a number of competing interests. First is the government who seem committed to a Big Australia agenda to keep Australia's GDP growing. Second is business interests who likewise seem committed to a Big Australia agenda in order to keep labour costs low and demand for products high. Third is the Trade Unions who are committed to keeping the number of skilled tradesmen at a level that maximises their members' wages. Finally is the university sector who want to see the number of overseas students kept at a high level to fund their research and maintain their high salaries. The suggestions I make here will undoubtedly be resisted by some of these competing interests, but a start must be made somewhere, or Australia may find itself involved in a popular uprising for political change.

Let's start with the Government agenda. To maintain a Big Australia immigration policy it will be necessary to base permanent immigration primarily on skills-based immigration. That is if the skills requirements of the housing industry and Australia's infrastructure projects were met first before consideration was given to others seeking immigration into Australia, including family reunion and our refugee intake. This would enable Australia to make more houses and take some of the pressure off the demand side of the housing availability ratio. Giving immigration preference to the building industry's skills requirement would result in more skilled workers for the building industry, currently unable to find workers to meet the demand for planned building projects. The current government immigration target, as previously stated, is for 185,000 immigrants with a 70:30 split between skill and family reunion. Of course, these are targets, not actual arrivals. Government immigration targets were last met in the 2019-2020 financial year (AI Overview, 2025).

In a nutshell, immigration should be determined by filling job offers that employers currently have available which cannot be filled by Australian workers; families that can reunite and support their loved ones; charities that want to and can sponsor refugees; and the accommodation that is available for immigrants and university students. It should not be determined by ideology or desired GDP targets. One other point: it is futile if political parties make promises to reduce mass-immigration numbers during an election only to ignore their promise after the election. Clearly, such a political tactic lacks veracity and integrity.

The Big Australia agenda of business interests may lead to higher profits from a continuous rise in housing costs, and an ever-increasing demand for their product, but this has created a housing price bubble, which could have serious consequences for Australia's economy if, or rather when, it bursts. For an example of the consequences of a real estate bubble burst look no further than what China is currently experiencing. China keeps its hapless population in check with repression. How would Australian governments keep its population in check? Business must accept that a dampening down of demand for real estate is now required, if Australia is going to avoid the misery inflicted on its people from a deep recession. If nothing is done, business interests may not be happy with a politically popular uprising which usually accompanies a deep recession.

The Trade Union's limited skilled tradesmen agenda is keeping the financial rewards for its tradesmen high, but is also contributing to higher house prices. Trade union members should accept that the current situation is not in their long-term best interests. No one is advocating for a flooding of the labour market with skilled tradesmen, but a better balance needs to be arrived at. Australia needs to build more houses, but we have reached a ceiling for the number of houses Australia can build, and one of the problems contributing to this ceiling is the number of tradesmen available to build the required number of houses.

> *Australia requires approximately 83,000 to 130,000 additional tradespeople to meet the national target of building 1.2 million homes by mid-2029, with the specific number varying between industry reports.*
>
> (AI Overview, 2025)

More houses must be built and demand for houses must be controlled if Australia is to solve this pressing problem.

> *Building an extra 50,000 homes a year for a decade could result in Australian house prices and rents being up to 20% lower than they would have been otherwise.*
>
> (grattan.edu.au, 2021)

So we need to build an extra 50,000 homes a year, and the Trade Unions need to get behind a national effort to achieve this target.

This brings us to the final interest group contributing to Australia's housing crisis: the Australian universities' agenda for excessive increases in foreign students.

One possible solution to this problem could be found by requiring all Australian universities to supply their foreign students with accommodation, be that dormitory, apartment, or housing. This would be property that the universities own; it would not be property that either the universities or their students rent on the property market. This requirement could be a gradual increase, say, from 30% of foreign student accommodation by the first three years to 60% by the next three years to 90% over the next three years and by 10% in the final year. This would mean that all Australian universities would be supplying all their foreign students with 100% of their accommodation needs within 10 years and not competing in the rental or property market to do so. This 10-year plan would enable the universities to meet the government requirement and gradually reduce the pressure on rental accommodation. Failure of any university to meet these requirements would result in a reduction of foreign students enrolled at that university until the percentage has been met.

Also, all foreign students in Australia under a student visa could be prohibited from buying into Australia's real estate market or renting separate accommodation. This means that over a 10-year period all foreign students would gradually be taken out of the rental and housing market. Thus, creating a gradual reduction in demand over the 10-year period and a corresponding temporary increase in university accommodation building projects.

Currently, a student visas can be a pathway to permanent residency (PR) through gaining a subsequent visa, which is a necessary step before gaining citizenship. The granting of citizenship requires someone to have lived in Australia for at least four years with the final 12 months as a permanent resident. Many Australian universities sell this point to attract overseas students. Student visa applications and grants are counted as temporary migrants not permanent residents. Those holding student visas are counted as temporary visa holders and are included in Net Overseas Migration (NOM) calculations. The permanent migration program numbers do not include the NOM calculations. As of June 2024, 8.6 million people born overseas are living in Australia, making up 31.5% of total population. Therefore, before overseas students, who enter Australia under temporary migration status, are granted permanent visas they should be subjected to the normal national requirements for Australian immigration, which includes fitting into the permanent migration program (190,000 places) and Australia's skill-based requirements. This is one of the reasons why immigration numbers keep exceeding the permanent migration program. In other words, universities should not sell a pathway to citizenship as part of their appeal to their prospective overseas students, nor should it be used as such.

Also, serious consideration should be given to limiting the number of negatively geared rental properties on the market. Under current negative gearing rules, investors in the property market can negatively gear an unlimited number of properties. Obviously, this arrangement means that first home buyers must compete against these investors for a limited supply of properties. This is undesirable, but so too would a reduction in rental properties be, if it led to a shortage of rental properties available on the rental market. Nevertheless, as demand for rental properties declines, owing to my suggested changes, limits on negative gearing should be introduced.

Finally, the amount of real estate being bought by overseas investors should be limited. If the number of houses, apartments etc.

available for purchase increases, so too would the limit. If the number stagnates, so too would the limit. Another consideration concerning overseas investment in Australia's real estate could be made on a reciprocal basis. That is, the laws governing Australia's participation in an overseas county's real estate market could be made identical to that of their citizens' participation in Australia's real estate market. If they restrict, we restrict; if they prohibit, we prohibit.

These measures would take some of the demand for housing out of the real estate market and help stabilise it. But what about supply? What can be done there? Can supply be increased?

The first reason inhibiting supply seems to be government taxes and regulations. So, reduce the taxes and regulations (especially green taxes and red, green, and black regulations) on new houses, so more can be built with shorter approval times. Easing planning restriction by local, state, and federal governments would see more and faster investment in housing supply. More investment in new housing could be achieved by providing new home buyers with grants to buy into the new housing market and not the existing housing market. This would drive down the price of existing houses but increase demand for new houses. This could be controlled by placing a limit on the number of negatively geared investment properties investors are allowed to make in the new home market.

Then there is the cost of building new houses. This is primarily driven by three factors: availability of workforce skills, the cost of land and materials, and inflation. The skills issue has already been addressed by giving priority to a home builder skills-based immigration policy. Australia could also produce more tradespeople by expanding recruitment into home builder skills apprenticeships. The cost of land is something easily addressed, just release more land for suburban development. The problem that arises here is the push by some politicians to limit such release of land. The only way to address this problem is to dissuade these politicians, through the ballot box, from holding back land release.

The cost of materials is driven by two factors. First is the cost of importing overseas materials and the reliability of its supply chain. Little can be done about this from Australia's end, so we need to look at producing our own materials at competitive prices which means lower labour and energy costs, achieved by an expansion of our skilled labour force in the supply chain and creating an energy system that is both reliable and affordable. The current government's push for a net zero economy through 100% renewable energy will not achieve this, regardless of what some politicians promise. The second is the inflation rate in Australia. When speaking at an interview, Reserve Bank Governor Michele Bullock said inflation is now largely a "homegrown" problem (Michele Bullock, 22nd Nov 2023). A homegrown problem requires a homegrown solution. Inflation can only be reduced by cuts to government spending. Something I have addressed earlier, remember Milton Friedman.

Having just said that government spending needs to be cut, what I am about to suggest may sound contradictory but it really comes back to trade-offs when talking about government spending. To encourage young people to enter the new home market the government has a First Homeowner (New Homes) Grant. New house and land packages vary in cost according to what state and location you are looking at, so it is very difficult to give any definitive cost here. However, whatever the cost first home buyers will need a 10% deposit with enough secure income to service the life of the loan. So this will depend on how much they have saved towards the deposit and their credit rating. All things considered, what I am suggesting is that Governments (Federal, State, and Local) should contribute 50% of the 10% deposit on the average price for a new home and land package in their new estate developments for first-time home buyers. The young people wanting to purchase a new home would then be required to have saved the remaining 50% of the 10% deposit. A saving programme that produced the owners' contribution to the house's deposit would give the owner the correct credit rating for the loan.

The government could invest directly in low-cost public housing which would not only produce higher supply for this sector, but also help reduce the growing number of homeless citizens in our country. Also, the occupants of these homes could be encouraged to purchase their homes once their financial situation changes.

The suggestions I have made above address the housing crisis in Australia. However, I am not suggesting that all these suggestions should be introduced immediately, because this could lead to a crash in the property market. What I am suggesting is to take these suggestions one at a time and introduce them slowly over time. The obvious place to start would be with reducing immigration numbers and increasing university-provided student accommodation. To overcome this crisis will take time, but if we don't start somewhere it will only get worse until it crashes anyway, in the same way as all real estate bubbles always eventually crash.

These are some suggestions you can consider when contemplating how to tackle three important problems facing young people today. Can you offer other proposals as possible solutions than the ones I have suggested here? Can you identify other problems I have overlooked? I'm sure there are many if you think about it.

Another consideration regarding Australia's future is Australia's aging population which is a serious, and very real, problem your generation will have to face. This will require raising the national birth rate (currently at 1.5) back up to at least replacement level (2.1). It even would be desirable to achieve a national birth rate of 3.0 or above to accommodate the kind of economic growth achieved by previous generations of Australians. Don't forget high levels of immigration is a temporary solution to the aging population problem, because today's immigrants will become tomorrow's old retirees much quicker than those born today. Without an increase in Australia's natural birth rate, this problem is going to grow more quickly, so why postpone it for the next generation to solve?

Why not turn your attention to this problem and propose your own solution. You could begin your research by addressing ways to encourage the young men and women of your generation to enter stable marriages and have more children. If you are a young woman, ask yourself what it would take to encourage you to have three or more children. Would allowing families to submit a joint income tax statement help? Should encouragement be limited to financial compensation alone?

Remember what Peter Costello's (Australia's Treasurer, 1996-2007) advice to young women contemplating motherhood was –

> *Have one for yourself, one for your husband,*
> *and one for your country.*

He also gave families a $3,000 lump sum payment for every child born after July 1, 2001, and it worked. Parents did have more children (smh.com.au, *Parents find third baby is a bonus*, March 2, 2009).

To Summarise

So you can see that you have inherited a lot of problems from my generation, your parents' generation, and have created a number for yourselves. What should be clear from our discussion is that a number of unintended consequences have arisen from reformists, with the best intentions, influencing changes that radicals have taken up and exacerbated to the point where undesirable structural changes have occurred to Australia's culture and economy. These structural changes have accumulated over time and now endanger Australia's future to an extent where prudent reforms are needed to realign Australia's integrity. Some social commentators today refer to the position that Australia finds itself in as the *managed decline* of Australia as a Nation State (ipa.org.au, *Australia's New Course is to be Managed Decline*, 2024). To reverse this trend will require decisive action be taken regarding Australia's moral integrity, its political integrity, its economic integrity, its cultural integrity, and its national integrity. To this end, the following issues need urgent attention.

Renewable energy is cheap but only when the wind is blowing and the sun is shining, then it relies on baseload power either stored or some other generating technology. So far the only reliable baseload power is achieved through either fossil fuels or nuclear. Storage technology is still a long way off being viable, even if its invention can be realised. One would think that a sensible approach would be to develop the storage and hydrogen generation technology *first* before Australia destroys its existing energy system.

Those promoting renewable energy avoid admitting the real costs of baseload power or even an examination of what has happened to

To Summarise

the economies of countries like Britain (that has now changed to a mixed energy system containing more nuclear power), Germany (that has the highest concentration of renewable energy in the world) and Spain where energy costs are among the most expensive in the world. Owing to the high cost of its energy, Australia is now having to subsidise its heavy industry or watch it transfer overseas. If this continues our economy will become deindustrialised while other overseas countries will industrialise theirs through the use of our fossil fuels and uranium.

Cutting off our export of fossil fuels and uranium will not halt the increasing release of carbon dioxide into the earth's atmosphere nor the spread of nuclear-powered electric generators. Australia is not the only potential supplier of fossil fuels and uranium, and increasingly large, multi-national companies are looking elsewhere for its supply. What they are finding are cheaper ways of gaining access to these commodities, some of which are more pollutant to earth's atmosphere than are Australia's. Australia is harming itself for no gain.

Currently, Australia sends its coal to China and imports solar panels, wind generators, and transmission towers and lines from China. What this entails is for Australian coal and iron ore to be transported to China, using trains and ships that burn diesel (the dirtiest of fossil fuels). The solar panels, wind generators, and transmission infrastructure are manufactured in factories in China using energy generated by fossil fuels. The solar panels, wind generators, and transmission lines are then transported to renewable energy construction sites in Australia using ships and trucks that burn even more fossil fuels. On top of this is the loss of rain and old-growth forests to renewal energy projects. This also reduces the release of oxygen into the atmosphere created by these rain and old-growth forests.

If the primary aim of renewable energy is to reduce the amount of carbon dioxide going into the atmosphere, while maintaining current production levels of oxygen, this makes no logical sense. If, however, the primary aim is to make money, from exporting mountains of iron ore and coal to China, receiving huge sums of money in the form of corporate welfare, or engaging in the highly profitable retail trade of renewable energy products, it makes perfectly logical sense. Clearly, if Australia was to use its own coal to power its generators or build new nuclear-powered generators to replace the coal-fired generators, there would be no need for solar panels, wind generators, or new transmission lines. Thereby reducing the amount of carbon dioxide going into the atmosphere and maintaining current levels of oxygen production from our existing rain and old-growth forests. Even better would be for Australia to create a mix of different energy sources, including nuclear energy; end all subsidies for energy generation and transmission; then, allow the private sector to determine what the most efficient, reliable, and affordable low-carbon emission energy source is, without the need for corporate welfare.

Another issue related to energy generation is that of a growth in the demand for energy. For example, the power demand for AI data centres in the USA alone is expected to reach 606 terawatt hours, up from 147 TWh in 2023 (mckinsey.com, 2024). If Australia is to participate in the development of AI it will need to generate a lot more energy than it currently does. The American government has allowed private AI companies to build their own generating capacity. These companies have chosen gas or nuclear over wind or solar energy as their source of energy (goldmansachs.com, Jan 2025).

One final consideration is the lifespan of solar panels and wind generators. Generally speaking, solar panels have a lifespan of around 25 years, provided they are kept clean and free from debris (skylinesolar.com.au, 2025). In Western Australia a solar farm and battery storage system was decommissioned after 7 years owing to its poor economic performance (AI Overview, 2025). On the other hand, wind turbines have a lifespan of around 20-30years (reneweconomy.com.au, 2025). In Victoria, the Codrington Wind Farm, containing 14 turbines, was decommissioned after 24 years (westvicbrolga.com.au, 2025). There is some contention over the genuine lifespan of wind turbines. Some say that the towers last longer than the turbines and that the turbines need replacing after just 3-4years (aap.com.au, *Wind Turbine Lifespan Claim Generates Misinformation*, 2025).

Then there is the cost of decommissioning. The cost of removing a single solar panel after the decommissioning of a solar farm is about $20-28, although this can be higher due to factors like market fluctuations, specific disposal and recycling costs, and regulatory compliance. Industry estimates vary significantly based on technology, equipment, and location of the solar farm (AI Overview, 2025). The average solar farm contains thousands to over a million solar panels AI Overview, 2025). A 100 MW solar farm contains between 300,000 and 400,000 solar panels (Stanwell.com, *Harvesting the sun: How solar farms are maintained*, 2025).

The removal of wind turbines and their towers is also expensive, ranging from $400,000 to $600,000. The final cost depends on things like the turbine's size, location, the complexity of removal, and the value of salvaged material (AI Overview, 2025). Australia currently has around 3,500 to 4,000 wind turbines across Australia. To meet the government's 2030 target of 82% renewable energy they will need to install approximately 40 wind turbines and 22,000 solar panels per month until 2030 (AI Overview, 2025).

It's time for Australia to take decisive reform to our energy system by halting our wind and solar expansion, using coal and gas as an intermediary energy source, lifting our moratorium on uranium and gradually replacing our fossil fuel energy system with nuclear power, the most environmentally friendly, and cleanest source available. It is also –

> *cost-competitive with other forms of electricity generation, except where there is direct access to low-cost fossil fuels.*
> (world-nuclear.org, *Economics of Nuclear Power*, 29 September 2023)

Australia must recognise the erosion of its social cohesion and do more than use words like 'unacceptable', 'intolerable' or 'un-Australian' as a method to regain its lost social unity. When multiculturalism leads to an attack on Australia's basic right to freedom of speech, equal justice, social harmony, and a breakdown in national unity, it is clear that Australia has let people into its society who are not willing to accept its values. Australia is a liberal democratic nation state that protects its citizens' liberty. It is not a communist dictatorship, nor is it an autocratic theocracy. If you prefer to fly the flag of another country over the flag of the country you are living in, or if you burn the flag of the country you are living in while holding aloft the flag of another country, perhaps you should find another country to live in. Then, there are those Australian children who have been educated by our educational institutions to feel ashamed of their country. One wonders exactly how many Australians now hate their country and want it destroyed.

In early June 2025, riots broke out in cities across America over the issue of illegal immigration. This involved assaulting law enforcement officers, burning privately owned cars, looting and destruction of private and public property. Burning the American flag while flying the Mexican flag is not accepting American values while living in America. Rather it is trying to introduce separatism into American society. Add to this the deep social divide emerging in Britain, where a huge number of protesters came out in London in opposition to Britain's illegal immigration policy, and you have a glimpse of what may happen in Australia which has already witnessed the burning of its flag while violent protesters fly the flags of other countries. The scale may not be the same, but the sentiment certainly is.

It's time for decisive reform to Australia's immigration policy from one of mass immigration and multi-culturalism to one of controlled immigration and cultural assimilation.

The biggest change to Australia's security is the emergence of China as a superpower and the CCPs assertive attitude towards its neighbours, including Australia. This has seen the CCP involved in territorial disputes, economic pressure on its trading partners, cyber-attacks, spying and diplomatic manoeuvring. The stability in our region is no longer as safe as it was.

It is time for Australia to undertake decisive reform by accepting the real threat to its security and spending more on its defence than it currently does. A movement towards more independence in Australia's security is now urgent, especially after the experience of some countries who over-relied on their American alliance. The alliance is necessary, but we must contribute more to it and rely less on American strength to come to our rescue.

It is also time to reform our educational curriculum. Australia must recognise that radicals have shamed non-Aboriginal Australians into accepting a race-based division of its society and take action to end not only the race division within Australia but also the *guilt* and *victim mentality* that arose from it. Australia must cease forcing identity politics on its children and citizens, and stop pandering to group identity. It is discriminatory and divisive. Discrimination is discrimination, regardless of what sex, race, gender or religion it is directed against. When it comes to special attention, there are only two groups in Australian society: those in genuine need and those who are not. Any other classification is based on *wants* not *needs* and pandering to wants only takes scarce resources from the truly needy.

It's time for decisive reform to Australia's treatment of its non-Aboriginal citizens and its preoccupation with identity politics. Australia must recognise the substandard performance in its education system and address its underlying causes and not its symptoms. Clearly, Australia's educational system is misguided when not only are standards deteriorating but our children are being taught to feel *shame, guilt,* and *victimhood* about their country's past as well as *climate anxiety* over a belief that they are all going to die from a catastrophic climate change emergency (look up the research done by Caroline Hickman, Laura Carter Robinson and The American

Psychological Association on climate anxiety). The dark chapters of Australia's past must be addressed and evaluated by students, but the examination must be truthful and balanced and not generate in their minds and hearts feelings of shame, guilt, and victimhood. Having empathy for the suffering of people from the past does not encourage such destructive consciousness in the living. Creating climate distress in the innocent minds our youth only leads to anxiety and not a constructive concern for their environment.

Yet another problem with our education system is how it is now failing our boys and young men. Teachers of, and learning styles for, boys need to change. The decline in male teachers needs reversing so boys are given a positive male role model in their classrooms; boys should not be subjected to prolonged periods of stillness and sedentary learning; a logical approach to the learning of the three 'Rs' needs reintroducing; a more active, hands-on, and visual learning strategy needs priority; and the cultural and societal condemnation and ridicule of the 'strong' man must be abolished. Furthermore, boys, and girls as well, need Australia's heroic narrative to inspire within them positive values like courage, kindness, and resilience.

The purpose of education is to provide a foundational knowledge base from which graduating students can think critically, evaluate differing opinions and draw their own conclusions. It is also to fill the students' hearts and minds with hope, optimism and enthusiasm about their future. It is not to crush their hopes and dreams with distress, confusion, apathy, indifference or lack of interest.

It's time for Australia to take decisive reform and show some moral clarity by addressing the harmful issues of student guilt, victimhood, climate anxiety, and male failure within our education system.

Let me conclude this section with the following observation –

No single study confirms that Australia achieved its highest level of home ownership and most equitable wealth distribution in the 1950s and 1960s: rather, historical data

> *and contemporary studies by institutions like The Australian Bureau of Statistics (ABS) and the Household, Income and Labour Dynamics in Australia (HILDA) show that home ownership was high during that period and that wealth was more evenly distributed before increasing inequality in more recent decades.*
>
> (AI Overview, 2025)

Australia achieved this through controlled migration and a policy of cultural assimilation, a liberal democratic government dedicated to protecting its citizens' liberty, a prudently regulated capitalist economy, and a national unity based on the heroic narrative of its foundation and the sacrifice of its citizens in its defence.

This was not a perfect system but a successful trade-off. If Australia continues to trade these proven successful policies for those of a globalist regional centre, or a vassal state for a communist dictatorship or authoritarian theocracy, its liberty, independence, and individual prosperity will be compromised, and it could fall victim to internal division and violent conflict. What a tragic end that would be for an illustrious nation whose succession of contemporary political leaders are deliberately destroying its once proud and successful unity and its economic strength.

Clearly, these lamentable structural problems are destroying Australia's once proud liberal democracy. Those who fail to address these pernicious problems are not just wrong; they are intellectually dishonest. Many of these problems have been created by a radical, socialist-inspired agenda which promotes a false narrative of liberation when in reality it produces the economic, political, and cultural destruction of liberal democracies. If Australians are not prepared to respond to these challenging problems, they will fall into a creeping, unstoppable malaise that will allow those pursing a radical socialist agenda to install their ideologically driven solutions to the problems they have deliberately created. Something Australia's ancestors would never have allowed. Remember, countries with fewer advantages than Australia have achieved better results and Australia can too, if it undertakes decisive reform and makes a course correction.

Chapter 9: Conclusion

We have come a long way in our discussion. I hope you have found it interesting and have stayed with me to the end. We began by observing the link between truth and freedom and detected a link between freedom and responsibility. My greatest wish is that you have gained some insights from our time together and are now better prepared to pursue a future committed to a logical, rational, wise, common sense, prudent, and empathetic search for truth, and an acceptance of personal responsibility for the choices you make in your life. I also hope you will devote yourself to the principles of national sovereignty and individual liberty that your ancestors sacrificed so much to bequeath you.

Before leaving, I want to mention one more important issue. As you venture through life, you will experience joy and happiness, pain and sorrow, anger and frustration. You will say and do things that, on later reflection, you will regret. If some of these things deeply trouble you, you will need to address them. Just remember that everyone is entitled to redemption, even you, and accept that redemption is achieved through five distinct steps: recognition, acceptance, contrition, forgiveness, and redemption.

First, you must recognise that you have done something wrong that continues to trouble you. Second you must accept that the fault for the wrongdoing is yours and not try to palm off the blame onto someone or something else. Next, approach this wrongdoing with contrition. This means that you must be so concerned about what you have done that you feel very sorry or guilty about it and are having difficulty moving on. With contrition in your heart you need to seek forgiveness from the person or organisation you have wronged. This may involve a genuine apology, restitution or compensation on your part. Finally, you achieve redemption when you have forgiven yourself. Yes, you do have to forgive yourself if you are going to move on and leave your guilt behind. This is truly the hardest part of redemption because it will be difficult to set aside your guilt, but you must find a way to stop punishing yourself if you are going to achieve not only redemption but a more fulfilling life and realise your full potential.

As a child, I remember my father saying to me before dispensing deserved discipline, *if you do something wrong, you have to take your whack*. I guess I'm trying to explain what my father so succinctly said to me all those years ago. Here are a few other sayings that were popular with my parents' generation, that I grew up hearing and believing in. The list is by no means complete, but they are the ones that had a lasting influence on me –

Talk to the butcher not the block. In Dad's day, butchers had a huge block of wood (a section of tree trunk) in the middle of their shop where they cut up the meat. So this saying meant only to talk with someone who can help you with your problem, otherwise your talk falls on deaf ears.

I was flat out like a lizard drinking. Meaning you had just put in a hard day's work.

A fair day's work for a fair day's pay. Meaning you worked for your wages and did not try to cheat your boss by putting in less than a satisfactory day's work.

He's about as useful as a hip pocket on a singlet. Meaning the person you are working with is useless at his job.

He's not worth his salt. The salt is a reference to his work ethic because work produces salty sweat, but it also meant he did not look after his family, usually because he drank too much which deprived his family of their share of his wages.

Never hit a woman. The meaning is obvious and I can remember my mother ingraining this saying into my character. Something I am grateful to her for teaching me.

He's a few sandwiches short of a picnic. Meaning he does not think clearly about important issues. He is perceived as being unintelligent, eccentric, or lacking common sense.

He's trying to pull the wool over my eyes. Meaning he is not being honest or genuine with me.

Put a sock in it. Meaning you are talking too much, so be quiet.

He's got Buckley's chance. Meaning he is unlikely to achieve what he is setting out to achieve.

Six of one, half a dozen of the other. Meaning two things mean the same thing. You are arguing over the same point. It also could mean that whatever choice you make between two choices you will likely end up with the same result.

It'll all come out in the wash. Meaning we will eventually find out the truth because the truth will always reveal itself.

Fish always rot from their head. Meaning corruption always starts at the top of any organisation.

And one my Uncle Colin favoured, *She'll be right, you'll find.* Meaning to stop worrying, life will work itself out.

Let me end our time together by stating that I hope you have found it valuable and are now more aware of the world that existed before your new world emerged. We have also explored some of the deep problems your new world faces. I hope you are now better equipped to handle them. Perhaps you have discovered that to find existential or archetypal truth you must be factually correct and not politically correct, because facts reveal truth while politics reveal ideology. Alternatively, the appreciation of beauty and goodness will reward you with moral clarity regarding transcendental truth. I leave you with a profound conviction that whatever emerges in your lifetime you will find the confidence and courage to face it, if you acknowledge and speak the truth. It is your duty as an Australian citizen.

> *But I have seen the lighted road*
> *stretching on and on.*
>
> Max Ehrmann, *Love and Faith*

Also By This Author

Broken Lives

Go into the trenches with the Australian troops of the 9th Battalion. Follow the exploits of Lieutenant Peter Bowen and Sergeant Craig Williams during the major battles of 1917 and 1918. Then go to the streets of Paris and London and observe the impact that the Great War had on the civilian population of these great cities. Follow Sister Ann Copley as she works selflessly to nurse the casualties of war. Observe some of the  changes that took place at this time regarding the relationships between men and women, as they struggled to make sense of the upheaval to their society, which was happening all around them. Empathise with Yvette, a young 'war widow' whose life is turned upside down, and her struggle to find companionship and to forge a future for herself.

Kokoda Mist

Join Australian soldiers, Stan and Billy, in their stubborn resistance against an overwhelming World War II Japanese force in Papua New Guinea as the Australians fight a tactical withdrawal along the Kokoda Track. The strategies and tactics used in this withdrawal created one of the most famous actions in the annals of Australian military

history and was to have a major impact on the collective psyche of all Australians.

Follow the magnitude of this impact as it played out on the streets of Brisbane. Link arms with Carol and Jean, two sisters who experience love and tragedy while struggling to fulfil their duties as waitresses in the Victory Café. Experience the full effect that tens of thousands of allied troops had on their home city of Brisbane. Put yourself in the middle of the Battle of Brisbane – a brief battle that broke out between Australian and American servicemen, which highlighted the tension that existed between these two allied forces. At war's end, you will realise how it was that this generation was able to face their future with such confidence and certainty as they built the foundations of the modern Australia that we all enjoy today.

All Our Yesterdays

Travel with Jason Freeman, a young Australian conscript, as he journeys from a loving home into the troubled times of a society blighted and torn apart by the Vietnam War. Witness a young generation struggle with the changes being wrought upon it from an emerging *sex, drugs, and rock 'n roll* culture. Follow David, a young man from the *old rich* section of Melbournian society, as he successfully navigates all the challenges that his changing society throws at him. Meet two young women of Melbourne: Sarah who shows us the dignity that comes from her compassion and understanding, and Clarissa who displays the confidence and outspoken independence of her new ideas. Watch as Nick and Toby try to lock themselves away from the personal suffering of their past. This period in world history became what John Kenneth Galbraith referred to as *The Age of Uncertainty*. An uncertainty that embraced the whole Free World, and, to a large extent, is still with us today.

www.ingramcontent.com/pod-product-compliance
Lightning Source LLC
Chambersburg PA
CBHW060347080526
44583CB00012B/208